THE VIRTUE OF SOLIDARITY

THE VIRTUES: MULTIDISCIPLINARY PERSPECTIVES

Series Editor

Nancy E. Snow

Professor of Philosophy and Director of the Institute for the Study of Human Flourishing, University of Oklahoma

Justice
Edited by Mark LeBar

Humility
Edited by Jennifer Cole Wright

Integrity, Honesty, and Truth-Seeking
Edited by Christian B. Miller and Ryan West

The Virtue of Sustainability
Edited by Jason Kawall

The Virtue of Harmony
Edited by Chenyang Li and Dascha Düring

The Virtue of Loyalty
Edited by Troy Jollimore

The Virtue of Solidarity
Edited by Andrea Sangiovanni and Juri Viehoff

THE VIRTUE OF SOLIDARITY

Edited by Andrea Sangiovanni
and Juri Viehoff

Oxford University Press is a department of the University of Oxford. It furthers
the University's objective of excellence in research, scholarship, and education
by publishing worldwide. Oxford is a registered trade mark of Oxford University
Press in the UK and certain other countries.

Published in the United States of America by Oxford University Press
198 Madison Avenue, New York, NY 10016, United States of America.

© Oxford University Press 2024

All rights reserved. No part of this publication may be reproduced, stored in
a retrieval system, or transmitted, in any form or by any means, without the
prior permission in writing of Oxford University Press, or as expressly permitted
by law, by license, or under terms agreed with the appropriate reproduction
rights organization. Inquiries concerning reproduction outside the scope of the
above should be sent to the Rights Department, Oxford University Press, at the
address above.

You must not circulate this work in any other form
and you must impose this same condition on any acquirer.

Library of Congress Control Number: 2024931145

ISBN 978–0–19–761275–0 (pbk.)
ISBN 978–0–19–761274–3 (hbk.)

DOI: 10.1093/oso/9780197612743.001.0001

CONTENTS

Series Editor's Foreword vii
Contributors ix

Introduction 1
Andrea Sangiovanni and Juri Viehoff

1. Solidarity: Concept, Conceptions, and Contexts 35
Rainer Forst

2. Solidarity and the Just Society 56
Philippe Van Parijs

3. Challenges to Solidarity 84
Andrea Sangiovanni

4. Solidarity as a Virtue of Equality 112
Avery Kolers

5. Personal Sacrifice and the Value of Solidarity 139
Juri Viehoff

CONTENTS

6. Transforming Interdependence into Social Virtue: Solidarity in Catholic Social Thought 170
   Meghan J. Clark

7. Pernicious Solidarities: Equity and Trust in Solidary Relations 194
   Sally J. Scholz

8. Rethinking Solidarity through the Lens of Critical Social Ontology 220
   Carol C. Gould

9. The Cost of Belonging: Universalism versus the Political Ideal of Solidarity 246
   Véronique Munoz-Dardé

10. Solidarity: The Link between Facts and Norms 284
    Margaret Kohn

11. Transnational Solidarity: A Durkheimian View 311
    Alexander Somek

12. A Tale of Two Tenths: Race, Class, and Solidarity 337
    Tommie Shelby

Index 365

SERIES EDITOR'S FOREWORD

Typically, having a virtue means being disposed to having certain kinds of perceptions, thoughts, motives, emotions, and ways one is inclined to act. The end of the twentieth and the beginning of the twenty-first centuries have seen an upsurge of interest in the topic of virtue. This is true not only in philosophy but also in a variety of other disciplines, such as theology, law, economics, psychology, and anthropology, to name a few. The study of virtue within disciplines is vitally important, yet the premise of this series is that the study of virtue in general, as well as of specific virtues, can be enhanced if scholars take into account work being done in disciplines other than their own.

Cross-disciplinary work can be challenging. Scholars trained in one field with its unique vocabulary and methods do not always move seamlessly into another discipline and often feel unqualified to undertake the task of serious cross-disciplinary engagement. The upshot can be that practitioners of disciplines can become "siloed"—trapped within their own disciplines and hesitant to engage seriously with others, even on important topics of mutual interest.

SERIES EDITOR'S FOREWORD

This series seeks to break the silos, with fifteen volumes on specific virtues or clusters of virtues. For each book, an introduction by the editor highlights the unity of writings by identifying common themes, threads, and ideas. In each volume, the editor seeks to include a chapter from a "wild card" discipline, a field one would not expect to see included in a collection of essays on a particular virtue. We do this both to highlight the diversity of fields in the study of specific virtues and to surprise and challenge readers to broaden their horizons in thinking about virtue.

The audience for this series is practitioners of different disciplines who seek to expand their thinking about virtue. Each volume contains chapters that are accessible and of interest to scholars from many disciplines. Though the volumes are not comprehensive overviews of the work on virtue that is occurring in any given field, they provide a useful introduction meant to pique the curiosity of readers and spur further engagement with other disciplines.

Nancy E. Snow
Professor of Philosophy and Director of the
Institute for the Study of Human Flourishing
University of Oklahoma

CONTRIBUTORS

Meghan J. Clark is an Associate Professor of Moral Theology at St. John's University (NY). In 2015, she was a Fulbright Scholar at the Hekima Institute for Peace Studies and International Relations at Hekima University College, Nairobi, Kenya. She has conducted fieldwork on human rights and solidarity in Sudan, Kenya, Ethiopia, and Tanzania. In May 2018, she was a Visiting Residential Research Fellow at the Centre for Catholic Studies at the University of Durham (UK). In 2022, she was Assistant Coordinator for the North American Working Group of the "Doing Theology from the Existential Peripheries" project of the Migrant & Refugee Section of the Dicastery for the Promotion of Integral Human Development of the Holy See. She is author of *The Vision of Catholic Social Thought: The Virtue of Solidarity and the Praxis of Human Rights* (Fortress Press, 2014) as well as numerous articles and chapters. Active in public theology, she is a columnist for *US Catholic* magazine and contributes to *NCR*, *America Magazine*, and other outlets.

Rainer Forst is Professor of Political Theory and Philosophy and Director of the Research Center "Normative Orders" at Goethe

University, Frankfurt. His research focuses on questions of justice, democracy, and toleration, as well as critical theory and practical reason. Important publications: *Contexts of Justice* (1994, Engl. University of California Press, 2002), *Toleration in Conflict* (2003, Engl. Cambridge University Press, 2013), *The Right to Justification* (2007, Engl. Columbia University Press, 2012), *Justification and Critique* (2011, Engl. Polity, 2013), *Normativity and Power* (2015, Engl. Oxford University Press, 2017), *The Noumenal Republic* (2021, Engl. Polity, 2024). In 2012, he was awarded the Leibniz Prize of the German Research Foundation.

Carol C. Gould is Distinguished Professor at the City University of New York, where she teaches in the Philosophy Department at Hunter College and in the Doctoral Programs in Philosophy and Political Science at the Graduate Center and is Director of the Center for Global Ethics and Politics at the Ralph Bunche Institute for International Affairs. She previously taught at Temple University and George Mason University and was a Member of the Institute for Advanced Study (2015–2016) and Fulbright Chair at the European University Institute (2000). Gould is Editor of the *Journal of Social Philosophy*. Her most recent books are *Interactive Democracy: The Social Roots of Global Justice* (Cambridge University Press, 2014), which received the Joseph B. Gittler Award of the American Philosophical Association, and *Globalizing Democracy and Human Rights* (Cambridge University Press, 2004), which won the David Easton Award from the American Political Science Association.

Margaret Kohn is a Professor of Political Theory at the University of Toronto. Her primary research interests are in the areas of critical theory, global justice, and urbanism. She is the author of *The Death and Life of the Urban Commonwealth* (Oxford University Press, 2016), which won the David Easton Award for Best Book in Political Theory and the Judd Award for Best Book in Urban and Local Politics. Her other books include *Radical Space: Building the House of the People* (Cornell University Press, 2003), *Brave New Neighborhoods: The Privatization of Public Space* (Routledge, 2004), and *Political Theories of Decolonization* (with Keally McBride, Oxford University Press, 2011). She was a Senior Braudel Fellow at the European University Institute. Her articles have appeared in such journals as *Political Theory*, *Perspectives on Politics*, *Journal of Politics*, *Polity*, *Dissent*, *Constellations*, *Theory & Event*, and *Philosophy and Social Criticism*.

Avery Kolers is Professor and Chair of Philosophy at the University of Louisville. He is the author of *Land, Conflict, and Justice: A Political Theory of Territory* (Cambridge University Press, 2009) and *A Moral Theory of Solidarity* (Oxford University Press, 2016), as well as numerous papers in applied ethics and social and political philosophy. He is working on a book about what political theory can learn from the individual and collective goods we realize in athletic activity and games. A recent paper in this vein is "Groundwork for the Mechanics of Morals," *Canadian Journal of Philosophy* (2021).

Véronique Munoz-Dardé is Professor of Philosophy at University College London, and she is also a member of the Department of Philosophy at University of California, Berkeley. Her research is in practical reasoning, ethics, and political philosophy. In recent years, she has written articles on a range of issues, worrying about ethical problems at different levels of abstraction: aggregation and numbers in practical reasoning; the transitivity of 'better than'; the social significance of risk; the justification of taxation; the nature of regret and what it reveals about the role of value in practical reasoning; the nature of social goods such as universities and museums; and the nature and importance of the political ideals of equality, fraternity, and solidarity. She has held visiting positions at the Department

CONTRIBUTORS

of Philosophy at Harvard and at the École des Hautes Études en Sciences Sociales. She is the author of *La justice sociale: Le libéralisme égalitaire de John Rawls* (Armand Collin, 2001), and is currently finishing a book manuscript provisionally entitled *The Regulation of Intimacy*.

Philippe Van Parijs is a Guest Professor at the Universities of Louvain and Leuven and a Simone Veil fellow at the European University Institute. He chairs the Brussels Council for Multilingualism and the advisory board of the Basic Income Earth Network. His books include *Real Freedom for All* (Oxford University Press, 1995), *Sauver la solidarité* (Cerf, 1995), *Refonder la solidarité* (Cerf, 1996), *Just Democracy* (ECPR Press, 2011), *Linguistic Justice for Europe and for the World* (Oxford University Press, 2011), and *Basic Income: A Radical Proposal for a Free Society and a Sane Economy* (with Y. Vanderborght, Harvard University Press, 2017).

Andrea Sangiovanni is Professor of Philosophy at King's College London. During 2018–2020, he was Professor of Social and Political Theory at the European University Institute, Fiesole. He received his BA and PhD from Harvard University. Before joining KCL, he was a Randall Dillard Research Fellow at Pembroke College, University of Cambridge (2005–2007). A monograph, entitled *Solidarity: Its Nature, Grounds, and Value* (with responses from five commentators) was published with Manchester University Press in 2023. This research is supported by a five-year ERC Consolidator Grant entitled 'Solidarity in Europe' (EUSOL). He is also the author of *Humanity without Dignity: Moral Equality, Respect, and Human Rights* (Harvard University Press, 2017), and numerous articles in journals such as *Philosophy & Public Affairs*, *Journal of Political Philosophy*, and *Oxford Journal of Legal Studies*.

CONTRIBUTORS

Sally J. Scholz is Professor of Philosophy at Villanova University. An award-winning teacher and researcher, Scholz works in social philosophy on solidarity, oppression, violence, and just war theory. Publications include the books *Political Solidarity* (Pennsylvania State University Press, 2008), *On de Beauvoir* (Wadsworth, 1999), *On Rousseau* (Wadsworth, 2000), and *Feminism: A Beginner's Guide* (Oneworld Publications, 2010). Scholz has co-edited numerous books and special issues, and served as editor for *Hypatia, Journal of Peace and Justice Studies,* and the *APA Newsletter on Philosophy and Feminism*. In addition, Scholz is a leader in the profession, serving on the board of the American Philosophical Association and as President of the North American Society for Social Philosophy.

Tommie Shelby is the Caldwell Titcomb Professor of African and African American Studies and Professor of Philosophy at Harvard University. Shelby's writings focus on racial justice, economic justice, and criminal justice and on the history of black political thought. He is the author of *Dark Ghettos: Injustice, Dissent, and Reform* (Harvard University Press, 2016), which won the 2018 David and Elaine Spitz Prize for best book in liberal or democratic theory and the 2016 Book Award from the North American Society for Social Philosophy. He is also the author of *We Who Are Dark: The Philosophical Foundations of Black Solidarity* (Harvard University Press, 2005). He and Derrick Darby co-edited *Hip Hop and Philosophy: Rhyme 2 Reason* (Open Court, 2005). Shelby and Brandon M. Terry co-edited *To Shape a New World: Essays on the Political Philosophy of Martin Luther King, Jr.* (Harvard University Press, 2018). Shelby's most recent book is *The Idea of Prison Abolition*, which is based on his 2018 Carl G. Hempel Lectures at Princeton University.

Alexander Somek is a Professor of Legal Philosophy in the Faculty of Law, University of Vienna. Prior to the present appointment, he held the Charles E. Floete Chair in Law in the College of Law, University of Iowa, and held visiting professorships at Princeton University and at the London School of Economics. He was a Law and Public Affairs Fellow at Princeton in the academic year 2012–2013 and a Fellow in the Institute for Advanced Study in Berlin during 2007–2008. His more recent publications include *Knowing What the Law Is: Legal Theory in a New Key* (Hart, 2021) and *The Legal Relation: Legal Theory after Legal Positivism* (Cambridge University Press, 2017).

Juri Viehoff is an Assistant Professor of Philosophy at the University of Utrecht in the Netherlands. Before taking up his current position, he was a permanent Lecturer in political theory at the University of Manchester and a research fellow at the Centre for Ethics, University of Zurich, and the European University Institute in Florence. He holds degrees from the London School of Economics and the University of Oxford (DPhil). He is currently completing a monograph on the political philosophy of the European Union (*Free and Equal: Political Morality for the European Union*). His work has been published in *The Journal of Political Philosophy*, *European Journal of Philosophy*, *Synthese*, *European Journal of Political Theory*, and several others.

Introduction

ANDREA SANGIOVANNI AND JURI VIEHOFF

Solidarity plays an important role in social and political life: historically invoked by socialist, nationalist, as well as Christian thinkers and activists, it is today perhaps the most prominent political ideal in which protest movements like Black Lives Matter[1] or #MeToo[2] couch their calls for action. And during the rapidly spreading coronavirus pandemic, there were widespread calls for solidarity with those most affected by the outbreak.[3] Moreover, solidarity is appealed to in order to justify decisions by political actors across a wide ideological spectrum, and legal and political institutions claim to implement communal solidarity among citizens, for example in relation to labor markets, healthcare, or old age pension schemes. Talk of solidarity, however, is not limited to political contexts: we can easily think of instances of

---

1. "George Floyd: Black Lives Matter Solidarity as England Buildings Go Purple," BBC News online, June 3, 2020, https://www.bbc.com/news/uk-england-52903747.
2. "700,000 Female Farmworkers Say They Stand with Hollywood Actors against Sexual Assault," *Time*, November 10, 2017, https://time.com/5018813/farmworkers-solidarity-hollywood-sexual-assault.
3. "Covid-19: People across the Country Are Delivering Groceries Free. It's 'Solidarity, Not Charity,'" *Washington Post*, April 27, 2020, https://www.washingtonpost.com/lifestyle/2020/04/27/people-across-country-are-delivering-groceries-free-its-solidarity-not-charity.

solidarity among colleagues or friends organizing some event, or fellow flight passengers hit by some unforeseen calamity. When used in such non-political contexts, solidarity is typically regarded as a personal disposition or standing attitude, and it is one among many concepts we use to evaluate the quality of individual character. But while philosophers working in moral psychology have over recent decades developed increasingly sophisticated accounts of important human virtues like honesty, integrity, humility and beneficence, so far no similarly systematic exploration of solidarity as a personal virtue of integral importance to human flourishing has emerged.[4] This reflects the fact that, in contrast to ideals of similar real-world significance—for example, justice, liberty, equality, and democracy—solidarity has received less attention from contemporary social, moral, and political philosophers. This is quickly changing: there has recently been a burgeoning interest in the nature, value, and grounds of solidarity among philosophers and social theorists (many of whom have contributed to this book). However, the literature is not, at the moment, unified around a set of central themes and controversies and is developed independently in various sub-fields.

This volume aims to remedy solidarity's relative neglect in social and political philosophy and moral theory, and to provide a unifying discussion of a range of central defining themes. By bringing together scholars from different disciplines and philosophical traditions that each contribute to our understanding of solidarity, we seek to explore some of the philosophical problems of solidarity, and we aim to better understand the connection between solidarity as a political phenomenon and solidarity as a personal and social virtue more generally. Different chapters of this volume address, respectively, solidarity's

---

4. Two recent exceptions to this are: Nicolas Bommarito, "Private Solidarity," *Ethical Theory and Moral Practice* 19 (2015): 445–455; Michael Zhao, "Solidarity, Fate-Sharing, and Community," *Philosopher's Imprint* 19 (2019).

nature and value, its role in our ethical life, its importance for our political and legal practices and institutions, and its connection to other important ideals and values.

We also believe that this book will contribute to debates regarding 'non-ideal theory.' Over recent years, 'mainstream' political philosophy has increasingly moved away from an exclusive focus on ideal theory. There has been a growing interest in applied normative analysis that starts its theorizing from prevailing conditions of injustice and oppression. We can see this trend in prominent publications that focus on the nature of oppression and domination, the ethics of protest and civil disobedience, and applied topics in global justice such as poverty or the exploitation of workers in global production chains. A nuanced philosophical discussion of solidarity, we believe, is ideally placed to benefit from these ongoing debates; but theorizing solidarity also promises to offer an important theoretical resource for those working on non-ideal theory. A moral theory of solidarity systematically explains the duties of the oppressed toward each other, and the requirements incumbent on the majority to stand by them in their struggle. Relatedly, the virtue theoretical perspective through which solidarity is also analyzed in this volume opens up a range of questions connected to the ethics of social activism: How do solidarity commitments reflect on personal character? And what contribution does solidarity with the oppressed make to the individual flourishing of the activist?

In this Introduction, our aim is to introduce the topic of solidarity and guide the reader through the themes that are taken up by contributors. We do so in a number of steps: First, we set out some of the core issues that arise when we think of solidarity as a philosophical topic and we describe some background assumptions shared by the various contributors. Next, we account for some important differences and disagreements that arise once we move beyond these shared initial ideas. We then lay out some core questions and puzzles that arise when we think of solidarity as a virtue, and then document what positions different contributors take in this volume. In the final section, we describe the structure of the book, briefly summarize each contribution, and close with a number of open issues and areas for future research.

ACCOUNTING FOR SOLIDARITY

The dispersed nature of existing contributions to the topic of solidarity in terms of philosophical traditions and (sub-)disciplines has meant that, to date, no unified body of literature to which those working on solidarity standardly refer has developed, and so there is no clearly defined set of arguments and debates in respect of which additions to the literature position themselves. Even more, philosophical understandings of what the concept of solidarity refers to (i.e., the extension of the term) range over a large array of social and political phenomena. Perhaps this is not especially surprising given the variegated linguistic use of the term. (And, as Philippe Van Parijs notes in Chapter 2, various European languages have developed meanings that differ from each other in at least some respects.) All of this raises the unwelcome possibility of scholars speaking past each other or failing to see how they are, in fact, asking identical questions. It is therefore important to elucidate a clear, overarching account of the core concept of solidarity, and to specify what such an account is meant to do. We do so by distinguishing below between the concept of solidarity and various conceptions of it, and by distinguishing between the content, ground, scope, and value of solidarity.

INTRODUCTION

Concept, Conceptions, and Types of Solidarity

In elucidating the concept of solidarity, one important initial observation is that the concept may not always match the word 'solidarity', both in the sense that different words may refer to the concept of solidarity and in the sense that some instances of 'solidarity' may refer to different concepts. Both are familiar ideas: the words 'liberty' and 'freedom' refer to the concept of freedom; and the word 'bank' refers to at least two concepts. In relation to solidarity, things are as follows (they also vary between European languages): Regarding the first phenomenon, both common usage and the literature frequently use the word 'fraternity'—*fraternité, Brüderlichkeit*, and so on—beside 'solidarity' to reference the social phenomena central to solidarity. As regards the latter, there are at least some polysemous usages of the term as well.[5] But if the use of the word 'solidarity' is neither necessary nor sufficient to track the *concept* of solidarity, then how can we demarcate that to which the concept refers? The best strategy, it seems, is to appeal to uncontroversial instances of solidarity and then work out what these phenomena have in common.

Of course, this is not always straightforward for, as we noted earlier, the practices and phenomena that authors have in mind when using the language of solidarity are wide-ranging, even if we limit ourselves to those who work in social and political philosophy. In order to avoid both 'merely verbal' disagreements and speaking past each other, philosophers have developed a number of tools and terms to keep track: One systematic distinction sometimes introduced here is that between the *concept* of solidarity and varying *conceptions* of it (see Forst, Chapter 1).[6] When two people share a concept, they

---

5. E.g., in French *solidaire* means 'parallel'; cf. Van Parijs, Chapter 2 in this volume.
6. John Rawls, *A Theory of Justice*, rev. ed. (Cambridge, MA: Belknap Press of Harvard University Press, 1999), 4; Ronald Dworkin, *Law's Empire* (Cambridge, MA: Belknap Press of Harvard University Press, 1986), 70. Rainer Forst, in Chapter 1 of this volume, also uses the concept/conception distinction for his central argument. By introducing the further notion of an

can have meaningful disagreements about it.[7] This is the case because (at least on this understanding, favored, e.g., by Rawls and Dworkin) sharing a concept entails that one agrees to a sufficient degree about the underlying aspect of the world that the concept picks out (e.g., both parties to a dispute might agree on what counts as paradigmatic instances of solidarity). And yet, sharing a concept of solidarity does not preclude, first, that they may disagree on what makes paradigmatic cases paradigmatic, disagree on how to deal with further cases, and disagree on the correct analysis of the concept. When people share the concept of solidarity but disagree about its boundaries and/or the nature of the things to which the concept refers (and perhaps other aspects), then they are putting forward diverging *conceptions* of solidarity.

One difficulty that we encounter with solidarity is that it is not always clear whether incompatible understandings amount to diverging conceptions, or whether authors really have in mind aspects of the social world so different that we should take them to not really disagree but just to address different topics using the same word, hence to be speaking past each other. For example, there is a huge difference between those who think of solidarity as encompassing literally any kind of pro-social attitude and behavior (e.g., Richard Rorty[8]) and those who think that solidarity is importantly different from other such concepts, for example, empathy, loyalty, or love.

    'account' of solidarity, we seek to sharpen the distinction between analytic/conceptual questions about solidarity and explanatory issues regarding the social phenomena that solidarity as a concept picks out.

7. We do not mean to imply that there aren't other ways of making sense of conceptual disagreement, e.g., metalinguistic disagreements about which terms to use; David Plunkett and Timothy Sundell, "Dworkin's Interpretivism and the Pragmatics of Legal Disputes," *Legal Theory* 19 (2013): 242–281. For this Introduction we aim to stay neutral between them. Our point is that whichever way of pointing to differences in concept use one likes, it is important, for conceptual debates to be productive, to clarify the nature of these disagreements.

8. Richard Rorty, *Contingency, Irony, and Solidarity* (Cambridge: Cambridge University Press, 1989).

INTRODUCTION

In spite of these legitimate worries, there is, we believe, sufficient common ground that allows for a shared topic and hence meaningful disagreement. At the most general conceptual level, solidarity's core applies to cases where the relations between persons satisfy some condition of *unity* or *togetherness*, or are characterized by some positive reciprocal attitude. This seems true for both micro (interpersonal) and macro (large-scale societal) contexts in which the concept of solidarity is paradigmatically invoked. It is also compatible with the descriptive, social-scientific use of the concept of solidarity in sociology and social psychology. For Auguste Comte and Emile Durkheim, for example, solidarity refers to the set of mutual attitudes, dispositions, and (cooperative) actions required to sustain social cohesion across a society.[9] Finally, this common core also reflects, as various authors have noted, solidarity's linguistic origins in Roman law as a jointly shared debt-liability (*obligatio in solidum*[10]).

TYPES OF SOLIDARITY

Of course solidarity today no longer has a primarily juridical connotation, but is used widely across ethical, social, and political contexts. This has led many writers on the topic to distinguish between different types of solidarity, for example, organic versus mechanical (Durkheim), social versus civic versus political solidarity (e.g., Bayertz, Scholz), unitary versus networking (Gould), civic versus democratic versus redistributive (Banting/Kymlicka), robust

---

9. Emile Durkheim, *The Division of Labor in Society* (New York: Simon & Schuster, 2014); Auguste Comte, *Discours sur l'esprit positif*, (Paris: Carilian-Goeury et V. Dalmont, 1844). For a detailed analysis of Durkheim's account, see Alexander Somek, Chapter 11 in this volume.
10. Kurt Bayertz, "Four Uses of 'Solidarity,'" in *Solidarity*, ed. Kurt Bayertz (Dordrecht: Kluwer Academic Publishers, 1999), 3–28, at 3; Arto Laitinen and Anne Pessi, eds., *Solidarity: Theory and Practice* (New York: Lexington, 2015), 1–29, at 1; Steinar Stjernø, *Solidarity in Europe: The History of an Idea* (Cambridge University Press, 2009).

versus expressive (Taylor), 'solidarity with' versus 'solidarity among' (Miller).[11] While such classifications can be helpful to categorize the diversity of social phenomena that make up solidarity, they also give rise to new questions: Is the relation between 'civic solidarity' and 'political solidarity' more like that between 'civil law' and 'criminal law,' or that between 'the law of the land' and 'the laws of physics' (i.e., referring to separate concepts)? If, much more plausibly, it is the former, then what is it in virtue of which civic and political solidarity are instances of the wider phenomenon of solidarity in general?[12]

Accounts of Solidarity

Concepts and conceptions of solidarity differ from what we would call (philosophical) *accounts* or *theories* of solidarity in that the latter amount to a systematic explanation of the phenomena that a concept/conception picks out.[13] More specifically, we suggest that for something to count as a philosophical account of solidarity it must answer, in a coherent manner, some basic questions about solidarity's nature, which includes a discussion of *content*, *ground*, *scope*, and *value* or *function*. This does not mean that in order to put

---

11. Sally J. Scholz, "Seeking Solidarity," *Philosophy Compass* 10 (2015): 725–735; Bayertz, "Four Uses of 'Solidarity' "; Carol C. Gould, "Transnational Solidarities," *Journal of Social Philosophy* 38 (2007): 148–164; Will Kymlicka and Keith Banting (eds.), *The Strains of Commitment: The Political Sources of Solidarity in Diverse Societies* (Oxford: Oxford University Press, 2017); Ashley E. Taylor, "Solidarity: Obligations and Expressions," *Journal of Political Philosophy* 23 (2015): 128–145; David Miller, "Solidarity and Its Sources," in *The Strains of Commitment: The Political Sources of Solidarity in Diverse Societies*, ed. Keith Banting and Will Kymlicka (Oxford: Oxford University Press, 2017), 61–79.
12. Similar concerns about excessive reliance on different types of solidarity are raised in [Sangiovanni 2023] [Viehoff ms].
13. Joseph Raz, "Two Views of the Nature of the Theory of Law: A Partial Comparison," in *Hart's Postscript: Essays on the Postscript to the Concept of Law*, ed. Jules Coleman (New York: Oxford University Press, 2001), 1–37, at 8ff.

forward an account of solidarity one must respond fully to each of these. But an account of solidarity will at the very least describe what count as paradigmatic instances of solidarity and *explain why* they are paradigmatic. Below, we describe what we mean by each of these features.

CONTENT

Philosophical accounts of solidarity will, at a minimum, elaborate how the notions of *togetherness*, *unity*, and so on, mentioned above, are exactly to be understood; that is, they will define more precisely the attitudes and dispositions (and perhaps further elements) that are paradigmatic of the relation 'being in solidarity with.' In doing so, they will respond to some fundamental questions: Is solidarity more than a disposition to empathize with another person, perhaps something like the belief that there is an obligation to assist someone in need? Does solidarity, in addition to some emotional and cognitive content, require something like an actual intention to act in appropriate ways? Does solidarity entail a desire to overcome some obstacle or adversity? Does 'being in solidarity' involve further mental elements? And: Is there a core sense in which 'full solidarity' really is more a type of (joint) *action* than a (combination of) mental state(s) and disposition(s)? In filling out the specific character of solidarity's requirements we arrive at a more determinate account of the *content* of solidarity.

GROUND

The attitudes that make up solidarity's content are not free-floating but are typically explained in terms of some background characteristic (e.g., shared humanity), some form of preexisting identification (e.g., gender- or race-based identification) or preexisting bond (e.g., of kinship) that those standing in solidarity with each other share. This is the question about solidarity's *ground(s)*: In virtue of which facts *should* and *do* individuals develop bonds of solidarity with each other? Among the grounds frequently invoked in the existing literature are facts about 'community,' 'shared sympathy,' 'shared oppression/adversity,' 'shared identity,' 'shared goals,' or indeed a combination of these. The way we understand the notion of 'ground' for the purpose of this volume is, first and foremost, normative: For some fact, say shared identity, to ground solidarity, shared identity must be an (objective or subjective, prudential or moral) reason to adopt or maintain the attitudes, dispositions, and so forth, that are constitutive of solidarity. The reasons can be reasons that one takes oneself to have to join with others (subjective reasons), or reasons that one really has (whether or not one recognizes them) to join with others. So when we explain how shared identity acts as a ground of solidarity, we explain why this kind of relation among members of a group provides those members with subjective or objective, as the case may be, reasons to develop solidarity among each other.

SCOPE

Issues regarding solidarity's grounds are clearly connected to the question about solidarity's *scope*: Between which agents, and under what circumstances, is solidarity possible? If, for example, one believes that the sole normative ground of solidarity is a basic recognition of one another's moral worth,[14] then the scope of solidarity is not restricted to anything short of humanity at large. Yet if one takes solidarity to require some concrete, shared experience of oppression or adversity, then the notion of 'human solidarity' will seem

---

14. David Wiggins, *Ethics: Twelve Lectures on the Philosophy of Morality* (Cambridge, MA: Harvard University Press, 2006).

farfetched, unless one adopts some religious assumptions about susceptibility to original sin or imagines humanity facing, collectively, a single threat (such as climate change).

VALUE/FUNCTION

Beyond the issues of what solidarity is and over whom it ranges, there are important axiological questions that a systemic explanation of the nature of solidarity must account for. First, at the most general level, what makes being in solidarity and having commitments characterized by solidaristic mutual concern valuable? Is this value non-instrumental or instrumental? Is solidarity good, for example, because of what further things it supports, enables, facilitates, or causes, or is it good in itself? (Others,[15] more cautiously, suggest that solidarity merely constitutes an important social ideal, which means, roughly, that it serves a distinctive function.) Beyond this fundamental axiological question, there are important questions about solidarity's relative force and its deontic status: How should we proceed if the value of solidarity conflicts with other values? And what role should the value of solidarity play in the design of social and political institutions? To make better sense of these questions, it is important to distinguish solidarity from other phenomena. How is solidarity different from loyalty, benevolence, sympathy, and love? How does it differ from other political ideals, such as justice, fairness, or community? All of these questions are taken up, in one way or another, by different authors throughout this book.

---

15. For example, Véronique Munoz-Dardé, Chapter 9 in this volume.

ANDREA SANGIOVANNI AND JURI VIEHOFF

SHARED ASSUMPTIONS ACROSS THE VOLUME

Having outlined the terrain in terms of concept/conception/accounts of solidarity, we are now in a position to say a bit more about some of the shared assumptions that run through the individual chapters of this volume. First, and most importantly, all authors agree that, as far as the concept of solidarity is concerned, we should think of it as both *unique* and *explanatory*. Solidarity is *unique* in the following two senses: First, our concept picks out a particular social phenomenon that is distinct from others that can be run under the broader label of 'pro-social behavior,' for example, loyalty or empathy. Second, authors assume that solidarity is unified across different domains of social life so that it can, at least to some extent, be captured in terms of necessary and sufficient conditions or paradigmatic conditions (the latter sets out conditions that most, though not necessarily all, instances of solidarity must satisfy). Put differently, solidarity is not too diffuse or amorphous to be amenable to analysis, and different uses of solidarity are not mere instances of polysemy.

Solidarity is also *explanatory*, in that knowing that A and B are in solidarity can help to explain both normative and non-normative further features of the world. By way of example, consider the case of friendship: Knowing that A and B are friends is explanatorily significant in that it can furnish an adequate explanation of their actions and feelings: the fact that B was A's friend is a good explanation of A's sadness when B passed away. Bonds of solidarity are similarly explanatorily significant when we try to understand how people act, feel, deliberate, and so on. And like the case of friendship, solidarity is also normatively explanatory in that "B is in solidarity with A" can, provided certain features obtain, serve as an appropriate explanation or justification of A being under certain obligations, requirements of aptness when it comes to certain emotions, and so on.[16]

The shared assumptions of conceptual uniqueness and explanatory relevance in turn shape how the authors assembled here understand the content, ground, scope, and value of solidarity: The attitudes necessary for individuals to be in solidarity are complex, and cannot be reduced to other phenomena, such as mere loyalty or empathy; and since solidarity is taken to be explanatorily significant for how people act, the dispositions and attitudes of solidarity must (if not always, then at least typically) be *action-guiding* and *practical*. While the authors importantly disagree about the grounds and value of solidarity (more on this below), there is, we think, a shared belief that something other than those basic features necessary for counting morally, for example sentience, capacity to reason, are required for solidarity to be a useful category. Even Clark, who takes up the Catholic tradition of thinking about solidarity as uniting human beings as such, suggests that solidarity is a response to the distinctive facts of human interdependence (see Chapter 6). Solidarity, for all authors, is an ideal that has purchase only between agents that have some capacity for self-directed moral agency and are therefore, at least in principle, capable of engaging with one another on terms of (perhaps counterfactual) reciprocity or mutuality. (How exactly this condition needs to be spelled out is, of course, subject to debate and disagreement.) Finally, there is broad agreement among all authors that we have decisive reasons, both practical and theoretical, to insist that solidarity is not coextensive with existing categories we use in that domain (e.g., 'justice' or 'community').

---

16. It is a substantive question about which contributors to this volume disagree whether solidarity is 'normatively dependent,' that is, whether solidarity is only obligation-generating in the presence of further deontic facts (cf. Forst, Chapter 1 in this volume).

DIVERGENCES AND DISAGREEMENTS

Our aim in the following paragraphs is to briefly point to a number of areas where the authors assembled here disagree with each other in developing a fuller account of solidarity. We do this with a view to identifying those areas that seem most promising for further discussion and future research.

One initial observation when it comes to the diverging positions within this volume relates, again, to conceptions of solidarity. While authors agree that solidarity is sufficiently unitary to merit philosophical analysis and debate, this does not mean that, when putting forward conceptions of solidarity, authors agree on what instances or cases count as (most) paradigmatic. One distinction we can discern in relation to the pieces assembled here relates to the primacy of micro versus macro cases: Those authors who investigate solidarity primarily as an individual personal attitude or virtue, or as a small-group phenomenon among people who know each other personally, take solidarity in these contexts to be central and see large-scale social or civic solidarity as less paradigmatic instances of the phenomenon (e.g., Viehoff, Chapter 5). Perhaps one good analogy here comes from the literature on trust, where philosophers tend to think of 'interpersonal trust' between two individuals as the core case through which we understand its distinctive nature (e.g., that trust differs from mere reliance, that it requires a distinctive set of emotional responses, etc.). 'Social trust,' on the other hand, refers to widely shared dispositions among society-at-large, but does not pick out exactly those features we have identified as central in small-scale scenarios. Other authors (e.g., Forst, Kohn, Somek, and Munoz-Dardé) start from society-wide dispositions. In addressing solidarity as a wider social phenomenon (e.g., something that can characterize societies at large), they deny, at least implicitly, the primacy of interpersonal solidarity. Typically, they rely on a 'thinner' conceptual core of solidarity, that is, whether solidarity applies among members of a group depends on a less expansive set of attitudes and dispositions. Interpersonal cases of solidarity that contain a fair amount of mental content are then classified as one distinct, but not explanatorily privileged, 'context' (see Forst, Chapter 1) of solidarity.

But even among those that take interpersonal behavior to be (most) paradigmatic for solidarity, there emerge some interesting fault lines: First, at least some authors believe that whether some instance of solidarity among members of a group counts as paradigmatic is tied to the objective moral status of their convictions, goals, and actions. Put differently, some authors—most notably Carol Gould (Chapter 8), but arguably also Sally Scholz (Chapter 7)—have *moralized* conceptions of solidarity: Perhaps we should not go as far as saying that solidarity among mafiosi is no solidarity at all (though Gould seems to come close to this), but mafiosi solidarity, these authors think, is clearly less paradigmatic than solidarity among members of, say, the 1960s civil rights movement. By contrast, those authors who believe that solidarity is, and ought to be, *non-moralized* maintain that there is nothing infelicitous about talking of mafiosi solidarity. (Accepting a non-moralized conception of solidarity is, of course, compatible with the idea that in classifying a case of solidarity as paradigmatic, we appeal to facts about the beliefs about what is wrong or right, good or bad, of the people whose solidarity we assess.)

A second fault line concerns the domain of action: both Avery Kolers (Chapter 4) and Andrea Sangiovanni (Chapter 3) have put forward (here and elsewhere[17]) accounts of solidarity that understand it as a kind of joint or cooperative action among members of a group. This seems to imply that cases of what we may call 'silent'

---

17. Avery Kolers, *A Moral Theory of Solidarity* (Oxford: Oxford University Press, 2016); Andrea Sangiovanni, "Solidarity as Joint Action," *Journal of Applied Philosophy* 32 (2015): 340–359.

or 'one-sided' solidarity—that is, cases where some agent develops those attitudes necessary for being in solidarity with a group or goal but no collective action ensues—are not (paradigmatic) instances of solidarity. Others (notably Viehoff in Chapter 5 and Van Parijs in Chapter 2) disagree: there is nothing unintelligible about cases of such silent solidarity, or solidarity without shared and interlocking intentions; indeed some such cases appear to be especially pure instances of solidarity.

Once we move beyond questions of definition and conceptual centrality, one recurring topic throughout the volume concerns the (normative) grounds of solidarity, that is, the reasons that explain why individuals are motivated to act in solidarity and why the performance of such acts of solidarity is indeed justified: Some authors adopt a pluralist view on solidarity's grounds—perhaps most explicitly Forst (Chapter 1), but also Gould (Chapter 8) whose two types of solidarity, unitary and networked, are grounded in different social ontologies. Tommie Shelby too advocates in Chapter 12 a pluralist position with regard to solidarity's grounds in that he seeks to establish a middle ground between a Marxist explanation of solidarity in terms of shared material interests or mutual dependence and the idea that solidarity amounts to a moral commitment to overcome injustice. Sangiovanni in Chapter 3 distinguishes five grounds of solidarity—solidarity on the basis of a shared cause, shared condition, shared set of experiences, shared way of life, and shared role—arguing that, depending on the context, one or more of these bases serves to underpin solidarity.[18] Van Parijs, on the other hand, in Chapter 2, favors a unitary approach in which 'counterfactual reciprocity' is tied to *identification* with the object of solidarity.

---

18. Andrea Sangiovanni, *Solidarity: Nature, Grounds, and Value* (Manchester: Manchester University Press, 2023).

INTRODUCTION

A further topic that runs through this volume concerns solidarity's scope: With whom can we, in principle, be in solidarity and what motivational and institutional constraints are there on solidarity as a political virtue? Somek, in Chapter 11, coming from the macro perspective of society-wide solidarity, questions whether the scope of solidarity bonds can simply be expanded to wider groups through deepening integration and interdependence among those groups. This view of social and political solidarity conflicts with the suggestion that solidarity can take a wide scope encompassing all of humanity (as promulgated by Clark and other cosmopolitan authors). Munoz-Dardé too stresses the particularist nature of solidarity and criticizes those who want to expand the scope of solidarity to humanity at large (see Chapter 9). Against accounts according to which solidarity stands in contrast to impartial morality, Kolers in Chapter 4 offers a novel gloss on David Wiggins's formulation of solidarity as "the root of the ethical": Even if it is right that solidarity requires partiality, then at least one kind of solidarity, to wit, fundamental solidarity that grounds all other moral requirements, is a kind of partiality toward all human beings.

A final cluster of issues that several contributions take up concerns solidarity's value, most notably whether solidarity action is non-instrumentally good and how solidarity is connected to justice. At one end of this spectrum we find Carol Gould's Chapter 8: as we suggested above, she *defines* solidarity as necessarily aimed at bringing about (true) justice. Read this way, solidarity's value is conditional and instrumental on realizing justice, and genuine solidarity is always valuable because it realizes that which is valuable (i.e., justice). Both Kohn (Chapter 10) and Scholz (Chapter 7) side with Gould on the connection between solidarity and justice; that is, they agree that solidarity is valuable because and only insofar as it contributes to the realization of justice. (Kohn and Scholz, however, differ from Gould on the conceptual issue in that they believe that 'pernicious' solidarity is solidarity, too.) On these accounts, then, solidarity is only *conditionally and instrumentally* valuable. Though Clark in Chapter 6 formulates her interpretation of solidarity's value in terms of "the common good," her view too seems most compatible with this conditional interpretation of solidarity's value. The close connection to moral requirements and justice is scrutinized by Viehoff (Chapter 5) and Kolers (Chapter 4): Viehoff notes features internal to solidarity behavior that make it morally good independent of its purposive aim (personal integrity, community, etc.), while Kolers emphasizes solidarity's internal connection to something that is intrinsically good, namely human virtue. In contrast to a purely instrumental understanding, these positions then see solidarity as non-instrumentally (but still conditionally) valuable: unless some disabling condition is in place, solidarity is either good in itself or good as a constitutive element of something else that is non-instrumentally good. In Chapter 3, Sangiovanni addresses several challenges to the idea that solidarity is a value at all.

SOLIDARITY AND VIRTUE

We suggested early on that talk of solidarity is at home both in our assessment of macro-level societal phenomena and interpersonal relations. A good philosophical account of solidarity should connect these different uses and explain their relation. One explicit aim of this volume is to connect reflection on solidarity in social and political philosophy to topics in moral psychology. It seems that in interpersonal cases, at least under normal circumstances, acting from motives of solidarity reflects well on the agent: The worker who resists a tempting offer by her boss in order to stand with his striking fellow union members, or the white person who refuses to sit in a "whites only" section of a bus during segregation in order to demonstrate her allegiance to the civil rights movement, is praiseworthy. Conversely, we deride those that we deem to act selfishly where solidarity is called for. These judgments provide some intuitive appeal to the notion that, like loyalty or beneficence, solidarity is a (moral) virtue. In the literature, this common-sense judgment has been taken up and developed by different authors. Perhaps most explicitly, Christian writers[19]—following Catholic social thought developed in papal encyclical letters[20]—as well as recent feminist authors[21] writing on solidarity have stressed that solidarity is (also) a moral virtue.

In this volume too, different contributors take up the idea that solidarity is a virtue and develop it in different directions. The assumption that solidarity is a moral virtue in its own right is taken up by Kolers in Chapter 4: unless we see solidarity as a distinctive moral virtue, namely as a "dedication to our coequal membership of the *party of humankind*," virtue theory lacks a clear commitment to the equal moral worth of persons. Thus, solidarity is a kind of meta-virtue in whose light others are to be (re)interpreted and applied. Kolers's argument is indebted to earlier discussions of solidarity by Philippa Foot and David Wiggins, who used the term to illuminate a type of virtuous attitude, namely one that resists consequentialist and aggregationist tendencies in ethical decision-making.[22] In Chapter 9, Munoz-Dardé criticizes Foot and Wiggins (and, by extension, Kolers) for postulating solidarity as such a fundamental virtue.

---

19. Gerald J. Beyer, "The Meaning of Solidarity in Catholic Social Teaching," *Political Theology* 15 (2014): 7–25; Meghan J. Clark, "Anatomy of a Social Virtue: Solidarity and Corresponding Vices," *Political Theology* 15 (2014): 26–39.
20. Benedict XVI, "Caritas in veritate," 2009; John Paul II, "Sollicitudo Rei Socialis," 1987; Paul VI, "Populorum Progressio," 1967.
21. Sally J. Scholz, "The Duty of Solidarity: Feminism and Catholic Social Teaching," *Philosophy in the Contemporary World* 4 (1997): 24–33; Sally J. Scholz, *Political Solidarity*, (University Park: Penn State University Press, 2008).
22. Philippa Foot, "Morality, Action and Outcome,'" in *Morality and Objectivity*, ed. Ted Honderich (London: Routledge, 1985), 23–38, at 36; Wiggins, *Ethics*, 243.

Any such reading, Munoz-Dardé contends, neglects the 'essentially partitive' dimension carried by our concept of solidarity. Of course, we can realign our understanding of solidarity to eliminate this logic of 'us' versus 'them'; but doing so would lose solidarity's distinctive flavor and render the concept redundant. There are many aspects of this discussion that merit further discussion: Is it really plausible to see solidarity's distinctive contribution to moral theorizing in its partitive or adversarial nature? And, even if true, does this fact rule out that solidarity is a virtue in its own right?

Viehoff, in Chapter 5, does not aim to classify solidarity as a virtue. Rather, his contention is that we can better understand solidarity's nature if we focus on acts of solidarity that require *self-sacrifice*. Sometimes self-sacrifice is both an instance of solidarity and expresses some well-known virtues like benevolence, integrity, humility, and courage. And sometimes, solidarity is the only morally virtuous thing for an agent to do. But what do solidaristic self-sacrifices and other acts of solidarity have in common, and when does self-sacrifice stop being good for the agent? Solidarity, Viehoff argues, is held together by a commitment to pursue solidarity goals under the guise of a communal commitment. Self-sacrifice stops being solidaristic (though not necessarily being virtuous) when the interests of the individual agent and the demands of the group diverge too drastically. Viehoff's contribution thus explores common ground with Kolers, who also argues that commitments of community stand at the heart of solidarity.

Others in this volume adopt a more indirect approach on the subject of virtue: In her discussion in Chapter 10 of the French solidarists, as well as Jürgen Habermas's writing on solidarity, Kohn takes up the idea that solidarity is a specifically civic and democratic virtue, one that consists in a "willingness to discharge a collective obligation to repair unjust social institutions." Similar to Kohn, Van Parijs (Chapter 2) suggests that solidarity is (at least) also a component of civic virtue. Solidarity, that is, is constituted by those traits and dispositions that, under normal conditions, allow a democratic polity and just social institutions to thrive. On this view, solidarity is primarily a political phenomenon that arises specifically in the context of mass society and the modern nation-state.[23]

Lastly, the solidarity-virtue nexus also bears on what we might say about solidarity's value. As Sangiovanni stresses in Chapter 3, seeing solidarity as a virtue opens avenues to better understand solidarity as a value: if virtues robustly dispose some agent to pursue some further good, then solidarity is clearly of instrumental value. But beyond that, if solidaristic action is itself virtuous, then that may explain why solidarity is also non-instrumentally valuable: as Thomas Hurka and others have argued, having appropriate attitudes and dispositions toward a state of affairs that is intrinsically good is itself intrinsically good (a thought that is taken up by Viehoff in Chapter 5 to make sense of the value of causally ineffective acts of solidarity).[24]

Beyond offering suggestions regarding what makes *solidarity good*, virtue theory may include distinctive suggestions on what makes *good solidarity*. At least according to the Aristotelean account of the virtues, virtuous actions occupy a kind of mean between two opposing vices, and it is at least in part the avoiding of these vices through *phronesis* (good practical judgment gained through experience, sentimental education, etc.) that makes virtuous action good. Thus, the person in possession of courage avoids two bad responses to risk, namely cowardice and recklessness. Similarly, the generous

---

23. A point that is repeatedly stressed by Jürgen Habermas, "Solidarität jenseits des Nationalstaats: Notizen zu einer Diskussion," in *Transnationale Solidarität: Chancen und Grenzen*, ed. Jens Beckert et al. (Frankfurt: Campus, 2004), 225–235; Jürgen Habermas, "Democracy, Solidarity and the European Crisis," lecture delivered at the University of Leuven, 2013.
24. Thomas Hurka, *Virtue, Vice, and Value* (Oxford; New York: Oxford University Press, 2001), chapter 1.

person avoids both stinginess and pointlessly squandering one's resources to benefit others.[25] Moreover, phronesis consists in more than the appropriate choice of means: a clever person knows how to pursue her ends effectively, but only the wise knows how to choose both means and valuable *ends*.[26] What may these claims about the Aristotelean account of virtue imply for good solidarity? One thought, entertained by Meghan Clark in Chapter 6, is that solidarity is the virtue that lies between the two deficiencies of 'excessive individualism' and 'excessive collectivism' about the common good. Interestingly, she suggests that these vices can be both the subject of an individual person's character and embodied in social and political institutions (free-wheeling neoliberalism vs. communism). Should we, alternatively, place solidarity between a lack of commitment to a just case ('turn-coatism') and the opposite vice of zealotry or fanaticism? A second point ties back to the earlier discussion of 'pernicious solidarities': if solidarity is a virtue, then this may indeed impose constraints on what can appropriately count as a solidarity goal or aim. This point can be developed into two directions: Gould, in Chapter 8, relying on the idea that solidarity is a virtue, deploys it to bolster her claim that some apparent solidarities aren't true instances of our core concept.[27] By contrast, Forst, in Chapter 1, relying on the thought that solidarity in the pursuit of evil purposes—say among mafiosi or white supremacists—is clearly possible, takes this to decisively imply that solidarity is not, in fact, a (moral) virtue.

---

25. Susan Wolf, "Moral Psychology and the Unity of the Virtues," *Ratio* 20 (2007): 145–167, at 149.
26. Philippa Foot, *Virtues and Vices and Other Essays in Moral Philosophy* (Oxford: Oxford University Press, 1978), 6.
27. Her conception of virtue thus seems to operate with something like the Aristotelean idea of the unity of (moral) virtues in the background. Aristotle, *Nicomachean Ethics*, trans. Roger Crisp, 2nd ed. (Cambridge: Cambridge University Press, 2014), 1145a 1–2.

INTRODUCTION

STRUCTURE OF THE VOLUME

A natural progression in the philosophical analysis of solidarity starts from conceptual clarification, then moves on to the elucidation of the content, ground, scope, and value of solidarity, and finally, engages questions regarding its realization in different social contexts and in light of potential conflicts with other values. Although this edited volume is not separated into parts, we have sought to organize chapters in light of this natural progression. In other words, we begin with those contributions most directly concerned with illuminating the concept of solidarity; we then move toward more axiological and deontic questions and, finally, to questions regarding the practical consequences of solidarity and its relation other areas in social and political philosophy. These latter chapters respond to solidarity as a topic in macro-level institutional reflection, broaching a number of issues ranging from the predominantly theoretical (e.g., whether solidarity is compatible with ethical universalism, whether solidarity is an important institutional virtue) to concrete applications and problems of solidarity in the context of social and political movements.

The first substantive chapter of this volume comes from Forst and seeks to clarify the concept of solidarity and locate it in relation to other normative concepts, such as justice. Forst thinks that we can isolate a general *concept* of solidarity that contains its essential features, and, on the other hand, describes how specific variants of this notion interpret these essential characteristics of solidarity to arrive at distinctive *conceptions* of it. The general concept of solidarity, according to Forst, refers to "a practical attitude" of "standing by" that some agent adopts toward others. The attitude is based on a normative connection grounded in a common cause or shared identity. Moreover, solidarity establishes that one is willing to engage in joint action with others "based on the motive of affirming the collective bond." Such action requires participants to set aside narrow self-interest in the pursuit of their joint goals. Those who belong to a solidaristic community must, furthermore, be disposed to a particular kind of reciprocity—"solidary reciprocity"—that exceeds any standard understanding of reciprocity in terms of receiving a fair return. Solidarity requires us to look beyond any one individual's contribution: What matters is whether someone is willing to contribute, not how much they contribute. Forst argues that the concept of solidarity is a "normatively dependent" concept in need of normative grounding by other values or principles, depending on context. He subsequently describes different contexts of solidarity, which he labels *ethical, legal, political,* and *moral,* and discusses their connection to other principles such as justice: In political and legal contexts, he suggests, our duties of solidarity are best "defined by justice," though that is a normative and not a conceptual claim. He closes with a note of caution against excessively streamlining solidarity to fit a particular model in terms of grounds, motives, content, scope, and form.

In Chapter 2, Van Parijs claims that solidarity is best understood as mutual responsibility between the members of a real or imagined community. On this view, strong interdependence among participants is neither necessary nor sufficient: It is insufficient because there can be interdependence among antagonistic parties (e.g., workers and capitalists) and because solidarity requires a disposition to go beyond tit-for-tat forms of reciprocity. It is unnecessary because we can 'share a fate' with people who are unable to shape our own destiny in any meaningful way: It is the simple bond of a thinly shared identity that is enough for solidarity to arise. Solidarity must be distinguished from variants of purely altruistic behavior because solidarity is, to a limited extent, self-interested. If such a disposition becomes widely shared within a social group, then it will become true that it also serves the person who displays solidarity. Having established this notion of solidarity, Van Parijs moves on to clarify its relation to social justice and its relevance for institutions. Solidarity as mutual responsibility can be displayed by individuals and by collectives. But it can also govern institutions. The institutionalization of solidarity plays a major role in the pursuit of social justice, but the two are neither identical nor always pulling identical directions.

Van Parijs's piece is followed by Sangiovanni's. Sangiovanni begins Chapter 3 by considering the value-laden character of solidarity. Understood provisionally as a form of standing together against adversity grounded in identification, it embodies an ideal of *unity* and *integrity*. It is opposed to division, rancor, strife, and discord. Those who exhibit solidarity with others exhibit a virtue of character and conduct. To act solidaristically is to act well. He then canvasses three main challenges to solidarity as an ideal. First, he responds to the objection that solidarity's demands for unity stifle liberty and encourage exclusion. Second, he responds to the those who believe that it is a wishy-washy, vague term whose meaninglessness is a beacon for demagogues and bad politics. Third, he seeks to allay the worry that, when given a more precise character, it becomes redundant, no different from similar ideas such as altruism, empathy, identification, fellow-feeling, or justice. His chapter therefore echoes both Scholz's and Gould's concerns with the darker sides of solidarity, and serves to foreground, like Forst, possible forms of skepticism.

The next contribution turns more explicitly to the question: Is solidarity a virtue? Kolers, in Chapter 4, points out that theorists of solidarity have used virtue terms such as justice, empathy, and generosity to characterize it, but have generally refrained from characterizing solidarity *itself* as a virtue in its own right. Conversely, philosophers writing on virtue have largely ignored solidarity. To overcome this mutual neglect, Kolers focuses on what he calls the 'hard case' of *violent* solidaristic struggle. He believes that in at least some hard cases, solidarity requires those jointly committed to a political struggle to endorse the use of violence against oppressors. His main theoretical claim is that virtue theorists—who have mostly focused on agential skills like courage, bravery, and kindness—cannot adequately account for the ethical requirement of dedicating oneself to the fundamental equal worth of persons. To enable virtue theory to affirm human equality of status, Kolers believes, we must postulate a virtue of solidarity. A person possessing the virtue of solidarity will have developed a type of 'skill' that allows one to navigate the thin line between using violence to stand up to the oppressors *and* respecting the fundamental inviolability of all persons qua members of humanity. Thus, the virtue of solidarity, for Kolers, is a basal commitment to our coequal membership in the 'party of humankind.' Moreover, in many instances, solidarity as a virtue imposes demands on the agent that are neither part of the 'intelligent caring' cluster of virtues (e.g., kindness, charity) nor part of the 'virtues of willpower' like courage, perseverance, and humility. Thus, solidarity unifies the virtues by reconstituting them and reorienting us to the task of living a life that repudiates structural advantage and affirms basic human equality.

Viehoff's Chapter 5 looks at one particular kind of solidarity behavior, namely cases of solidaristic sacrifice, that is, cases where an agent voluntarily suffers a setback to their interests in order to stand in solidarity with others. Viehoff begins by formulating a twofold conceptual puzzle: The first part of the puzzle is that, while some instances where individuals suffer setbacks to their interests for the sake of others intuitively seem to count as instances of solidarity, other such cases do not. In virtue of which features are some self-sacrifices solidaristic? The second puzzle is this: Since many instances of solidarity do not involve any obvious personal sacrifices, in virtue of which features are self-sacrificial and self-interested instances of solidarity part of a unified phenomenon? To make progress on this issue, Viehoff suggests, we must think about solidarity's function in our lives. As a practice that ties us into specific projects and relationships, solidarity helps us to live a good life. But as a practice that

INTRODUCTION

selects its cause by reference to moral demands, solidarity improves our moral performance. Whether some behavior counts as solidaristic, Viehoff argues, ultimately depends on whether or not it can realize this function of 'positive alignment' between our ethical and our moral reasons. Once we have described the function of solidarity in this way, we can also make progress on solidarity's value and virtuousness.

In Chapter 6, Clark develops and elaborates the account of solidarity at the core of Catholic social thought. For her, solidarity names a virtue that is a response to the demands of social interdependence. Acting with solidarity requires us to see how our actions as members of families, communities, nations, and wider networks have an impact on the fate of others. We realize the virtue of solidarity, in turn, when we take responsibility for our actions by seeking, together with others, to alleviate the suffering caused by our interdependence. Clark's chapter shows us how close Catholic teaching on solidarity is, in fact, to the earlier French Solidarists, including Léon Bourgeois: solidarity, on such accounts, is the virtue we realize in discharging a social debt we owe to others—a debt acquired in virtue of our place in a vast division of labor. Clark's chapter therefore also speaks directly to the issues raised in chapters by Kohn (on the importance of interdependence) and Sangiovanni (on the idea of identification based on a role). Her humanistic account of solidarity also raises similar issues to those noted by Kolers.

Chapter 7, by Scholz, and Chapter 8, by Gould, both address the important question of how theorists should think about those instances where groups display solidarity but pursue morally problematic aims or end up creating social risks and harms. Scholz, in her chapter, urges us to think more carefully about how the virtue of solidarity plays out *within* social movements. According to her, solidarity, considered as a virtue, requires us to act in the right way, at the right time, and for the right reasons. She focuses on cases in which actors involved in a social movement have good intentions—they are moved by the right reasons—but their actions have consequences that unwittingly increase the *social risk* to which other actors are subject. This kind of dynamic is likely when the privileged participate in movements intended to end the oppression of the less privileged. In these circumstances, Scholz pleads for the virtues of equity, trust, and dialogue: Those who enter into political struggles must make themselves aware, and must be prepared to respond adequately to, the concerns of those most likely to be negatively affected by their actions. She suggests that scrutinizing pernicious solidarities helps to identify some of what is at stake in solidarity and whether solidarity is a conditional or unconditional social and political virtue, as well as whether the practices of solidarity ought to be mitigated with other virtuous practices.

Gould, after clearing the way for forms of 'networked' solidarity in which participants are united by a shared commitment to overcoming injustice and oppression (rather than a preexisting identity), argues that solidarity is—as a virtue—an essentially *moralized* concept. Individuals who stand in solidarity with one another share a characteristic set of dispositions, commitments, and goals. The most important of these are a commitment to mutual aid, equality, and the realization of human rights. Solidarity among ultra-nationalists and violent gangs therefore cannot exist, since these groups fundamentally aim at injustice. Thus, Gould covers similar ground to Scholz and echoes concerns raised by Kolers.

Munoz-Dardé's Chapter 9 acts as something of a counterpoint to the more virtue-embracing accounts of solidaristic action of previous chapters. According to her, solidarity is essentially *partitive*: it requires an 'us' defined in relation to, and in exclusion of, a 'them.' This makes it problematic from a liberal perspective. Because of its essentially exclusionary nature, solidarity cannot be non-instrumentally valuable. It cannot, therefore, be a virtue, since the virtues, as traditionally conceived, are always non-instrumentally valuable. Munoz-Dardé, however, does not argue that we should reject solidarity. Solidarity, she claims, is *instrumentally* valuable for creatures like us, who are weakly motivated by general forms of benevolence or love of humanity. Solidarity is an essential tool for preserving a sense of unity and purpose among diverse populations, and so essential for the realization of political justice. Munoz-Dardé's argument speaks to the same worries as Shelby's rejection of 'thick' solidarity in favor of 'thin,' where solidarity is prized above all for its instrumental benefits in rallying people against oppression. It also explores similar territory as Kohn (on Bourgeois and civic solidarity) and Gould, Kolers, Sangiovanni, and Scholz (on the negative aspects of solidarity and solidarity's scope).

Rather than particular groups and social movements, the next three chapters approach solidarity as a society-wide macro phenomenon. Kohn's Chapter 10 focuses on solidarity as a *civic* virtue, as a disposition to mutual aid and concern among citizens. She reconstructs and revives the arguments for solidarity made by the late nineteenth-century French Solidarists (most importantly, Léon Bourgeois and Alfred Fouillée). According to the Solidarists, the obligation to redistribute resources among citizens arises from the fact that we are each the lucky beneficiaries of a social, cultural, linguistic, and institutional inheritance. This inheritance makes it possible for us to make use of our talents and abilities in ways we could not have if acting in isolation. The disposition to share resources among citizens, then, is understood as the discharge of a *social debt*. Mutual recognition of this social debt—realized by our support for each other and for just institutions—constitutes, on this picture, the heart of solidarity as a virtue. In defending solidarism against three important liberal-pluralist criticisms, she also points to concerns raised in the chapters by Van Parijs (on institutionalized solidarity), Forst (on the normative demands of different contexts of solidarity), and Somek (on the possibility of civic solidarity on a European scale).

In Chapter 11, Somek investigates the supposed ability of macrostructures of cooperation to create sentiments of solidarity that can, in turn, sustain enhanced modes of sharing social goods. He does so through a detailed analysis and explanation of Durkheim's famous distinction between mechanical and organic solidarity. He conducts this analysis in order to clarify a site of solidarity that has been much discussed in recent political theory, namely the (purported) formation of a form of organic European solidarity through intensified economic integration and interdependence among European societies. Somek suggests that this idea, one of the most fundamental ideological commitments underlying the project of European integration since its implementation after 1945, is flawed: Solidarity beyond the state is composed of three elements, namely *doux commerce*, cosmopolitan concern for individual suffering, and faith in future union. However, none of these is capable of maintaining *organic* solidarity among participants. Organic solidarity is constituted when each individual sees their own well-being as bound up with the collective, and when each sees how their individual work, despite being highly specialized, contributes to the overall flourishing of society. If organic solidarity is present, individuals are more likely to accept redistribution and collective burden-sharing. But organic solidarity requires some mutual identification on the basis of a shared way of life. Where such identification is missing, interdependence in the form of a division of labor will not lead to organic solidarity, but only to a general disposition to behave peacefully toward those with whom one engages in economic activities (*doux commerce*) or a generic form of piety and compassion with human suffering of any kind (cosmopolitan concern).

The final chapter in the volume comes from Tommie Shelby. He approaches the question about solidarity's grounds through a concrete and pressing political issue that he takes to be one of the biggest challenges to contemporary black political solidarity in the United States: How should theorists of black solidarity account for class differences among blacks? Most Marxists, for example, are sharply critical of race-based solidarity and antiracist identity politics. They believe that this form of politics is often instrumentalized in the interests of the black professional-managerial class, and tends to obscure or sideline working-class issues. The black working class, these leftists argue, should seek allies among the broader (multiracial) working class and in the labor movement. Such Marxists also maintain that race-based politics wrongly subordinates class to race, rather than viewing race and class as inextricably related and fundamentally structured by capital-labor relations. Though Shelby shares some of the skepticism that thinkers on the left have toward identity politics, he maintains that they often take their criticisms too far. Shelby goes on to defend black solidarity against the most powerful Marxist critiques of it. Shelby shows how black solidarity can be grounded, not on 'thick' forms of black ethnocultural identity, but on a commitment to antiracism and antipoverty. This mutual commitment, he argues, can serve to bridge the divide between black elites and the marginalized black poor. In examining the grounds of solidarity, Shelby's chapter explores territory that is also addressed by Gould (in her discussion of 'networked' rather than 'unitary' solidarity), Sangiovanni (on challenges to solidarity) and Van Parijs (on the special role of identification in solidarity).

CONCLUDING THOUGHTS

Though one of the most widely claimed values in actual political discourses, solidarity has for a long time been ignored in theoretical discussions in social and political philosophy. Fortunately, this has started to change in recent years with an increasing number of scholars incorporating reflection on solidarity in their work. In closing this Introduction, we want to suggest a number of thoughts on the prospects of philosophical theorizing on solidarity and list a few areas where we believe future research might be fruitful.

It should not come as a surprise that those who have written on solidarity have tended to think of solidarity and solidaristic social relations as, by and large, a good thing, something that we have reason to aspire to and, wherever possible, to promote. As a result, there has to date been rather little engagement with those voices critical of the very ideal. Yet in order to vindicate solidarity as a bona fide subject, authors writing on it will have to address these objections to solidarity. Two such criticisms seem particularly prevalent: first, a value-based criticism, according to which solidarity, as a political value, has no place in a liberal democracy because of its illiberal, anti-individualist, and fundamentally communitarian elements;[28] second, a theoretical-cum-conceptual challenge: solidarity, some have argued, is conceptually redundant, that is, there is nothing new or interesting there that cannot just as easily be expressed in the language of justice, community, equality, and so on. Friends of solidarity, we think, are well advised to respond to these root-and-branch criticisms, not least because it will force them, on the one hand, to clarify how solidarity differs from objectionably illiberal social relations and, on the other

---

28. Jacob Levy, "Against Fraternity," in *The Strains of Commitment: The Political Sources of Solidarity in Diverse Societies*, ed. Keith Banting and Will Kymlicka (Oxford: Oxford University Press, 2017), 107–125, at 114; George Kateb, "Democratic Individuality and the Meaning of Rights," in *Liberalism and the Moral Life*, ed. Nancy Rosenblum (Cambridge, MA: Harvard University Press, 1989), 183–206, at 200; Stephen Holmes, "The Permanent Structure of Antiliberal Thought," in *Liberalism and the Moral Life*, ed. Nancy Rosenblum (Cambridge, MA: Harvard University Press, 1989), 227–253, at 229–231.

hand, to demonstrate how solidarity does not simply collapse into the more familiar terms and concepts of liberal theory.

A connected second area for future research concerns the *limits* of solidarity. There are really two issues here: One question relates to solidarity's 'external' moral constraints. What considerations impose limits on our reasons to act in solidarity? If being in solidarity provides us with agent-relative moral reasons to jointly act with a specified group of fellows in the pursuit of a cause, then what general moral considerations may undermine or cancel such reasons? What ends cannot permissibly be made the object of a solidarity group, and the choice of which means renders exercises of solidarity impermissible? Put more generally: What are the limits of solidaristic partiality? Scholars working on this relatively underexplored facet of solidarity could productively engage with the existing literature on permissible/required partiality in other, perhaps more intimate relationships. Tackling this issue might also advance our understanding of how solidarity, both axiologically and deontically, *differs* from more intimate social relationships. A second question concerns solidarity's *internal* limits: What prevailing self-understandings and what group-level decision-making procedures would disqualify a group from counting as solidaristic? Even if most authors believe that solidarity requires some disposition to accept burdens in the pursuit of a common aim, this minimal condition may not be sufficient for relations of solidarity; that is, something more demanding in terms of burden-sharing and shared decision-making may be necessary. And yet, it does not seem right that solidarity is only realized when members of a group realize a strongly democratic and egalitarian ethos in their mutual interaction. So how much inequality is compatible with being in solidarity? Various chapters in this volume make some initial suggestions that, hopefully, will with time lead to more sustained treatments of these and other issues. At the very least, we hope that the essays assembled here will bring home to the reader that solidarity is both an extraordinarily rich topic and one that contains many questions yet to be explored in more detail.

Chapter 1

Solidarity

Concept, Conceptions, and Contexts

RAINER FORST

A CONTESTED AND ELUSIVE CONCEPT

Solidarity is an elusive and contested concept, and debates about it abound:[1] Is it a moral value or a virtue, or can it also be found in groups of criminals, and can the solidarity of some violate the rights and standing of—and the solidarity with—others? Is solidarity a feeling, or can it be motivated by rational considerations of self-interest

---

1. See, for example, the various contributions to Kurt Bayertz, ed., *Solidarity* (Dordrecht: Kluwer Academic, 1999), and to Keith Banting and Will Kymlicka, eds., *The Strains of Commitment: The Political Sources of Solidarity in Diverse Societies* (Oxford: Oxford University Press, 2017); also the important works by Larry May, *The Socially Responsive Self: Social Theory and Professional Ethics* (Chicago: Chicago University Press, 1996), Avery Kolers, *A Moral Theory of Solidarity* (Oxford: Oxford University Press, 2016), Sally J. Scholz, *Political Solidarity* (University Park: Pennsylvania State University Press, 2008), Steinar Stjernø, *Solidarity in Europe: The History of an Idea* (Cambridge: Cambridge University Press, 2005), Hauke Brunkhorst, *Solidarity: From Civic Friendship to a Global Legal Community* (Cambridge, MA: MIT Press, 2005), Tommie Shelby, *We Who Are Dark: The Philosophical Foundations of Black Solidarity* (Cambridge, MA: Harvard University Press, 2005), Simon Derpmann, *Gründe der Solidarität* (Münster: Mentis, 2013), Andrea Sangiovanni, "Solidarity as Joint Action," *Journal of Applied Philosophy* 32, no. 4 (November 2015): 340–359.

or moral reflection? Is solidarity necessarily of a particular communal nature, or can it also take on universalist forms? Is it based on social relations and expectations of reciprocity, or does it have its place in relations of asymmetry, one-sided dependence, and non-shared vulnerability? Can solidarity be combined with or even be based on demands of justice, or is it the "other" of justice, going beyond it in altruistic or supererogatory ways? Can it be institutionalized by law, or does it presuppose intrinsic motives and voluntary action to which one cannot be coerced? In short, the very nature of solidarity—its grounds, motives, content, scope, and form—is the subject of numerous disagreements, not just in light of the different histories and trajectories of the concept, but also in light of the different uses we make of it in our normative vocabulary.[2]

If we want to make some headway in understanding the concept and overcome its elusiveness, we should avoid certain dead ends of analysis. It seems inappropriate to argue that there are different "concepts" of solidarity in play, since we would then no longer be able to explain what is supposed to qualify all of them as concepts of *solidarity*.[3] Similarly, we should avoid being "held captive"[4] by a particular picture of solidarity, say the one associated with the socialist tradition

---

2. For an illuminating analysis of the different trajectories of the concept, see Andrea Sangiovanni's Chapter 3 in this volume. With respect to the dominant usages of the concept, Kurt Bayertz, "Four Uses of 'Solidarity,'" in *Solidarity*, ed. Kurt Bayertz (Dordrecht: Kluwer Academic, 1999), 3–28, is very useful.
3. For an argument against employing different "concepts" with regard to liberty (commenting on Isaiah Berlin), see Rainer Forst, "Political Liberty: Integrating Five Conceptions of Autonomy," in *Autonomy and the Challenges to Liberalism: New Essays*, ed. John Christman and Joel Anderson (Cambridge: Cambridge University Press, 2005), 226–242 (also in my *The Right to Justification* (New York: Columbia University Press, 2012), ch. 5); and also, with respect to toleration, Rainer Forst, *Toleration in Conflict: Past and Present* (Cambridge: Cambridge University Press, 2013), §1.
4. Ludwig Wittgenstein, *Philosophical Investigations* (Oxford: Basil Blackwell, 1968), §115, 48.

or with social activism, and avoid declaring it to be the "true" or "authentic" form of solidarity.[5]

I suggest instead that we use the distinction developed by John Rawls between a "concept" and various "conceptions"[6]—the concept contains the essential features of a term, whereas conceptions are thicker interpretations of these features—and situate the different conceptions of solidarity in the social and normative contexts where they play a special role. Following this methodological approach, however, requires particular care. For neither can one start from a quasi-Platonic, conceptual *eidos* and derive the criteria for every legitimate usage of the term from it, nor can one inductively examine all semantic usages of the word for common features which would then constitute the core concept. The former approach is dogmatic, the latter uncritical and in any case unrealistic. Rather, we should aim to achieve a "reflective equilibrium" (to use another Rawlsian term, although in a different sense than he did) by going back and forth between paradigmatic examples of forms of solidarity in certain contexts, historical and contemporary, on the one hand, and a determination of basic features they share, on the other. This process is in principle an open-ended one, as one can always go back and re-enter the hermeneutical-analytical circle: Was the concept defined too narrowly or broadly? Are the different conceptions appropriately determined? The general aim is to provide the definition of a concept that reveals meaningful distinctions between different conceptions of solidarity. In that way, we might be able to answer some of the questions outlined above and, most of all, avoid declaring a particular conception of solidarity as the general concept—a mistake occasionally

---

5. See, for example, Rahel Jaeggi, "Solidarity and Indifference," in *Solidarity in Health and Social Care in Europe*, ed. Ruud ter Meulen, Wil Arts, and Ruud Muffels (Dordrecht: Kluwer, 2001), 287–308.
6. John Rawls, *A Theory of Justice*, rev. ed. (Cambridge, MA: Harvard University Press, 1999), 5.

made in corresponding debates, especially when it comes to politically charged concepts such as solidarity (or toleration, justice, liberty, etc.).

THE CONCEPT OF SOLIDARITY

The general concept of solidarity refers to a special *practical attitude* of a person toward others. It involves a form of "standing by"[7] each other (from the Latin *solidus*)[8] based on a *particular normative bond* with others constituted by a *common cause* or *shared identity*. The two latter notions are not mutually exclusive, because a shared identity can be correlated with a common cause. Still, sometimes, such as in the case of working-class solidarity, the common cause determines the commonality more than a particular social situation or identity marker (e.g., you do not need to be a worker to be solidary with the cause of the working class).

Solidarity expresses a willingness to act with and for the sake of others, based on the motive of affirming the collective bond, that is, of furthering the common cause or the shared identity (or both), when this is required. Solidarity as a practical attitude exists as long as this bond is perceived to be important and binding, and it materializes when corresponding action is felt to be required, especially in

---

7. In German, *füreinander einstehen*.
8. In the tradition of Roman law, the term referred to a particular kind of collective liability of a group for the costs generated by one member and vice versa. That meaning is still preserved in the term today. The history of the concept is reconstructed by Andreas Wildt, "Solidarität," in *Historisches Wörterbuch der Philosophie*, ed. Joachim Ritter, Karlfried Gründer, and Gottfried Gabriel (Basel: Schwabe Verlag), 1004–1015, and in Andreas Wildt, "Solidarity: Its History and Contemporary Definition," in *Solidarity*, ed. Kurt Bayertz (Dordrecht: Kluwer Academic, 1999), 209–220.

the face of threats or particular challenges.[9] Solidarity is not generally, on the basic conceptual level, a fighting creed, but it is required as a practice when "needed" (i.e., when called for to affirm or defend the common project). Solidary action is voluntary and based on inner conviction because it springs from the motive of the common bond as felt and perceived by those who act (which does not exclude motivational forces that, in their view, leaves them with no alternative other than to be solidary, especially if connected with strong social expectations to act loyally).[10]

It is important to note that solidary action is expected of members of the collective precisely when it is costly, also when narrow self-interest might actually deem it to be too costly. This is when reasons rooted in the "deeper" bond come into play as justifying and motivating forces. As far as the basic concept of solidarity is concerned, however, it is not justified to add to its defining features that its demands are always supererogatory,[11] since costly actions can also be demanded by duties of reciprocal, symmetrical solidarity. At the general conceptual level, it is difficult to determine the point at which the call for particular actions by some members overstrains the bonds of solidarity uniting the collective, especially given that people usually belong to various overlapping, but also possibly conflicting, contexts of solidarity (family, nation, and class, for example—which is, in other words, the classic material of drama). The general concept of solidarity entails no particular metric of what solidarity requires in concrete contexts. That is determined by the various conceptions of the collective bond that grounds particular contextual instances of solidarity.

---

9. This is stressed by Sangiovanni, "Solidarity as Joint Action," 343–345. It seems to me, however, that solidarity as a practical attitude, as a willingness to act if required, is essential, independent of whether it finds expression in action or not.
10. The point of loyalty is stressed by Shelby, *We Who Are Dark*, 69–70.
11. As Wildt, "Solidarity: Its History and Contemporary Definition," 213, does.

There is some reciprocity involved, since *each* member of a solidary communal context is expected to act in solidarity if they have the opportunity; however, this is far from a straightforward economic form of reciprocity in which one (ideally) receives an equivalent for one's contribution or in which contributions have to be roughly equal. *Solidary reciprocity* rather means: One's own contribution serves the general, common cause, and those who can contribute more or something special do it to further that cause, so that when they act in such ways, they feel neither superior nor exploited (and those who contribute less do not feel like second-class members). Such solidarity can reach so far that one feels bound to save the body or execute the last will of a deceased comrade or friend, assuming that he or she *would* have done the same. Solidary reciprocity can take imagined and yet real, highly asymmetrical forms. This also includes solidary support for people struggling in a certain way for a cause (such as human rights) that I feel committed to, even though I may not know them personally or they may be in a position where they could not possibly reciprocate what I do (and vice versa). Nevertheless, there is a common cause between us, for which we work together, each doing their share.[12]

It is often said that solidarity is owed most to the weakest member of a collective, but this is only half of the truth: It is *owed* to the collective and its general cause and common good, but it may *materialize* in the shape of a particular concern for those who are weakest, depending on the specific nature of the common bond. There are many historical layers that have been stored in the term and which need to

---

12. This notion of imagined reciprocity exceeds the notion of reciprocity and joint action that Sangiovanni, "Solidarity as Joint Action," 350, thinks defines solidary action. For an argument about transnational solidarity, see Carol C. Gould, "Transnational Solidarities," *Journal of Social Philosophy* 38, no. 1 (Spring 2007): 148–164. I hesitate to call that kind of solidarity less "robust," as Ashley E. Taylor, "Solidarity: Obligations and Expressions," *The Journal of Political Philosophy* 23, no. 2 (June 2015): 128–145, does.

be distinguished here, ranging from Catholic social doctrine to the communist movement or to forms of nationalism.

So these are, to summarize, the components of the general concept of solidarity, abstracted from concrete contexts and conceptions: a *practical attitude* which takes the form of a willingness to act based on a *common bond* that implies a common *cause* or shared *identity* that ought to be furthered. The bond *itself* is the motivating force, and it can call for particular actions *beyond* narrow self-interest. The *reciprocity* involved can take many forms, including asymmetrical ones, as long as the bond justifies what it means to do one's share. If these features appear in a certain practical context, we encounter a form of solidarity.

NORMATIVE DEPENDENCY

So far, solidarity sounds like a virtue, and with respect to its character of overcoming one's narrow self-interest to further a common cause it surely is. But that does not make it a *moral* virtue or something intrinsically good, since a Mafia family may also depend quite a lot on the solidarity of its members. And nationalist movements have historically used the language of solidarity effectively for many purposes, including aggressive ones.[13] Hence, solidarity is a morally neutral virtue that can be used for good or bad concerns and goals; in this respect, it is similar to courage, for example.

The concept itself is, therefore, a *normatively dependent* one, which means that normative conceptions of solidarity are in need of interpretive supplementation by other normative principles (such as justice) or values (such as national welfare or serving God's honor). The

---

13. See Cornelia Schmitz-Berning, *Vokabular des Nationalsozialismus* (Berlin: de Gruyter, 2007), 602f., on the use of the term "national solidarity" during National Socialism.

concept of solidarity is contextually and normatively promiscuous—it can serve many ends and does not contain any particular ends in itself, neither moral nor political ones. Such ends must be connected with the idea of solidarity—that is, of standing in for others based on a particular shared bond and common cause—and the bond or cause in question must be spelled out independently as something worth caring about. Here the relevant justifying reasons can be specific and relative to particular social contexts, but they can also be of a universalist nature. Religious forms of solidarity often combine particularistic and universalistic claims because they are rooted in a particular faith, but may (and often do) regard the truths and imperatives of that faith as being universally valid.

This means that reasons of solidarity are *not* reasons of a normative kind categorically distinct from reasons of morality, justice, religion, friendship, and so on.[14] They are of a particular nature, however, insofar as reasons of political solidarity, for example, are reasons to promote the *particular* political cause of a concrete collective one feels bound to and identifies with, even though there may be other political collectives that are similar in nature. Still, the bond that justifies solidary actions is not binding in virtue of the mere fact of membership.[15] Rather, it is binding for a person because she values the cause or identity of the collective for particular normative reasons. She sees certain values *embodied* in a particular way by this community with which she identifies and not by others (though this may change). Reasons of solidarity thus combine *independent* evaluative considerations with a special attachment and bond to a *concrete* collective one identifies with. This bipolar nature of solidarity can create a dynamic of critique of one's collective in light of the relevant

---

14. The opposite view is defended by Derpmann, *Gründe der Solidarität*.
15. A view held by Richard Rorty, *Contingency, Irony, and Solidarity* (Cambridge: Cambridge University Press, 1989), ch. 9.

evaluations and possibly of changing solidarities between collectives. At the level of basic conceptual analysis, it is not possible to define the proper ratio between particular combinations of the fact and history of membership and identification, on the one hand, and independent evaluative components, on the other, as these vary with contexts and conceptions of solidarity.

Once again, it should be emphasized that this conceptual analysis does not imply that the reasons for valuing the bond through which solidarity arises are good moral reasons; a one-sided and nationalist, perhaps even chauvinistic affirmation of a national identity can be just as much a basis for solidarity as a postconventional antinationalist solidarity with marginalized groups. A religiously based form of solidarity can lead to a solidarity with the exploited in foreign parts of the world or to a hostile isolation against "foreign infiltration" by other religious groups of one's own country.

Our normative vocabulary contains other, similar terms, such as toleration or legitimacy, that only express a personal or institutional moral virtue if they are accompanied by independently grounded good reasons and justifications.[16] Unlike justice, for example, they do not stand for intrinsically justified virtues.[17] To be sure, a particular interpretation of justice may not be well founded, but it can be criticized in terms of the core concept of justice *itself* as a matter of overcoming arbitrariness in social relations (which is the core meaning of justice), whereas such a reflexive critique is not possible in the case of solidarity or toleration (although it has often been tried). One can criticize a particular act of solidarity for not being sufficiently

---

16. See the discussions of toleration and legitimacy as normatively dependent concepts in Forst, *Toleration in Conflict*, §3, and Rainer Forst, *Normativity and Power: Analyzing Social Orders of Justification* (Oxford: Oxford University Press, 2017), ch. 8, respectively.
17. See my argument in Rainer Forst, "Justice: Procedural and Substantive," in *The Cambridge Handbook of Constitutional Theory*, ed. Richard Bellamy and Jeff King (Cambridge: Cambridge University Press, forthcoming).

solidary, but that does not tell us anything about the value of the cause that shall be furthered. Whether an act or attitude of solidarity is well founded depends on such additional values.

The idea of normatively dependent concepts is different from that of "essentially contested concepts,"[18] because the normative conceptions, but not the concept itself, are contested and conflict with each other. In fact, I doubt whether there really are any essentially contested concepts all the way down. For if there were, as argued above, it would not be clear whether a contest between normative interpretations of a concept really was a contest about the *same* concept. If it is, there is a non-contested core concept that unites the contending positions.

NORMATIVE CONTEXTS AND CONCEPTIONS OF SOLIDARITY

One can distinguish various *conceptions* of solidarity depending on the values or principles that lend normative substance to the bond of solidarity in certain *practical contexts*. That renders my account contextualist in a certain conceptual, non-relativistic way and takes seriously the multiplicity of what could be meant by a "common bond," "shared identity," or "common cause." As we saw above, it has to express something of value to all members of the solidary community; but what that value is and what exactly it entails depend on the respective context.

So "context" here is a complex notion involving the following aspects: It specifies the *normative nature* (or the point) of the solidary bond and demarcates the *community* of solidarity. It is not just

---

18. Walter B. Gallie, "Essentially Contested Concepts," *Proceedings of the Aristotelian Society* 56, no. 1 (1955–1956): 167–198.

a context of action but a normative context of self-understanding, both individually and collectively. Most notably, it is a *context of justification* that determines the relevant reasons for solidary action. At the same time, it is a context of normatively binding social relations of *mutual recognition*.[19] Which actions in particular are required depends on a further step of contextual specification; for example, there is a conception of solidarity among friends, but what exactly a concrete friendship requires friends to do or not depends on the history and particular nature of their relation. The context of justification has to be spelled out at various levels (i.e., that of a general conception and that of a particular case).

Ethical Contexts

In *ethical* contexts of family and intimate partnerships, friendships, or other forms of community, solidarity is based on particular communal bonds centered on a notion of the shared and mutually enjoyed good. These bonds ground concretely what it means to be solidary or to lack solidarity. I call such contexts "ethical" because the communally affirmed notion of the good relevant here is (at least in part) constitutive of one's ethical-personal identity, one's form of life or *ethos*. When you act in solidarity with others in this context, you affirm your own identity, you recognize who and what you are, and the common project is part of yourself—and that motivates you to do what is required. The personal investment in this form of solidarity can be very high, depending on the level of identity involvement.

The nature of the commitment and of the actions that are required and justifiable, as well as the scope of the community of solidarity, depend on these particular identity contexts. In this realm,

---

19. See my distinction between contexts of recognition and of justification in Rainer Forst, *Contexts of Justice: Political Philosophy beyond Liberalism and Communitarianism* (Berkeley: University of California Press, 2002), ch. 5.

one usually is a member of multiple ethical contexts, which may lead to priority issues or conflicts, for example between loyalty to and solidarity with your family and to your religious community or to a friend who is in need of support. None of these contexts of solidarity is self-justifying or takes natural precedence; it is all a question of ethical justification, where the question of who you are and what you owe to others with whom you share a strong communal bond is essential. Such a practice of justification, searching for what you "really care about,"[20] will also determine what exactly acting in solidarity means, including whether it requires you to sacrifice something important or to take risks. The main "currency" of justification here is the "ethical identity investment" (as we may call it) you share with concrete others.[21]

Legal Contexts

It may sound surprising to list the legal domain as a context of solidarity, since this does not seem to cohere with the notions of "common bond" or "solidary reciprocity" and the idea that solidarity is a voluntary, non-coerced act. And indeed, many people think that solidarity must be located outside the bonds of legal duties and obligations or, for that matter, of what justice demands.[22] However, as we know since Hegel and Durkheim, modern social systems presuppose certain forms of institutionally mediated solidarity, where one contributes one's share without expecting a narrow *quid pro quo*.[23] Social insurance schemes are an example of such systems, which is why in

---

20. Harry Frankfurt, *The Importance of What We Care About* (Cambridge: Cambridge University Press, 1988).
21. Cf. Taylor, "Solidarity: Obligations and Expressions" (although not in these terms).
22. Wildt, "Solidarity: Its History and Contemporary Definition," 223–242.
23. Emile Durkheim, *The Division of Labour in Society* (London: Palgrave Macmillan, 1984), and Axel Honneth, *The Struggle for Recognition: The Moral Grammar of Social Conflicts* (Cambridge: Polity Press, 1995).

German they are called *Solidargemeinschaften*, that is, communities of solidarity.[24] Leibniz can be seen as a pioneer of such solidary schemes of "institutionalized solidarity,"[25] because he argued for an insurance scheme (in cases of fire and flooding)—*assecurazione contra casus fortuitos*—in which society as a whole should stand in for those affected by such disasters.[26] He compared society to a ship whose welfare is the responsibility of all, so that we have to help each other in case of need for the sake of the general context of cooperation— adding that the need in question should not be the result of one's own blameworthy behavior.

Many social insurance schemes are built on such ideas, including social welfare and healthcare schemes, and it remained a matter of dispute whether carelessness and other vices disqualify one from the scheme of solidarity or not. These are issues that are still relevant today, in practice as well as in theory, if you think, for example, of luck egalitarianism and its (too) strict distinction between individual responsibility and the circumstances for which one cannot be held responsible.[27] In any case, whether it is a private insurance scheme (e.g., car or home insurance) to which one contributes without ever necessarily receiving an equivalent in return, while others are bailed

---

24. Karl H. Metz, "Solidarity and History: Institutions and Social Concepts of Solidarity in 19th Century Western Europe," in *Solidarity*, ed. Kurt Bayertz (Dordrecht: Kluwer Academic, 1999), 191–207, and Ulrich K. Preuß, "National, Supranational, and International Solidarity," in *Solidarity*, ed. Kurt Bayertz (Dordrecht: Kluwer Academic, 1999), 281–289.
25. Frank Nullmeier, "Eigenverantwortung, Gerechtigkeit und Solidarität – Konkurrierende Prinzipien der Konstruktion moderner Wohlfahrtsstaaten?," *WSI Mitteilungen* 4 (2006): 175–180, and Gøsta Esping-Andersen, *Social Foundations of Postindustrial Economies* (Oxford: Oxford University Press, 1999).
26. Gottfried Wilhelm Leibniz, "Öffentliche Assekuranzen," in his *Sämtliche Schriften und Briefe* IV/3 (Berlin: Akademie Verlag, 1986), 421–432. See also Cornel Zwierlein, *Prometheus Tamed: Fire, Security and Modernities, 1400–1900* (Leiden: Brill, 2021).
27. See Rainer Forst, "The Point of Justice: On the Paradigmatic Incompatibility between Rawlsian 'Justice as Fairness' and Luck Egalitarianism," in *John Rawls: Debating the Major Questions*, ed. John Mandle and Sarah Roberts-Cady (Oxford: Oxford University Press, 2020), 148–160.

out from emergency situations resulting from bad behavior or bad luck, or whether it is a socially obligatory scheme (say of general public health insurance), some form of solidary reciprocity is always involved, since it is generally accepted that those in need will receive more benefits than those who are not in need. Although free-riding is not explicitly accepted, it is for the most part tacitly tolerated for the sake of maintaining the overall integrity of the scheme.

The legal form does not preclude solidarity properly speaking, even in a mandatory scheme. For, as Durkheim argued, its members are asked to accept the system not only and not primarily because of its sanctioning force but because of its justification, its raison d'être, and the way it functions—which means they should not exploit it, even if they could, nor long for changing it politically for their own benefit, even if they could do so with the support of a majority. Both as subjects of the law who could cheat but do not do so and, more importantly, as lawgivers in a democratic legal state, its members accept the solidary scheme as justified and as an expression of a common civic bond. Otherwise, we would run into the paradox that the social struggles of solidary workers and others for such social insurance schemes throughout the nineteenth and twentieth centuries were really struggles to overcome "true" solidarity based on voluntary action by institutionalizing social rights. This institutionalization, however, is not beyond solidarity, but retains it as a claim to recognize and accept the social, solidary sense of such systems.[28]

It is true that those libertarians, for example, who would rather abolish such schemes are, as members of these systems, legally obliged to act in accordance with norms of solidarity without really being in solidarity, and here we should recognize that certain external actions conforming to solidarity can be enforced, although the

---

28. Cf. T. H. Marshall, *Citizenship and Social Class* (Cambridge: Cambridge University Press, 1950); Hauke Brunkhorst, *Solidarität unter Fremden* (Frankfurt am Main: Fischer, 1997).

internal attitude cannot be. Yet one cannot infer from the fact that the law is coercive that all those who are subject to it follow it *because* it is coercive. Some do, some don't. It is always difficult to infer the nature of motivating reasons from actions. One cannot, for example, assume that acts of solidarity in ethical contexts were in fact motivated by the right reasons; maybe group pressure was the driving force. As far as legal contexts are concerned, if the laws were only followed out of fear of being caught when violating them, functioning legal states would have to take the form of repressive police states. And from a political perspective, the assumption that "the state" as a separate agent installs legal systems of obligations independently from the political will of citizens and forces its subjects to comply with them is a remnant of a pre-democratic notion of law. The institutionalization of a system of social solidarity can and should be a political act of solidarity, as well as its maintenance and improvement; and its neoliberal dismantling can rightly be criticized with good reasons as an act of de-solidarization.[29]

Political Contexts

In *political* contexts, we encounter various forms or conceptions of solidarity:

An *ethical-political* form of solidarity refers to national bonds and a shared history, or perhaps even an ethnic-historical identity interpreted as a political identity and as a project to be pursued and continued, for example, through national independence. The fact that such communities, their histories, and meanings are often "imagined"[30] or fabricated does not mean that the motivating force of such ideas or communities is any less powerful. Nationalism, whether it assumes

---

29. Wendy Brown, *Undoing the Demos* (Princeton, NJ: Princeton University Press, 2015).
30. Benedict Anderson, *Imagined Communities: Reflections on the Origin and Spread of Nationalism* (London: Verso, 2016).

more benign or more malicious forms, remains a major normative source of solidary practical motivation.

A *political-social* form of solidarity exists where there is less ethical investment in a particular communal identity that is regarded as valuable, but where a common cause and project motivates people to act in solidarity, such as the creation of a new form of life or a new society. In most cases these are fighting creeds, as in the struggles for class liberation, democracy, or ecological transformation. The nature of the project can be seen as moral or self-serving; interpretations of class struggle, for example, can come in Hegelian-Marxist or in Nietzschean guises.

Political-social solidarity often aims at establishing a *just* society, as in movements for gender and racial equality or for overcoming class and caste exploitation as grave forms of injustice—*Unrecht schlechthin* (absolute injustice), in Marx's words.[31] Such movements may share certain elements with ethical-political collectives, involving a positive valuation of marginalized or exploited forms of life; yet the thrust of these communal struggles is to establish a new, more just society. That is what calls for solidarity; it is grounded in justice as a *general* principle to be realized in a *particular* social context. Justice-based conceptions of solidarity come in two forms: those that demand solidarity in order to *establish* a just political and social order, and those that require solidarity in order to *preserve* it—where preserving justice also implies to promote and improve it.

It is important to distinguish the forms of solidarity involved in struggles for justice from more institutionalized forms of solidarity which presuppose that a certain level of justice has already been

---

31. Karl Marx, "Zur Kritik der Hegelschen Rechtsphilosophie. Einleitung," in *Marx-Engels-Werke* I (Berlin: Dietz, 1976), 390. Cf. Rainer Forst, "Noumenal Alienation: Rousseau, Kant and Marx on the Dialectics of Self-Determination," *Kantian Review* 22, no. 4 (2017): 523–551.

established (as rare as this may be the case). For the former, solidarity is required to combat injustice, and it is difficult to determine to what extent that struggle should itself be bound by principles of justice (as I think it should). The second form of solidarity is clearly guided by principles of justice, for example, when it is a question of realizing a demanding form of social justice, say one that accords with Rawls's difference principle. This necessitates an ethos of justice that gives people reasons not to act or vote on their short-term self-interests, an ethos that cannot be fully realized in the form of legal duties.[32] It implies a form of solidary reciprocity which is based on the conviction that social justice involves a balance between contributions and benefits that does not serve the optimization of one's self-interest in the narrower sense.[33]

In contemporary societies, solidarity is often required in a way that combines the motives of establishing and preserving justice, because the existing institutions realize justice at best partially, while undermining it at the same time. Justice in its true sense—a notion on which I cannot elaborate here[34]—means using existing institutions (such as nation-states) to overcome the obstacles to establishing transnational institutions of democratic justice, given existing transnational realities of global injustice. The community of solidarity with respect to social and political justice must be broader than the nation-state, because states are part of transnational schemes of cooperation and, most importantly, of enforced and asymmetrical

---

32. G. A. Cohen, Jürgen Habermas, and John Rawls agree on this point. See, for example, Rawls, *A Theory of Justice*, §79; G. A. Cohen, *Why Not Socialism?* (Princeton, NJ: Princeton University Press, 2009); Jürgen Habermas, *Im Sog der Technokratie* (Berlin: Suhrkamp, 2013), ch. 5.
33. See Sangiovanni, "Solidarity as Joint Action."
34. See especially my work on transnational justice in Forst, *The Right to Justification*, part 3; Forst, *Normativity and Power*, part V; and Forst, "A Critical Theory of Transnational (In-)Justice: Realistic in the Right Way," in *The Oxford Handbook of Global Justice*, ed. Thom Brooks (Oxford: Oxford University Press, 2020), 451–472.

"cooperation" that include relations of political, social, and economic exploitation which ought to be overcome by institutions of transnational justice. From a comprehensive perspective of justice, we recognize that national solidarity must not be realized at the price of a lack of solidarity with others who are exploited and dominated.[35]

In this context, the reasons for drawing the line around a justification community or a community of solidarity are different from those in ethical contexts. There, the basis for solidarity is the ethical investment in a communal context; in the case of justice, the basis is a moral-political conception of what one owes to others as members of a shared normative order, which may transcend national ones.[36] This implies a normative (and graduated) notion of solidarity that is grounded in the principle that no one ought to be subjected to a normative order (including the global economy) of which they cannot be a coauthor with equal standing. Bound by claims of justice, we owe solidarity to those who are denied such standing and should not accord our fellow nationals normative priority in a way that is detrimental to this duty.

Solidarity in contexts of (in-)justice is a duty based on the basic right of persons to be respected as equal normative authorities in all those normative orders they are subjected to. In cases where we share such orders with them—whether it is a state or an encompassing, global economic scheme—we have duties of justice as participants in such orders which are, at the same time, duties of solidarity defined by justice. In those (unlikely) cases where we are not implicated (however indirectly) in such orders in which persons are being denied equal standing as justificatory agents, we nevertheless have a "natural duty"[37] of justice (and solidarity) to help them overcome

---

35. Stephan Lessenich, "Doppelmoral hält besser: Die Politik mit der Solidarität in der Externalisierungsgesellschaft," *Berliner Journal für Soziologie* 30 (2020): 113–130.
36. See Habermas, *Im Sog der Technokratie*, 102–111.
37. Rawls, *A Theory of Justice*, §19.

that injustice. In both cases, existing injustice and shared projects of justice ground duties of solidarity, but in different ways depending on the context.

A special case of duties of solidarity based on considerations of justice is ensuring that refugees are treated respectfully in the normative orders they reach.[38] They are fellow human beings who are fleeing from injustice or from living conditions that are intolerable, especially given the existing global possibilities for the redistribution of resources, and members of better-off countries owe them a standing as agents of justice who have claims upon them as cosmopolitan compatriots and participants in a transnational normative order of resource distribution. Here, as elsewhere, it is important to be clear about whether we are talking about general moral, legal, or moral-political duties of solidarity. All of these categories are involved in this case.

Moral Contexts

In *moral* contexts, finally, solidarity is based on our common humanity and calls for actions ranging from morally obligatory assistance in cases of need to supererogatory actions beyond any assumption of reciprocity—except, perhaps, for the hope that, should we ever find ourselves in a similar situation, others would do something similar for us as well. Solidarity covers all of these cases, from "ordinary" help to extremely costly forms of assistance, although supererogatory action is an especially praiseworthy service of solidarity. The realm of solidarity thus allows for an additional space for extremely solidary and laudable actions and efforts; and I should add that this is generally the case, also in other contexts.

---

38. David Owen, *What Do We Owe to Refugees?* (Cambridge: Polity Press, 2020).

Moral solidarity, traditionally called *Brüderlichkeit*[39] (brotherhood) by idealists like Schiller or Beethoven (either ignoring women or including them as "brothers"), is not the "other" of morality in the sense of an opposite, even when morality is understood along Kantian lines;[40] rather, it is an *aspect* of morality that recognizes others as vulnerable beings one must "stand in for," given their finitude and frailty and the fact that we all share a human form of life. Morality, after all, is a form of caring for and about others, even if one does not share a more particular form of life or identity with them. Respecting the uniqueness and vulnerability of the "concrete other"[41] while also respecting and treating them as an equal is precisely what morality demands.[42] Acts of solidarity are always concrete acts, but that does not mean that the reason for performing them cannot be universalistic in nature. From the moral point of view, we have no good justifying reason not to show solidarity with others in need.

CONCLUSION

The foregoing analysis intends to contribute not only to illuminating the various meanings of the term "solidarity" (and the different normative conceptions of solidarity) but also to avoiding some of its pitfalls. The latter stem especially from mistaking a particular conception of solidarity for the whole concept, for example by assuming that solidarity must always be ethical or political in nature, that it is categorically

---

39. Véronique Munoz-Dardé, "Fraternity and Justice," in *Solidarity*, ed. Kurt Bayertz (Dordrecht: Kluwer Academic, 1999), 81–97.
40. Jürgen Habermas, "Justice and Solidarity: On the Discussion Concerning 'Stage 6,'" in *Philosophical Forum* 21, no. 1 (1989): 32–52. He retracts this in favor of a political understanding of solidarity in *Im Sog der Technokratie*, 104, fn. 23.
41. Seyla Benhabib, *The Rights of Others: Aliens, Residents, and Citizens* (Cambridge: Cambridge University Press, 2004).
42. Lutz Wingert, *Gemeinsinn und Moral: Grundzüge einer intersubjektivistischen Moralkonzeption* (Frankfurt am Main: Suhrkamp, 1993).

different from justice, or that it is always supererogatory. Solidarity comes in many forms and with many justifications and grounds. One must not reduce this plurality, but instead describe it properly.

As indicated, this opens up the possibility of conflicts between the contexts and dimensions of solidarity mentioned—among friends, comrades, citizens, or all those suffering from injustice. My main point in this regard is that the normatively dependent concept of solidarity does not tell us to which form we ought to accord priority. This is where we reach bedrock in a dispute between, for example, a Humean and a Kantian view. Drawing on Hume, one might argue that the forms in which the identity investment is greatest, thus possibly the ethical ones, should take precedence.[43] Or one might develop a moral theory of the worst evils to be avoided, thereby according priority to the moral aspect (depending, however, on the ethical identification with such priorities).[44] Kantians understand the emotional and social appeal of ethical forms of solidarity, but believe that forms of solidarity based on the categorical imperative of equal respect should have greater normative weight.[45] The reason for this is that, in a Kantian framework, solidarity is a virtue only if founded on practical reason, based on the best justification among equal human beings. Seen in this light, the question of solidarity points to larger questions about who we are as moral beings.[46]

---

43. Rorty, *Contingency, Irony, and Solidarity*.
44. Andrea Sangiovanni, *Humanity Without Dignity* (Cambridge, Mass.: Harvard University Press, 2017).
45. Barbara Herman, *Moral Literacy* (Cambridge, MA: Harvard University Press, 2008); Forst, *The Right to Justification*, part I.
46. Many thanks to the participants of the Florence Workshop "Solidarity: Its Nature and Value" at the European University Institute in May 2019 for helpful comments and questions, especially to the organizers of the conference and editors of this volume, Andrea Sangiovanni and Juri Viehoff, and to Margaret Kohn and Tommie Shelby for their commentaries. Thanks also to Ciaran Cronin, Felix Kämper, and Amadeus Ulrich for their valuable suggestions and help in preparing this text.

Chapter 2

Solidarity and the Just Society

PHILIPPE VAN PARIJS

SOLIDARITY AS MUTUAL RESPONSIBILITY

Under the shock of the pandemic, solidarity was, more than ever, in fashion.[1] "Solidarity" (or its near-homonyms in other languages) was used to refer to what people were expressing by applauding from their balconies every evening, to what member states of the European Union showed or failed to show in response to proposals for a partial mutualisation of national public debts, as well as to the working of national health care systems and the measures taken to buffer the impact of the lockdown on people's livelihood. What does "solidarity" mean in these very diverse contexts? And how does solidarity, duly defined, relate to the pursuit of social justice?

The conceptual clarification with which I need to start bears some relationship with what dictionaries aim to do. But it is not

---

1. Just one quantitative illustration: during the six weeks that followed the local outbreak of the coronavirus crisis in mid-March 2020, the word "solidariteit" was used 3236 times in Belgium's Dutch-language newspapers, compared to only 548 times in the corresponding weeks of 2019 (De Lobel 2020).

meant as a contribution to the lexicography of the English language. The nineteenth-century French words *solidarité* and *solidaire* and their subsequent adaptations in other languages are commonly used to refer both to individual and collective actions and feelings and to social institutions. It is quite possible that *solidarité, solidarity, Solidarität, solidaridad, solidarietà,* and so on, do not cover exactly the same semantic fields in their respective languages. More specifically, it is quite possible that the best explication of *solidarité* and its quasi-homonyms in other languages may differ significantly, depending on which uses are perceived as paradigmatic or as limiting cases in the idiolects one is most familiar with. In the languages I am acquainted with, however, it is clear that "solidarity," "insurance," "charity," and "justice" (and the corresponding words in other languages) are not used interchangeably, whether when they are applied to actions or to institutions. It is for this differential use that I need to offer a characterization.[2]

The Latin expression *obligatio in solidum* was used in Roman law to refer to a debt that was held jointly by several people, with each of them liable to have to pay the whole of it. In addition to having coined the expression *socialisme*, the French philosopher Pierre Leroux claims to have been the first to extract the word *solidarité* from

---

2. In this enterprise, I shall be guided by my own linguistic intuitions, and hence probably by the way the relevant words are used in French more than in other languages. This may account for differences with what readers more familiar with other languages may regard as the best explication of the concept: discussions of earlier versions of this text suggest that such differences are quite tenacious. The fact that the modern notion of *solidarité* originated in French gives speakers of French no authority to dictate the way in which the corresponding word should be used in other languages. I conjecture, however, that percolation across Western languages has been sufficiently intensive for the relevant segment of the semantic map of English to resemble the corresponding French one more than enough for my purposes. Note, however, that Keith Banting and Will Kymlicka (2017: 4) use the term "solidarity" so as to cover "civic solidarity" (or mutual respect) and "democratic solidarity" (or support for equal rights) in addition to what they call "redistributive solidarity." This may reflect a different use of the word "solidarity" (and its quasi-homonyms in other languages) in North America and in Europe.

the legal vocabulary and to give it a "philosophical" sense in his book *De l'Humanité* (1840).[3] From then on, solidarity started being understood in the contemporary moral sense of "mutual responsibility." According to Auguste Comte (1866: 382), for example, "solidarity rests on the fact that men represent each other to such a degree that they are responsible for each other."[4] And the 1877 edition of Littré's dictionary defines solidarity as "mutual responsibility between two or more people."[5] Here, *solidarité* no longer refers to a legal obligation, but to a moral sentiment, motive, disposition, or duty—as it does today.

In parallel, however, the word *solidarité* was also used—including in the booklet that most contributed to spreading its moral meaning, Léon Bourgeois's *Solidarité* (1896)—to refer to the sheer fact of "mutual dependence."[6] This use of *solidarité* as mutual dependence has now largely been overshadowed by the moral sense of mutual responsibility. But it has not disappeared.[7] And for Bourgeois, what links the two concepts is far more than a fortuitous homonymy. He claimed to "establish on the scientific doctrine of natural solidarity

---

3. On the first uses of the word, see Gide (1932: 32–36) and Le Bras-Chopard (1992).
4. "En fait, l'homme qui prétend ne représenter que sa propre personnalité, se trompe. Il porte, quoi qu'il veuille l'empreinte de la société où il a appris à parler, à penser, à agir, voire même à croire ou à douter. Il n'y a que les idiots qui ne représentent rien. La solidarité repose précisément sur ce que les hommes se représentent les uns les autres au point d'être responsables les uns pour les autres."
5. "Littré, en 1877, ne donne encore de ce terme, en dehors des acceptions juridique et physiologique, qu'une définition 'de langage courant,' c'est-à-dire sans précision et sans portée: 'c'est, dit-il seulement, la responsabilité mutuelle qui s'établit entre deux ou plusieurs personnes'" (Bourgeois 1896: 6).
6. Bourgeois (1896: 21–23) mentions, for example, "the general law of reciprocal dependence, that is of solidarity, of the elements of universal life," "the law of gravity, the law of solidarity of the celestial bodies," and the "bond of solidarity that unites man with the rest of the world".
7. It is in this sense, for example, that the word *solidarité* was famously used in an often quoted sentence featuring both in the Schuman declaration of May 9, 1950, and in the preamble of the treaty that created in the following year the European Coal and Steel Community: "*L'Europe* [...] *se fera par des réalisations concrètes créant d'abord une solidarité de fait.*" ("Europe [...] will be built through concrete achievements that will first create a de facto solidarity.")

a practical doctrine of moral and social solidarity" and believed that "the knowledge of the natural laws of solidarity among beings leads to a comprehensive theory of the rights and duties of man in society" (1896: 30, 53). His attempt at providing a "scientific foundation" to a "positive morality" can rightly be rejected as a clear case of naturalistic fallacy.[8]

The moral sense of solidarity as mutual responsibility must be distinguished from the sense in which Emile Durkheim used it in his classic *De la Division du travail social*, published just a few years before Bourgeois's booklet. As he used the expression, the only feature common to all forms of social solidarity is "a general tendency to sociability" (Durkheim 1893: 30–31) that is "symbolized" or "expressed" in distinct bodies of law. The laws that express "mechanical solidarity" serve to maintain similarity between all members of society through the repression of crimes. The laws that express "organic solidarity" serve to organize the division of social labor. Both sets of laws produce "social cohesion," by enforcing conformity in one case, by organizing interdependence in the other. As the division of social labor deepens, social cohesion relies increasingly on organic solidarity. In one formulation, Durkheim (1893: 394) equates the "source of solidarity" and "what forces man to take others into account, to adjust his movements to something other than the impulsion of his selfishness." In this very broad sense (which covers the repression of religious heresy as well as the regulation of commercial transactions), one could say that he understands solidarity as "mutual responsibility."[9] But this is a

---

8. See Ewald (1996: 1514, 1517) on Bourgeois's fascination with Pasteur's pioneering study of contagious diseases and how it inspired his ambition to found his *solidarisme* as a "*morale positive*" rooted in the mutual dependence illustrated most vividly by an epidemic. Rejecting the fallacy should not prevent us from recognizing that mutual dependence can be a major factor of solidarity as mutual responsibility, a point to which we shall return below.
9. Note that Durkheim, like Bourgeois, occasionally uses *solidarité* in the purely factual sense of "interdependence" (Durkheim 1893: XLIII, 24). But elsewhere, he speaks of a "sentiment of

far broader sense than the one captured in Comte's or Littré's formulations and the one in which solidarity is used today—and to which we now turn our attention.

According to Bourgeois (1896: 59–60), the "rigorous duty of social solidarity" should "replace the moral duty of charity formulated by Christianity and the more precise yet still abstract and sanctionless notion of fraternity." But what is it exactly that distinguishes solidarity from charity, compassion, or pity and makes it a modern version of fraternity? Under each of these labels, there is generosity involved, benevolence, altruism, care for others: one does something at some cost to oneself for the purpose of benefiting someone else. What is distinctive of solidarity, I submit, is the symmetry captured by the expression "mutual responsibility," responsibility for each other as members of some (more or less imagined) community. When I help you out of solidarity, I do so because you are "one of us," because "I could have been you," because, in this sense, I "identify" with you. This identification is not a cause of solidarity but part of its meaning. Without it, there can be generosity or altruism, but not solidarity. When acting out of solidarity, I am also trusting—more or less firmly—that, precisely because you are "one of us," you would have done for me, had our respective positions been swapped, what I am now doing for you. It is this symmetry that gives solidarity its egalitarian flavor, in contrast with the demeaning, sometimes even offensive connotations associated with "charity," "pity," or "compassion." On the other hand, since the symmetry of mutual responsibility presupposes membership in something like a community, small or large, it implies a closure, a discrimination between members and non-members. And it requires this community to be sufficiently homogeneous in relevant respects for the assumption of

---

solidarity" (Durkheim 1893: 19) and clearly refers to social solidarity as a "moral phenomenon" (Durkheim 1893: 28).

reciprocation under similar conditions to be plausible. There is, however, no limit—except, arguably, mankind itself—to the scope of this community. I can conceivably express solidarity, or act out of solidarity, with all the victims of exploitation in the world, for example, or even with all the victims of climate change in the present and future generations.

SOLIDARITY'S MANY SHAPES

Solidarity so characterized can take many forms. Exploring their variety will help explain why some plausible candidates as ingredients of its definition are here being discarded. In nearly all cases, the benefit provided out of solidarity takes the form of help in what can be described as a situation of adversity, trouble, misfortune. But this is not necessarily the case. Solidarity can drive us to help a colleague preserve his privileges, or to help a member of our clan not only to get a job if unemployed, but also to be promoted to the top job from a position that is already quite enviable. The size of the cost incurred out of solidarity can vary greatly. It can be very high, as when soldiers risk their lives to come to the rescue of fellow soldiers. It can be tiny, as when you pick up a lost wallet and contact its owner. It can take the form of an action, as in all these examples, but also of an abstention. For example, customers can abstain from buying goods produced in the Israeli colonies out of solidarity with Palestinians. Solidarity often takes the form of joining a struggle against some other human beings, but it can also be triggered by a natural misfortune striking an individual person or a group. It can be shown by individuals acting alone, for example when a mountain climber goes to the rescue of another mountain climber. It can be shown by individuals acting together, as when workers join together in a strike or consumers in a boycott. And it can be shown by a collective entity such as a youth club or a member state of the European Union: mutual responsibility then applies between the members of a community of collectives. Solidarity often relates to material circumstances, but it does not need to. One can act out of solidarity with people whose religious freedom is being threatened or with populations whose traditional language is at risk of disappearing.

Sometimes, the consciousness of forming a community, the "we-feeling" associated with a shared identity, is obvious. This is typically the case when a strong national identity has emerged through successful top-down nation building. But it can also be the case when a minority identity has been reinforced by segregation, discrimination, or persecution, or when an enterprise, a profession, or a municipality has managed to instill a strong sense of belonging into their stable membership. But sometimes this shared identity is far from obvious and has to be rhetorically asserted, as when John F. Kennedy declared, "I am a Berliner," when T-shirts started asserting *"Je suis Charlie,"* or when Western Christians wear Palestinian scarves. These are all ways of saying: despite the appearances, we do belong to the same community and therefore your struggle is our struggle. The shared identity of individuals often consists of membership of actual communities, understood as sets of people interacting to some extent with one another, from extended families to neighborhoods, cities, alumni associations, labor unions, or nations. But it can also consist of membership in categories of people who need not have had any contact with each other—say, backpackers, academics, people of the same "race," or practitioners of the same religion spread all over the globe.

The extent to which people share these collective identities—and are therefore disposed to show solidarity with the corresponding "us"—can of course vary enormously. One way of measuring the strength of this mutual identification is by assessing the intensity of the pride or shame people feel for something they have not done themselves but by some other person or group sharing that collective identity. The disposition that stems from this identity does not need to amount to a duty. But it may turn into a duty if the cost to oneself is small, the benefit to the other large, and the shared identity strong. Under such circumstances, it can be taken for granted that others would have done for you what you are now expected to do for them. If you then do what solidarity requires, no particular gratitude will be triggered. If you do not, it will be resented and sometimes punished as a form of free-riding, a reprehensible failure to do your share in a reciprocal practice. On the other hand, the higher the cost and the weaker the shared identity, the less self-evident the duty and consequently the more admirable the act of solidarity when it occurs.

In today's world, whom one identifies with, and hence who might benefit from our solidarity, is more than ever a matter of the story one is telling about oneself: Shall I choose to view myself to a significant extent as a Brusseler, a Belgian, or a European, as a Mac user, a cyclist, or a grandfather, as a philosopher, an Oxonian, or a Louvaniste, as a Francophone, a Fleming, or a basic income supporter? But there are no doubt objective factors that help create or strengthen a collective identity. One of them is the salience of visible similarities that causes you to be perceived by others as belonging to a particular group. If everyone around you categorizes you as a woman, a *Maghrébin*, or a dwarf, this greatly increases the chance that you will regard yourself as such, identify with others categorized in the same way, and therefore be disposed to show solidarity with them. Another factor is the sharing of the same predicament or fate or challenge: being stuck on the same ship facing a storm, working in the same firm under the same boss, in the same city plagued by the same epidemic.[10] A community

---

10. For example, in Albert Camus's *The Plague*, the dwellers of the confined city of Oran are said to have been compelled by the illness to a solidarity of besieged people: "Ainsi la maladie qui, apparemment, avait forcé les habitants à une solidarité d'assiégés, brisait en même temps les associations traditionnelles et renvoyait les individus à leur solitude" (Camus

of fate is not automatically a community of belonging, but if the commonness of fate is (made) sufficiently salient, mutual identification can easily develop, both spontaneously and by design: when addressing the challenges of a common fate, it is often of great help to be able to count on the solidarity made possible by such identification.

Sharing a fate or a predicament is often associated with interdependence, but not always: think of widely scattered wilderness lovers, academics at risk, or speakers of endangered languages. And there are powerful forms of interdependence which cannot plausibly be framed as sharing the same fate and therefore show no tendency to generate the egalitarian shared identity that underlies solidarity as mutual responsibility: think of the interdependence between masters and slaves, capitalists and proletarians, teachers and pupils, parents and children, shepherds and sheep.[11] Yet there are causal connections in both directions between mutual dependence and the collective identity that underlies mutual responsibility. A common identity, especially if perceived as such by outsiders, can be a source of interdependence, most dramatically when a minority group is stigmatized, ostracized, or persecuted. And some types of mutual dependence, for example the increasing interdependence between the member states of a currency union, can support a strong case for mutual responsibility, and therefore for strengthening the common identity it requires.[12]

1947: 188–189). In a letter to Roland Barthes, Camus (1955) emphasizes the central place of solidarity in his novel: "Comparée à L'Étranger, La Peste marque, sans discussion possible, le passage d'une attitude de révolte solitaire à la reconnaissance d'une communauté dont il faut partager les luttes. S'il y a évolution de L'Étranger à La Peste, elle s'est faite dans le sens de la solidarité et de la participation."

11. This is why I have consistently resisted Andrea Sangiovanni's (2019) intriguing attempt to make interdependence (*solidarité de fait* in the old French sense) part of the definition of solidarity. Making concepts too fat, by packing too many components in it, makes it more difficult to perceive that these various components do not always go together, indeed can sometimes clash.

12. See, for example, Offe (2006: 127) on the functional necessity of wider "operative solidarity" to match the widening "supranational interdependencies" within the European Union. This functional necessity may or may not lead to the necessary becoming reality.

A PECULIAR SORT OF ALTRUISM

As mentioned above, solidarity in all these instances can be regarded as a form of altruism or care or generosity. But it is distinct from what might be regarded as pure altruism: doing for others what they would like us to do for them. And it is also distinct from what is enjoined by the golden rule: doing for others what we would like them to do for us—which is not necessarily what they would like us to do for them. Acting out of solidarity consists more narrowly in doing for others within our (real or imagined) community what we presume (precisely because we belong to that same community) that they would do or would have done for us in similar circumstances. This more circumscribed form of altruism can be regarded as self-serving for several reasons not shared by other forms of altruism. There are several familiar strategies for reducing all instances of altruism to self-interest. One can claim than an altruist simply maximizes a utility function that has the welfare of some other people among the variables that affect it. Or one can point out that it is the positive social sanctions that accrue to altruistic behavior and the negative ones that accrue to selfish behavior that make people behave altruistically in their own self-interest, all things considered. Or one can argue that even acting purely out of duty—unseen by anyone and for the benefit of people whose happiness does not make us any happier—still provides some sort of "selfish" gratification.[13] The altruism involved in solidarity, however, is self-serving in a sense that goes beyond these various quasi-tautological reductions of altruism to selfishness.

The suggestion, here, is in the same vein but less deterministic and more specific that the neo-functionalist theory of European integration. The latter claims that the growing interdependence created by integration—Jean Monnet's "*solidarité de fait*" quoted in an earlier footnote—is bound to lead to further integration, whether or not the latter takes the form of greater solidarity as mutual responsibility.

13. See Amartya Sen's (1977) classic discussion of "sympathy" and "commitment."

The first dimension of this specific connection between solidarity and self-interest is a corollary of the link between solidarity and insurance. The insurance motive can be understood as probabilistic reciprocity: I help you because I believe that I may one day be in your position and want to be able to count on your help in that case. The solidarity motive can be understood as virtual or counterfactual reciprocity: I help you because I assume that I could have been you—even though I know that I am not you and may also know that I shall never be in the sort of trouble in which you are now.[14] It is because of the counterfactual nature of the assumption that solidarity, unlike insurance, is not purely selfish. However, while not reducing to insurance, an established practice of solidarity within a community provides to its members a reduction of individual vulnerability analogous to the one provided by insurance schemes: all can trust that the others will help them when they are in trouble.

By virtue of this insurance effect, an established practice of solidarity is not only welfare-enhancing for its practitioners as a result of reducing individual vulnerability, but also because of the public goods it generates. It will increase the welfare of a community because of the benefits the latter derives from some of the risky activities in which it enables some its members to engage. For example, the members of a tribe can take more risks when hunting because they know that fellow tribe members will look after them if they are injured, or a family member can engage on a risky professional track because she knows the family will provide a safety net.

More than insurance, solidarity also creates goodwill: it increases not only the probability of being helped in similar circumstances but

---

14. I propose such a characterization of solidarity versus insurance in Van Parijs (1996: chapter 1). This characterization is largely consonant with David Miller's (2017: 62–66) thorough discussion of the concept of solidarity. Unlike him, however, I do not believe that there is a significant distinction to be made between "solidarity with" and "solidarity among," nor that there is any conceptual connection with the idea of limiting distributive inequality.

also the likelihood of willing cooperation in other domains, such as mobilization against (and hence deterrence of) external threats. Sheer insurance would have difficulty creating the same level of goodwill because it is purely self-interested, and other forms of altruism may not do as well because of their demeaning character. It is therefore not surprising that practices of "parochial altruism"—as Bowles (2008) characterizes solidarity—should provide an evolutionary advantage to the societies that develop them.[15]

Finally and most fundamentally: to the extent that one identifies with the others one is helping out of solidarity, what one does for them or for the community to which we all belong is something that one also does, to that extent, for oneself. When this identification distinctive of solidarity is maximal, when the "I could have been them" imposes itself as a self-evident truth, the other is perceived as so undistinguishable from oneself that altruism merges into egoism: there is no "alter" left to be altruistic with. This might well be the main reason why the rhetoric of solidarity—if available owing to a sufficiently strong "we-feeling"—can be more effective than the rhetoric of justice at inducing altruism, generosity, indeed sometimes self-sacrifice, and is therefore more often used.

Solidarity as mutual responsibility can thus be viewed as both altruistic and self-serving. This also applies to a distinct interpretation of "solidarity" proposed by John Roemer (2017, 2020) as the defining feature of socialist ethics. Solidary action, on this

---

15. "Thus, in ancestral humans, evolutionary pressures favoured cooperative institutions among group members as well as conflict with other groups. These were complemented by individual dispositions of solidarity and generosity towards one's own, and suspicion and hostility towards others. The potent combination of group and individual attributes is as characteristic of the contemporary welfare state in a system of heavily armed and competitive nations—in short, modern nationalism—as it was among our ancestors" (Bowles 2008: 327). See also Bowles and Choi (2004), Bowles and Gintis (2011).

interpretation, is acting on the assumption that others will be acting in the same way. Choosing what to do under this assumption requires one to follow universalizable maxims or to be "Kantian optimizers" rather than individualistic optimizers. Such solidary action is not restricted to doing something for others out of solidarity with them. Abstaining from lying, stealing, or overfishing, spending time carefully recycling one's refuse, adopting a common stance in negotiations are all typical cases of solidary action so defined while fitting uneasily under the label of mutual help. Conversely, there are practices of solidarity that a Kantian optimizer is unlikely to choose, for example—arguably—the dilapidation of any economic surplus to help relatives pay for expensive funerals and other festivities sometimes invoked as one of the causes of stagnation in sub-Saharan Africa. Hence, the two notions are not coextensive, but there is a large set of practices that can fall under both notions, and each of these articulates altruism and self-interest thanks to the assumption that other members of some relevant set will be acting in similar fashion. Despite the language of "universalizability," the Kantian notion of solidarity is no less dependent on such a set than solidarity as mutual responsibility: as a unionized bank employee, it makes a difference whose "universal" interest I am meant to pursue: the staff of my bank, all workers in the financial sector, the working class of my country, all workers in the world. Using the term "solidarity" for this Kantian notion can be intuitive enough, but it is the distinct (and on the whole narrower) notion of solidarity as mutual responsibility that is operative, I believe, in most of our everyday uses of the term and, as we shall see shortly, it is also that notion that is most relevant to the description of some of our institutions as being governed by a principle of solidarity.

SOCIAL SOLIDARITY AND SOCIAL JUSTICE

This should suffice by way of conceptual clarification. Let us now turn to the relationship between solidarity and justice. Although these two terms are often closely associated in everyday discourse, our conceptual exploration has not made justice part of the definition of solidarity.[16] One link has been mentioned in passing, however: a lack of solidarity is sometimes a clear case of cooperative injustice. In circumstances in which it is obvious that others in your community would have helped you, not helping them is unfair even if you yourself have never been helped: you are free-riding on a cooperative practice. In many circumstances, however, one can easily imagine that solidarity can clash with what some compelling notion of fairness requires. Suppose I am a doctor in charge of admission to an intensive care unit. Out of solidarity, I might be tempted to give priority to one of my relatives, or colleagues, or neighbors—just as they would have done for me in similar circumstances. Yet, fairness requires that I should stick instead to a protocol that applies impartial criteria. In other situations, solidarity would even demand a murderous revenge while justice would call for reconciliation. This suffices to show that there is no pre-established harmony between the parochialism of solidaristic altruism and the impartial demands of justice.

And yet, there is a robust relationship between solidarity and justice, or more precisely between some major instances of social solidarity and social justice plausibly interpreted as the equalization of opportunities (or possibilities or real freedom) among the members of the relevant community. One might first think of invoking the fact that a group is strengthened by the solidarity that binds its members, and if that group consists of exploited workers, or harassed women,

---

[16]. In contrast with the characterization of (true) solidarity by Arnsperger and Varoufakis (2003) and by Viehoff (2019).

or despised minorities, its greater strength can contribute to greater social justice. But the privileged can also show solidarity toward each other, for example in order to keep poor households or ethnic minorities out of their neighborhoods, or to share monopoly rents, or to keep each other in power. Similarly, the EU member states may show solidarity in helping Italy or Greece protect their coasts against the arrival of economic migrants from Africa. But this can hardly be interpreted as a contribution to global social justice.

More promising is the alliance between solidarity at the level of a whole society and (domestic) social justice. Social solidarity so understood can arise when the salient common identity crosses the boundaries between the social classes of a nation, as it can most easily do during or after a military conflict. Then solidarity can inspire the consensual dismantling of unjust privileges. But the strength of this common identity and the associated spontaneous solidarity may soon wither away, as net contributors attempt to retain the benefits of the positive externalities of solidarity while cutting down their contributions. The pursuit of sustainable justice requires the institutionalization of this mutual responsibility (i.e., the hardening of "warm" into "cold" solidarity).

The word "solidarity," as it is used today, refers not only to a disposition, a motive for individual or collective behavior. It also refers to a principle that governs some of our social institutions, a value they aim to realize, a character they possess. To clarify the content of this principle, it is convenient to start with the principle of social insurance, which presided over the origins of the modern welfare state. As neatly explained by Condorcet (1795), it is possible to provide income security to the sick and the old on favorable terms thanks to the contributions of those who never get sick or old. Thanks to an actuarially fair setup—that is, one that equalizes the contributions paid and the benefits received, weighted by the probability of the occurrence of the risks (of illness or old age) that triggers them—everyone is made better off than if they had to save individually for periods of illness or old age. Even though such a setup is in everyone's interest, it may not develop spontaneously at the optimal level because of the possibility of adverse selection (i.e., the attraction exercised by specific schemes on people aware of running specific risks). This is one reason why sickness, invalidity, unemployment, or old age insurance schemes were soon made compulsory for all or at least for large categories of the population. But there are further reasons for making social insurance compulsory. As mentioned above in connection with informal practices of solidarity, insurance also generates positive externalities. This holds even more for country-wide institutionalized insurance. These positive externalities then include macroeconomic stabilization, social peace, and the availability of a healthy workforce, in addition to "good moral hazard," that is, the encouragement of risky behavior that can be beneficial for the community, such as engaging in a training with an uncertain return or accepting a job with uncertain prospects.[17]

It did not take long, however, for such systems of social insurance to stop conforming to the criterion of actuarial fairness, if they ever did. Several factors led to the development redistribution ex ante—not only ex post, as in any insurance—from the wealthier and more immune to the poorer and more vulnerable. First, it is not easy for administrative procedures to assess risk profiles nor therefore to implement actuarial fairness. Second, the enlightened self-interest of ex ante contributors could be reconciled with some degree of ex ante loss thanks to more or less plausible arguments to the effect that this loss is more than offset by the positive externalities listed above. Third, relatively disadvantaged sections of the working class could fight, sometimes successfully, not only for higher wages or shorter

---

17. See Germany's rich debate, already in the 1930s, about the "wirtchaftiche Wert der Sozialpolitik" (see Vobruba ed. 1989).

working hours but also for better social protection (i.e., more ex ante redistribution within the so-called social insurance system). The outcome is the sort of welfare state we are familiar with. Typically, social benefits and social services are funded through social contributions proportional to earnings and/or a progressive taxation of incomes, while social services are provided according to needs, irrespective of contributions and risk profiles, and social benefits distributed, under specific conditions, as a function of contributions, but with both a floor and a cap.[18]

By appealing to sufficiently strong positive externalities, one can try to sell such a system to all classes of society on the ground that all of them benefit, including those that make the largest net contributions to the system. If one wishes to avoid fragile empirical claims, however, it is safer to appeal frankly to a principle of solidarity. As explained earlier, whereas insurance can be understood as probabilistic reciprocity, solidarity can be understood as counterfactual reciprocity: "I help you not so as to ensure that you will help me, but because I could have been you." If the working-class movement manages to create a strong common worker identity, it no longer matters if some pay more into the system than what they get out of it (probabilistically): this is precisely what solidarity among all workers requires. But the development of the welfare state went along with the building of modern nations. And it is the common identity as citizens of a nation that provided the moral basis for the development of national welfare states. These encompass not only the social insurance systems that grew out of mutual insurance among industrial workers but also the social assistance systems that grew out of the older discretionary poverty-relief schemes. In its first centuries of existence, public assistance was explicitly framed and justified as

---

18. On the interwovenness of insurance and ex ante redistribution in contemporary welfare states, see Baldwin (1990) and Vandenbroucke (2020: 7–14).

public charity.[19] It is now presented, along with social insurance, as social solidarity. France's means-tested non-contributory minimum income scheme, for example, is now called *Revenu de solidarité active*, and Chile's *Chile Solidario*. The perceived legitimacy of ex ante redistribution in the eyes of the net contributors depends no doubt in part on their belief in the positive externalities that may indirectly serve their self-interest. But it depends above all on their being able to look at national transfer systems as solidarity between people who could have been in each other's place by virtue of being members of the same nation.

Understood in this way, the solidarity that is embedded in our welfare states can be viewed as the institutionalization of solidarity understood as the moral disposition of mutual responsibility. This disposition is being solidified through being turned into a legal obligation, with corresponding legal rights. The "cold" solidarity implemented by our institutions is less heart-warming than the "warm" solidarity of spontaneous gestures. But it has the advantage of being more reliable. Yet it remains dependent on the moral disposition of solidarity in two ways. This disposition must be sufficiently present in the population both for the institutions of solidarity to be politically achievable and sustainable and for willing compliance with the legal obligations of solidarity to be widespread. The more this disposition is present, the more pride people will derive from contributing to the system and not abusing it. The less it is, the more people will try to cheat on both the contributors' and the beneficiaries' side, and thereby jeopardize the system's viability.

19. Part 1 of the first systematic defense of public assistance to the poor is framed entirely in terms of Christian charity (Vives 1526: part 1). And even in Jeremy Bentham's 1796 proposal for a thorough reform of the English Poor Laws, the management of public assistance should be entrusted to a "National Charity Company" (see Kelly 1990: 114–136).

In order to preserve its viability, institutionalized solidarity will need to equip itself with mechanisms that can make up for dwindling loyalty. Like any other formal or informal insurance scheme, it must be made resistant to moral hazard (i.e., the effect on people's behavior of the fact that some risks they run are covered by an insurance scheme, whether or not the latter involves ex ante redistributive solidarity). As pointed out earlier when listing the positive externalities of insurance and solidarity, some forms of moral hazard are desirable, and indeed aimed at by insurance schemes. The fact that shipwrecks could be insured led to the expansion of international commerce. The development of pension systems enabled people to save less for their old days and thereby enjoy a higher level of consumption. The availability of a common reserve of medical equipment enables each unit to stock less of it. But there is also undesirable moral hazard. If theft insurance or sickness insurance increase massively the number of people who get robbed or sick or who fake it, there is a problem both for the viability of the scheme and for its fairness. The same holds for institutionalized solidarity. It is guided by the idea of taking responsibility for others, but these others need to act in a "responsible" way. This corresponds to a second important and very different sense in which solidarity and responsibility are closely linked.

There are contexts of high mutual trust in which this responsible behavior is adopted spontaneously. But with cold solidarity more than with warm solidarity, bad moral hazard will need to be kept under check through mechanisms of "responsibilization." There are two such mechanisms. One is copayment: the misfortune is only partly compensated, just as is the case, for example, when a car insurance contract includes a deductible. Thus, patients are expected to pay part of the price of a medicine or of a medical appointment, unemployment benefits are lower than the wages they replace, and the per capita tax revenues of Germany's unequally affluent *Länder* are only partially equalized through the *Finanzausgleich* mechanism.

The problem with copayment is that it limits the extent to which solidarity protects the unfortunate and weeds out good moral hazard no less than a bad one. The other mechanism consists in imposing conditionalities: the aid is only forthcoming if the beneficiaries "deserve" it by behaving in an appropriate way. Thus, the unemployed do not get their benefits unless they are being "activated," and the countries that are heavily indebted do not get international aid unless they engage in "structural reforms." Unlike the copayment mechanism, conditionality is in principle consistent with full compensation, but it relies on a characterization of "responsible" behavior that can easily be contentious and breed resistance among the beneficiaries of solidarity against what they see as the contributors trying to micromanage their way of life. And in the absence of an agreement about what this proper behavior would be, the conditionality mechanism cannot work.[20]

If designed so as to sustainably reduce disadvantages for which its beneficiaries cannot be held responsible, a system of institutionalized solidarity uncontroversially contributes to social justice as the equalization of possibilities—unlike pure insurance schemes, which exclude ex ante redistribution. It definitely improves the life chances of people with lower earning power and/or less favorable risk profiles. However, the pursuit of social justice through redistributive institutions cannot be conflated with institutionalized solidarity. Free universal basic education, child benefits, a universal basic income, or enjoyable public spaces are equally relevant to this objective. But unlike the social insurance and social assistance components of our welfare states, they cannot be best construed as the institutionalization of mutual responsibility, of the disposition to do for others what

---

20. This plays no doubt a role in explaining why there is far wider support for transnational solidarity in the area of natural disasters than for debt relief (see Cicchi et al. 2020 on the basis of the EUI-YouGov annual solidarity survey).

we trust they would do for us in similar circumstances. This does not prevent them from having, like any institution that affects the predictable distribution of entitlements, an impact on the behavior of its beneficiaries: people may work less, for example, as a result of receiving child benefits or of not having to paying school fees. But it would be misleading to characterize such impact as moral hazard. The fundamental criterion for assessing the justice of social institutions is the equal distribution of possibilities—deviation from which can be justified on the ground that it boosts the possibilities that can be sustainably offered to the worst off.[21] Institutionalized solidarity is only one set of instruments in the service of meeting this criterion as well as possible. And the disposition on which one must be able to rely to support the broader set of institutions required by social justice is not mutual responsibility among the members of a community of identification but the need to justify distributive claims in the community of justification created by the functioning of a deliberative democracy.

---

21. In this light, Rawls's difference principle can be seen as a concession by egalitarians to efficiency considerations—something to be deplored on grounds of fraternity or solidarity by egalitarians more radical than Rawls, like G. A. Cohen (2000, 2009). But in a passage which includes a rare use of the term "solidarity," Rawls (1971: 105) presents instead the difference principle as the embodiment of the value of fraternity (with the other two principles of justice embodying the values of liberty and equality): "Those better circumstanced are willing to have their greater advantages only under a scheme under which this works out for the benefit of the less fortunate." This ties in with the notion of "noblesse oblige" mentioned by Rawls as the only formulation of the difference principle prior to his own, in a footnote on Santayana (Rawls 1971: 74 fn 12). Whether inequalities justified on maximin grounds should be understood as denials or expressions of fraternity depends on whether what is taken as the relevant baseline distributes the resources that are up for redistribution equally among all (in which case maximin-compatible inequalities are the reflection of ransoming by the lucky) or leaves them with those who happen to possess them (in which case agreeing to shrink inequalities down to their maximin level is the expression of generosity on the part of the lucky).

THE CHALLENGE OF DIVERSITY

Seeing that social justice does not reduce to social solidarity is particularly important in the context of increasingly diverse societies.[22] As modern nations become more heterogeneous, it becomes more difficult to maintain the plausibility of a common identity and thereby to turn the population covered by the transfer systems into an imagined community: the assumption that "I could have been any of them" is under pressure. In order to address this challenge, one strategy consists in nurturing, from the local to the European level, an inclusive collective identity and a corresponding imagined community that does not require a common ancestry, religion, or native language. This inclusive identity can take shape and flourish if there are enough opinion leaders, role models, journalists, bloggers, artists, and politicians to illustrate and propagate it. It can be fostered by multiplying contacts across cleavages, by developing bridging in addition to bonding social capital, by promoting the sharing of public spaces and public transport, crèches and schools, medical centers and hospitals, sport clubs and cultural activities. It can be further strengthened by developing both the reality and the perception of *solidarité de fait*, of interdependence, of a community of fate, of sitting in the same boat or the same fortress, even (but hopefully not) in the same bunker or the same tank. And it can also be strengthened by erecting an institutional framework that articulates a coherent multilevel citizenship status.[23] The conjunction of these strategies can help preserve, despite growing

---

22. For an assessment of these challenges and a discussion of the ways to address them, see the essays collected in Van Parijs ed. (2004) and in Banting and Kymlicka eds. (2018).
23. These four strategies correspond largely to the theories about the sources of solidarity listed by David Miller (2007: 69–75): the identity theory, the associational theory (Tocqueville-Putnam), the interdependence theory (Durkheim), and the institutional theory. This last one is neatly exemplified by Bauböck (2017).

diversity, citywide and countrywide collective identities, and some of them can even help build, despite international diversity, a stronger common European identity. Such mutual identification is required if institutionalized mutual responsibility at the corresponding levels is to be politically sustainable and its obligations voluntarily complied with. It is, however, unlikely to ever reach the level it can reach in homogeneous populations.

Moreover, this strategy does not address the second challenge faced by solidarity in the presence of diversity: cultural divergence as to what solidarity should cover and what can be reasonably expected from its beneficiaries. Culturally diverse societies may host significantly diverging conceptions of what counts as a misfortune that institutionalized solidarity ought to cover. Should an inability to have children, for example, or an unwanted pregnancy, enter this category? Even more likely are significant divergences as to what can be reasonably expected from the beneficiaries of solidarity, both to prevent the misfortune from occurring and to get out of it when it strikes. For example, do single parents who persistently refuse to take a full-time job do what can be "reasonably expected" from them to escape from poverty? Or does Greece do what it can be "reasonably expected" to do in order to reduce its public debt if it persistently refuses to tax the Orthodox Church? And when cultural norms differ, how confident can one be that the other would have helped us if the places had been swapped? Solidarity as mutual responsibility then becomes problematic: "If you keep behaving like this, OK with me. I can respect your way of life, just as I want you to respect mine. But then, do not expect my solidarity." The more cultural diversity, the likelier the resentment of the net contributors about the net beneficiaries behaving in "irresponsible" fashion and the likelier the resentment of the net beneficiaries about the net contributors being "meddlesome." This does not warrant much optimism about the power of solidarity, as cultural diversity keeps swelling in our countries as a result of immigration and as we need to lift solidarity to a higher and therefore more heterogeneous scale, owing to the mounting competitive pressure on the aspects of our national welfare states that go beyond strict insurance.

These difficulties do not evaporate, but they become less central if the equalization of possibilities, rather than social solidarity, is taken as the fundamental principle that should govern our redistributive institutions. Mutual identification and convergent conceptions of misfortune and responsibility are then no longer fundamental.[24] Support for redistribution is expected to be rooted, rather than in the spontaneous sentiments of solidarity that link the members of a community to each other, in the power of deliberation. Its possibility hinges on our political institutions managing to enable and induce ourselves and our representatives to talk to each other and justify our aims, proposals, and decisions to all the people potentially affected by them. What must then do the work is the civilizing force of common deliberation rather than the solidarizing force of mutual identification. The hope is that a community of justification can thrive even under conditions in which, owing to cultural diversity, a strong collective identity is no longer or not yet within reach. At the same time, the very functioning of the political institutions that structure the community of justification may slowly contribute to the emergence or strengthening of a shared identity and the solidarity resting on it.

---

24. Even if the guiding principle is the equalization of possibilities and not solidarity, there are good reasons for wanting part of the fair distribution of resources to take the form of universal insurance packages against illness or handicaps. Configuring these requires some degree of consensus in the population concerned. But there is less at stake, as the fall-back option is a fair distribution of cash, rather than no redistribution at all.

PHILIPPE VAN PARIJS

WARM SOLIDARITY AND THE JUST SOCIETY

Even from this perspective, which emphasizes the irreducibility of social justice to social solidarity, the nurturing and enactment of warm solidarity, of the moral disposition of mutual responsibility between individuals and between collectives, remain important for several reasons. First, any successful call for solidarity across national borders, not least among such collectives as the member states of the European Union, not only prompts acts of solidarity of an ephemeral nature but also paves the way for their institutionalization in the service of lasting greater social justice at a scale on which little exists by way of institutions for the equalization of possibilities.

Second, as explained above, the institutionalized solidarity embodied in our welfare states is a major instrument for social justice, and whatever support they can keep receiving from feelings of solidarity despite the increasing heterogeneity of our societies is most welcome.

Third, the deliberative process on which the pursuit of justice must be able to rely must not be thought of as just a polite conversation. The civilizing force of discussing with each other will not produce the desired effects if those who stand to gain from greater justice do not mobilize and struggle to get their voices heard and their interests taken into account. And the success of these struggles will constantly demand solidarity among those involved in them.

Finally, even the most just formal institutions cannot work in such a fine-grained way that they can identify and address all situations of obvious injustice. To help fill these gaps, to help reduce the injustices which formal institutions cannot hope to mend, warm solidarity at the local level is far from redundant: it is indispensable. The fraternal feelings displayed in such solidarity-driven actions are both a reflection of and a contribution to the quality of human relationships that prevail in a society. They do not provide an alternative to the development of "cold" just institutions, but they are an essential complement to them, and one that provides living in a community with a warm glow that even the best institutions could not keep alight.[25]

For all these reasons, the virtue of solidarity, as practiced both by individuals and collectives, is of great importance to social justice. But this should not make us praise this virtue unconditionally: it can serve wicked aims and clash with fairness. Nor should this make us forget that the institutions central to the pursuit of social justice cannot all be conceptualized as institutionalized solidarity, even in those circumstances in which the population for which social justice is being sought coincides with the community among which the mutual responsibility of solidarity prevails.[26]

WORKS CITED

Arnsperger, Christian, and Yanis Varoufakis. 2003. "Toward a Theory of Solidarity." *Erkenntnis* 59: 157–188.

Baldwin, Peter. 1990. *The Politics of Social Solidarity: Class Bases of the European Welfare State*. Cambridge: Cambridge University Press.

---

25. In September 1985, the September Group (then consisting of Robert Brenner, G. A. Cohen, Jon Elster, Adam Przeworski, John Roemer, Hillel Steiner, Robert van der Veen, Philippe Van Parijs, and Erik Olin Wright) played a little game requiring each member to rank the following five values: liberty, equality, fraternity, self-realization, and efficiency. Four of us ranked liberty first, three self-realization, one equality, and one fraternity. I was the one who gave priority to fraternity. Yet the conception of justice I proposed ten years later in *Real Freedom for All*, while articulating equality, liberty, and efficiency, gives no role to fraternity. The final paragraphs of the present piece indicate how I believe this can be made consistent.

26. I am most grateful to Andrea Sangiovanni, Frank Vandenbroucke, Roberto Veneziani, and Juri Viehoff for very useful written comments, to the organizers (Paul de Beer, Mette Eistrup-Sangiovanni, Ayelet Shachar, Antonio Riva) and participants in conferences on solidarity in Amsterdam (9/25/2014), Cambridge (5/5/2018), Göttingen (6/14/2019), and Milan (9/17/2019), and to all participants in the 2020 meeting of the September Group (8/30/2020) for instructive and stimulating discussions.

Banting, Keith, and Will Kymicka. 2017. "Introduction." In *The Strains of Commitment: The Political Sources of Solidarity in Diverse Societies*, ed. K. Banting and W. Kymicka. Oxford: Oxford University Press, 1–58.

Banting, Keith, and Will Kymicka, eds. 2017. *The Strains of Commitment: The Political Sources of Solidarity in Diverse Societies*. Oxford: Oxford University Press.

Bauböck, Rainer. 2017. "Citizenship and Collective Identities as Political Sources of Solidarity in the European Union." In *The Strains of Commitment: The Political Sources of Solidarity in Diverse Societies*, ed. K. Banting and W. Kymicka. Oxford: Oxford University Press, 61–79.

Bourgeois, Léon. 1896. *Solidarité*. Paris: Armand Colin.

Bowles, Samuel. 2008. "Conflict: Altruism's Midwife." *Nature* 456: 326–327.

Bowles, Samuel, and Jung-Kyoo Choi. 2004. "The Co-Evolution of Love and Hate." In *Cultural Diversity versus Economic Solidarity*, ed. P. Van Parijs. Brussels: De Boeck Université, 81–98.

Bowles, Samuel, and Herbert Gintis. 2011. *A Cooperative Species: Human Reciprocity and Evolution*. Princeton, NJ: Princeton University Press.

Camus, Albert. 1948. *La Peste*. London: Methuen.

Camus, Albert. 1955. "Lettre à Roland Barthes," 11 janvier 1955, https://philofrancais.fr/camus-lettre-a-roland-barthes#:~:text=Sans%20doute%20est%2Dce%20l%C3%A0,est%20de%20l%C3%A9gitimer%20une%20tyrannie.

Cicchi, Lorenzo, Philipp Genschel, and Anton Hemerijck. 2020. *EU Solidarity in Times of Covid-19*. Policy Brief 2020/34, Robert Schuman Centre, European University Institute.

Cohen, G. A. 2000. *If You're an Egalitarian, How Come You Are So Rich?* Cambridge, MA: Harvard University Press.

Cohen, G. A. 2009. *Why Not Socialism?* Princeton, NJ: Princeton University Press.

Coman, Ramona, Louise Fromont, and Anne Weyembergh, eds. 2019. *Les solidarités européennes: Entre enjeux, tensions et reconfigurations*. Bruxelles: Bruylant.

Comte, Auguste. 1844. *Discours sur l'esprit positif*. Paris: Carilian-Gœury

Comte, Auguste. 1866. *Traité de politique et de science sociale*. Paris: Amyot, 1866, Tome 2.

Condorcet, Antoine Caritat, Marquis de. 1795. *Esquisse d'un tableau historique des progrès de l'esprit humain*. Paris: Garnier-Flammarion, 1988.

De Lobel, Peter. 2020. "De terugkeer van de solidariteit." *De Standaard*, April 30, 2020, 10.

Durkheim, Emile. 1893. *De la Division du travail social*. Paris: P.U.F., 1967.

Ewald, François. 1996. "Solidarité, Protection, Assurance." In *Dictionnaire d'éthique et de philosophie morale*, ed. Monique Canto-Sperber. Paris: P.U.F., 1513–1520.

Gide, Charles. 1932. *La Solidarité: Cours au Collège de France 1927–1928*. Paris: P.U.F.

Kelly, Paul J. 1990. *Utilitarianism and Distributive Justice: Jeremy Bentham and the Civil Law*. Oxford: Clarendon Press.

Le Bras-Chopard, Armelle. 1992. "Métamorphoses d'une notion: La solidarité chez Pierre Leroux." In *La Solidarité: Un sentiment républicain?*, ed. Jacques Chevalier and Dominique Cochart. Paris: P.U.F., 55–69.

Leroux, Pierre. 1840. *De l'Humanité, de son principe et de son avenir*. Paris: Perrotin.

Miller, David. 2017. "Solidarity and Its Sources." In *The Strains of Commitment: The Political Sources of Solidarity in Diverse Societies*, ed. K. Banting and W. Kymicka. Oxford: Oxford University Press, 61–79.

Offe, Claus. 2007. "Obligations versus Costs: Types and Contexts of Solidary Action." In *European Solidarity*, ed. Nathalie Karagiannis. Liverpool: Liverpool University Press, 113–128.

Roemer, John E. 2017. "Socialism Revised." *Philosophy & Public Affairs* 45, no. 3: 261–315.

Roemer, John E. 2020. "Market Socialism Renewed." *Catalyst Journal* 4, no. 1: 9–57.

Sangiovanni, Andrea. 2019. "Solidarity." European University Institute and King's College London.

Sen, Amartya. 1977. "Rational Fools: A Critique of the Behavioral Foundations of Economic Theory." *Philosophy & Public Affairs* 6: 317–344.

Van Parijs, Philippe. 1996. *Refonder la solidarité*. Paris: Cerf.

Van Parijs, Philippe. 1998. "Fairness." *Boston Review* 23, no. 6: 15–16.

Van Parijs, Philippe ed. 2004. *Cultural Diversity versus Economic Solidarity*. Brussels: De Boeck Université.

Vandenbroucke, Frank. 2020a. *Solidarity through Redistribution and Insurance of Incomes*. University of Amsterdam: ACES Research Paper 2020/1.

Vandenbroucke, Frank. 2020b. "Solidariteit in Europa." In *Wetenschap in een veranderende wereld. Lezingen voor de XXIste eeuw*. ed. Pieter D'Hoine and Bart Pattyn. Leuven: Leuven University Press, 141–167.

Viehoff, Juri. 2019. "Solidarity: A Functional Explanation." European University Institute.

Vives, Johannes Ludovicus. 1526. *De Subventione Pauperum*. English translation: *On the Relief of the Poor, or of Human Needs*, in *The Origins of Modern Welfare*, ed. Paul Spicker. Oxford: Peter Lang, 2010, 1–100.

Vobruba, Georg, ed. 1989. *Der wirtschaftliche Wert der Sozialpolitik*. Berlin: Duncker & Humblot (Sozialpolitische Schriften no. 60), 1989.

Chapter 3

Challenges to Solidarity

ANDREA SANGIOVANNI

Whatever else it is, solidarity is an ideal. It describes something that has value, something toward which we should aspire. Understood provisionally as a form of standing together against adversity, it embodies an ideal of *unity* and *integrity*. It is opposed to division, rancor, strife, and discord. Those who exhibit solidarity with others exhibit a virtue of character and conduct. To act solidaristically is to act well. Flourishing lives that are lived in solidarity with others are all the more flourishing for it.

We will need to say more about what solidarity is and why it is supposed to have value and function as an ideal. We will come to that. But first we need to state a series of challenges, because not everyone agrees that solidarity is a good, or a virtue, or an ideal. Many believe that solidarity is not an appropriate aspiration for a modern, diverse, and individualistic people; its demands for unity stifle liberty and encourage exclusion. Others believe that it is a wishy-washy, vague term whose meaninglessness is a honey trap for demagogues and bad politics. Others still worry that, when given a more precise character, it becomes redundant, no different from similar ideas, such as altruism, empathy, identification, fellow-feeling, or justice. In this chapter,

I will address these challenges; I will address, that is, the challenge that solidarity is (i) *illiberal*, (ii) *exclusionary*, (iii) *empty*, or (iv) *redundant*.

WHAT IS SOLIDARITY, AND WHY IS IT VALUABLE?

To address these challenges, we first need to specify an account of solidarity that can serve as a counterpoint. In other work, I have defended an account of solidarity that has the following form.[1] I argue that solidarity is a form of acting together to overcome significant adversity grounded in identification. We act solidaristically when, that is, (a) we identify with one another on the basis of a shared way of life, cause, set of experiences, condition, or role; (b) we are, as a result, committed to doing our part in overcoming significant adversity and to setting aside, in a range of cases, narrow self-interest in its pursuit; (c) we have a settled, reliable disposition to come to others' aid in support of our goal, and are disposed not to bypass one another's wills in that pursuit; and (d) we trust one another with respect to (b) and (c) (where trust is reliance plus a normative expectation that others will indeed be committed and come to our aid when necessary). On this reading, solidarity does not name an emotion, such as fellow-feeling, and it cannot be reduced to mere support for a noble cause (e.g., donating money to Oxfam). It is also omni- rather unilateral: acts of charity, altruism, or humanitarian aid do not, as such, count as instances of solidarity. Solidarity, furthermore, cannot be merely passive: the dispositions and commitments mentioned above must be dispositions and commitments displayed

---

1. Sangiovanni 2023.

in a form of irreducibly joint action. We cannot *be* in solidarity unless we *act* in solidarity.

In defense of this view, I argue that this account can provide an explanatory and normative structure to the five main traditions of thought that have shaped solidarity (as a practice), namely socialism, solidarism, nationalism, Christianity (especially Catholicism), and contemporary social movements.[2] Each one grounds solidarity among workers, citizens, nationals, human beings, and disadvantaged groups (women, African-Americans, disabled, and so on), in a distinctive notion of identification, and advocates a distinctive kind of collective action designed to overcome significant adversity. Within socialism, solidarity among workers, for example, is grounded in identification based on a shared condition as exploited, and is realized through collective action designed to overthrow capitalism. Within Christianity, solidarity among human beings is grounded in identification with one another on the basis of a recognition of our interdependent vulnerability, and is realized through forms of organization and cooperative action (e.g., family, community, country, church) designed to alleviate the suffering that interdependence brings in its train. A similar pattern unites all the other cases.

As I have already mentioned, solidarity is a *value-laden* practice. While it is possible to speak of solidarity among, say, right-wing nationalists (when employing the concept for descriptive purposes), solidarity is usually seen to be both instrumentally and non-instrumentally valuable. In the mouths of advocates, it is a rallying cry describing an ideal of human cooperation. This value-laden background provides another important perspective for evaluating different accounts of solidarity. For a particular account of solidarity to be successful, it must, that is, be able to capture the distinctive values associated with it. Any successful theory of solidarity must then

---

2. Sangiovanni 2023, Section 2.

characterize those values, and explain how the account of the concept proposed captures those values.

It is evident that solidarity, where it exists, can have *instrumental* value. When solidarity is present, we are able to achieve things together that we wouldn't have otherwise been able to achieve. But what non-instrumental values, if any, does solidarity realize? I argue that this value has three components, each of which captures the sense in which solidarity realizes a kind of *social unity* among actors.[3] (i) Solidarity instantiates the non-instrumental value of, inter alia, *mutual commitment*, where what is valued is not just my standing by you, or your standing by me, but the conjunction of the two. The value of this kind of mutual commitment is evident in thinking through cases in which we prefer struggling together against adversity than surrendering, even if we know we will be overwhelmed. (ii) Solidarity instantiates a form of non-instrumentally valuable cooperation in which we each participate in the complementary excellences of all, and take pleasure in the collective realization of ends that none of us could achieve alone. (iii) When we act in solidarity, we also rightly take pleasure in the fact that we can see our collective agency reflected in our joint, coordinated, and beneficial activity; we can say, for example, not only that justice was done, but that *we* did it. Each of these forms of non-instrumental value are reflected in the five main traditions I mentioned above. These values are, however, *conditional* on the goodness of the ends promoted by solidaristic action: while right-wing nationalists might exhibit solidarity, because the ends promoted through their solidarity are wicked, the solidarity ceases to have value.

---

3. Sangiovanni 2023, Section 4. For a different account of solidarity as non-instrumentally valuable, see Kolers 2016, ch. 6.

With this brief summary, we are in a better position to assess our main question: Can an account of solidarity that has the form outlined in this section answer all four challenges?

DOES SOLIDARITY UNDERMINE LIBERTY?

Does solidarity muffle liberty? In her celebrated essay, the "Liberalism of Fear," Judith Shklar claims it does. Echoing Isaiah Berlin, she writes:

> We must therefore be suspicious of ideologies of solidarity, precisely because they are so attractive to those who find liberalism emotionally unsatisfying, and who have gone on in our century to create oppressive and cruel regimes of unparalleled horror. The assumption that these offer something wholesome to the atomized citizen may or may not be true, but the political consequences are not, on the historical record, open to much doubt. To seek emotional and personal development in the bosom of a community or in romantic self-expression is a choice open to citizens in liberal societies. Both, however, are apolitical impulses and wholly self-oriented, which at best distract us from the main task of politics when they are presented as political doctrines, and at worst can, under unfortunate circumstances, seriously damage liberal practices. For although both appear only to be redrawing the boundaries between the personal and the public, which is a perfectly normal political practice, it cannot be said that either one has a serious sense of the implications of the proposed shifts in either direction.[4]

---

4. Shklar 1989, p. 36.

CHALLENGES TO SOLIDARITY

There is, one might think, an element of truth in what Shklar says here. I, too, have emphasized that an ethic of solidarity becomes important for us now and around here when and because we sense the need for collective resistance and unity of purpose in the face of adversity. I have also emphasized the non-instrumental (albeit conditional) value in setting aside self-interest in a horizontal identification with others ('community') on behalf of a shared goal, where part of what is valued is our seeing, together, our collective agency reflected in the ends we pursue ('self-expression').

The element of identification may seem particularly problematic. Identification requires, among other things, coming to see others as 'like oneself,' and taking that similarity as a basis for joint concern, empathy, and normative orientation. So, for example, when I identify with you *as a worker*, I see our common role as providing an important orientation in my life. It matters to me what 'being a worker' means, what struggles we face, what happens to us as workers. My well-being is tied up with you as a worker: when we, as workers, do well, I do well. I also feel concern for you as a worker, and am moved to come to your aid when you are under attack. But identification of this kind, especially when it underpins solidarity, and hence joint action, also brings with it a demand for *loyalty*—for setting aside self-interest when this is required by the group, setting aside smaller differences for the success of our plans, setting aside individual concerns for the well-being of all. In this sense, an ethic of solidarity demands that one set aside the personal for the political (thus 'redrawing the boundaries' between them).

The worry is that, in politics, this demand for similarity, commitment, and loyalty leads to tyranny. Liberals like Shklar prize the freedom that comes from a vigilant distrust of politics. Politics should aim to provide good fences, to secure personal rights and personal space against incursion. It should not aim to forge a common purpose or identity, or a devotion to a whole in which each can feel themselves realized. Hannah Arendt famously captures this diagnosis. Total terror, she writes in the *Origins of Totalitarianism*,

> substitutes for the boundaries and channels of communication between individual men a band of iron that holds them so tightly together that it is as though their plurality had disappeared into *One Man* of gigantic dimensions. To abolish the fences of laws between men—as tyranny does—means to take away man's liberties and destroy freedom as a living political reality; for the space between men as it is hedged in by laws, is the living space of freedom.[5]

Solidarity, Shklar fears, is like the 'band of iron,' dissolving plurality and hence stifling individual liberty.

George Kateb finds solidarity troubling for similar reasons. He warns us against it, and celebrates the democratic individuality championed by Thoreau, Whitman, and Emerson in its stead. In the same volume that contains Shklar's essay, Kateb writes:

> The weakening of traditional enclosure in status, group, class, locality, ethnicity, race—the whole suffocating network of ascribed artificial, or biological but culturally exaggerated, identity opens life up, at least a bit. The culture of individual rights has lightness of being; free being is light.... Nothing is worse than the horrors that do or would come from the unqualified prestige of participation in sovereign politics, the society-wide bond of community, the

---

5. Arendt 1973, 465–466. Arendt herself, it should be noted, was not a critic of solidarity, and not a liberal either. She is better classified as a republican, and views the communicative power generated by collective action as necessary for freedom. See Arendt 1990 [1963], 84. I mention her in connection with Shklar because Shklar believes that the same impulse underlies both the yearning for solidarity and the yearning for individual transcendence that totalitarianism seeks to satisfy.

solidarity of the armed group, and the project of socialized self-realization. They are horrors in themselves and are auxiliaries to the further horrors of statism. The remedies for the troubles must be found, at least in any democratic setting, within rights-based individualism and the aspiration to democratic individuality.[6]

'Enclosures' of status, group, class, locality, ethnicity, and race are, Kateb claims, suffocating. And so solidarities based on them, by extension, must also be suffocating: they rest and rely on seeing one another—for the sake of our common action—as bound together not primarily as individuals but as members of a group, whether of, say, workers, women, citizens, immigrants, or African-Americans. The democratic individualist can allow for coordinated action and resistance (here Kateb cites Thoreau on civil disobedience), but it should be temporary, shifting, improvised, and based on independent affirmation rather than identification.

As criticisms of solidarity, I find these challenges unconvincing for two reasons. First, they treat a commitment to solidarity as incompatible with a commitment to liberalism. To be sure, solidarities organized to promote illiberal ends by illiberal means (one might think here of xenophobic nationalisms or alt-right racists) are, well, illiberal by definition. But their disregard for individual rights or freedom or equality is not entailed or required (although it may be facilitated) by their solidarity. Solidarity makes, we might say, their common actions all the worse, but this is compatible with all that I have said so far: recall that the non-instrumental value of solidarity is only realized when the ends in view and the means taken to those ends are not wicked. The presence of solidarity amplifies the goodness of the ends and means when they are good, but, at the same time, amplifies the badness of the ends and means whey they are bad.

6. Kateb 1989, 188, 204.

Indeed, liberalism, I want to argue, *requires* solidarity rather than being at odds with it. If, as Shklar and Kateb repeatedly emphasize, liberalism demands vigilance, hatred of injustice, and a readiness to resist power when necessary, then liberalism requires solidarity. What Shklar and Kateb overlook is that resistance is most effective when it is conducted by *groups* whose grievances are shared, and known to be shared. The grievances—when they are shared and known to be shared—provide a spring for joint action, and a powerful source of identification. Such identification is necessary to overcome fear, and to lead people to look beyond their immediate self-interest to the larger task at hand. Identification also promotes pro-social and altruistic behavior among those engaged in the joint task: when you identify with others in the cause, you are more likely to come to their aid when necessary.[7] Furthermore, individual resistance is rarely, if ever, successful. Isolated acts of resistance aren't either. From this point of view, it is no surprise that Kateb cites Thoreau on civil disobedience. Thoreau's speech is a paean to the individual standing alone, fortified by his conscience, against an unjust state. The speech, although it invites its listeners to act as he did (i.e., to cease paying general taxes), is not a call to rise up *together* against the state. It is not a call to organized rebellion, coordinated resistance, or collective protest.[8] Its central moral message is: do not make yourself a tool of injustice by blindly supporting an unjust state.

This brings me to the second reason why these challenges strike me as unconvincing. In both Shklar and Kateb, the target is what we

---

7. See Bowles and Gintis 2011, 35–38 and ch. 8. See also Tajfel et al. 1971. Yamagishi et al. 1999 argues that ingroup favoritism is explained by expectations of generalized reciprocity within groups derived from shared norms. See also note 7, and accompanying text, below.

8. It is important to note that Thoreau did not deny that collective resistance was often necessary. Indeed, in his defense of John Brown, he lauded the raid at Harpers Ferry. But in such cases, he did so at a distance—as someone whose conscience had been moved by the actions of others.

might call *state-level* solidarity. Though they do not name it, their target is nationalism or patriotism—solidarity as invoked by those who have political power and who aim to rally the people against an enemy (whether internal or external), or solidarity as it is invoked by those who believe that active, partisan political participation is essential for a flourishing life. The first response is simply to point to the fact, as I have above, that solidarity can be at the heart of social movements and bottom-up political action. It need not be solely focused on or through the state. The second response is that even state-level solidarity need not be so pernicious. In particular, state-level solidarity, or civic solidarity as I will call it, need not enforce blind conformity, disrespect difference or disagreement, or raze plurality.

The key is in identifying a form of solidarity among a people that is neither a form of nationalism nor constitutional patriotism. Using the account of solidarity I reviewed in the first section of this chapter, I will give a sketch of such an account here. It is often said that welfare state institutions, for example, are products of solidarity, or are governed by a principle of solidarity, but it is just as often unclear what is meant.[9] If solidarity is understood as simply a willingness to share resources, or a commitment to social justice, then it is too unspecific. There are many instances of sharing resources that do not count as instances of solidarity, and identifying solidarity with social justice dissipates the theoretical and practical interest of solidarity as a value *distinct from* social justice. The distinctive nature of civic solidarity, however, can be preserved if we understand it as grounded in the identification of citizens with one another. But on what basis? The nationalist will say that the identification that binds citizens together is an identification based on a shared way of life. But there is another way

---

9. I draw here on Sangiovanni 2023, Section 3. On welfare state solidarity and its relation to justice, see also Bayertz 1999, 21–26.

that I want to defend here, that does not ground civic solidarity in identification rooted in *sharing a culture* but in *sharing authorship of a set of institutions*. The moral pressure to act in solidarity will depend on the presence of identification, but will be ultimately derived from demands of fairness.[10] On this view, solidarity *supports* demands of justice by grounding such demands in the nature of civic identification, rather than in general, natural duties to support just institutions. (I return to the relationship between justice and solidarity below.)

Citizens who identify with their role as citizens conceive of their joint participation in reproducing, reforming, and authoring common institutions as providing normative orientation. The argument is an analogue of Léon Bourgeois's case for solidarity as interdependence.[11] Where Bourgeois emphasizes our myriad contributions, through work, to the joint social product, this account emphasizes a more fundamental contribution to the basic structure that makes our contribution through work to the joint social product possible in the first place. We recognize, as citizens, that it is not only through our state's official political acts—its legislative, executive, and adjudicative output—but also through our support of informal conventions and norms that we collectively author the basic institutions that both constrain and enable individuals' pursuit of the good life. When citizens identify with one another *as citizens* in this sense, they recognize that their ability to generate a marginal product of labor, or to invest in productive resources, and thereby to gain, depends on the contributions of millions of others in a complex division of labor

---

10. See also Yamagishi et al. 1999, who argue that ingroup favoritism is explained by expectations of generalized reciprocity within groups derived from shared norms. If no generalized reciprocity is expected within the group, ingroup favoritism, Yamagishi shows, disappears.
11. Bourgeois 1902 [1896]. I discuss Bourgeois at greater length in Sangiovanni 2023, Section 2.

that is backed by a set of basic social and political institutions.[12] They therefore recognize that their public, civic, economic, cultural, and political activity has a cumulative effect on the prosperity of the state as a whole, and are disposed to seek an understanding of how their coordinated actions impact on the prospects of other citizens. When things go well, their collective achievements as authors contribute to their own sense of well-being; when things go poorly, they perceive their own lives as less flourishing as a result.

While there is, of course, profound disagreement about the character and requirements of the values and ideals that underlie common institutions, citizens who identify share a readiness to define them through deliberation (and sometimes more open conflict); this process of reflection, deliberation, and conflict reflects a disposition to see common institutions as their own, as reflecting their collective deliberation and disagreement. Indeed, it is more often than not the characteristic lines and modes of *dis*agreement—rather than areas of consensus—that form the focus of identification among citizens. This is a direct result of the fact that identification is not, on this understanding, grounded in a shared culture or in a shared set of values, but in the exercise of shared agency as a people.[13] Citizens recognize that their peers come from multiple, sometimes only thinly overlapping cultural backgrounds.[14] Their attachment to common institutions is founded on what they *do* together, which defines, in part, who they *are*. (Note that nationalists have it the other way around: who we *are* should define what we *do* together.)

Solidarity becomes a demand of citizenship, then, when citizens recognize that sustaining and reproducing common social and

---

12. I make this argument in the context of the global justice debates at greater length in Sangiovanni 2007.
13. Cf. Jodi Dean's conception of reflective solidarity Dean 1995, 123.
14. See also Miller 2017, 68.

political institutions require commitment to overcoming, together, the adversity created by imperfect markets; legacies of racism, sexism, colonialism, and other forms of arbitrary exclusion and oppression; poverty and (especially work-related) illness; vulnerability to foreign interference, disruption, and economic dependence; pandemics; and so on. Solidarity also requires mutual trust, which, in this context, implies a tolerance for difference and a recognition that sustaining a common life requires respect for (sometimes foundational) disagreement, and a willingness to meet others halfway.[15] Solidarity, finally, demands a disposition to come to each other's aid in overcoming adversity, which, in this case, can be interpreted as a willingness to divide the joint social product fairly and in a way that recognizes the contributions of each to the functioning of the whole.[16] There are two sources of rational pressure at work here. First, there is prudential pressure from our identification with the project; to fail to act in solidarity with others with whom we identify is then a failure of integrity. But there is also moral pressure from a sense of fairness: should citizens who identify fail to act in solidarity with others—by failing, say, to support policies that divide the social product fairly, or not be disposed to engage others with tolerance and respect, or not to do their part in maintaining, reproducing, and reforming common institutions that are just or nearly just—they would not only be contributing to injustice but also free-riding on the efforts of others to maintain the public good.

One might think my rendering of civic solidarity bears some similarity to constitutional patriotism.[17] There is a crucial difference. According to the constitutional patriot, what binds individual citizens into a people is a shared commitment to constitutional

---

15. On meeting others halfway, see the Introduction to Banting and Kymlicka 2017.
16. Bourgeois 1902. For more discussion, see Kohn 2018.
17. See, e.g., Habermas 2001; Ingram 1996; Müller 2007.

principles and values, such as justice and liberty—where, importantly, this commitment takes particular historical forms in different polities according to their specific histories and political cultures. By contrast, on my account, civic solidarity is based *not* on a shared affirmation of principles and values, but on the basis of a horizontal identification with other citizens (and, indeed, residents) for the role they play in authoring and reproducing common institutions. Often such shared authorship will involve a shared commitment to values and principles but it need not. As I mentioned previously, it is possible for there to be deep disagreement about which such principles and values ought to govern our cooperation; as long as there is a shared intention to continue political and social life together, and there continues to be horizontal role-based identification, commitment to overcoming significant adversity, dispositions to share one another's fate, and trust, then there is enough for civic solidarity.[18] There is, therefore, no reason to believe that solidarity, even state-level solidarity, and liberalism need to be at cross-purposes.

IS SOLIDARITY EXCLUSIONARY?

Solidarity is grounded in identification, where identification, in turn, can be grounded in a shared cause, role, condition, set of experiences, or way of life. And so solidarity, it seems, must be exclusionary: those

---

18. Cf. Levy 2005, 107: "[The inhabitants of a political community] are not what nationalists falsely claim co-nationals to be: members of some pre- or extra-political social whole that can make its will felt through politics. . . . They are not the particular subset of humanity united by allegiance to some particular political ideal, at any level of abstraction; even if most people had sufficient political knowledge and sufficiently coherent views to qualify as holding an ideal, politics contain a perennial diversity of such ideals. . . . There is no polity made up entirely of liberals or social democrats or civic republicans, and each of those is found in more than one polity." The account of civic identification I defend in the text, which relies only on our role as collective authors, does not fall prey to this criticism.

who do not share the grounds of identification with us cannot be in solidarity with us. Solidarity is, furthermore, often (though not necessarily) oppositional:[19] when we seek to overcome together some significant adversity, that adversity—more often than not—will be created and maintained by other individuals acting against us. When we struggle in solidarity, we struggle, therefore, against *them*. We might struggle, for example, against slave-owners, members of a government, racists, or the occupiers. What we want to explore here is whether and when solidarity is *objectionably* exclusionary (from here on I will drop 'objectionably').[20] It seems self-evident that solidarity need not *always* and *necessarily* be exclusionary (we could, after all, stand in solidarity together as the human race battling climate change). But it also seems evident that it can often be exclusionary precisely in virtue of its demand for trust, mutual commitment, and unity of purpose. The best way to proceed is not by trying to enumerate all the particular instances when and where solidarity is exclusionary. Rather, I will use an example to work through how the problem of exclusion emerges, and how it can be addressed, within particular solidaristic groups.[21] My example will be the idea of *sisterhood*. Although I do not do so here, it should be clear by the end of the discussion how the argument can be extended to other contexts, too.

It seems uncontroversial today to assert that, given diversity among women, the basis for sisterhood should *not* be shared experiences of womanhood. This has, by now, become a staple of the feminist literature: the experiences of African-Americans, working-class, Egyptian, Irish, lesbian, trans-women (including the intersections among any of these categories) will be vastly different—so different

---

19. On the oppositional character of solidarity, see Sally Scholz 2010.
20. On problems of exclusion and inclusion within solidarity movements, see also Sally Scholz, Chapter 7 in this volume; Shelby forthcoming.
21. I draw here on Sangiovanni 2023, Section 1.

that it would be exclusionary and divisive to base identification and, in turn, a politics of solidarity on a canonical list of such experiences. Trying to come up with such a list will, more often than not, turn out not to represent something universal about women but something altogether more partial, namely the perspective of those privileged few who have the power and access to forge and disseminate the list as 'canonical' in the first place.[22] In *Ain't I a Woman?*, bell hooks calls out Adrienne Rich, who writes:

> An analysis that places the guilt for active domination, physical and institutional violence, and the justifications embedded in myth and language, on white women not only compounds false consciousness; it allows us all to deny or neglect the charged connection among black and white women from the historical conditions of slavery on, and it impedes any real discussion of women's instrumentality in a system which oppresses all women and in which hatred of women is also embedded in myth, folklore, and language.[23]

The problem is that, in attempting to create and invite solidarity among women *as such*, white feminists like Rich either didn't realize, or self-consciously ignored, how they themselves participated in the system of oppression they were criticizing. hooks mentions, for example, Betty Friedan's seminal *The Feminine Mystique*, which identified the central problem for feminists as the exclusion of women from the world of (male) work. hooks and other black feminists were quick to point out that black women were always expected to work, and work, often, for white women. hooks also shows how,

---

22. For seminal contributions on this point, see, among others, Lorde 2009, 219–220; King 1995; Collins 2002 [1990]; Spelman 1988; Crenshaw 1990.
23. Adrienne Rich cited in hooks 2015 [1981], 168.

throughout the history of the women's movement, black women's particular concerns were marginalized and silenced; they were welcomed only insofar as they were willing to fight for, what were, in the end, white women's concerns.

For hooks (as for many other feminists), the response is to acknowledge (rather than repress) the radical diversity among women (including the ways in which race, class, sexuality, nationality, and gender intersect[24]), to confront racism and other exclusions within the women's movement head-on, and to build solidarity on commitment to a *cause* rather than on a *shared set of experiences*.[25] She writes:

> We understood that political solidarity between females expressed in sisterhood goes beyond positive recognition of the experiences of women and even shared sympathy for common suffering. Feminist sisterhood is rooted in shared commitment to struggle against patriarchal injustice, no matter the form that injustice takes.[26]

---

24. For a useful overview of recent debates on intersectionality, see Carastathis 2014.
25. See, e.g., "The Master's Tools Will Never Dismantle the Master's House" in Lorde 1984, 111–112 and "Difference and Survival" in Lorde 2009, 201.
26. hooks 2015, 15. Cf. de Beauvoir 2012, 18, who writes, "The proletarians have accomplished the revolution in Russia, the Negroes in Haiti, the Indo-Chinese are battling for it in Indo-China; but the women's effort has never been anything more than a symbolic agitation. They have gained only what men have been willing to grant; they have taken nothing, they have only received. The reason for this is that women lack concrete means for organizing themselves into a unit which can stand face to face with the correlative unit. They have no past, no history, no religion of their own; and they have no such solidarity of work and interest as that of the proletariat. They are not even promiscuously herded together in the way that creates community feeling among the American Negroes, the ghetto Jews, the workers of Saint-Denis, or the factory hands of Renault. They live dispersed among the males, attached through residence, housework, economic condition, and social standing to certain men—fathers or husbands—more firmly than they are to other women."

Ending patriarchal injustice, on this picture, requires an acknowledgment that such injustice will take different forms in different circumstances, and that sisterhood requires coming to terms with the way that race, class, nationality, and so on, can divide and exclude women among themselves.

This way of framing the question raises a puzzle. If the best way to understand sisterhood is to see it grounded in commitment to a *cause* or *coalition* against injustice, then what distinguishes, if anything, solidarity among *feminists* and solidarity among *women*? After all, men can (and should be) feminists. Men can (and should) recognize the marks of patriarchal injustice and fight against it. Emphasizing a common commitment to fighting patriarchal injustice gives rise to a solidarity grounded in identification based on a *cause*. But, once any kind of common experience (or common essence) is rejected as uniting women, what role is there for a politics of solidarity grounded in identification among *women*? What kind of identification, if any, ought to ground *sisterhood* among women *as* women?

Referring to critiques of the category *woman* as united by a set of shared experiences (of the same kind I mentioned above), Iris Marion Young writes:

> I find the exclusively critical orientation of such arguments rather paralyzing. Do these arguments imply that it makes no sense and is morally wrong to talk about women as a group or, in fact, to talk about social groups at all? It is not clear that these writers claim this. If not, then what does it mean to use the term *woman*? More importantly, in the light of these critiques, what sort of positive claims can feminists make about the way social life is and ought to be? I find questions like these unaddressed by these critiques of feminist essentialism.[27]

---

[27]. Young 1994, 717. See also Zack 2005, 7, and Alcoff 2005, 143: "What can we demand in the name of women if 'women' do not exist and demands in their name simply reinforce the

I mention Young at this point because I find her discussion of what might unite the type *woman* illuminating as a possible basis for identification and solidarity among women as women—a basis that, in turn, promises to be less vulnerable to the diversity and exclusion critiques briefly alluded to before.

According to Young, women as a group form what she calls a *series*. A series is united neither by a set of intrinsic properties possessed by all members of a group, nor by a shared recognition of constituting a group, nor by a shared set of goals or experiences; it is united, rather, by a relation between persons and a set of socially conditioned material objects around which they orient their activity. The group of bus riders—who orient their activity around objects like bus stops, buses, and so on, and the norms, expectations, and patterns of behavior surrounding them—constitute a series. Similarly, radio listeners—who orient their activity around the radio and the norms, expectations, and patterns of behavior enabling and conditioning radio listening—are a series. And so are women. The primary material object around which women are expected to orient their activity is the sexed body. This is not the body understood as possessing a vagina, clitoris, breasts, and so on. Rather, it is the body as conditioned by social rules and expectations.[28] Young mentions menstruation, lactation, pregnancy, and childbirth as examples. Each of these activities is not just a brute biological fact but is shaped by social practices that condition possible meanings and opportunities. The norms, expectations, and patterns of behavior surrounding

---

myth that they do? How can we speak out against sexism as detrimental to the interests of women if the category is a fiction? How can we demand legal abortions, adequate child care, or wages based on comparable worth without invoking the concept of 'women'?"

28. One might wonder here whether another exclusion is in the wings: what about trans-women? But even in this case, one might argue, in defense of Young, that trans-women as women are also expected to comply with the social rules and expectations that have built up around the sexed female body. This threatens further forms of exclusion and subordination if they cannot meet those expectations.

the body, in turn, give rise to a range of further socially conditioned physical objects (such as clothes, cosmetics, tools, spaces, and so on), and hence further social practices. Together these reinforce two overarching social structures that position women as subordinate to men: heterosexuality (who desires and who is desired, who possesses and is possessed) and the sexual division of labor (who does what, where, and how).

On this picture, women are those individuals marked out by the system of objects and social practices as occupying a particular position vis-à-vis men. The category *woman* is defined, that is, by the relation of individuals to gendered social structures rather than by any intrinsic properties they share. Young is keen to emphasize that a particular individual's *response* to how the structure positions her/him will be as variable as you like. Some will resist and challenge the positioning and expectations, others may internalize them, others still will waver and become alienated. And, even more importantly for our purposes, some individuals' response to the structure will be further conditioned by other aspects of their circumstances, including race, class, nationality, sexuality, and so on. There is no expectation, then, that women's (or men's) particular experience of the structure will be the same. What *is* the same is *subjection* to the structure, which is reproduced through myriad daily interactions, characteristic scenarios, institutionalized forms of behavior, expectation, and habit, and so on.[29]

The analysis of women as a series also provides a possible basis for identification among women grounded in a *condition* shared by women: subjection to a subordinating gendered social structure. This does not imply, as we have seen, that women who identify in this way with one another have had the same *experience* of such subjection. Here we can draw contrast to identification among cancer survivors,

---

29. Cf. Haslanger 2012, 239.

which *is* based (we are imagining) on sharing a set of experiences. Identifying with others as a cancer survivor is identification that presupposes that others with whom one identifies have had cancer. The common experience is what motivates mutual sympathy, understanding, and an attempt to make sense together of that experience. But, as we have seen, making particular experiences the basis of identification among women is unnecessarily exclusionary given the wide diversity of ways in which women experience their subjection to a gendered social structure. Identification based on *condition* promises to avoid these problems. Subjection to an oppressive social structure is like subjection to a system of law: two different individuals can be subject to the law—can be addressed by the system—without experiencing the weight of the law in the same way.[30]

Notice that I shifted above from speaking of the concept *woman* (in my elaboration of Young's account) to the possibility of identification among women as women. The two ideas can come apart. One may, indeed, come to believe—as many feminists do—that there is *no* unified concept *woman*, or that the concept is unified, but not by the idea of oppressive subjection to a gendered structure. It would still be possible, on the picture I have drawn, to identify with other women who *are* oppressed by the gendered system on the basis of their shared condition.[31] There is, that is, no necessary congruence between the concept *woman* and the basis for identification among women. To illustrate: suppose you believe it is *possible* for there to be *non-oppressed* women—women who are not subordinated vis-à-vis

---

30. Cf. Haslanger 2012, 239: "So women have in common that their (assumed) sex has socially disadvantaged them; but this is compatible with the kinds of cultural variation that feminist inquiry has revealed, for the substantive content of women's position and the ways of justifying it can vary enormously. Admittedly, the account accommodates such variation by being very abstract; nonetheless, it provides a schematic account that highlights the interdependence between the material forces that subordinate women, *and* the ideological frameworks that sustain them." See also Alcoff 2005, 148.

31. On this point, see Mikkola 2007, 375–380.

men.[32] It is, on this view, not a necessary part of being a woman that one is oppressed. It might nonetheless be true that, in *our* world, all women are (contingently) oppressed, and come to identify with each other on that basis.[33]

An intersectionality theorist may object that it is a mistake to say that there is a *single* gendered social structure. Each person, depending on their circumstances, is addressed by the gendered social structure in a fundamentally different way—so different that there is no sense in speaking of it as a single system. A black woman's body, for example, will be gendered and positioned vis-à-vis men in different ways than a white woman's body, the body of a working-class woman in a different way than an upper-class woman, and so on. The objector concludes that it would be just as arbitrary and inevitably exclusionary to identify with other women, who are positioned so differently, on the basis of a common *condition* as it would be to identify on the basis of a common *set of experiences*.[34]

This is, I believe, a difficult objection to meet successfully. In a Youngian spirit, one might respond to the objection in the following way: Just as it would be mistaken to say that an *employed* and an *unemployed* immigrant within a single society are subject to entirely different systems of law, it is a mistake to say that *white* and *black* women are subject to entirely different gendered structures. Within a single society and system of law, employment law and immigration law are *interlocking* and *overlapping*.[35] To be sure, there is no way to understand how unemployment affects immigrant rights without understanding how immigration and welfare law *interact*. However, although the employed and the unemployed immigrants' legal rights will differ in

---

32. Cf. Stone 2007, 160–163, on Haslanger. And see also Stoljar 1995, 281.
33. I thank Jude Browne for helpful discussion.
34. Crenshaw 1990, 1299; Spelman 1988, 167. See also Stone 2004.
35. Cf. the Combahee River Collective on the interlocking character of oppression (Collective 1983).

basic ways (including their rights to stay, their right, in some cases, to access welfare, and so on), there are other ways in which they are addressed in the *same* way by immigration law (including their rights to access emergency care, their rights to appeal immigration decisions, and so on). Drawing the analogy, we can say that the same is true of black and white women in, say, the United States. While it is certainly true that black women's bodies are positioned by the gendered social structure in different ways than white women's bodies, there are many dimensions of the gendered social structure that address black and white women in the same way. The objects, norms, expectations, and practices of the gendered social structure address black and white women, across many dimensions, *in common* (which is not to say that their *experience* of that subjection will be the same). That common subjection, the response concludes, can be a basis of identification among women *as* women, just as the common subjection to immigration law of an employed and unemployed immigrant can be the basis of their resistance to that law *as* immigrants.

I am not sure what to make of this kind of response, since it will certainly meet with the following counter: the response begs the question about whether there really is only *one* gendered system of subjection with different manifestations (analogous to a complex system of law with different parts), or rather many more such systems (analogous to different systems of law each with its own internally complex structure). Indeed, it is difficult to come up with examples that survive the objection: norms and practices regarding beauty, the sexual division of labor, the way heterosexuality is enforced, and so on, all *do* seem to address black and white women differently (and upper- and lower-class women, and women of different religious backgrounds). One cannot, I believe, adjudicate between the two views by employing solely empirical criteria. Adjudicating requires asking: What is the *point*—politically, socially, and ethically—of insisting on one or the other reading? If one believes that the struggle for woman's liberation needs more solidarity among women *as* women, then one might be attracted to the Youngian view.[36] On this view, solidarity among women is based on identification grounded in a *condition*. If, on the other hand, one believes that, historically, the call for sisterhood has been exclusionary, partial, blinkered, and divisive, and that it is more important to focus on fighting injustice than to seek an elusive common ground, then one will more likely opt for the intersectional-coalitional view. On this view, there is also possibility for solidarity, but it must be solidarity grounded in a *cause* rather than in a condition or set of experiences. For our purposes, we need not come to a conclusive judgment; it is enough if we see how a politics of solidarity founded on identification, but that is alive to the problem of exclusion, can proceed without abandoning solidarity as an ideal worth fighting for.

IS SOLIDARITY EMPTY OR REDUNDANT?

I will address the challenges from *emptiness* and *redundancy* together. With respect to the former, the best defense is offense: solidarity is not an empty concept if we can show both that it plays an important role in real-world politics across time, and that it is determinate enough to give shape and structure to debate today. The best response, that is, is simply to defend an account of solidarity (as I have outlined above), and see if it can do some work in important political and social disputes in which the term figures.[37]

And, once we have a determinate account in hand, we can then address the redundancy critique. I will give a quick summary, via

---

36. Cf. Schor 1994; Riley 1988.
37. For more on the history of solidarity (and its significance), see Blais 2007 and ch. 2 in Sangiovanni 2023.

a series of contrasts, of the ways in which the account of solidarity I have singled out is not redundant. First, we can draw up a list of the most relevant, adjacent concepts: fellow-feeling, altruism, empathy, community, and justice.

Solidarity is not merely fellow-feeling (and not, by extension, merely an emotion). While it is no doubt true that fellow-feeling or camaraderie will often accompany solidarity, solidarity is not reducible to it. It is possible for actors to be in solidarity—to meet all of the conditions I have outlined in the first section of the chapter—while not feeling any camaraderie at all. As long as they identify with one another, act to overcome significant adversity, are willing to set aside narrow self-interest, do not bypass each other's wills, are disposed to share one another's fate, and trust one another, they are in solidarity. Their feelings or emotions about their solidarity can come and go without their solidarity coming and going along with those emotions.

Solidarity is not merely altruism. While one must be disposed to share another's fate (and so behave altruistically) to be in solidarity with them, altruism is not sufficient for solidarity. Unilateral acts of humanitarianism—such as aiding someone injured by the side of the road—are not, on the account I have defended, acts of solidarity.

Solidarity is not merely empathy. While one of the key features of *identification* is a disposition to feel heightened empathy toward those whom one identifies with, identification is not sufficient for solidarity, and empathy is not sufficient for identification. I might empathize with someone, yet not act in solidarity with them; I may simply be overcome with the emotion they are feeling, or project myself in their situation. I also may identify with someone without ever acting together with them to overcome some significant adversity. In that case, my identification is not sufficient to make it the case that we are in solidarity.

Solidarity is not merely community. Whatever it is that 'community' is, I may relish my neighborhood and its lively sense of community, but this is not sufficient to say that I stand in solidarity with them. Until we work together to overcome some significant adversity that threatens us *as* neighbors, we do not count as being in solidarity as a community.

And solidarity is not merely justice. Unjust groups can act in solidarity. Justice also usually refers to a set of principles; solidarity to a way of acting together. Justice also comprehends a range of negative duties that we would not normally speak of as duties of solidarity (such as a duty to refrain from violating others' rights).

Indeed, the fact that the account outlined in the first section does not collapse into any one of these notions should strengthen our confidence in the overall account as an accurate picture of a distinctive practice.

WORKS CITED

Alcoff, L. M. 2005. *Visible Identities: Race, Gender, and the Self.* Oxford: Oxford University Press.
Arendt, H. 1973. *The Origins of Totalitarianism.* New York: Harcourt Brace & Jovanovich.
Arendt, H. 1990 [1963]. *On Revolution.* London: Penguin Books.
Banting, K., and W. Kymlicka. 2017. *The Strains of Commitment: The Political Sources of Solidarity in Diverse Societies.* Oxford: Oxford University Press.
Bayertz, K. 1999 "Four Uses of "Solidarity." In *Solidarity*, ed. Kurt Bayertz. London: Springer, 3–28.
Blais, M.-C. 2007. *La Solidarité: Histoire d'une idée.* Paris: Gallimard.
Bourgeois, L. 1902. "Rapport de M. Léon Bourgeois au Congrès d'éducation sociale en 1900." In his *Solidarité.* Paris: Armand Colin, 159–188.
Bourgeois, L. 1902 [1896]. *Solidarité*, 3rd ed. Paris: Armand Colin.
Bowles, S., and H. Gintis. 2011. *A Cooperative Species.* Princeton, NJ: Princeton University Press.
Carastathis, A. 2014. "The Concept of Intersectionality in Feminist Theory." *Philosophy Compass* 9: 304–314.
Collective, T. C. R. 1983. "A Black Feminist Statement" [1977]. In *Home Girls: A Black Feminist Anthology,* ed. Barbara Smith. New Brunswick: Rutgers University Press, 272–292.

Collins, P. H. 2002 [1990]. *Black Feminist Thought: Knowledge, Consciousness, and the Politics of Empowerment*, 2nd ed. London: Routledge.
Crenshaw, K. 1990. "Mapping the Margins: Intersectionality, Identity Politics, and Violence against Women of Color." *Stanford Law Review* 43: 1241–1300.
de Beauvoir, S. 2012 [1949]. *The Second Sex*. New York: Vintage.
Dean, J. 1995. "Reflective Solidarity." *Constellations* 2: 114–140.
Habermas, J. 2001. "The Postnational Constellation and the Future of Democracy." In *The Postnational Constellation: Political Essays*, ed. Max Pensky. Oxford: Polity Press, 58–113.
Haslanger, S. 2012. *Resisting Reality: Social Construction and Social Critique*. Oxford: Oxford University Press.
hooks, b. 2015. *Feminism Is for Everybody: Passionate Politics*. London: Routledge.
hooks, b. 2015 [1981]. *Ain't I a Woman*, 2nd ed. London: Routledge.
Ingram, A. 1996. "Constitutional Patriotism." *Philosophy and Social Criticism* 22: 1–18.
Kateb, G. 1989. "Democratic Individuality and the Meaning of Rights." In *Liberalism and the Moral Life*, ed. Nancy Rosenblum. Cambridge, MA: Harvard University Press, 183–207.
King, D. 1995. "Multiple Jeopardy, Multiple Consciousness: The Context for Black Feminist Ideology." In *Words of Fire: An Anthology of African-American Feminist Thought*, ed. Beverly Guy-Sheftall. New York: New Press, 294–317.
Kohn, M. 2018. "Solidarity and Social Rights." *Critical Review of International Social and Political Philosophy* 21: 616–630.
Kolers, A. 2016. *A Moral Theory of Solidarity*. Oxford: Oxford University Press.
Levy, N. 2005. "The Good, the Bad and the Blameworthy." *Journal of Ethics and Social Philosophy* 1: 1–16.
Lorde, A. 1984. *Sister Outsider*. Trumansburg, NY: Crossing.
Lorde, A. 2009. *I Am Your Sister: Collected and Unpublished Works of Audre Lorde*, ed. Rudolph Byrd, Johnnetta Betsch-Cole, and Beverly Guy-Sheftall. Oxford: Oxford University Press.
Mikkola, M. 2007. "Gender Sceptics and Feminist Politics." *Res Publica* 13: 361–380.
Miller, D. 2017. "Solidarity and Its Sources." In *The Strains of Commitment: The Political Sources of Solidarity in Diverse Societies*, ed. Keith Banting and Will Kymlicka. Oxford: Oxford University Press, 61–80.
Müller, J.-W. 2007. *Constitutional Patriotism*. Princeton, NJ: Princeton University Press.
Riley, D. 1988. *"Am I That Name?": Feminism and the Category of "Women" in History*. Basingstoke: Macmillan.
Sangiovanni, A. 2007. "Global Justice, Reciprocity, and the State." *Philosophy & Public Affairs* 35: 2–39.
Sangiovanni, A. 2023. *Solidarity: Nature, Grounds, and Value*. Manchester: Manchester University Press.

Scholz, S. 2010. *Political Solidarity*. Philadelphia: Penn State Press.
Schor, N. 1994. "This Essentialism Which Is Not One: Coming to Grips with Irigaray." In *Engaging with Irigaray: Feminist Philosophy and Modern European Thought*, ed. Carolyn Burke, Naomi Schor, and M. Whitford. New York: Columbia University Press, 57–79.
Shelby, T., ed. Forthcoming. *A Tale of Two Tenths: Race, Class, and Solidarity*. Oxford: Oxford University Press.
Shklar, J. N. 1989. "The Liberalism of Fear." In *Liberalism and the Moral Life*, ed. Nancy Rosenblum. Cambridge, MA: Harvard University Press, 21–39.
Spelman, E. 1988. *Inessential Woman: Problems of Exclusion in Feminist Thought*. Boston: Beacon Press.
Stoljar, N. 1995. "Essence, Identity, and the Concept of Woman." *Philosophical Topics* 23: 261–293.
Stone, A. 2004. "Essentialism and Anti-Essentialism in Feminist Philosophy." *Journal of Moral Philosophy* 1: 135–153.
Stone, A. 2007. *An Introduction to Feminist Philosophy*. Cambridge: Polity.
Tajfel, H., M. Billig, R. P. Bundy, and C. Flament. 1971. "Social Categorization and Intergroup Behavior." *European Journal of Social Psychology* 1: 149–177.
Yamagishi, T., N. Jin, and T. Kiyonari. 1999. "Bounded Generalized Reciprocity: In-Group Boasting and In-Group Favoritism." *Advances in Group Processes* 16: 161–197.
Young, I. M. 1994. "Gender as Seriality: Thinking about Women as a Social Collective." *Signs* 19: 713–738.
Zack, N. 2005. *Inclusive Feminism: A Third Wave Theory of Women's Commonality*. Lanham, MD: Rowman & Littlefield.

Chapter 4

Solidarity as a Virtue of Equality

AVERY KOLERS

INTRODUCTION

Is solidarity a virtue? Clearly the mere disposition *to act together with others for shared ends* is not; it all depends on how one does so, and for what ends. Further, if solidarity were a "virtue" like punctuality or good humor, it might be of minor interest as an aside in an introductory textbook, but hardly worth considering at length. So to show that solidarity is a virtue of any significance one would need to do three things: first, identify a crucial gap in virtue theories, that is, an essential and important part of good character that virtue theories cannot account for; second, explicate an account of solidarity as a character trait or skill set that could fill this gap in virtue theories; and third, show that solidarity so understood can fit within a conception of the virtuous character the way (other) virtues do, namely, by contributing to flourishing and being unified in the right way with the other virtues. These are my three aims in the current chapter.

I want to start with the question of whether virtue theory needs solidarity at all: What is missing from virtue theory that solidarity (or something) might add? The answer, roughly, is equality: virtue theorists focus so hard on individual character excellence that they neglect fundamental status equality and its implications. Then, following David Wiggins, I propose a way in which solidarity can provide this, namely, through the idea of coequal membership of "the party of humankind," and the inviolability built on this party unity.[1] Wiggins's conception is, however, in two ways unsuited to this task. First, it is deontological and so seems to treat inviolability as the wrong kind of rule for virtue ethics; and second, he proposes only a very thin human solidarity and draws few specific implications that would help us fill the gap. I therefore build out Wiggins's conception by appeal to Leonard Harris's powerful "insurrectionist" challenge to ethics.[2] I argue that solidarity can embrace insurrection and even violence, under specific circumstances and in a way that turns Wiggins's deontological rule into a rule of skill that is more congenial to virtue ethics. Rather than the *root* of the ethical, a virtue of solidarity may be part of the *point* of the ethical. Finally, I show how a virtue of solidarity can in fact serve this role, by explaining its place in the unity of the virtues and in individual flourishing.

One prefatory note about the conception of virtue and virtue theory at issue here. My quarry is the broadly eudaimonistic tradition associated with Aristotle and the Stoics, on which virtues are (or are analogous to) practical skills; on this view, virtues properly so-called are not merely a congeries of distinct habits but are somehow interconnected (if not fully unified) aspects of individual character, and such virtuous character is connected to the happiness of the virtuous

---

1. David Wiggins, "Solidarity and the Root of the Ethical," *Lindley Lecture*, 2008. I am grateful to Véronique Munoz-Dardé for some clarifications on how to understand Wiggins's view.
2. Leonard Harris, "Honor and Insurrection or a Short Story about Why John Brown (with David Walker's Spirit) Was Right and Frederick Douglass (with Benjamin Banneker's Spirit) Was Wrong," in *A Philosophy of Struggle: The Leonard Harris Reader*, ed. Lee A. McBride III (London: Bloomsbury, 2020), 161–173. See also Harris, "Insurrectionist Ethics: Advocacy, Moral Psychology, and Pragmatism," in the same volume at 175–187.

agent.³ This tradition has emerged as a leading conception of virtue in contemporary ethical theory and is widely thought to be the most promising alternative to other main schools such as Kantianism, Care Ethics, Discourse Ethics, and Consequentialism. My discussion is therefore intended as a contribution to eudaimonistic virtue ethics. I shall argue that this tradition's shocking inattention to fundamental equality is tantamount to its lacking a vital organ. Implanting a virtue of solidarity may, however, be just the surgery it needs.

VIRTUE ETHICS AND STATUS EQUALITY

Many critics (and even some defenders) of eudaimonistic virtue ethics have charged that this view is egoistic.[4] At worst, its egoistic character causes an intolerable inversion in the account of moral wrongness: murder is wrong first because of how it affects the perpetrator, and only secondarily the victim. Julia Annas has convincingly repudiated this charge by emphasizing that virtue is a skill set directed not at the *agent's* good but at the *moral* good.[5] So understood, virtue's contribution to the agent's good is the "flow" experience of excellent performance; this self-directed benefit supervenes on excellent production of the moral good.

---

3. For this characterization of the tradition I follow Julia Annas, *Intelligent Virtue* (New York: Oxford University Press, 2011), 1. I am grateful to Jasmin Özel for pressing me to clarify this point.
4. For discussion of this charge, see Christopher Toner, "Virtue Ethics and Egoism," in *The Routledge Companion to Virtue Ethics*, ed. Lorraine Besser-Jones and Michael Slote (New York: Routledge, 2015), 345–357.
5. Annas, *Intelligent Virtue*, 72. Liz Gulliford and Robert Roberts hold that some, but only some, virtues are directed at "moral reality," which I take to be equivalent to "the good" as Annas has it. I will discuss their account below. See Liz Gulliford and Robert C. Roberts, "Exploring the 'Unity' of the Virtues: The Case for an 'Allocentric Quintet,'" *Theory & Psychology* 28 (2018): 208–226.

Granting Annas's refutation, however, an underlying part of the egoism objection nonetheless remains: virtue theories are not built around recognition of, or acting upon, our *fundamental moral equality*. Equality is mysteriously missing from virtue ethics.[6]

To show this I want to start by recalling a different critique of virtue ethics, namely, the charge of moral conservatism or conventionalism. The charge is that, because the adult attainment of the virtues depends on the context in which one is reared and educated and the institutions within which one is able to develop one's moral capacities, the putatively virtuous agent will be overly bound to the particular, unjust contexts in which they live.[7] Their capacity for moral critique and commitment to moral reform will be limited by the bounds of convention. Annas presents this critique using the example of slave-owners:

> Slave-owners . . . [may be] unquestionably fair and generous as they have learned to be by that society's lights, but . . . may never reflect that there may be something seriously inadequate at best, about the ways in which they are fair and generous.[8]

To refute this charge, Annas powerfully discusses two contexts in which a language of virtue was applied to the problem of enslavement. The Roman Stoics, she notes, argued repeatedly for treating slaves humanely and seeing their equal humanity. Though they fell short of abolitionism (or even humanitarian legal reforms when they

---

6. Interestingly, perusing the *Routledge Companion* one finds that the only authors dedicated to showing that virtue theory is compatible with or committed to equality are the ones explicating Confucian virtue ethics, which has often been accused of being hierarchical. Equality is otherwise mostly missing and nowhere explicated as a significant aspect of the tradition. Nor is equality much discussed in leading works on virtue ethics, including Annas's.
7. The root of this objection is Aristotle, *Nicomachean Ethics*, trans. David Ross, rev. Lesley Brown (New York: Oxford World's Classics, 2009), II.i.25.
8. Annas, *Intelligent Virtue*, 53.

had the chance), she argues, the Stoics "achieved a universal viewpoint of ethical community on equal terms with the slave":[9] "As rational beings interacting as members of a community of rational beings, owner and slave realize that the barriers between them are completely conventional."[10] That said, the conventions of the time were particularly rigid, and abolition or even manumission would, Annas claims, have been impossible if not counterproductive. Thus it was "the circumstances of ancient society that limit[ed] the ways Stoics could act with regard to slavery, not the limitations of thinking in terms of virtue."[11] In the eighteenth century, by contrast, the abolitionists overcame those circumstances and ultimately won a fundamental transformation of society—one that should have been, by all rights, just as unthinkable then as it was to the Stoics. As Annas writes, quoting the historian Adam Hochschild: "anyone looking back in time would have seen little but other slave systems."[12] Even so, she writes, "no new way of thinking about ethical matters was needed."[13] To the contrary, they held that "if the general condition of man is ever to be ameliorated, it can only be through the medium of BELIEF IN HUMAN VIRTUE."[14]

I share Annas's reading of Stoic ethics: the Stoics saw master and slave as moral equals separated only by convention. What she does not show in this context or in that of the modern abolitionists, however, is whether the capacity to see slaves as equal or to be moved by that fact is connected to a virtue-centered "way of thinking about ethical matters"; for all she shows, the virtues may have been inert or

---

9. Ibid., 60.
10. Ibid., 59.
11. Ibid., 60.
12. Ibid., 61, quoting Adam Hochschild, *Bury the Chains: Prophets and Rebels in the Fight to Free an Empire's Slaves* (Boston: Houghton Mifflin, 2005).
13. Annas, *Intelligent Virtue*, 61–62.
14. Ibid., 62, quoting Thomas Love Peacock, *Melincourt* (capitalization in original).

even have held them back from genuinely perceiving or acting as they might have. Further, I reject Annas's claim that the Stoics perceived or still less did all that could be expected of a virtuous agent based on their recognition of fundamental equality. So even if their moral egalitarianism was connected to being virtuous, virtue ethics did not move them to perceive or act on this doctrine. On this issue, virtue fails the convention test; it was, I shall argue, at best ineffectual and at worst counterproductive.

Take first the Roman Stoics. Annas shows that the Stoics viewed the difference between master and slave as purely conventional. Seneca, for his part, held, contrary to the practice of the time, that slaves should be treated in ways that are kindly and respectful; that they should be free to speak and eat with their masters; that the household should be a site of love and respect for all who live and work there, slaves included.[15]

This argument, however, fails to show two crucial points that would be required to link virtue and equality. First, Annas does not show that the Stoics did or advocated all that could reasonably be thought to follow from these commitments to natural equality. Although it might have been idle or counterproductive to advocate for abolition, manumission was a live option. Seneca could have recommended that Lucilius free his own slaves. But he did not do so. Annas defends his omission:

> It was not open to a slave-owner, as it was later to an American slave-owner in the South, to free his slaves and adopt another approach; in the ancient world there was nowhere else to go, no way to opt out and move into a more just system.[16]

---

15. Seneca, "How We Treat Our Slaves," in *Letters on Ethics: To Lucilius*, trans. Margaret Graver and A. A. Long (Chicago: University of Chicago Press, 2017: 136–137).
16. Annas, *Intelligent Virtue*, 60. As the second half of the sentence indicates, by "and adopt another approach" she seems to have in mind something like the white Southern US slave

Roman slave-owners did, though, have the power to free their slaves, and many did so.[17] Many who did not do so dangled the "carrot" of manumission in front of their slaves to induce good behavior, which implies that they were very much aware they had the power to do so.[18] In fact, whereas Annas implies that Roman society was more rigid in this respect than the US South, the opposite seems to be true. Freedmen became citizens—a status that was denied to freed US slaves until the ratification of the Fourteenth Amendment. Yet Seneca fails to recommend manumission. To the contrary, he treats the prospect of slaves' going free as a straw man objection to his view, and rebuts it.[19] Thus Seneca did not advocate for the maximum that highly restrictive institutions allowed, he advocated for a mild form of conventional mastery.

Nor, second, is there any evident internal connection between virtue per se, as a driver of moral perception, and the Stoics' recognition that nothing moral or natural separated slave and free. Seneca sums up his argument for treating slaves kindly not with any appeal to virtue but with a "Golden Rule" test:

> **11** ... But all my instructions can be summed up in this: live with an inferior the same way you would want a superior to live with you. Each time you remember the extent of power over a slave, remember also that your own master has that same amount of

owner's option to free his slaves and move north or west or to England or Canada. This interpretation preserves the truth of the second conjunct—the Roman had no option of moving somewhere that slavery had been abolished—but the crucial first conjunct remains false. As I show in the text, the Roman slave owner was perfectly free to manumit his slaves and employ freedmen to do the same work.

17. See Leonard Schumacher, "Slaves in Roman Society," in *The Oxford Handbook of Social Relations in the Ancient World*, ed. Michael Peachin (New York: Oxford University Press, 2011), 589–608; 593. See also Matthew J. Perry, *Gender, Manumission, and the Roman Freedwoman* (New York: Cambridge University Press, 2013).
18. Schumacher, "Slaves in Roman Society," 593.
19. See Seneca, *Letters*, 138.

power over you. **12** "But I have no master," you say. You're still young—perhaps someday you will. Don't you realize how old Hecuba was when she became a slave? Don't you realize how old Croesus was? The mother of Darius? Plato? Diogenes?[20]

In itself, a Golden Rule test uses the mechanism of inversion rather than appeal to virtuous character or the moral good. Seneca imagines Lucilius rejecting the inversion test by denying that the roles could be reversed, so he affirms that the test is apt by referencing free persons captured and sold into slavery. It is by making salient the prospect of inversion that Seneca justifies and attempts to motivate kindly treatment of slaves. But that is what one would have thought *virtue* was for: to spur the perception that manumission was honorable and just, that keeping slaves was self-indulgent and grasping and cowardly, and to generate the motivation in slaveholders to free their slaves. Stoic virtue is missing in action.

The case of the Roman Stoics thus does not overcome the objection from conventionality or conservatism. Seneca's recognition of the natural equality of slave and free does not require appeal to the insight provided by virtue; that is needed only to drive his insistence that one should act on this by treating one's slaves in a friendly and respectful manner. In any event there is a disconnect between virtue ethics and fundamental equality. The limits of what the Stoics could think to be virtuous were restrained by their social environment in a way that a moral rule of equal status would repudiate.

This disconnect carries over to Annas's argument about the modern abolitionists. Given the widespread acceptance of slavery across all strata of white European and settler-colonial societies during the seventeenth and eighteenth centuries, and the deep integration of the triangular trade into the European economy, the existence,

---

20. Ibid., 136.

let alone success, of a mass social movement against slavery needs to be explained. A change like this needs to be explained by something that also changed. It is perhaps possible that the English public's moral views changed, and drove the rise of abolitionism. Yet the vocabulary of the virtues was older than Christianity itself. If moral explanations are to be found they more likely run to what was morally or philosophically new and thus potentially explanatorily significant: innovations such as the doctrine of natural rights, the liberal economic critique of mercantilism, or the rise of evangelical strains of Protestantism.[21]

But it seems more likely that moral reform did not happen of its own accord, and must itself be explained by appeal to something else that changed. Hochschild's explanation for the movement's "eruption" (chapter 15) runs to geographic, social, educational, political, and other considerations far more than moral or religious ones. His great insight is the role of Britons' fear of naval impressment as a spur to their ability to empathize with slaves—a striking fact reminiscent of the central role that Seneca gave to, in effect, the same Golden Rule test.[22] In short, there is little reason to think that virtue as such played any role in enabling the abolitionists to see that African and African-descended people had a right to be free and that slavery was immoral, or motivated them to act on these perceptions.

To be sure, Annas claims only that "[n]o new way of thinking about ethical matters was *needed*,"[23] that is, the wrongness of slavery

---

21. "Britons' confidence in their rights ran proud and deep. Without it, the abolitionists could never have convinced them that slaves had rights as well" (Hochschild, *Bury the Chains*, 221). On the nineteenth-century US context, see John Cumbler, *From Abolition to Rights for All* (Philadelphia: University of Pennsylvania Press, 2008). For philosophical discussion, see Elizabeth Anderson, "Social Movements, Experiments in Living, and Moral Progress: Case Studies from Britain's Abolition of Slavery," *Lindley Lecture*, University of Kansas, 2014.
22. See Hochschild, *Bury the Chains*, 222.
23. Annas, *Intelligent Virtue*, 61–62. Emphasis added.

is *explicable* in virtue terms, and abolitionist motivation was *compatible* with virtue ethics. This seems to put the burden of proof on her opponent to show that virtue somehow militated against abolition. But the fact that virtue language can retroactively and anachronistically be applied to endorse today's views as against those of an earlier era is just what we should expect if virtue is conventional. Of course a twenty-first-century virtue ethicist thinks slavery is wrong; the test will be what they think about some *currently* widely accepted immorality, or how they are motivated regarding the socioeconomic residue of classical slavery and the stubborn persistence of modern slavery.[24] And as we noted above, it does not even seem to be factually true that no new moral framework was required. Natural rights seem to have been required, and although the Golden Rule test was not new, its visceral salience in the form of large-scale impressment was.

Annas thus fails to show that virtue theory avoids the conventionalism objection, specifically with respect to the belief in—or the capacity to act on—human equality. Beyond this one case, it is striking that fundamental equality is basically absent from the main examples of virtue that run through Annas's book and for that matter the wide swath of virtue ethics that has emerged in recent decades. Bravery, kindness, and other sophisticated agential skills make no essential reference to recognition of fundamental equality. It may seem that there is an obvious reason for this, namely, that fundamental equal worth is *implied* by the "cardinal virtues" of the ancients, namely courage, temperance, wisdom, or (most likely) justice, or some combination of them, and so there is no need to belabor it. But I shall argue that this is not the case; these virtues, even justice, are

---

24. On the residue, see William A. Darity and A. Kirsten Mullen, *From Here to Equality: Reparations for Black Americans in the Twenty-first Century* (Chapel Hill: University of North Carolina Press, 2020). On the persistence, see Kevin Bales, *Blood and Earth: Modern Slavery, Ecocide, and the Secret to Saving the World* (New York: Spiegel and Grau, 2016).

compatible with a denial of fundamental equality and, by extension, of any motivation to stand against inequitable treatment.

On its face, justice is egalitarian: *legal* justice is about treating like cases alike and unlike cases unlike; *distributive* justice is about returns based on contribution as a share of the joint product; and *retributive* justice is about equality in exchange when returning good for good or bad for bad.[25] From the fact that justice involves treating the parties to a transaction equally, however, we cannot infer that justice treats persons as equals. Aristotelian justice requires returning payment, punishment, or social rewards equivalent to the actions or contributions which merit them. This is justice as regularity or the fact of commensurability, not any substantive commitment to equality:

> For it is not two doctors that associate for exchange, but a doctor and a farmer, or in general people who are different and unequal; but these must be equated. This is why all things that are exchanged must be somehow comparable.[26]

Aristotle's most important engagement with equality is his account of equity, which serves as the fine-tuning aspect of the virtue of justice.[27] Because justice must be the subject of legislation and general practice, it is inevitably coarse-grained and must be supplemented by the more fine-grained and precise measuring tool of equity if it is to get the right answer in hard or specific cases, with a degree of accuracy that legislation alone cannot realize.[28] Yet despite its capacity

---

25. See Aristotle, *Nicomachean Ethics*, V.iii–v.1131a–1134a.
26. Ibid., V.5.1133a.
27. I have emphasized two Aristotelian senses of equity in my account of solidarity. But these both presuppose what I call Kantian equity—the fundamental equality of status. See Avery Kolers, *A Moral Theory of Solidarity* (New York: Oxford University Press, 2016), ch. 6.
28. For discussion, see Allan Beever, "Aristotle on Equity, Law, and Justice," *Legal Theory* 10 (2004): 33–50.

to modulate general rules for the sake of particular circumstances, equity is no more likely to find in favor of the slave than of the master. The reason is that fine-tuned equalizing is carried out against the backdrop of a social ontology that determines which cases are "like" and which are "unlike" such that equity requires treating them accordingly. Given information about particulars, judges may draw status distinctions based on their views about natural differences that the legislature has overlooked, for instance when legislation speaks only of "persons" or "citizens."[29] Or contrariwise, they may conflate kinds of things that they think the legislature has wrongly separated, like citizens and corporations.[30] And equity would allow a judge to fairly divide outputs between master and slave, rather than emancipate the slave and rectify the wrong of enslavement in the first place. Simply put, if the question of Aristotelian equity is how to return to each party more precisely the same or exactly the proportionate amount that each brought to the transaction or shared endeavor, then to redress the unequal status of the parties is to answer an entirely different question. Aristotle would accurately accuse such a judge of having changed the subject: "Your Honor, I didn't mean, 'should this man be a slave,' I meant, 'should this slave get the reward he was promised in return for the work he did?'"

A final concern about the ability of eudaimonistic virtue ethics to account for status equality comes from Leonard Harris's

---

29. This is of course a foundational insight of critical race theory, but one hardly needs to be a critical race theorist to make the point. A particularly outrageous instance is the *Dred Scott* case, in which Justice Taney, writing for the Court, found that a Black man has "no rights and privileges which the white man was bound to respect." *Dred Scott v. Sandford*, 60 US 393 (1856), online: https://www.law.cornell.edu/supremecourt/text/60/393. See also "the Persons Case," *Edwards v. A.G. of Canada*, where the Supreme Court of Canada found, in 1928, that women were not "persons" for purposes of appointment to the Senate. The U.K. Privy Council overruled in 1930. See 1929 CanLII 438 (UK JCPC), online: https://www.canlii.org/en/ca/ukjcpc/doc/1929/1929canlii438/1929canlii438.html.
30. See *Citizens United v. FEC*, 558 US 310 (2010).

"insurrectionist ethics." Like Wiggins, Harris proposes equal dignity as the foundation of ethics. But he takes the point further, toward affirmative steps to realize equal dignity:

> If the advice a [moral theory] would give to persons in a society of racial slavery did not include insurrection and honor for those engaged in insurrection—if no more than as a form of self-defense—then [that moral theory] ... is woefully inadequate.[31]

Eudaimonistic virtue ethics fails this test—so much so that those who have tried to theorize virtue in the context of oppression have found that they must propose different virtues altogether, or give up on the internal connection between virtue and flourishing.[32]

For all that, I shall argue, the failure of eudaimonistic virtue ethicists to account for equality does not show that eudaimonistic virtue ethics fails as an enterprise, but that its development has been skewed in a peculiar way. Although the traditional "egoism" objection was wrong, its kernel of truth was that virtue theorists' emphasis on individual excellence and character development distracted them from a fundamental condition of humanity, namely, our equality, and the fundamental importance of egalitarianism as a feature of a good human social life. My claim in the remainder of this chapter is that this failure is remediable, provided we add a virtue of *solidarity*, on a par with the classical "cardinal virtues." Borrowing Wiggins's terminology, I understand this virtue as *coequal membership of the party of humankind*; a virtuous person would recognize and be motivated

---

31. Leonard Harris, "Insurrectionist Ethics: Advocacy, Moral Psychology, and Pragmatism," in *A Philosophy of Struggle*, 175–187; 186. Harris is discussing pragmatism in particular but intends this as an adequacy criterion for any ethical system. I am grateful to Alberto Urquidez for discussion.
32. Harris, "Insurrectionist Ethics"; See also Lisa Tessman, *Burdened Virtues* (New York: Oxford University Press, 2005).

to act on that coequal membership or party unity, whereas a vicious person would lack the motivation or the recognition altogether.

A virtue of solidarity would go beyond the extant resources of eudaimonistic virtue ethics by causing us to countermand and repudiate the status hierarchies that serve powerful interests. Such a virtue meets Harris's insurrectionist challenge: by fighting as or alongside the oppressed, by refusing the wages of their exploitation and expropriation, by seizing opportunities to stand against oppressors, and by honoring those who live in this way. This virtue adds the essential missing element to the critique of slavery, and decisively breaks free from convention.

SOLIDARITY: WHAT KIND OF RULE?

An immediate problem arises for a virtue-theoretic reading of solidarity. For Wiggins, solidarity is deontological in that it establishes a primitive prohibition on violations of others' bodily integrity or other comparably basic interests. He insists that this prohibition is not a *disvalue*, as a utilitarian would have it, such that it could be entered on one side of the ledger and counterbalanced by enough entries on the other. For the same reason, we might add, it cannot be an Aristotelian mean. Rather, the prohibition conditions all other ends. It is in recognition of the inviolability of the other, as a fellow human being, that we restrict our choice set to preempt or rule out violative courses of action.[33]

In the current section I want to ask how it is possible to reconcile this peremptory inviolability with two elements that seem required for the revision to virtue ethics that I have suggested: a

---

33. Experimental support for the primitivity of this prohibition is discussed in Fiery Cushman et al., "Simulating Murder: The Aversion to Harmful Action," *Emotion* 12 (2012): 2–7.

non-deontological virtue theory, and Harris's insurrectionist criterion of adequacy for ethical theories. I shall argue that these aims can be combined if Wiggins's rule of inviolability is understood not as a deontological rule (or constraint) but as a *practice-structuring* rule. A virtue of solidarity would then not be the *root* of the ethical, it would be part of the *point* of the ethical.

Wiggins develops his account of the force of solidarity in critique of neoliberals who press forward with globalization in a form that, they realize, will force millions of people from their homes and land as the world is built anew.

> "Always there will be winners and losers," people sometimes say. Under one aspect this is a truism; under another it is an unscrupulous way of making injury, rapine and injustice sound as if they were logically inevitable and in no way the responsibility of those who devise the proposals that the truism is meant to justify. But look for another plan, solidarity will say.... The time has come for human beings to be more inventive, more resourceful, more sensitive to the issue of compensation or amends, and more patient in their grand plans for the reconstruction of the human condition.[34]

Against such grand plans, Wiggins suggests, human solidarity calls for "defence of anyone or everyone affected." Yet the idea of (self-)defense is, frankly, in tension with the idea of inviolability; Leonard Harris would surely ask, *by what means* might the trampled and oppressed defend themselves or be defended by third parties? This grounds an insurrectionist objection: Wiggins seems to rule out violence; but insurrectionist violence is violence; and so Wiggins's proposal seems to put us on the wrong side of Harris's criterion.

---

34. Wiggins "Solidarity," 12.

Although he speaks of an absolute prohibition on "intentional assault," Wiggins's rule has space for insurrectionist self-defense: "a space surrounds another; and the preservation of that space forbids *unprovoked* injury, murder, plunder, or pillage."[35] Insurrectionists like Nat Turner and John Brown could rightly justify their violence by appeal to self-defense or the defense of others, for which reason their violent uprisings were *provoked*.[36] In this way Wiggins's conception might pass Harris's insurrectionist test.

Yet this may be too quick. A relaxed commitment to inviolability must not allow us to be *cavalier* about violence, defensive or otherwise. If we follow Ronald Dworkin in regarding rules as binary—they are either valid or not in a given instance, and if invalid, have zero weight[37]—then the inviolability rule simply does not apply to Nat Turner and John Brown. Thus I propose to recast Wiggins's prohibition not as a rule of prohibition but as a rule of *skill*: part of the "mechanics" of morals rather than its rule-book.[38] Such a reading would not only fit better with a virtue orientation, but would also align with Wiggins's call to be "more inventive, more resourceful, more sensitive to the issue of compensation or amends, and more patient." Wiggins here recasts inviolability as a *productive constraint* that reorients our patterns of thinking, even if it does not rule out violence altogether. So understood, the real ethical work of solidarity will be in the creativity and inventiveness that the constraint demands and thereby makes possible. This resolution also makes sense of the "last resort" criterion on traditional accounts of disobedience and

---

35. Ibid., 12; emphasis mine.
36. Harris affirms the defensive character of insurrectionist violence at "Insurrectionist Ethics," 186.
37. Ronald Dworkin, "The Model of Rules," *University of Chicago Law Review* 35 (1967): 14–46; 27.
38. On the rules/mechanics distinction, see Avery Kolers, "Groundwork for the Mechanics of Morals," *Canadian Journal of Philosophy* 50 (2020): 636–651.

resistance. Such accounts never actually insist that the precipitous action be the *absolute last* resort, but rather, that one would have avoided the precipitous action if there were any reasonable likelihood of success by doing something else that it would be reasonable to expect someone to try first.[39]

To summarize: solidarity is less the *root* of the ethical than part of its *point*: to live our lives in affirmation of fundamental equal status and shared membership of the party of humankind, which implies that violence could be acceptable only as a "last resort" to repulse an attack on our own or another person's equal status or party membership, and even then the most skillful among us will recognize modes of action that minimize or avoid violence altogether. In its abhorrence of violence, solidarity is similar to other virtues, such as courage and justice, which can condone coercion or violence but never celebrate it. And conceiving this "prohibition" as a rule of skill rather than of obligation also explains why we ought to de-escalate wherever possible, rather than exact all the violence that we can morally get away with.[40]

THE UNITY OF THE VIRTUES

I have argued that eudaimonistic virtue ethics has an equality problem, and that a virtue of solidarity can solve that problem. Understood as the virtue of *coequal membership of the party of humankind*, solidarity

---

39. For example and discussion, see Alejandra Mancilla, *The Right of Necessity* (Lanham, MD: Rowman & Littlefield, 2016), 91–92.
40. Insofar as justice is also a rule of skill, then clemency, restorative practices, and pardons may be built into the virtue of justice even in a retributive context. The challenge would be to get complete justice using as little violence as possible. For reflection, see Dan Markel, "State, Be Not Proud: A Retributivist Defense of the Commutation of Death Row and the Abolition of the Death Penalty," *Harvard Civil Rights-Civil Liberties Law Review* 40 (2005): 407–480.

not only seems to count as a virtue but plays an essential role in completing standard accounts of the virtues, which lack this commitment to fundamental equality. When we additionally recast Wiggins's core deontological "prohibition" as a rule of skill, what starts to come into focus is the idea of solidarity as part of the point of the ethical. The function in human life of an ethical system is, in part, to enable us to live in a way that affirms our equality.

If this virtue-ethical account of solidarity is to succeed, in a eudaimonistic system it should do some work in unifying the virtues and in linking virtue with flourishing. To be sure, if solidarity is only *part* of the point of the ethical then it need not do *all* the work of unification. Thus in the current section I develop the suggestion that solidarity functions as a unifying force on otherwise disparate virtues. To provide this account I must first explicate a recent insightful account of what the "unity" of the virtues amounts to.

In their groundbreaking interdisciplinary work on the moral psychology of virtue, Liz Gulliford and Robert Roberts argue that the virtues exhibit a complex, structured Aristotelian unity.[41] The "life of virtue" depends on our exemplifying three distinct virtue "clusters": virtues of intelligent caring, virtues of willpower, and virtues of humility. The clusters are functionally distinct one from another and functionally unified internally. Virtues of intelligent caring track "moral reality" and connect our recognition of it to a motivation to act accordingly. For instance, virtues of fair play such as justice and reciprocity exemplify intelligent caring about the quality of social relations, and to have these virtues is to value such relations and be motivated to support and uphold them.[42] A sub-class of intelligent

---

41. Annas defends a similar unity thesis. I work with the Gulliford-Roberts view because it is empirically supported and the links among virtues are worked out with some specificity, whereas Annas's is more conjectural. See Annas, *Intelligent Virtue*, 89.
42. Gulliford and Roberts, "Exploring the 'Unity' of the Virtues," 210.

caring virtues is the *allocentric* virtues, that is, virtues that involve caring about (other) *people*. The four properly allocentric virtues are all forms of benevolence: compassion, truthfulness, generosity, and kindness.[43]

By contrast, "virtues of willpower," such as courage, perseverance, and self-control, are "powers of self-management."[44] Unlike virtues of intelligent caring, willpower virtues do not orient us to concern about the moral world but to our ability to follow through with our ends and achieve self-mastery. Perseverance, for instance, "will consist partly in self-management skills, partly in a kind of psychological muscle for resisting impulses contrary to one's more fundamental goals."[45] Finally, definitive of humility is neither an orientation to the moral world nor a mastery of the self but simply the absence of vice, specifically of the vices of pride such as "arrogance, vanity, hyper-autonomy, domination, snobbery, envy, and . . . racism, sexism, and homophobia."[46] Although this kind of humility is a standalone virtue, in avoiding the vices of pride it affirms that we are no more important than others. Consequently humility underlies intelligent caring about other people, and hence Gulliford and Roberts make it an "honorary member" of what becomes the "allocentric quintet."[47] I shall suggest that Gulliford and Roberts's conception of humility is actually a partial account of the content of solidarity.

Gulliford and Roberts's account gives the virtuous life a unified structure: three top-level virtue-clusters (intelligent caring, willpower, humility), subdivisions within the clusters (allocentric, etc.), and individual virtues within each subdivision (generosity, kindness, etc.). Within clusters, virtues are functionally unified by how

43. Ibid., 216–217.
44. Ibid., 214.
45. Ibid., 212.
46. Ibid., 213.
47. Ibid., 217.

they orient us: respectively, toward moral reality, toward the unity of the self, and away from pridefulness. Across clusters, the virtues are linked by causal relations such as mutual support. The more courage we have, the more effective we will be at standing up for justice even when it's risky; the more we care about good social relations, the easier it will be to return a favor even if we would rather have done something else.[48] And so on.

The anomaly in their account, however, is humility. Humility is a lack of the vices of pride, and hence a source of insight into one's own importance relative to others—that is, into our fundamental equality. In this limited respect, humility seems to capture part of the role that I carved out for a virtue of solidarity, namely, dedication to fundamental equal worth. But it is only a part. For we might ask what humility would have us *do* with this insight into our equal significance. The answer seems to be, *nothing in particular*; Gulliford and Roberts insist that humility "supplies no motive or self-management ability."[49] They recognize that this makes it an outlier, but go on to defend the idea of a "virtuous absence," assimilating humility to other such fortunate lacks as purity in water (lacking toxins) and not being infected with a disease (lacking pathogens). Just as the absence of salt in water enables the water to slake your thirst, so the absence of identity-based pridefulness enables you to intelligently care about others. Hence humility's honorary status in the "allocentric quintet."

Gulliford and Roberts's defense of humility as a virtuous absence is not fully convincing, however. On a personal level, not having the vices of pride does not do much for those lacking a sense of self-worth or on the bottom of each of these hierarchies, who, quite the contrary, need self-esteem and proper pride to countervail a learned shame and deference to power. We need a virtue that not only denies we are

---

48. Compare Annas, *Intelligent Virtue*, 91 and 98–99.
49. Gulliford and Roberts, "Exploring the 'Unity' of the Virtues," 213.

better-than, but insists we are as-worthy-as. Humility as a mere lack cannot do this. At the structural level, in a world of "racism without racists," anti-racism and other orientations need to be not just lacks of the vices of pride but affirmative efforts to overcome affected ignorance and conventional status differences that indoctrinate children from the youngest ages into a world of advantages and disadvantages, and that taint quotidian rational choices with the consequence of exacerbating oppression.[50]

Finally, inasmuch as the virtues of intelligent caring are about making contact with moral reality, solidarity does not merely causally support these virtues but reshapes the reality they make contact with. In this sense solidarity corrects the social ontology underlying Aristotelian justice and equity, so that that virtue's mathematical implements can provide accurate measurements rather than solidify distortions. For example, solidarity reshaped Ruth First's experience of the world; it placed her alongside Black militants, and enabled her to see Apartheid society through the eyes of her close associates, who were among its most oppressed victims, but with whom she interacted as equals.[51] It enabled her to live in a way that in one respect embodied the world she was trying to build. In the absence of solidarity, no other virtue, nor all the others realized together, would have enabled this, because she would have found herself, like a latter-day Roman Stoic, stuck in a world of racialized advantage. She would have been structurally prevented from living the life of equals, no matter how fervently she desired it. No amount of personal humility or recognition of the merely conventional difference between herself and the rightless people who served her or tended

---

50. See Eduardo Bonilla-Silva, *Racism without Racists*, 5th ed. (Lanham, MD: Rowman & Littlefield, 2017). On quotidian choices being tainted with oppression see, again, Bales, *Blood and Earth*.
51. My knowledge of Ruth First's life is mostly based on Alan Wieder, *Ruth First and Joe Slovo in the War against Apartheid* (New York: Monthly Review Press, 2013).

her lawn could have changed this. Where Seneca saw the prospect of slaves overthrowing their masters as a potential *reductio ad absurdum* of his conventional ethic of enlightened superiority, Ruth First saw, correctly, that such an overthrow was morally laudable, an outcome to be hoped for and a struggle to be joined. Without solidarity, virtue might have *criticized* the life of structural advantage, but could not break her free of it.

FLOURISHING

All this said, solidarity poses a worrisome challenge for eudaimonistic virtue ethics. The anti-racist soon recognizes that the life of solidarity is continual, perpetual, struggle.[52] Most often, "the people" lose. Most justice movements fail, or see their initial success met with powerful backlash, and even "astonishingly swift" victories like the abolition of slavery or the end of European colonialism take "more than one lifetime."[53] And anyway, solidarity can shorten lifetimes: Ruth First and John Brown paid with their lives for daring to live in affirmation of fundamental equality.

Struggles, even losses, have their joys, but in many ways are not pleasant while they are happening. Even small-scale struggles are often unpleasant, for instance, if they require us to violate typical interpersonal conviviality by refusing to shake the hand of a friend who is on the other side of a conflict.[54] This puts solidarity in tension

---

52. For compelling reflections on this fact, see Kathryn Norlock, "Perpetual Struggle," *Hypatia* 34 (2019): 6–19.
53. Annas *Intelligent Virtue*, 61, citing Hochschild. Also note that, according to Bales, there are some 37 *million* people enslaved today, the vast majority in "modern" slavery that uses debt and government corruption to hold families in bondage for generations, and their labor is no less integrated into our economy than was the labor of enslaved persons in the economies of ancient Rome or industrializing Europe and Anglo-America.
54. Certainly, effective social movement organizers will create opportunities for fellow-feeling and camaraderie, and will also celebrate incremental wins. But these are movement

with eudaimonistic virtue ethics. Simply put, solidarity is often unpleasant; but the virtuous life is the most pleasant life; so solidarity seems to be ruled out.

The eudaimonist must see the virtuous life as the most pleasant life, but this is not because every virtuous act is itself pleasant. Being just in a way that sacrifices one's own or one's friend's interests typically does not feel good. Courage in battle, too, may feel however bad it feels to get killed in battle. These are not instantaneously pleasant experiences. Similarly for the things one might do in solidarity when the police are bearing down or when powerful actors break the group's unity through selective incentives. But what is often even more painful than acting virtuously is failing to do so. A person who claims to support the cause but fails to hold the picket line is ashamed and feels like a phony. They swear to do right the next time and feel self-disgust until they do. In this sense, lack of solidarity is shameful, like lack of courage, and as Aristotle suggests, what makes courage pleasant in its own way is one's embrace of what matters more over what matters less, when the two conflict.

CAN'T WE ALL JUST BE FRIENDS?

Before concluding I need to address a final objection about solidarity's place in eudaimonistic virtue ethics. Solidarity might be thought of as a kind of friendship. Like solidarity as I have sketched it here, Aristotelian virtue friendship involves the affirmation of the equality of self and other.[55] Expanded as far as "civic friendship," it might be thought that friendship could suffice for the affirmation of

---

strategies to ease the psychological burden or demandingness of solidarity; they are not solidarity itself.

55. Aristotle, *Nicomachean Ethics*, VIII.i.1155a.

fundamental equality in general. To be sure, Aristotle is ambiguous about the exact relationship between friendship and the virtues, but eudaimonistic virtue ethicists have said a great deal about friendship and its place in the best human life. Thus if solidarity is a kind or aspect of friendship, we do not need this independent account of it.

There are, however, two basic differences between Aristotelian friendship and solidarity. First is that friendship presupposes, whereas solidarity does not, an antecedent relationship between self and other, and this relationship is the basis of the commitment to the other's good for its own sake. Even civic friendship is limited in scope to that of the political community: "the extent of their association is the extent of their friendship, as it is the extent to which justice exists between them.... [F]riendship depends on community."[56] In solidarity we affirm the equality of each and stand up for and with the other for their own sake even in the absence of any relationship. It might be this commitment to stand for their equality that leads us to seek out a relationship, but the relationship is not necessary for solidarity. Nor is it sufficient: one can betray a friend or, despite loving them for their virtue, fall into patterns of unequal treatment and power imbalances. Second, friendship seems to be a symmetric relationship, whereas a virtue of solidarity is not. A virtuous person could be the only one around, and would be "in solidarity with" everyone in the sense of affirming and acting on everyone's fundamental equality, even if no one reciprocated by also affirming the virtuous person's equality.

I admit that it is possible to say that the "party of humankind" is the object of one's "universal friendship," and if we are inclined to say this, then we can say that to have the virtue of solidarity is to affirm this universal friendship. However, we must remember that this is friendship only in an extended sense. Moreover this sense of

---

56. Ibid., VIII.ix.1159b.

friendship seems to be derivative on human solidarity rather than the other way around.

CONCLUSION

Eudaimonistic virtue ethics has an equality problem. This problem is connected to the egoism and conventionality/conservatism objections familiar in the literature. Virtue ethicists' orientation toward individual character excellences arguably leads them to ignore an essential part of the point of the ethical, namely, to affirm, believe in, and be motivated by our fundamental equality. In the current chapter I have suggested that the equality problem has a straightforward solution, namely, to affirm a virtue of solidarity, understood as *coequal membership of the party of humankind*. Placed on a par with the classical "cardinal" virtues of justice, self-control, courage, and wisdom, solidarity completes the image of excellence of character. In addition, solidarity provides a partial account of the *point* of the ethical, and thereby helps to unify the virtues.

While David Wiggins's thin notion of human solidarity is not itself an account of political solidarity in the sense of shared struggle, the case of Ruth First allows us to see the radical—insurrectionist—potential of choosing to live one's life according to a virtue of fundamental equality. Ruth First was offered a life of racialized advantage and gendered disadvantage, and refused to live it. Under Apartheid, the only way to refuse to live that life was to join the struggle against it. Whereas a deontological reading of Wigginsian solidarity might absolve us from taking action against oppression if we are not (willing) agents of it, a virtue of solidarity does not let us off so easily. Affirmatively living the life of a coequal entails intervening in and standing up against subjugation, not just refraining from participating in it. Nor is First's context of Apartheid South Africa the only place where this lesson holds. In general, in an unjust world, a virtue of (Wigginsian human) solidarity entails a project of political solidarity. This is no less true in societies that are liberal in form yet unjust than it was under Apartheid.[57]

WORKS CITED

Anderson, Elizabeth. "Social Movements, Experiments in Living, and Moral Progress: Case Studies from Britain's Abolition of Slavery." *Lindley Lecture*, University of Kansas, 2014.

Annas, Julia. 2011. *Intelligent Virtue*. New York: Oxford University Press.

Aristotle. 2009. *Nicomachean Ethics*, trans. W. D. Ross and Lesley Brown. Oxford: Oxford World's Classics.

Bales, Kevin. 2016. *Blood and Earth: Modern Slavery, Ecocide, and the Secret to Saving the World*. New York: Random House.

Beever, Allan. 2004. "Aristotle on Equity, Law, and Justice." *Legal Theory* 10: 33–50.

Bonilla-Silva, Eduardo. 2017. *Racism without Racists*, 5th ed. Lanham, MD: Rowman & Littlefield.

Citizens United v. FEC, 558 US 310 (2010).

Cushman, Fiery, et al. 2012. "Simulating Murder: The Aversion to Harmful Action." *Emotion* 12: 2–7.

Darity, William A., and A. Kirsten Mullen. 2020. *From Here to Equality: Reparations for Black Americans in the Twenty-first Century*. Chapel Hill: University of North Carolina Press.

Dred Scott v. Sandford, 60 US 393 (1856). Online: https://www.law.cornell.edu/supremecourt/text/60/393.

Dworkin, Ronald. 1967. "The Model of Rules." *University of Chicago Law Review* 35: 14–46.

Edwards v. A.G. of Canada. 1929 CanLII 438 (UK JCPC). Online: https://www.canlii.org/en/ca/ukjcpc/doc/1929/1929canlii438/1929canlii438.html.

Gulliford, Liz, and Robert C. Roberts. 2018. "Exploring the 'Unity' of the Virtues: The Case of an Allocentric Quintet." *Theory & Psychology* 28: 208–226.

Harris, Leonard. 2020a. "Honor and Insurrection or a Short Story about Why John Brown (with David Walker's Spirit) Was Right and Frederick Douglass (with

---

57. I am grateful to an audience at the University of Nevada–Las Vegas for lively discussion of a predecessor of this paper. I am also grateful to Andrea Sangiovanni and Juri Viehoff for comments on a previous draft.

Benjamin Banneker's Spirit) Was Wrong." In *A Philosophy of Struggle: The Leonard Harris Reader*, ed. Lee A. McBride, III. London: Bloomsbury, 161–173.

Harris, Leonard. 2020b. "Insurrectionist Ethics: Advocacy, Moral Psychology, and Pragmatism." In *A Philosophy of Struggle: The Leonard Harris Reader*, ed. Lee A. McBride, III. London: Bloomsbury, 175–187.

Hochschild, Adam. 2005. *Bury the Chains: Prophets and Rebels in the Fight to Free an Empire's Slaves*. Boston: Houghton Mifflin.

Kolers, Avery. 2016. *A Moral Theory of Solidarity*. Oxford University Press.

Kolers, Avery. 2020. "Groundwork for the Mechanics of Morals." *Canadian Journal of Philosophy* 50: 636–651.

Mancilla, Alejandra. 2016. *The Right of Necessity*. Lanham, MD: Rowman & Littlefield.

Markel, Dan. 2005. "State, Be Not Proud: A Retributivist Defense of the Commutation of Death Row and the Abolition of the Death Penalty." *Harvard Civil Rights-Civil Liberties Law Review* 40: 407–480.

McBride, Lee A. III., ed. 2020. *A Philosophy of Struggle: The Leonard Harris Reader*. London: Bloomsbury.

Norlock, Kathryn. 2019. "Perpetual Struggle." *Hypatia* 34: 6–19.

Perry, Matthew J. 2013. *Gender, Manumission, and the Roman Freedwoman*. New York: Cambridge University Press.

Schumacher, Leonard. 2011. "Slaves in Roman Society." In *The Oxford Handbook of Social Relations in the Ancient World*, ed. Michael Peachin. New York: Oxford University Press, 589–608.

Seneca. 2017. *Letters on Ethics: To Lucilius*, trans. Margaret Graver and A. A. Long. Chicago: University of Chicago Press.

Tessman, Lisa. 2005. *Burdened Virtues*. New York: Oxford University Press.

Tilly, Charles, and Sidney Tarrow. 2015. *Contentious Politics*, 2nd ed. New York: Oxford University Press.

Toner, Christopher. 2015. "Virtue Ethics and Egoism." In *The Routledge Companion to Virtue Ethics*, ed. Lorraine Besser-Jones and Michael Slote. New York: Routledge, 345–357.

Wieder, Alan. 2013. *Ruth First and Joe Slovo in the War against Apartheid*. New York: Monthly Review Press.

Wiggins, David. 2008. "Solidarity and the Root of the Ethical." Lindley Lecture, University of Kansas.

Chapter 5

Personal Sacrifice and the Value of Solidarity

JURI VIEHOFF

In a portrait of John McCain published in *Rolling Stone*, David Foster Wallace recounts the story of McCain's plane being shot down over Hanoi in 1967. He then has to say the following about McCain's ordeal as a prisoner of war in an infamous North Vietnamese camp:[1]

> He was delirious with pain for weeks, and his weight dropped to 100 pounds, and the other POWs were sure he would die; and then after a few months like that after his bones mostly knitted and he could sort of stand up they brought him in to the prison commandant's office and offered to let him go. This is true. They said he could just leave. They had found out that McCain's father was one of the top-ranking naval officers in the U.S. Armed Forces [. . .], and the North Vietnamese wanted the PR coup of mercifully releasing his son, the baby-killer. McCain, 100 pounds and barely able to stand, refused. The U.S. military's Code of

---

1. https://www.rollingstone.com/politics/politics-features/david-foster-wallace-on-john-mccain-the-weasel-twelve-monkeys-and-the-shrub-194272/ (accessed June 15, 2023).

Conduct for Prisoners of War apparently said that POWs had to be released in the order they were captured, and there were others who'd been in Hoa Lo a long time, and McCain refused to violate the Code. The commandant, not pleased, right there in the office had guards break his ribs, rebreak his arm, knock his teeth out. McCain still refused to leave without the other POWs. And so then he spent four more years in Hoa Lo like this, much of the time in solitary, in the dark, in a closet-sized box called a "punishment cell."

Maybe you've heard all this before; it's been in umpteen different media profiles of McCain. But try to imagine that moment between getting offered early release and turning it down. Try to imagine it was you. Imagine how loudly your most basic, primal self-interest would have cried out to you in that moment, and all the ways you could rationalize accepting the offer. Can you hear it? If so, would you have refused to go? You simply can't know for sure. None of us can. It's hard even to imagine the pain and fear in that moment, much less know how you'd react. But, see, we do know how this man reacted. That he chose to spend four more years there, in a dark box, alone, tapping code on the walls to the others, rather than violate a Code. Maybe he was nuts. But the point is that with McCain it feels like we know, for a proven fact, that he's capable of devotion to something other, more, than his own self-interest.

People often make sacrifices for others. And at least some people, on some occasions, make tremendous sacrifices: Some people donate a kidney to a stranger when they could just have ignored a plea. Others get hurt defending the innocent from attack when they simply could have walked past. Yet others, like John McCain, spend years in a torture prison when they could easily have avoided it. Cases of sacrifice vary in terms of the setback to self-interest that a person knowingly and willingly accepts. But they also differ along other dimensions: Many, but perhaps not all, significant sacrifices are morally discretionary. And many, but perhaps not all, are morally praiseworthy, displaying virtues like courage, benevolence, and personal integrity to different degrees. They also differ in terms of the goal or goals that the person making the sacrifice pursues and the relationship in which the one making the sacrifice and the person benefiting stand. Sacrifices, especially those that involve enormous and irreversible setbacks to a person's interest, raise interesting philosophical issues in their own right.[2] But cases of self-sacrifice also play a role in thinking about solidarity: If A is in solidarity with B with regard to some plight *p*, then A must at least be willing to incur some costs or forgo some benefit for the sake of B's improvement with regard to *p*. This assumption, many would say, comes close to a truism about what solidarity is or what attitudes are necessary for being in solidarity to obtain. And if 'being willing to incur some costs' is equivalent to being prepared to make a sacrifice, then there is a clear connection between solidarity and sacrifice.

The purpose of this chapter is to investigate that connection. More specifically, I analyze what sacrifice cases of solidarity can teach us about the nature and value of solidarity in general. I suggest that we can make better sense of solidarity's nature by explaining why some but not other cases of sacrifice are instances of solidarity. And we can learn something important about solidarity's value or function

---

[2]. Jean Hampton, "Selflessness and the Loss of Self," *Social Philosophy and Policy* 10 (1993): 135–165; Andrea C. Westlund, "Selflessness and Responsibility for Self: Is Deference Compatible with Autonomy?," *The Philosophical Review* 112 (2003): 483–523; Douglas W. Portmore, "Welfare, Achievement, and Self-Sacrifice," *Journal of Ethics & Social Philosophy* 2 (2006): [i]; George Kateb, "Morality and Self-Sacrifice, Martyrdom and Self-Denial," *Social Research* 75 (2008): 353–394; Alfred Archer and Marcel van Ackeren, eds., *Sacrifice and Moral Philosophy* (New York: Routledge, 2020).

by understanding which instances of solidaristic sacrifice fail to be morally valuable or virtuous. Ultimately, I will suggest that these two issues, solidarity's nature and value, are related: we understand what counts as solidarity by thinking about the value or function that having a practice that conforms to certain norms has for people like us. Where sacrifices fail to realize this function, we should not speak of core examples of solidarity.

The argument unfolds as follows: After some preliminaries, the next section turns to the issue of solidaristic personal sacrifice and presents two sets of cases. Some of these intuitively register as instances of solidarity, while others do not. And some cases of solidaristic behavior contain personal sacrifice, while others do not. Understanding the nature of solidarity, I suggest, turns among other things on solving this twofold conceptual puzzle: First, in virtue of which features are some self-sacrifices *solidaristic*? Second, since some instances of solidarity do not involve sacrifice, in virtue of which features are self-sacrificial and non-self-sacrificial instances of solidarity part of a unified phenomenon? The third section looks at two recent motivation-based accounts that start from the second puzzle of explaining what unifies sacrificial and non-sacrificial cases of solidarity. To understand solidarity, we must explain the precise content of the attitudes and motives that agents in solidarity have. While I suggest that each account captures important features of solidarity, they fail on the first conceptual puzzle: neither can explain why some cases of self-sacrifice do not count as solidaristic. The following two sections develop and apply an alternative, functionalist account. Solidarity is not simply concerned with fostering 'concern' or establishing 'community,' but it serves a specific function, to wit, that of mitigating a conflict in our outlook between complying with our moral duties and living a life that contains valuable projects and relationships. In solidarity, we build projects and relationships based on morality-given criteria. According to my functionalist proposal, whether some behavior counts as solidaristic depends on whether or not it realizes solidarity's function and not (or only derivatively) on the particular motivation with which the agent acts. This suggests a solution to the puzzle of non-solidaristic sacrifice: where the agent's self-interest diverges too drastically from the course of action recommended by the moral cause, there simply is no way of realizing the described function and, therefore, we should not speak of cases of solidarity.

Before I proceed, some preliminaries are in order. First, while solidarity is used as a term both in ordinary discourse and in more specific (social) scientific contexts, for example in sociology, psychology, and sociobiology, the purpose of this chapter is not to offer an explanation of it that reflects its use in all these domains. Rather, my goal is to illuminate solidarity as a useful category in moral and political theorizing. Solidarity would be a useful category if the practice the term picks out constitutes an interesting, independent phenomenon. Conversely, solidarity would not be worth exploring in much detail if our existing repertoire of terms and concepts is fully adequate, that is, if talk of solidarity can just as well be captured by more established theoretical notions like 'justice' or 'community.' Second, an account of solidarity is a good one if it offers a unified, illuminating explanation of the underlying phenomenon. Here is one upshot for what follows: even though I make extensive use of cases and initially classify them as intuitively being instances of solidarity or not, these intuitive judgments are preliminary—what ultimately matters is whether or not the theoretical explanation that I offer in latter sections succeeds in the sense of advancing our understanding of an interesting, independent phenomenon.

JURI VIEHOFF

SACRIFICE AND SOLIDARITY: CASES

I want to introduce the twofold puzzle of solidarity and sacrifice by presenting two sets of cases. The first two cases are cases of significant personal sacrifice. The second two cases are instances of solidarity. But not both of the former cases are *also* cases of solidarity; and the two latter cases contain no clear instances of sacrifice.[3] Before presenting them, it will be helpful to clarify the notion of sacrifice I have in mind. I will adopt a definition by Douglas Portmore that strikes me as sufficiently broad and non-prejudicial on the topic under consideration. According to this definition, "an act x is a self-sacrificing act if and only if there exists an available alternative y such that the agent would be better off were she to perform y, and yet she performs x, knowing that this means that she will be worse off, because she wants to bring about some end that she believes has a greater chance of being realized if she performs x than if she performs y."[4] Thus, an agent does not make a sacrifice when she erroneously thinks that the action she performs is in fact the one self-interest would recommend, nor is an act self-sacrificial if, believing that the chosen action is not the one most recommended by self-interest, the action is the one that best advances it. This latter point suggests that the status of an action can change after it has occurred. For example, an action may later turn out to have been in the agent's best interest and hence no longer be an instance of a sacrifice. Some may find this perplexing. Luckily, we need not resolve this issue because, as I will argue, what matters for solidarity are actions that agents undertake with a certain attitude

---

3. Since my overarching aim is to identify an interesting phenomenon rather than to police language around solidarity, I am not concerned with whether or not less paradigmatic cases should not be named cases of solidarity at all or whether they are just that: less paradigmatic.
4. Portmore, "Welfare, Achievement, and Self-Sacrifice," 14.

or motivation that connects to sacrifice, not actions that are (and remain) instances of sacrifice. Here then are two cases of sacrifice:

Milton: While on a dangerous jungle mission during the Vietnam War in 1965, Private First Class Milton Lee Olive III sacrificed his life to save four members of his platoon by smothering a live grenade. He posthumously received the Medal of Honor.

John: Having been captured, John McCain refused to be released from prison unless all other POWs that arrived earlier than him were released. After his refusal, he was kept in solitary confinement and tortured for several more years.

Both cases are cases where the protagonist makes a significant sacrifice: they each could have done something different that would have been better from the standpoint of what would make their life go best. Moreover, they were both—let us assume—fully aware of this. Of course, they differ in crucial respects. Perhaps most obviously they differ in terms of how much inferior the agent's chosen option was from a prudential point of view and thus how much well-being each actually sacrificed. But they also share certain elements: each episode occurs against the backdrop of political adversity and violent struggle, and in each of them the protagonist's actions are intended to further not just a personal or idiosyncratic goal, but one that the protagonist deems *morally* significant. Moreover, these actions seem morally praiseworthy.[5] Now despite these similarities, I want to suggest that, intuitively, these cases differ with regard to whether or not we would classify what the agent does as acting from, or being an instance of, solidarity. As far as solidarity is concerned, it seems clear to me that while *John* is a paradigmatic instance of solidarity, *Milton* is not. This judgment is confirmed by those writing on solidarity. Michael Zhao, for example, uses a case like *John* as a clear-cut case

---

5. I think this holds true even if we maintain, as we should, that the US's military engagement in Vietnam lacked a moral justification, was in fact deeply immoral.

of solidarity, yet he also recognizes that a case like *Milton* does not register as similarly paradigmatic.[6] And Nicolas Bommarito explicitly addresses the challenge that cases where an agent makes a sacrifice as huge as *Milton* do not seem to be clear-cut instances.[7]

The second set of cases are instances of non-sacrificial solidarity. Again, I want to rely at this stage merely on individual judgments about these cases without going into any theoretical explanation of why we might think they exhibit solidarity:

Xenia: Xenia is a seasonal agricultural laborer picking fruits for an agriculture conglomerate. One day she is informed in a secret meeting that many of the all-female workforce are about to go on strike to fight for the right to unionize, force the adoption of rules regarding regular breaks, and so on. Even accounting for all risks, taking part in the strike is in Xenia's self-interest.

Yvonne: Yvonne is an affluent student who reads about the agriculture laborers' strike. Yvonne joins a local support group that raises awareness of farm exploitation in the agro industry by distributing leaflets, staging boycotts, organizing concerts whose proceeds will support the workers' families while on strike, and so on. Yvonne's life goes better because of her activism compared to what pursuing other options would have brought about.

Now what is noteworthy about these two cases is that, although each an instance of solidarity, neither case is, according to the earlier definition, a clear-cut case of personal sacrifice. While Xenia's participation in the strike surely counts as a case of solidarity, that course of action is also the one that is best from her own self-interested perspective. Put differently, any rational Xenia would participate in the

---

6. Michael Zhao, "Solidarity, Fate-Sharing, and Community," *Philosopher's Imprint* 19 (2019): 10. Zhao calls these cases of self-deprivation. He thinks that they also rule out some prominent accounts of what solidarity is.
7. Nicolas Bommarito, "Private Solidarity," *Ethical Theory and Moral Practice* 19 (2015): 445–455, at 451.

strike, whether or not she cares (non-instrumentally) about the fate of her co-workers. And since she is doing what is in her own best interest, Xenia is not making a sacrifice. As far as Yvonne is concerned, we have another, if significantly different scenario that is not a case of sacrifice. In this case, the chosen solidaristic action later *turns out* to be in the agent's best interest. As stipulated, pursuing any other activity would not have matched the personal benefits (say in terms of a sense of purpose and meaning in life) that Yvonne receives from being in solidarity. So again, there is no sacrifice here.

Our two sets of cases and the intuitive judgments proposed give rise to two conceptual puzzles. The first one is the puzzle of *non-solidaristic sacrifice*: In virtue of what features are some instances of personal sacrifice acts of solidarity while others are not? Put in terms of our examples: What distinguishes *John* from cases of sacrifice that are not—or anyway less clear-cut—solidaristic, such as *Milton*? The second puzzle is that of *non-sacrificial solidarity*: What is it that unites acts of solidarity that do contain actual sacrifices with those that do not? In other words, what is it that *John* shares with *Xenia* and *Yvonne* that makes each a case of solidarity? A good explanation of the nature of solidarity, I want to suggest, must establish a criterion for distinguishing which cases are cases of solidarity and why they are.

One response may be this: There is no connection. What examples like the ones presented demonstrate is that, contrary to what was hypothesized in the beginning, there just is no deeper connection between sacrifice and solidarity. Some cases of sacrifice are solidaristic, others are not. And some cases of solidarity contain sacrifices, but others do not. There is nothing to explain here. The upshot of this would be that in cases like *John* (i.e., cases that are both instances of personal sacrifice and of solidarity), it is some other factor besides the sacrifice that renders the action solidaristic. But I think it would be a mistake to abandon the idea that there is an important nexus between solidarity and sacrifice so quickly: After all, it is a tempting thought that John McCain was in solidarity with the other American POWs *because* he refused to leave, that is, *because* he made the sacrifice that he did.

As already hinted at above, I think we can make some progress by focusing on attitudes and motives rather than the classification of actions: Many practices are distinguishable from others not by what we do, but only by the attitudes and motives we have when engaging in certain acts. Such attitudes can be diverse and complex. For example, one can attend a rally to protest the unjust imprisonment of political activists in a foreign country because one cares about them and their cause, but also, at the same time, because one has a love interest in the leader of the protest.[8] Importantly, one can act for a reason while also having a commitment that, if things were differently, one would do the same thing for a different reason. Thus, one can attend a strike both for the reason that doing so advances one's self-interest and, at the same time, for the reason that one cares about the cause and those individuals picked out by it. Now the suggestion is that as far as solidarity is concerned, the necessary condition for being in solidarity is a commitment to make sacrifices for the cause (or those picked out by it). Where acting in solidarity is also in one's best self-interest, then the relevant attitude of solidarity is counter-factual: one would remain committed to doing what solidarity demands even if things were to change and acting in one's own best self-interest and doing what is required by the cause would come apart. Moreover, one is in solidarity at t_1 when one believes that one is making a sacrifice for an object of solidarity, even if, at t_2, it turns out that what one did was in fact in one's best interest.

This proposal is also attractive in that it implies, very plausibly, that agents who act 'as if' they were in solidarity but do so *only* because it

---

8. Ibid., 449. Bommarito uses the example to show that one is not in solidarity if one's sole reason is the romantic interest.

is in their best self-interest are not in fact in solidarity: Imagine that Xenia takes part in the strike, but is willing to go back to work if she alone were offered better working conditions. While she would be acting 'as if' she were in solidarity, she would not in fact be, even while taking part in the strike. And conversely, it shows why people who cannot (either because they are simply prevented or because their action is non-sacrificial for reasons of self-interest), but would make a sacrifice for the cause if they could, are in solidarity.

EXISTING EXPLANATIONS

The present proposal is that what unites cases of solidarity (John, Xenia, Yvonne) is that an agent is in solidarity either (a) when they make such a sacrifice for the object of solidarity or (b) when, counterfactually, they would make a sacrifice if they could or needed to do so. If we describe the sacrifice-solidarity-nexus in this way, then we have an initial answer to the second puzzle of what sacrifice and non-sacrifice cases of solidarity have in common: they each contain a commitment to making a sacrifice when needed. But of course, this amounts to nothing more than a stipulative definition so far. To vindicate this proposal, we need some explanation of why this should be a relevant feature in virtue of which behavior counts as solidaristic. Moreover, and importantly, we need an explanation of the features that distinguish solidarity cases from non-solidarity cases. In this section, I discuss two recent accounts that do just that. These accounts are motivation-based: they each assume that, in order to see what unifies solidarity and distinguishes it from other phenomena, we need to attend to the specific attitudes and motives with which the agent acts. Below I describe both these accounts in more detail and explain how they ultimately each fail because they have no principled response to the conceptual issue just mentioned, namely the puzzle of non-solidaristic sacrifice.

In "Private Solidarity," Nicolas Bommarito's primary goal is to establish that instances of what he calls 'private solidarity' count as solidarity. Consider the following scenario:

Zoe: Zoe is a cashier at a supermarket carrying fruits from the agricultural conglomerate that exploits the farm workers. Zoe sympathizes with the workers, but knows that if she were to openly demonstrate this, she would be fired and could no longer support her family. Yet in order to stand with the farmworkers, Zoe resolves to not take bathroom and cigarette breaks during the strike.

In *Zoe*, we have an agent that engages in causally non-effective, non-public behavior that is directed toward some object of concern. Cases like Zoe tend to elicit a diverse set of intuitive responses: Whereas Bommarito and others think of them as clear instances of solidarity, others doubt this.[9] What is clear is that *if* cases like *Zoe* are instances of solidarity, then they disconfirm certain accounts of solidarity, namely those that see some form of acting jointly with others or sharing some reciprocal and interlocking set of intentions as a necessary condition for solidarity to obtain.[10]

Since Bommarito maintains that private solidarity is solidarity, he proposes an alternative suggestion about its nature. According to his 'concern account,' what all instances of solidarity share is a desire to establish 'concern' or 'unity' with others, and to manifest and develop such concern. When we either make a sacrifice or have a commitment to making it (in cases where we cannot reasonably do so at the moment, e.g., Zoe), it is the concern that our actions and thoughts

---

9. Andrea Sangiovanni, *Solidarity* (Manchester University Press, 2023), 118–120.
10. *Zoe* also shows that *making* a sacrifice is not necessary for solidarity: since her actions cannot improve the situation of the striking workers, and Zoe knows this, they cannot be intended to benefit the workers, and hence cannot count as a sacrifice for their sake according to definition.

express that accounts for it being an instance of solidarity. Though Bommarito does not offer a precise definition of concern, it seems plausible to think of concern along the following lines: A shows concern for B if (and only if) B's well-being plays a special role in A's mental life. This may manifest in different ways: where A can act in ways that make a practical difference for B's well-being, doing so will have special weight in A's practical deliberation. Where A cannot make such a practical difference, B's well-being will still be an object of reflection and emotional responses: if B's life goes well, A is elated; if B is harmed, A will feel pain and sorrow, and so on. And importantly, we express such concern for others when we deprive ourselves of goods with the desire to be emotionally close to those who are the objects of our concern.

Bommarito's account is attractive: First, it can explain why various cases we have discussed, including sacrifice-cases, are instances of solidarity. In refusing to leave his fellow POWs behind, John McCain showed/expresseed concern for them. Likewise, by committing not to abandon the strike unless all workers receive just benefits, Xenia shows concern for her fellow workers. Yvonne, too, by investing time and emotional energy, demonstrates concern. And so does Zoe, through her symbolic act of standing with the workers. Second, a lack of concern for those one professes to be in solidarity with disables any claim to solidarity. Think again of the person who only wants to be close to the protest leader; or imagine that John McCain's sole reason to refuse release from Hỏa Lò prison was his desire for military honors and his wish to live up to family tradition. Since these agents' actions would not be motivated by concern for the relevant group, their actions would not count as instances of solidarity.

The reason why Bommarito's account nonetheless fails as an explanation of solidarity is that it cannot provide a coherent criterion why some but not other cases of sacrifice are instances of solidarity (i.e., the first conceptual puzzle). Consider *Milton*: while we would not say that he acted from solidarity, he showed concern for his fellow soldiers by smothering a grenade to protect them from being killed. Yet if concern is both a necessary and sufficient criterion for solidarity, then contrary to the stated intuition, we should say that he was in solidarity with them. Or, alternatively, we might try to reject the claim that Milton showed concern for those members of his platoon whose lives he saved. Faced with other cases where an agent makes a very significant sacrifice, Bommarito gestures toward this possibility: In order to show concern for others, one must protect one's own agency, for if one did not, one would relinquish one's ability to benefit one's object of concern on an ongoing basis.[11] But while this suggestion may ring true for some cases (e.g., when benefiting another person is best served by continuously being around), 'being around' seems at most like a contingent condition of expressing concern. Sometimes the clearest and perhaps only way of showing concern for another will consist in a course of action whereby one disables (or, more drastically, terminates) one's own agency and hence deprives oneself of the ability to show further concern in the future. *Milton* seems like a clear case of this kind: Can we think of any more obvious way of showing concern for others than sacrificing one's life for them in the situation he faced? But if his act was not an instance of solidarity, then Bommarito's account of solidarity fails on account of not providing an adequate explanation of the puzzle of non-solidaristic sacrifice.

Let us look at another recent explanation of solidarity's nature that may help to solve the two conceptual puzzles, namely one by Michael Zhao.[12] Zhao's threefold goal is to illuminate (i) what motivations those in solidarity have, (ii) what "unifies acts of solidarity,"[13] and (iii) what kind of a value solidarity is. (We can set aside (iii)

---

11. Bommarito, "Private Solidarity," 451.
12. Zhao, "Solidarity, Fate-Sharing, and Community."
13. Ibid., 1.

for the moment.) Zhao, like Bommarito, believes that the correct response to (ii) hinges on a precise answer to (i), that is, on defining and explaining an encompassing motivational characteristic that all instances of solidaristic action have in common. And like Bommarito (and myself above), Zhao considers cases of sacrifice. Specifically, he starts with cases like *Zoe* where an agent acts in a non-public, causally ineffective, and uncoordinated way, yet seems to act in solidarity with some object of concern in virtue of the motivation with which these actions are executed or the attitudes that such actions express. Once we have clearly stated the motives of agents acting in solidarity in these cases (Zhao calls them private, self-depriving acts of solidarity), we are in a position to "point [...] to something more general whose presence explains both these cases and other cases of solidarity." The more general attitude that Zhao identifies as the common denominator of all forms of acting in solidarity is an "attitude of community." When one has this attitude of community with a group, one has a broad range of distinctive practical responses to its members. For example, one is disposed to consider the self/other distinction among group members as insignificant for certain practical purposes such as the distribution of goods or bads; or one comes to see the group as a 'collective entity' that can "subsume the agency of the individuals that make it up."[14]

Zhao's suggestion is that the attitude of community required by solidarity manifests itself in different ways when we think about self-depriving versus non-self-depriving (or self-sacrificial) cases: As somebody in solidarity, one identifies with those one is in solidarity with, and, seeing the group and its members' well-being tied to one's own, one will act to advance the group's aims and goals. In non-self-depriving cases, this will typically amount to actions that benefit the group and its members, even if it comes at a price to one's own,

---

14. Ibid., p. 7.

group-membership-independent prudential interest. But sometimes the agent simply cannot act in ways that would benefit the group. In such self-depriving cases, the agent attitude of community manifests itself in a 'commitment to share fate.' When one has a commitment to share fate with a group, then one desires that "what happens to part of the group should happen to the entire group."[15] This, precisely, is what we see in cases like *John* or *Zoe*: the agent in solidarity accepts significant cost to their own well-being so that what happens to them is also what happens (at least symbolically) to the other members of the group, even if their actions do not contribute in any clear-cut way to the group's aims or its members' well-being.

Does this account of fate-sharing and community fare better than the previous account based on concern? Though we are offered a plausible story about what unifies different instances of solidarity, to wit, an attitude of community, there remains, again, a question about the puzzle of non-solidaristic sacrifice: Zhao is clear that cases like *Milton* are not instances of solidarity.[16] But the difficulty is that, at least based on what he says about the attitude of community, Milton's self-sacrifice does seem to correspond closely to the stated elements. For example, the best rationalization of somebody's choice to give up their life for a group is, precisely, identification with the group and a disregard for the self/other distinction among members of the group: "I am saving my platoon!" or "I am protecting my fellow soldiers!" seems the most plausible thought running through Milton's mind the second before he used his body as a shield.

But if Milton does act with an attitude of community, then what makes it the case that his action is not an instance of *solidarity*? Zhao himself is aware of this conundrum. He considers—but then rejects—the possibility that the attitude necessary for solidarity

---

15. Ibid., 5.
16. Ibid., 10.

requires *both* identifying with/acting in the interest of the group and fate-sharing (i.e., undergoing the same predicament as one's fellows). But such a compound motivational requirement would rule out too many cases of solidarity (e.g., *Yvonne* does not really desire to undergo what the farm workers undergo—she wants to improve their plight). So, in the end, he merely concludes that "the class of acts of solidarity is vague and [. . .] at the edges, acts of solidarity blend into other things one might do out of an attitude of community."[17]

But the problem here runs deeper than the vagueness of peripheral cases: What is puzzling is the fact that we can identify cases that perfectly satisfy the stated conditions and yet, inexplicably, clearly fail to register as instances of solidarity. Though intellectually honest, Zhao's admission that he cannot think of a good explanation why *Milton* isn't a case of solidarity amounts more to an admission of defeat than a solution to the goal of explaining the nature of solidarity in terms of the motivation with which an agent undertakes such acts.

AN ALTERNATIVE EXPLANATORY STRATEGY: FUNCTIONALISM

Both accounts we have so far looked at attempted to come up with an explanation of solidarity by means of investigating the precise set of motives or attitudes necessary for an action to count as solidaristic. In this section, I want to propose a different account that relies on an alternative explanatory strategy, namely one that is functionalist. I take my cue from recent discussions about the nature of blame where, faced with a complex configuration of very diverse instances of blaming attitudes and contexts, some authors have advocated such

---

17. Ibid., 10.

an alternative approach. In relation to blame, Shoemaker and Vargas explain the functionalist strategy as follows:

> On *content-based* accounts, blame is a distinctive attitude or activity. The practice of blame—that is, blaming—is then understood in terms of where and how that attitude or activity occurs. Our proposal inverts that relationship: it is the *function* of blame—a signal about our normative commitments—that determines which attitudes and activities are instances of blame when they are.[18]

My approach below follows Shoemaker and Vargas's: rather than trying to work out some intricate set of attitudes and motives that need to be present for some act to count as an instance of solidarity, we should start by investigating the purpose(s) that solidarity practices serve individuals like us. Specifically, functionalism pursues the task of explaining a practice through a three-step method. First, we lay out core features of the practice. Second, we formulate a hypothesis about the point of such a practice given the needs that agents engaging in it have in light of some set of circumstances they face. We then work out the *point* of this social practice by dissecting the central (and perhaps unique) functions that it serves those in the predicament described.[19]

One way to think about this is in terms of *difference-making*: What would be lost if we lacked such a practice in our lives? For example,

---

18. David Shoemaker and Manuel Vargas, "Moral Torch Fishing: A Signaling Theory of Blame," *Noûs* 55 (2019): 581–602, at 587. Other broadly similar functionalist accounts of blame are: Miranda Fricker, "What's the Point of Blame? A Paradigm Based Explanation," *Noûs* 50 (2016): 165–183; Paulina Sliwa, "Reverse-Engineering Blame," *Philosophical Perspectives* 34 (2020): 200–219.
19. A more comprehensive explanation and defense of both the functionalist approach and its application to solidarity is offered in Juri Viehoff, "What's the Point of Solidarity?" (unpublished ms).

a social practice may enable beings like us to form and revise attachments to others and create shared understandings regarding wrongdoing (blame), or it might help us by improving our epistemic position (testimony). Once we have worked out solidarity's specific role in our life, we can explain which attitudes are central or necessary to realize this purpose, and we should be able to explain why, in cases we would not typically consider instances of solidarity (e.g., *Milton*), this purpose is served less well. Finally, with some luck, we should also be in a position to understand why there is genuine disagreement for other cases, for example instances of private solidarity like *Zoe*'s case. (Of course, the functionalist strategy of explanation can also have, in some cases, revisionist implications: Perhaps we should reject some uses of the concept of solidarity that do not live up to the point of solidarity identified.)

Core Features of Solidarity Practices

If we follow the three-step method laid out above, then what are the core features of solidarity? Setting out the explanandum is not straightforward because, as we saw, there is also disagreement among those writing on solidarity whether certain cases count as instances of solidarity. Nonetheless, I think we can list four features that all writing on solidarity consider to be necessary or at least central elements in paradigmatic cases. First, solidarity is, at least in some sense, will- or attitude-dependent: unless an agent's inner configuration satisfies some criterion, they are not in solidarity.[20]

Second, solidaristic actions express some form of unity or closeness with others. This is true in 'solidarity among' cases (e.g., *John*, *Xenia*), that is, cases where solidarity occurs among members of a

---

20. As we saw in the previous section, it is very difficult to specify the content of solidaristic attitudes precisely—but that does not preclude general agreement that some set of mental conditions is necessary.

socially salient group in which members think of each other as sharing some common feature.[21] But it is also true in 'solidarity with' cases, for example, *Xenia* or *Zoe*: it is through their solidaristic actions that both Xenia and Zoe express closeness to those suffering from an injustice. There is then, without a doubt, some deep connection between solidarity and the existence of some communal spirit (e.g., through identification, fellow-feelings, concern, or a belief in group agency).

However, and third, there is also something rather unique about solidarity that is not commonly associated with other forms of community and close bonds of group identification we share: Unlike other communal bonds, solidarity typically involves some plight, obstacle, or situation of adversity, and, consequently, some cause or aim that picks out those with whom the agent is in solidarity with. Put differently, we are in solidarity *with* others, but our solidarity is typically *over* some predicament that they (or that we, as a group) confront. And in central cases, it is some morally significant predicament that those we are in solidarity with face.

A final fourth point is more taxonomical: Most philosophers writing on solidarity agree that solidarity differs from behavior that is either purely self-interested or purely other-regarding (altruistic).[22] Since our aim is to develop solidarity in a way that makes it a useful concept for moral and political theory, we should aim to incorporate this aspect. It would be theoretically unsatisfactory if we came up with an explanation of the nature of solidarity that did not explain this "most distinctive, attractive, and challenging feature of solidarity

---

21. Simon Derpmann, "Solidarity, Moral Recognition, and Communality," in *Solidarity: Theory and Practice*, ed. Arto Laitinen and Anne Pessi (New York: Lexington, 2015), 105–124.
22. Christian Arnsperger and Yanis Varoufakis, "Toward a Theory of Solidarity," *Erkenntnis* 59 (2003): 157–188.

[namely] that it seems somehow to transcend the very dichotomy between altruistic and egoistic motivations."[23]

The Function of Solidarity

Having 'triangulated' central features of solidarity, I can now develop my thesis about its purpose. To do so, I begin by outlining a predicament and a concurrent need that agents like us face. Our predicament consists in the fact that in trying to respond to Reason, we encounter two kinds of demands on us. On the one hand, we aim to live autonomous lives in which we pursue self-chosen, valuable projects and establish and maintain valuable relationships to others. Such projects and relationships generate what we might call 'ethical' reasons. But on the other hand, we also face 'impersonal' concerns that do not stem from our relationships and self-chosen projects. Most notably (but perhaps not exclusively), these are the demands of morality, so we can call these our 'moral' reasons. Now our predicament consists in the fact that our 'ethical' and or 'moral' reasons do not neatly align: Perhaps not unavoidably, but certainly under present social, economic, political, and environmental conditions, there are conflicts between responding to the fullest to our ethical reasons while, at the same time, satisfying the demands of morality. This should be most obvious in instances where both reasons require actions that are not compossible. For example, we can easily imagine scenarios where one morally ought to invest time and energy into fighting for some important cause (say avoiding a climate catastrophe), but doing so proves incompatible with having a flourishing family life. After all, both activities require some positive investment in terms of time and energy and, given our finite amount of both, they cannot both be

---

23. Henry S. Richardson et al., *Social Progress: A Compass* (Cambridge: International Panel on Social Progress, 2017), 1–122, at 32.

satisfied. This conflict between our responsibility to live both moral and ethical lives is what I want to highlight as our predicament.

What we need, faced with this predicament, is a mechanism to mitigate its force in our lives. One such mechanism characteristic of much liberal moral theory is what we may call 'negative alignment': Individuals discharge their general moral duties by way of delegating them to institutions. With our obligation to satisfy general moral demands satisfied at the collective level, we are then each free to pursue our own projects and relationships—so long, of course, as exercising our 'personal prerogative' does not undermine this division of labor.[24]

My hypothesis about solidarity is that it amounts to a second, less frequently acknowledged mechanism to lessen the force of the predicament: The central idea is that through exercises of our will ('commitments'), we can *transform* general moral demands into something we then also have agent-relative, project- and relationship-given reasons to pursue. In contrast to the institutional strategy of a division of labor, I want to call this mechanism one of 'positive alignment.' My core hypothesis is that given solidarity's characteristics, its distinctive function consists in 'positive alignment.' When we commit to solidaristic action, we create a type of harmony between our reasons stemming, on the one hand, from general moral demands that apply to us and, on the other hand, from our self-chosen project and valuable interpersonal relationships. Once we have the idea of 'positive alignment' in focus, we can understand why solidarity has the features we have identified above as central to our practice, that is, we see why, in order to serve this function, it is imperative that solidarity is (i) commitment-based, (ii) cause-generated, (iii) expressive

---

24. Samuel Scheffler, *Equality and Tradition: Questions of Value in Moral and Political Theory* (Oxford: Oxford University Press, 2010) ch. 4.

of community or interpersonal unity, and (iv) transcends received notions of self-interest and altruism in an interesting way.

How Solidarity's Form Follows Its Function

Let us first reflect on why solidarity, in light of the function of 'positive alignment' I have proposed, requires an act of will or a commitment. This is not difficult to grasp: If solidarity helps us to transform acts we previously had only moral reason to perform into something that we also care about as our own valuable project, then it seems clear that some voluntary element should play a role. When we act in solidarity, we make some plight or adversity an object of special concern for us, and we do so through the mental act of committing ourselves.[25] Think of other, non-moral projects that make our life valuable: We form special relationships like friendships or love relations not by merely getting close to others and spending time with them, but through voluntary commitments to them.[26] Same when it comes to our significant autonomy-enhancing projects: Whether it is about being a good pianist, a professional biologist, or a recognized literary critic, such projects are more than just habitually repeated activities in which we find pleasure. Instead, they amount to long-term plans that structure our lives. We typically (though not always) *embark* on such projects as a result of our own choosing and, importantly, they remain our projects so long as, and because, we are committed to them.[27]

---

25. I explain the notion of commitment and its reason-generating force in more detail in Viehoff, "What's the Point of Solidarity?" (ms).
26. Ruth Chang, "Commitments, Reasons, and the Will," *Oxford Studies in Metaethics* 8 (2013): 74–113.
27. On projects, see: Samuel Scheffler, "Projects, Relationships, and Reasons," in *Reason and Value: Themes from the Philosophy of Joseph Raz*, ed. R Jay Wallace (Oxford: Oxford University Press, 2004), 247–269.

If solidarity has the function I described above, then it will naturally also require some form of commitment. Commitments can take two forms: We commit both to projects and to other people. Solidarity is typically a commitment to both of these in that we commit to a special relationship to a particular group of people based on a cause or goal (i.e., a project). Think of Yvonne: in committing to the project of ending farm exploitation in Central America, she also comes to see herself as standing in a special relationship to those individuals picked out by the project, as well as to those who have chosen this project as their own.

How does the second feature of paradigmatic solidarity, namely its unique *cause*-generated aspect, connect to the functionalist explanation? The point here is that, while the commitment element caters to our need to see solidarity as an expression of our autonomous agency, the fact that solidarity flows from a distinctive, morality-grounded cause caters to our responsibility to satisfy such moral demands. Because solidarity binds us to others with the goal of addressing a cause, it helps us to better comply with impersonal moral demands that apply to us. Think about it like this: If solidarity had no aim grounded in impersonal, moral demands, then it would not really amount to anything more than community with others. But we do not use it interchangeably with 'community.'

Let us turn to the third element of solidarity, namely community and unity with others. If we see ourselves as being in solidarity with some group characterized by some injustice or adversity, then we feel a special bond with those picked out by that characteristic. From the functionalist perspective I have adopted, what is the point of this sentiment? The idea is that developing such sentiments of closeness of unity with others helps us to alleviate the force of the predicament with which we started. On the one hand, forming close social bonds with others is typically valuable for our own self-realization: It makes our life go better to stand in relationships characterized by such phenomena as 'concern' or 'community,' provided they satisfy certain criteria. But what is special about the communal bond of 'fellows in solidarity' is that, unlike in the case of, say, friendship, those fellows in solidarity are selected in virtue of a distinctive solidarity cause. So while standing in relations of unity with others is valuable as such from a self-regarding perspective, it also becomes instrumentally valuable from a moral point of view. Why is that? A sense of community, I want to suggest, alleviates two standard problems we face when it comes to robustly pursuing moral aims.

The first problem is this: One barrier that often prevents people from continuously doing what is morally required is *motivational* fatigue: Even if we are in general motivated by moral concerns, we find it hard to continuously invest large amounts of our time and energy when we perceive such action as primarily serving the interests of others. But where the target of our actions is something or someone with which we identify in some special way, we typically find it much less odious to follow through. Solidarity, by requiring us to form a sense of unity with those whose injustice or suffering we have moral reason to address, draws us closer to them and thereby boosts our motivation to do what morality demands.

To understand the second reason why solidarity requires community to improve our moral performance, it is important to keep in mind that many of the instances of suffering and injustice that we find in the world leave us, as individuals, in a somewhat peculiar situation: While we *collectively* share a moral responsibility to address these issues, each single one of us will at most have an obligation to proactively fight some of them. But how should we pick the moral fights that we individually ought to fight when there are endless options, each giving rise to an imperfect duty to get involved? My suggestion is that through the act of committing to a particular group and forming community, we can, to some extent, engage in an act of 'rational bootstrapping': while our initial choice for some moral cause rather than some other may be idiosyncratic, this is no longer true once we have made a choice and, thereby, have established a form of special bond to those that it selects. This, I want to suggest, makes it rational, over time, to continue on this issue. By picking and committing to particular causes and then forming bonds of community with one's fellows, we avoid, at least to some extent, the difficulty of continuously being thrown back and forth between equally valid moral causes that pressure us into action.

This third element of solidarity (a sentiment of unity with others) also offers an inroad to understanding the taxonomical desiderata for solidarity, to wit, that we should be able to attribute it an interesting position in the continuum between self-interested and altruistic actions. Solidarity "transcends the dichotomy between self-interested and altruistic motivation" because we tag something that matters to how well our life goes for us (our projects and relationship) to moral demands that are grounded in the value of other people's well-being and agency.

HOW FUNCTIONALISM RESOLVES THE TWO CONCEPTUAL PUZZLES

I began this chapter with a twofold conceptual puzzle: First, what is it that all instances of solidarity, including those that contain sacrifices and those that do not, have in common (the *puzzle of (non-)sacrificial solidarity*)? Second, what explains that some cases of personal sacrifice do not intuitively register as cases of solidarity (the *puzzle of non-solidaristic sacrifice*)? Looking at the cases I have presented earlier, we can now answer this question based on the functionalist account of solidarity that I have presented as an alternative to motivation-based accounts: First, both sacrifice and non-sacrifice cases of solidarity realize solidarity's function of bringing into harmony reasons stemming from our ethical responsibility and from our moral responsibility. This solves the puzzle of sacrificial solidarity. Second, non-solidaristic sacrifice cases fail to be cases of solidarity because they do not realize this function to the same degree as those other cases. This solves the puzzle of non-solidaristic sacrifice. To vindicate this proposal, let us go back to the cases I presented and explain how the functionalist account categorizes each of them.

Intuitively, *Xenia* and *Yvonne* were both clear-cut cases of solidarity, even though they did not contain actual instances of sacrifice (both acted in their own best interest in doing what solidarity required). This, we now see, is the case because in each of them the agent combines ethical and moral responsibilities in a way that improves her performance on each score: In Yvonne's case, the agent chooses the agricultural laborers' cause as her own and thereby establishes a valuable personal project of her own that makes her life go better. So in virtue of realizing solidarity's function, we should say that this is a clear-cut case of solidarity. Though the case is slightly different because Xenia is a member of the group suffering from injustice, the same kind of reasoning applies here. Xenia faces two kinds of reasons in this situation: first, reasons of self-interest that instruct her to organize with others to end the harmful treatment by her unjust employer; second, reasons of justice or fairness to do her fair share in confronting the adversity they collectively face. As it happens, these reasons suggest the same course of action in the present situation (participate in the strike). But this need not be the case, and things could change quickly—recall the variation I proposed earlier where the employer, in order to sow discord, offers improved working conditions, but only to Xenia. Xenia turns into a person in solidarity with her fellow workers not as a result of going on strike, but as a result of committing to the moral cause and building a cause-generated sense of community with the other workers. Now that she has the commitment, her reasons are better aligned than they were before. For it is now true that even if she alone were offered the benefits, there would not be a conflict between self-interest and moral duty because she made the interests of her co-workers her own.

What should we say about the two cases that did contain sacrifice? Can the functionalist explanation of solidarity vindicate the idea that John McCain's decision to remain in the Vietnamese prison with other POWs amounted to an instance of solidarity, whereas Milton's choice to sacrifice his life for his fellow soldiers did not? I think it can. It turns out that for the functionalist account, classifying Milton's case as not one of solidarity is in fact not very hard at all: While his actions were clearly morally motivated and praiseworthy, they did not bring about greater harmony between his agent-relative perspective (his personal projects and relationships) and what would be best impersonally. While it is clearly morally good that only one soldiers died from the grenade, saving his comrades was not the course of action that allowed Milton to continue pursuing his projects and valuable relationships in any meaningful way. What cases like Milton show is that where the conflict between self-interest and the pursuit of morality-given aims is too stark, solidarity is simply not an option to be had. I think this insight not only helps to understand why we do not see Milton as a clear-cut case of solidarity, but also why we have such an intuition in somewhat different cases. Imagine, for example, that his fellow soldiers, once Milton jumped on the grenade, refuse to run for safety and, instead, opt to stay with him and equally suffer from the explosion. I submit that in this case, we are not inclined to talk of solidarity either because the sacrifice to each one's self-interest is so huge.

Now one might worry that there is a flipside to the ease with which the account I have put forward can rule out cases like *Milton* as instances of solidarity: wouldn't the same logic apply to *John*'s case and, therefore, lead to the conclusion that—contrary to the intuition I have relied on all along—we are not dealing with a case of solidarity here? I think we can avoid this classification. In order to do so, it is important to highlight the core differences between *John*'s case and *Milton*'s, focusing in particular on how their actions affect their projects and relationships. First, though, let me explain how John's actions do in fact serve some agent-neutral concern, for this may seem harder to grasp than the good that is realized through Milton's sacrifice. John's refusal to leave his fellow soldiers behind, one might think, fails to advance any goal dictated by morality. And if it does not, then it could not be an action through which John resolves a potential conflict between projects and relationships and these agent-neutral demands. My suggestion is that even though John's refusal to leave is not *morally required* and does not *benefit* anybody, it nonetheless realizes something that is impersonally valuable. By analogy, think of acts of futile resistance to an unjust tyrant where those resisting know that their fight is a lost cause. I would submit that, despite their futility, such resistance achieves something valuable; it makes the world a better place because *some* people appropriately responded to the tyrant's evil acts. A similar thought, it seems to me, can explain why John's refusal, both an act of protest against the injustice suffered by his fellow POWs and a gesture of standing in a kind of egalitarian community with them, realizes impersonal value.

This leaves open the question of how John's sacrifice differs from Milton's, specifically, how his, but not Milton's, sacrifice can be seen to make a (sufficiently) positive contribution to John's personal (project- and relationship-given) reasons. One first thing to note is that whether or not something counts as making a positive contribution to our life depends in part on the projects and relationships we care about. When I choose ultra-marathon running as my project, then the pain that realizing this project contains may not significantly make my life worse for me. My suggestion here is that even though his refusal to be released did cost him dearly in terms of well-being, it also allowed him to uphold—and arguably deepen—a powerful bond of comradery with his fellow POWs. Put differently, there is a sensible perspective from which, in retrospect, John can stand up and talk to his fellow POWs and from which he can now claim, sitting back home, that "I did it for *us*!" This, it seems to me, constitutes to a fundamental difference from Milton, whose ultimate sacrifice cannot be rationalized in terms of a first-personal 'We' but only as an instance of giving oneself for the sake of others.

CONCLUSION

The goal of this chapter was to investigate what cases of significant personal sacrifice can teach us about the nature of solidarity. In a first step, I suggested that some prominent account of solidarity's nature, namely those that attempt to reveal its conceptual core through a detailed analysis of the specific motives and attitudes with which an agent must act, cannot explain why some but not other cases of personal sacrifice count as instances of solidarity. In a second step, I proposed an alternative approach to explaining solidarity, namely one that draws on the idea that 'form follows function': solidaritistic practices serve as distinctive human need, and we should categorize something as an instance of solidarity by reference to how well it realizes the stated function, which I identified as that of creating 'positive alignment' between or project- and relationship-given personal reasons and the impersonal demands of general morality. In a third step, I showed how the functionalist explanation meets the intuitive data points laid out in the beginning. Clearly, my methodological approach requires a much more elaborate defense than I have been able to provide here. And even if successful, there are certainly other functions to which one could appeal in thinking about solidarity, yielding different criteria for assessing the centrality of different cases. But I hope that, at least for the limited case of solidaristic and non-solidaristic sacrifices, my explanation has been shown to be more convincing than existing alternatives.

Chapter 6

Transforming Interdependence into Social Virtue

Solidarity in Catholic Social Thought

MEGHAN J. CLARK

Catholic social thought (CST) is a current incarnation of Roman Catholicism's official moral reflection on contemporary social, political, and economic questions. Over the past sixty years, amidst growing recognition of globalization and interdependence, solidarity has emerged as a central and constitutive touchstone for how CST both interprets and challenges contemporary society. This chapter will examine the way in which CST proposes solidarity as a social virtue and calls for transforming interdependence into communities of solidarity. First, looking at Pope Francis's response to the Covid-19 pandemic, it will begin with a brief primer on CST to contextualize and locate solidarity. Second, it will examine the development of solidarity from an attitude and duty to a virtue within the tradition. And finally, this chapter will examine Pope Francis's *Fratelli Tutti* and its examination of the Good Samaritan as one way in which

CST's approach to solidarity contributes to the broader global moral imagination.

COVID CATECHESIS: A PRIMER ON CATHOLIC SOCIAL THOUGHT

On January 3, 2020, China notified the World Health Organization of an outbreak of a new coronavirus (Covid-19). By March 11, 2020, the United Nations reported that an estimated 20% of schoolchildren worldwide were out of school and the WHO officially declared the Covid-19 outbreak a pandemic. As of November 23, 2023, there have been more than 772 million confirmed cases globally and over 6.9 million deaths.[1] From 2020 through December 2023, the United States had confirmed more than 103 million case with over 1.14 million cumulative deaths. On August 5, 2020, Pope Francis launched an eight-week series of reflections on Catholic social teaching in light of the ongoing pandemic. These brief messages provide a succinct and helpful primer into the method, function, and core content of Catholic social teaching. Focusing on these messages, this section will offer a brief summary of CST as a moral framework in order to situate its specific approach to the virtue of solidarity. The moral framework of CST centers around a series of intersecting ethical principles: the dignity of the human person, the common good, the preferential option for the poor, the universal destination of goods, subsidiarity, care of our common home (formerly framed as stewardship), and that which is the focus of this volume, solidarity.

---

1. Covid-19 data all from: WHO coronavirus (Covid-19) dashboard, https://covid19.who.int/.

Often lamented as Catholicism's *best kept secret*,[2] Catholic social teaching is the Catholic Church's official public moral reflection on contemporary global social realities. Since the first Christian communities, churches have always sought to apply the Gospel to the social and economic context within which they lived.[3] In different formats and with varying strengths and weaknesses, Christian theologians and churches have actively engaged in ongoing moral reflection on the social, economic, and political contexts continuously throughout history. Beginning in 1891, modern Catholic social teaching is one particular sub-tradition within this broader social tradition. As the Industrial Revolution rapidly changed economic realities of how people worked and lived, there were dynamic calls for the dignity of work among young people (most notably the Young Christian Workers), growing unions (or worker associations like the Knights of Labor in the US), and individual leaders across Europe and the United States. In Europe, Cardinal Manning (England), Frederick Ozanam (France), and Bishop von Kettler (Germany) wrote and organized on behalf of workers' rights. Firmly upholding the rights of workers to form unions, as well as the good of private property, Pope Leo XIII issued the encyclical *Rerum Novarum*, literally "of new things," given the English title, *On the Condition of Labor*.[4] With this encyclical, Leo XIII sparked a tradition of papal social teaching, that continues today. Over the last 130 years, Catholic social teaching has

---

2. Catchphrase originated in the 1970s with Peter Henriot, SJ. In addition to his book so titled, it has continuously been invoked by advocates of CST. Forty years later, scholars and advocates still lament a seeming lack of familiarity among the faithful of the CST tradition.

3. Earlier Christian moral reflection continues to be source for modern Catholic social teaching today. For example, *Fratelli Tutti* cites the work of Thomas Aquinas, John Chrysostom, and others from the patristic and medieval periods.

4. For more information, see Thomas A. Shannon, "Commentary on Rerum Novarum (The Condition of Labor)" in *Modern Catholic Social Teaching: Commentaries and Interpretations*, 2nd edition, ed. Kenneth R. Himes et al. (Washington, DC: Georgetown University press, 2018), 133–157.

largely centered around papal encyclicals, augmented by other magisterial teachings from episcopal conferences, papal audiences, and in 2005 a "social catechism": the *Compendium of the Social Doctrine of the Church*.[5]

Methodologically, CST aims at deep contextuality and responsiveness to the historical moment while also drawing upon and contributing to a much broader tradition of moral principles. *Rerum Novarum* urges: "Nothing is more useful than to look upon the world as it really is, and at the same time to seek elsewhere . . . for the solace to its troubles."[6] Thus, it is imperative for CST to seek out and engage concrete and accurate data not only from theology but from the social sciences, politics, science, and at times, medicine. Over time, this method becomes increasingly systematic. In 1961, Pope John XXIII formally incorporated Pierre Cardjin and the Young Christian Worker's approach and shorthand: *see-judge-act*.[7] See: observe the world as it truly is; judge: engage in moral discernment using Catholic social tradition; and act: then Christians will be able to determine actions to further justice in the world. This is the method of CST succinctly demonstrated by Pope Francis's Covid Catechesis series. In introducing the series, he notes that the church "is not an expert in the prevention or the cure of the pandemic"; however, he continues, "nevertheless, over the centuries, and by the light of the Gospel the Church has developed several social principles which are fundamental . . . that can help us move forward in preparing the future that we

---

5. Pontifical Council for Justice and Peace, *Compendium of the Social Doctrine of the Church* (2005).
6. Leo XIII, *Rerum Novarum*, 18 http://www.vatican.va/content/leo-xiii/en/encyclicals/documents/hf_l-xiii_enc_15051891_rerum-novarum.html.
7. Kevin Ahern, *Structures of Grace: Catholic Organizations and the Global Common Good* (Maryknoll, NY: Obis, 2015), 66–73.

need."[8] While the primary audience is believers, CST also simultaneously seeks to engage all people of goodwill.

The coronavirus pandemic provides a concrete moment of crisis within which to examine human vulnerability, inequality, and a commitment to human dignity. The principle of human dignity is the basis for all the theological and philosophical claims within CST. Its moral vision begins with its philosophical and theological anthropology: the human person as created in the image and likeness of God (Genesis 1:27). Drawing on a Thomistic natural law tradition, CST understands all human persons to be created equal and endowed with freedom and rationality, called "to live in communion with our brothers and sisters, with respect for all creation."[9] As Francis notes, "in modern culture, the closest reference to the principle of inalienable dignity of the person is the Universal Declaration of Human Rights. . . . Rights are not only individual, but also social; they are of peoples, nations."[10] Explaining human dignity within the broader human rights tradition, Francis engages both believers and nonbelievers to work together to combat the coronavirus and "to commit ourselves seriously and actively to combat indifference in the face of violations of human dignity," which did not begin nor will they end with the pandemic.

CST recognizes that prioritizing human dignity has deep political, social, and economic import for all aspects of our social lives. The Covid-19 pandemic, "while it does not distinguish between people it has found, in its devastating path, great inequalities and

---

8. Francis, "To Heal the World: 1. Introduction," August 5, 2020, http://www.vatican.va/content/francesco/en/audiences/2020/documents/papa-francesco_20200805_udienza-generale.html.
9. Francis, "To Heal the World: 2. Faith and Human Dignity," August 12, 2020, http://www.vatican.va/content/francesco/en/audiences/2020/documents/papa-francesco_20200812_udienza-generale.html.
10. Francis, "To Heal the World: 2. Faith and Human Dignity."

discrimination. And it has exacerbated them!" Thus, the priority of human dignity leads directly into what CST calls the preferential option for the poor and vulnerable. Ultimately, as Christine Firer Hinze notes, "solidarity and the option for the poor disclose the very identity of the church."[11] If one holds equal and universal human dignity of every person, practically that demands particular concern for those whose dignity is most ignored or violated.[12] Examining the scandal of poverty, Bryan Massingale explains, "because what they possess is undesirable and they don't possess much, and can't get more, the poor are literally and figuratively 'worthless'—unwanted, unnecessary, and expendable. In a consumer society, the poor are at best, irrelevant; at worst they are a burden."[13] It is precisely this precarious nature of human dignity that leads Pope Francis to strongly condemn a *throwaway culture* of *globalized indifference* in which "human beings are themselves considered consumer goods to be used and then discarded."[14]

The Covid-19 pandemic is a crisis which acts as a spotlight revealing the vulnerabilities, inequality, and weaknesses already present. For example, in the United States, communities grappling with higher rates of poverty and racial discrimination are significantly more vulnerable to hospitalization and death from Covid-19. Native Americans are 4.0 times more likely to be hospitalized than White non-Hispanic persons and 2.6 times more likely to die of the virus. Additionally, Black or African-Americans are 3.7 times more likely

---

11. Christine Firer Hinze, "Over, Under, Around, and Through: Ethics, Solidarity, and the Saints," *CTSA Proceedings* 66 (2011): 33–60; 35.
12. See *Gustavo Gutierrez: Essential Writings*, ed. James Nickoloff (Minneapolis, MN: Fortress, 1996).
13. Bryan Massingale, "The Scandal of Poverty: 'Cultural Indifference' and the Option for the Poor Post-Katrina," *Journal of Religion and Society* Supplement Series 4 (2008): 58.
14. Pope Francis, *Evangelii Gaudium* (2013), 7, http://www.vatican.va/content/francesco/en/apost_exhortations/documents/papa-francesco_esortazione-ap_20131124_evangelii-gaudium.html.

to be hospitalized and 2.8 times more likely to die from Covid-19.[15] Infectious diseases exacerbate existing vulnerabilities and injustices; thus, health and human rights scholar Dr. Paul Farmer has argued that the diseases themselves make a preferential option for the poor and we need to respond accordingly.[16] Within CST, Francis highlights the preferential option for the poor to "inspire us to conceive of and design an economy where people, and especially the poorest, are at the centre."[17]

Similarly, thinking through the commitment to universal human dignity, the next principle is the principle of the universal destination of goods, which holds that the goods of creation are meant for the flourishing of all. Reflecting back upon the creation narratives in Genesis, CST holds that both the bounty of and responsibility for the goods of the earth belong to all persons. Like human dignity, this is a primary principle of CST from which other more specific clarifications emerge. In particular, private property is considered a derived or secondary principle of the universal destination of goods.[18] Within the context of the pandemic, the principle of the universal destination of goods applies not only to economic matters but epidemiological ones. Progressively, CST builds from the priority of universal human dignity through the preferential option for the poor and the universal destination of goods, to the principle of solidarity, in which humanity faces the pandemic together or not at all. While solidarity will be examined in great detail later in this chapter, here I simply

---

15. CDC data, https://stacks.cdc.gov/view/cdc/99332.
16. Paul Farmer, *Pathologies of Power: Health, Human Rights and the New War on the Poor* (Berkley, CA: University of California Press, 2005).
17. Francis "To Heal the World: Option for the Poor and Charity" (August 19, 2020), http://www.vatican.va/content/francesco/en/audiences/2020/documents/papa-francesco_20200819_udienza-generale.html.
18. Franics, *Laudato Si'* (2015), 93, http://www.vatican.va/content/francesco/en/encyclicals/documents/papa-francesco_20150524_enciclica-laudato-si.html.

note where it falls within Pope Francis's approach in his primer on CST and response to the pandemic.

Pope Francis's moral response to the Covid-19 pandemic develops with a concerted focus on upholding human dignity, not simply in the general sense, but particularly the dignity of those otherwise ignored, excluded, or denigrated by existing systems of power. Similarly, the theological anthropology of CST holds that human persons are also inherently social; therefore, concern for the common good is an intersecting yet twin foundational principle alongside human dignity. "In CST, society has been viewed as an organic unity," explains Agnes Brazal, "a body with different parts but still one."[19] Somewhat diffuse and easily misunderstood, Vatican II explains that "the common good embraces the sum total of all those conditions of social life which enable individuals, families, and organizations to achieve complete and effective fulfillment."[20] Rejecting both utilitarian and collectivist understandings of the common good, within CST, "the common good requires everyone's participation."[21] In *Evangelii Gaudium*, Francis explained the deep and universal inclusivity of the common good: "It is the convergence of peoples who, within the universal order, maintain their own individuality; it is the sum total of persons within a society which pursues the common good, which truly has a place for everyone."[22]

Within the context of Covid-19, Francis urges approaching health within the context of the common good such that health is

---

19. Agnes Brazal, "East Asian Discourses on Harmony: A Mediation for Catholic Social Teaching," in *Catholic Social Teaching in Global Perspective*, ed. Dan McDonald (Maryknoll, NY: Orbis, 2010), 118–146; 132.
20. Vatican II, *Gaudium et Spes* (1965), 74. https://www.vatican.va/archive/hist_councils/ii_vatican_council/documents/vat-ii_const_19651207_gaudium-et-spes_en.html.
21. Francis, "Healing the World: Love and the Common Good" (September 9, 2020), http://www.vatican.va/content/francesco/en/audiences/2020/documents/papa-francesco_20200909_udienza-generale.html.
22. Francis, *Evangelii Gaudium*, 236.

viewed as a public good and "to build a healthy, inclusive, just and peaceful society we must do so on the rock of the common good."[23] Methodologically, the principle of the common good should be interpreted within the context of CST's overarching method and scope. In place of specific policies, David Hollenbach posits that the principle of the common good offers three strategic priorities, "1. The needs of the poor take priority over the wants of the rich; 2. The freedom of the dominated takes priority over the liberty of the powerful; 3. The participation of the marginalized takes priority over the perseveration of an order that excludes them."[24] It proposes neither a scientific formula for a vaccine nor a political program for vaccine distribution. Instead, it prompts moral discernment and establishes criteria by which to evaluate any public health, social protection, or vaccine distribution program.

Linked to the common good, CST's concern for the environment has been reframed by Francis as the principle of care of the common home, which incorporates environmental stewardship and sustainability.[25] While CST, as examined here, has a decidedly anthropocentric thrust, care for our common home simultaneously emphasizes both the dignity of non-human creation and positions human beings as inseparably part of creation.[26] Condemning the sin of "exploiting creation" in which "we become predators, forgetting our vocation as custodians," Francis emphasizes that "we are inside nature, we are

---

23. Francis, "Healing the World: Love and the Common Good."
24. David Hollenbach, *Common Good and Christian Ethics* (Cambridge: Cambridge University Press, 2002), 195.
25. While outside the scope of this chapter, the principle of care of our common home is the component of CST to which Francis has contributed most greatly to the CST tradition as his encyclical *Laudato Si': On the Care of Our Common Home* centered the ecological crisis and its effects on both planet and people as an urgent moral crisis.
26. Creation is a theological concept but in this context is inclusive of the earth as well as the wider universe of existence.

part of nature."[27] The wider lens of future generations and moral obligations of solidarity and intergenerational justice intersect not only with questions of the common good but care of the common home. In particular, Francis expands the lens of solidarity to include all of creation into a "new and universal solidarity" linking the virtue of solidarity and the principle of care of our common home.[28]

Thus far CST comprises moral principles that can seem somewhat idealistic and aspirational. Human dignity and the common good (and by extension solidarity as well) aim the moral imagination toward a theological and philosophical anthropology in which human persons, as individuals and communities, flourish. The option for the poor and universal destination of goods pull that moral imagination back toward eliminating inequalities and vulnerabilities. The final principle, subsidiarity, is of a different type. Fundamentally an instrumental principle, subsidiarity is a principle designed to practically guide moral discernment for implementing the other principles and navigating conflicts between individuals and groups in society. Influenced by CST, the principle of subsidiarity was codified in the charter of the European Union as that which "ensures that decisions are taken as closely as possible to the citizen and that constant checks are made to verify that action at Union level is justified in light of the possibilities available at national, regional or local level."[29]

Developed by CST, the principle of subsidiarity states that "a community of higher order should not interfere with the life of a community of a lower order, taking over its functions. In the case of

---

27. Francis, "Heal the World: Care of our common home and the contemplative dimension" (September 16, 2020), http://www.vatican.va/content/francesco/en/audiences/2020/documents/papa-francesco_20200916_udienza-generale.html.
28. Pope Francis, *Laudato Si'* (2015), 14. http://w2.vatican.va/content/francesco/en/encyclicals/documents/papa-francesco_20150524_enciclica-laudato-si.html.
29. European Union. *Glossary of Terms*, "subsidiarity," http://europa.eu/legislation_summaries/glossary/subsidiarity_en.htm (accessed August 2013).

need it should, rather, support the smaller community and to help coordinate its activities in the rest of society for the common good."[30] As Francis notes, "this principle has a double movement . . . there is a collaboration from the top to the bottom, from the central State to the people, and from the bottom to the top: from the institutions of the people to the top. . . . To emerge better from a crisis, the principle of subsidiarity must be implemented, respecting everyone's autonomy and capacity to take initiative, especially that of the least."[31] Concerned with both forms of socialism or collectivism (where the state takes over all functions) and libertarianism or other forms individualism (which denies the proper role of larger communities and the common good), CST uses subsidiarity to argue that all levels of human society have a role in contributing to the common good.[32]

In urging global collaboration in the midst of the pandemic, Francis implores, "either we work together to emerge from the crisis, at all levels of society, or we will never emerge from it . . . and true change is done by everyone, all the persons that form a people."[33] Finally, the Covid catechesis message on subsidiarity circles back around to solidarity, reminding that practicing solidarity occurs when "we are taking the path of subsidiarity." This examination of Pope Francis's application of CST to the Covid-19 pandemic offers a brief primer on the method and principles of Catholic social teaching as background for examining the virtue of solidarity.

---

30. John Paul II, *Centesimus Annus (On the Hundredth Year)* (1991), 48, http://w2.vatican.va/content/john-paul-ii/en/encyclicals/documents/hf_jp-ii_enc_01051991_centesimus-annus.html (accessed June 2015).
31. Francis, "Heal the World: Subsidiarity and the Virtue of Hope" (September 23, 2020), http://www.vatican.va/content/francesco/en/audiences/2020/documents/papa-francesco_20200923_udienza-generale.html.
32. Francis, *Laudato Si'* (2015), 196.
33. Francis, "Heal the World: Subsidiarity and the Virtue of Hope."

TRANSFORMING INTERDEPENDENCE INTO SOLIDARITY: DEVELOPING A SOCIAL VIRTUE

Solidarity has become a dominant and elastic moral frame for grappling with the nuance and complexity of the globalized reality of human communities.[34] As Gerald Beyer notes, "The reality of interdependence should have ethical implications for all human interactions in the economic, cultural, political, and religious spheres of social life."[35] CST's answer is an evolving ethic of solidarity. The *Compendium of the Social Doctrine of the Church* offers the following definition: "Solidarity highlights in a particular way the intrinsic social nature of the human person, the equality of all in dignity and rights and the common path of individuals and peoples towards an ever more committed unity."[36] Identified as an attitude, a duty, a principle, and culminating in its status as a moral virtue in which persons and communities make "a firm and persevering determination to commit oneself to the common good; that is to say the good of all and of each individual because we are all really responsible for all."[37] As one can see, a concise definition does not quite seem to capture that to which solidarity aims, which is an adequate moral response to interdependence.

---

34. For more detail on the development of solidarity in CST, see Gerald Beyer, "The Meaning of Solidarity in Catholic Social Teaching," *Political Theology* 15, no. 1 (2014): 7–25, Marie Vianney Bilgrien, *Solidarity: A Principle, an Attitude, a Duty or the Virtue for an Independent World?* (New York: Peter Lang, 1999). Meghan J. Clark, *The Vision of Catholic Social Thought: the Virtue of Solidarity and the Praxis of Human Rights* (Minneapolis, MN: Fortress, 2014),
35. Beyer, "The Meaning of Solidarity," 15.
36. Pontifical Council for Justice and Peace, *Compendium of the Social Doctrine of the Church* (2005), 192, http://www.vatican.va/roman_curia/pontifical_councils/justpeace/documents/rc_pc_justpeace_doc_20060526_compendio-dott-soc_en.html.
37. John Paul II, *Sollicitudo Rei Socialis* (December 30, 1987) 38, http://www.vatican.va.

While Pius XII is the first pope to use the word "solidarity," it is John XXIII who introduces it into modern CST.[38] In *Mater et Magistra*, St. John XXIII invokes the growing "spirit of solidarity" among rural agriculture workers as a natural outgrowth of the Catholic social tradition's support for worker associations (*MM* 146, *MM* 23).[39] Both John XXIII and Paul VI point out a growing "spirit of solidarity" born out of the recognition of increasing interdependence and globalization. This development was influenced as well by the work of Henrich Pesch, SJ, and Oswald von Nell-Bruening, SJ (who worked on the drafting of *Quadragesimo Anno*). Both Pesch and Nell-Breuning, notes Beyer, "bequeathed CST with an understanding of solidarity as anthropological 'datum' (i.e. 'factual solidarity') and as a normative obligation governing interpersonal relations, as well as social, political, legal, and economic institutions."[40] It is also worth noting that prior to John XXIII, the word "solidarity" was sometimes viewed with suspicion within European Catholic circles as potentially problematic given historical connections to the French Revolution and, in the modern period, to socialism.[41] At the same time, the concept of solidarity also took root in Latin America through the work of El Consejo Episcopal Latinoamericano y Caribeño (CELAM) and theologians emphasizing the connection between solidarity and the option for the poor.[42] Additionally, explains Gerald Beyer, "the

---

38. Beyer, "The Meaning of Solidarity," 9. In his 1939 encyclical Summi Pontificatus, he argues "the first page of Scripture" (Gen. 1:26–27) undergirds the law of "human solidarity and charity," revealing our common origin and that all human beings are created in the image of God.
39. John XXIII, *Mater et Magistra* (May 15, 1961), 23, 146, http://w2.vatican.va/content/john-xxiii/en/encyclicals/documents/hf_j-xxiii_enc_15051961_mater.html.
40. Beyer, "The Meaning of Solidarity," 13.
41. For more on this history, see Steinar Stjernø, *Solidarity in Europe: The History of an Idea* (Cambridge: Cambridge University Press, 2005), 75–85.
42. Bilgrien, *Solidarity*, 49. See also Oscar Romero, *Voice of the Voiceless: The Four Pastoral Letters and Other Statements* (Maryknoll, NY: Orbis, 1985); Jon Sobrino and Hernandez, *Theology of Christian Solidarity* (Maryknoll, NY: Orbis, 1985).

Solidarność movement's struggle for freedom in John Paul's native Poland provided the crucible in which many of his ideas about solidarity were born."[43]

Interdependence, for CST, is both an observable condition as well as a moral question connected to issues of human dignity. The full and equal human dignity of each individual person provides a base foundation for solidarity; as Paul VI explains, "there can be no progress toward the complete development of man without the development of all humanity in the spirit of solidarity."[44] This is the first context of solidarity—interdependence and a growing sense of interconnectedness within the global community.[45] For CST, all persons are called to reflect upon interdependence within the framework of our universal and equal human dignity and the concept of "one human family." CST identifies this as an awareness, spirit, or attitude of solidarity. As Kevin Doran notes, "When the solidarity of a person is described as an attitude, it has a significance which has to do primarily with its outward direction towards other persons, their needs, and the structures of society within which they are called to be and to act."[46] This emerging sense recognizes, as Saji George Kochutha notes, "Injustice done anywhere in the globalized world will adversely affect peace, harmony, and development in other parts of the world. Globalization leads to real development only when it is sought in solidarity."[47] When Paul VI links the development of the individual to the development of all humanity, he envisions human

---

43. Beyer, "The Meaning of Solidarity," 14. See also Gerald Beyer, *Recovering Solidarity: Lessons from Poland's Unfinished Revolution* (South Bend, IN: University of Notre Dame Press, 2010
44. Paul VI, *Populorum Progressio* (1967), 43. https://www.vatican.va/content/paul-vi/en/encyclicals/documents/hf_p-vi_enc_26031967_populorum.html.
45. Vatican II, *Gaudium et Spes*, 4.
46. Kevin P. Doran, *Solidarity: A Synthesis of Personalism and Communalism in the Thought of Karol Wojtyla / Pope John Paul II* (New York: Peter Lang, 1996), 191.
47. Shaji George Kochuthara, "Globalization in Solidarity," *Political Theology* 15, no. 1 (2014): 53–73; 62

flourishing as something expansive and inclusive. Each and every human person living now and in future generations is included. There is a harmony envisioned: "the concept of solidarity presupposes that society is a community of diverse elements where all are called to cooperate together for the common good."[48]

Human dignity, as it is understood in CST, is both gift and responsibility. Theologically, Anna Rowlands notes, "Believing that we live within an unfolding economy of salvation means that dignity is something seen as something we *possess* and something we *become*. Dignity is something we can seriously debase in ourselves or for others but it is not something we can fundamentally lose or completely alienate."[49] In his philosophical writings, Karol Wojtyla explained, "as human beings we are capable of participation in the very humanity of other people, and because of this every human being can become our neighbor" and that "a human being finds fulfillment of himself by adding to the fulfillment of others."[50] Marie Vianney Bilgrien argues that "compassion, empathy, and mercy move solidarity into action and help sustain the disposition."[51] One challenge is to distinguish solidarity from other virtues like justice and charity within the tradition. This is not aided by a propensity of popes to use words like "love," "charity," "social friendship," and even "solidarity" as if interchangeable within Catholic social encyclicals.[52] A hallmark of human dignity, as specifically foundational for solidarity, is the dialogical

---

48. Brazal, "East Asian Discourses on Harmony," 132.
49. Anna Rowlands, *Towards a Politics of Communion: Catholic Social Teaching in Dark Times* (London: T&T Clark, 2021), 55.
50. Karol Wojtyla/John Paul II, *Toward a Philosophy of Praxis: An Anthology*, ed. Alfred Bloch and George T. Czuczka (New York: Crossroads, 1981), 49.
51. Bilgrien, *Solidarity*, 105–106.
52. John Paul II does this in *Centesimus Annus* 10: "This principle is frequently stated by Pope Leo XIII, who uses the term 'friendship,' a concept already found in Greek philosophy. Pope Pius XI refers to it with the equally meaningful term 'social charity.' Pope Paul VI, expanding the concept to cover the many modern aspects of the social question, speaks of a 'civilization of love.'"

possibilities of human agency. In the process of becoming "neighbor" in solidarity we each become more fully human together. Thus, the scope of human dignity within the horizon of solidarity reveals "a duty of all towards all."[53] While it is not fully fleshed out, there is a conscious mutuality and reciprocity of human dignity with respect to one's positionality that is one element characteristic of solidarity that is not simply identical with charity, social friendship, or justice.[54]

Without the equality and universality of human dignity, notes Charles Taylor, the rhetoric of solidarity becomes easily twisted so that "we feel a sense of moral satisfaction and superiority when we contemplate others."[55] This danger is particularly acute in the aid from the Global North to the Global South that claims solidarity but in which the rhetoric of solidarity masks bias and attitudes of superiority. At the same time, there is a danger if the emphasis on universality fails to appreciate cultural context, notes Agbonkhanmeghe Orobator. Catholic social teaching encyclicals "presume a common understanding" of solidarity, which "in situations of desperation, calamity, and impoverishment" is ethically significant; "yet we may not ignore the possibility that the appeal to the notion of solidarity can assume specific nuances depending on the particular cultural context, the outcomes of which may be ethically problematic."[56]

A second step in CST's development of solidarity requires identifying and clarifying our responsibilities for others and "a desire to make the conditions of life more favorable to all."[57] Practically, John Paul II identified "the need for a solidarity which will take up

---

53. John Paul II, *Sollicitudo Rei Socialis* (1987), 32. https://www.vatican.va/content/john-paul-ii/en/encyclicals/documents/hf_jp-ii_enc_30121987_sollicitudo-rei-socialis.html.
54. For more on this, see Clark, *Vision of Catholic Social Thought*.
55. Charles Taylor, *A Secular Age* (Cambridge, MA: Belknap Press, 2007), 696.
56. Agbonkhanmeghe E. Orobator, SJ, "Caritas in Veritate and Africa's Burden of (Under) Development," *Theological Studies* 71 (2010): 328.
57. Vatican II, *Gaudium et Spes*, 57.

interdependence and transfer it to the moral plane."[58] For this reason, the recognition of interdependence alone is not sufficient for an ethic of solidarity, for "when this interdependence is separated from its ethical requirements, it has disastrous consequences for the weakest."[59] Identifying the lure of selfishness, Francis notes in discussing the pandemic that "there is a long journey between interdependence and solidarity."[60] Most of the Catholic social tradition in the past sixty years has focused on developing the theory and application of these first two aspects: the descriptive awareness of interdependence and the normative obligations for all which flow from it. David Hollenbach notes, "Solidarity leads members of a community to recognize their well-being is shared. The relationships linking them with other members of the 'we' are themselves key aspects of the common good they share."[61]

The synthesis of the above culminates in solidarity as a virtue applying to both individuals and communities. As such, the common good is present "in a community of solidarity among active equal agents," explains Hollenbach, and "when these relationships form reciprocal ties among equals, the solidarity achieved" should be considered as "a good that cannot otherwise exist."[62] In *Sollicitudo Rei Socialis*, John Paul II defined the virtue of solidarity "as a firm and persevering determination to commit oneself to the common good; that is to say the good of all and of each individual because we are all really responsible for all."[63] In order for solidarity to be a virtue, it must be

---

58. John Paul II, *Sollicitudo Rei Socialis* (1987), 26.
59. Ibid., 17.
60. Francis, "Heal the World: Solidarity and the Virtue of Faith" (September 2, 2020), http://www.vatican.va/content/francesco/en/audiences/2020/documents/papa-francesco_20200902_udienza-generale.html.
61. David Hollenbach, SJ, "The Glory of God and the Global Common Good: Solidarity in a Turbulent World," *CTSA Proceedings* 72 (2017): 51–60; 56.
62. Hollenbach, *Common Good and Christian Ethics*, 189.
63. John Paul II, *Sollicitudo Rei Socialis* (1987), 38.

practiced. It must be learned.[64] Solidarity is not a preexisting condition, nor is it automatic; it must be freely chosen and actively built. The virtue of solidarity is both personal and communal. As Uzochukwa Jude Njoku notes, "solidarity requires a balanced understanding of the personal and the social (structural). Both ought to regulate the other . . . [and challenge] the structural to create such enabling conditions that promote the dignity of each person."[65] As I have argued elsewhere, "for solidarity, the formal object is our common humanity. The end of solidarity is participation in the universal common good. To be more specific, it is the participation by all in the universal common good."[66] The practices by which one habituates the virtue of solidarity is by practicing respect for human dignity and human rights.[67] The combination of human agency, human dignity, and human rights are mutually essential to achieve solidarity.

Practically, participation is key: "Active participation is required in order for the equality, mutuality, and reciprocity of human dignity to be present."[68] Duties of solidarity cannot be one directional. As Gerald Beyer argues, "Participation in Catholic social thought denotes a substantive contribution to society; it is not just a formal, procedural task to be valued in abstract from the ends served by it."[69] Thus, in addressing the Covid-19 pandemic, Francis insists, "this is everyone's task, not only that of a few specialists. Saint Thomas Aquinas used to say that the promotion of the common good is a duty of justice that falls on every citizen. Every citizen is responsible

---

64. Clark, *Vision of Catholic Social Thought*, 111–124.
65. Uzochukwu Njoku, "Re-thinking Solidarity as a Principle of Catholic Social Teaching: Going Beyond *Gaudium et Spes* and the Social Encyclicals of John Paul II," *Political Theology* 9:4 (2008): 525–544; 540.
66. Clark, *Vision of Catholic Social Thought*, 112–113.
67. Ibid.
68. Meghan J. Clark, "Anatomy of a Social Virtue," *Political Theology* 15, no. 1 (2014): 26–39; 30
69. Beyer, "The Meaning of Solidarity," 17.

for the common good."⁷⁰ Solidarity, like the common good, does not admit the possibility of excluding or sacrificing any individual or group.

Participation is crucial to understanding the virtue of solidarity's relationship to both justice and subsidiarity. Justice is a basic requirement, for as Benedict XVI notes in *Caritas in Veritate*, "I cannot 'give' what is mine to the other, without first giving him what pertains to him in justice. If we love others with charity, then first of all we are just towards them."⁷¹ Where justice is aimed at our duty to the other, solidarity "is based on the recognition that in the violation of another's human rights, my own are at stake. In a real way, the denial of another's human dignity is a denial of my own."⁷² Francis's own development of CST's understanding of our common humanity is influenced by *ubuntu* theology and the work of Desmond Tutu.⁷³

The principle of subsidiarity is practically important for developing the social virtue of solidarity. Reflecting on the pandemic, Francis notes, "there is no true solidarity without social participation, without the contribution of intermediary bodies: families, associations, cooperatives, small businesses, and other expressions of society. Everyone needs to contribute, everyone."⁷⁴ Subsidiarity offers a practical guide for living out a social virtue within many levels of community, from one's family to the one human family. According to CST, participation lived out via the virtue of solidarity resists the throwaway culture and negative aspects of the often faceless but powerful negative consequences of globalization. Given the reality of social media and

---

70. Francis, "Healing the World: Love and the Common Good" (September 9, 2020).
71. Benedict XVI, *Caritas in Veritate* (2009), 6, http://w2.vatican.va/content/benedict-xvi/en/encyclicals/documents/hf_ben-xvi_enc_20090629_caritas-in-veritate.html.
72. Clark, *Vision of Catholic Social Thought*, 123.
73. Agbonkhanmeghe E. Orobator, "Fratelli Tutti Is Ubuntu by Any Other Name," *National Catholic Reporter* (October 6, 2020), https://www.ncronline.org/news/opinion/fratelli-tutti-ubuntu-any-other-name.
74. Francis, "Heal the World: Subsidiarity and the Virtue of Hope" (September 23, 2020).

increasing digital consumerism, Vincent Miller's cautions against seeing "virtual solidarity" as sufficient for the virtue in which the digital or virtual becomes "a substitute for concrete political solidarity," which must be lived as an embodied reality is even more important.[75]

WHO IS MY NEIGHBOR? SOLIDARITY AND GLOBAL OBLIGATIONS IN 2020

The global pandemic is merely one crisis faced by the global community in 2020. Amidst ongoing ecological crisis and migration crisis, a particular threat to solidarity is rising nationalist sentiment. Under the Trump administration, the United States largely withdrew from previously standard international engagement. Repressive and protectionist governments along with extrajudicial killings are on the rise (for example in the Philippines, Nigeria, Brazil, and other countries).[76] In contrast, Francis's pandemic messages posit "diversity in solidarity" as possessing "antibodies that heal social structures and processes that have degenerated into systems of injustice, systems of oppression. . . . Either we go forward on the path of solidarity or things will worsen."[77] Similarly, hope is found in growing social movements calling for environmental justice (students' global school strike for climate), racial justice (Black Lives Matter), and gender justice (#metoo), especially among young people. CST posits solidarity

---

75. Vincent J. Miller, *Consuming Religion: Christian Faith and Practice in a Consumer Religion* (New York: Continuum, 2005), 76.

76. Vincent J. Miller, *Consuming Religion: Christian Faith and Practice in a Consumer Religion* (2005), 76.
  For a specific CST reflection on rising populism and violence in the Philippines, see Daniel F. Pilario, "Martyrs at the Margins: Rethinking Martyrdom in Violent Populist Regimes," in *Put Away Your Sword: Gospel Nonviolence in a Violent World* (Eugene, OR: Cascade Books, forthcoming).

77. Francis, "Heal the World: Solidarity and the Virtue of Faith" (September 2, 2020).

as that path forward, but journeying together first requires considering more the question of global obligations. In his new encyclical *Fratelli Tutti: On Fraternity and Social Friendship*, Francis offers an urgent vision of solidarity, imploring, "we need to think of ourselves more and more as a single-family dwelling in a common home"[78] and we begin by asking, who is my neighbor? In doing so, he challenges the global community to consider once more obligations to our neighbor.

On April 3, 1968, in his last speech, Martin Luther King, Jr., invited a full auditorium in Nashville, Tennessee, to join him on the road from Jericho to Jerusalem. Recounting the Parable of the Good Samaritan (Luke 10:25–37), King argued that the Samaritan practiced a "dangerous unselfishness." Considering the priest and the Levite, King imagines that the men may not have been callous but simply afraid, asking themselves, "'If I stop to help this man, what will happen to me?' But then the Good Samaritan came by. And he reversed the question: 'If I do not stop to help this man, what will happen to him?'"[79] In calling for solidarity with the sanitation workers' strike for racial and economic justice, King even cautions against only being concerned with "root causes" but failing to show compassion to the brother or sister on your path. There are echoes of this iconic reflection on the Good Samaritan's "dangerous unselfishness" and refusal to be "compassionate by proxy," representative of King's deep faith and hope in the possibility of solidarity, at the theological core of Pope Francis's encyclical *Fratelli Tutti*. An entire chapter is dedicated to a moral and theological contextualization and reflection

---

78. Francis, *Fratelli Tutti* (2020), 17.
79. Martin Luther King, Jr., "I Have Been to the Mountaintop Speech," April 3, 1968, Nashville, TN, Video: Parable of the Good Samaritan, https://www.youtube.com/watch?v=74nWJRsmxyM.

on the Parable of the Good Samaritan, which serves as the narrative animating his persistent call for solidarity "in these dark times."

The Parable of the Good Samaritan, as understood by King and by Francis, demonstrates what is at stake and acknowledges the real risk involved, in practicing dangerous unselfishness. It is easier to ignore the person on the side of the road than it is to risk our own safety, security, and property and "become neighbor" to the wounded.[80] Francis issues a stark and difficult challenge: "We need to acknowledge that we are constantly tempted to ignore others, especially the weak."[81] The parable "is clear and straightforward, yet it also evokes the interior struggle that each of us experiences as we gradually come to know ourselves through our relationships with our brothers and sisters.... Each day we have to decide whether to be Good Samaritans or indifferent bystanders."[82]

The parable is clear, and yet, still individuals and communities fail to practice the solidarity demonstrated in the parable. While it may seem strange, Francis uses the Good Samaritan as an overarching frame through which to resituate individual positionality vis-à-vis others. In *Fratelli Tutti*, he recognizes the importance of persons, reaching out to individuals but at the same time pushing against any individualized interpretation of the parable.[83] Passing the wounded man is a matter of both personal and social sin. It is within the reflection on the Good Samaritan that Francis explicitly names the failure of the Catholic church to practice the Gospel message. "I sometimes

---

80. For more on the challenge to "become neighbor," see Josh McElwee, "Gutierrez at Vatican: Church Must Be Samaritan, Reaching out to Others," *National Catholic Reporter*, 2/24/2014, https://www.ncronline.org/blogs/ncr-today/gutierrez-vatican-church-must-be-samaritan-reaching-out-others.
81. Francis, *Fratelli Tutti* (2020), 64.
82. Ibid., 69.
83. Francis sees interdependence and connection where traditionally people have not, while at the same time building upon solidarity as tied to *neighbor*, as John Paul II did in *Sollicitudo Rei Socialis*, 38–40.

wonder why," says Francis, "in light of this, it took so long for the Church unequivocally to condemn slavery and various forms of violence. Today with our developed spirituality and theology we have no excuses."[84] In order to deflect the implications of the parable, Christians have often ignored the parable's own answer to the question, who is my neighbor? In English, argues Cecelia Gonzales-Andrieu, one obstacle is that there is only one word for neighbor. Drawing on the word *semejante* in Spanish, we begin to see that "your neighbor is close and also far, needy and also comfortable, known and also unknown. Because your neighbor is precisely every single human person. We could say, using theological language, that the neighbor here is the one who, as made by God, shares our *imago Dei*."[85]

The "merciful solidarity" called for by the Good Samaritan, "directs our attention toward the flourishing and suffering of both human and non-human neighbors," notes Nichole Flores.[86] Solidarity, as it is envisioned by Francis, requires reconfiguring the ways both individuals and specific communities envision responsibility and how the international community approaches obligations to the distant other. While lamenting "insufficiently universal human rights," Francis argues for concrete positive moral obligations to promote the flourishing of others. For CST's vision of solidarity, it is not enough to avoid harming my neighbor; one also has a duty to promote their dignity and flourishing. This moves from simply "do no harm" to a robust beneficence, distinguishes CST's virtue of solidarity from the way secular Western philosophy tends to approach

---

84. Franics, *Fratelli Tutti* (2020), 86.
85. Cecelia Gonzales-Andrieu, "Who Is My Neighbor?," *America Magazine*, 10/31/2016, https://www.americamagazine.org/politics-society/2016/10/17/we-often-ask-who-my-neighbor-why-does-answer-always-surprise-us.
86. Nichole Flores, "Our Sister, Mother Earth: Solidarity and Familial Ecology in *Laudato Si*,'" *Journal of Religious Ethics* 43, no. 4 (2018): 463–478; 470,

obligations. Therefore, when considering the global migration crisis as one particular ethical issue, Kristin Heyer notes, "an understanding of solidarity with *near and distant strangers* can help move beyond the liberal-communitarian impasse and orient considerations of migrants' rights in terms of broader relationships abetting forced movement."[87]

CST accepts that we live in a finite and broken world, while raising the moral expectations of our responsibility for our neighbor. *Fratelli Tutti* provocatively challenges, "if all people are my brothers and sisters, and if the world truly belongs to everyone, then it matters little whether my neighbor was born in my country or elsewhere. My own country also shares responsibility for his or her development, although it can fulfill that responsibility in a variety of ways,"[88] and goes on to critique not only immigration policies but economic policy that does not adequately value the equal dignity of non-citizens. For CST, argues M. Shawn Copeland, "solidarity is a wrenching task: to stand up for justice in the midst of injustice; to take up simplicity in the midst of affluence and comfort; to embrace integrity in the midst of collusion and co-optation; to contest the gravitational pull of domination."[89]

---

87. Kristin Heyer, "Migrants Feared and Forsaken: A Catholic Ethic of Social Responsibility," *Interdisciplinary Journal for Religion and Transformation in Contemporary Society* 6, no. 1 (2020): 58–170.
88. Francis, *Fratelli Tutti*, (2020) 125.
89. M. Shawn Copeland, "Toward a Critical Christian Feminist Theology of Solidarity," in *Women and Theology*, ed. Mary Ann Hinsdale and Phyllis H. Kaminski (Maryknoll, NY: Orbis, 1995), 18.

Chapter 7

Pernicious Solidarities

Equity and Trust in Solidary Relations

SALLY J. SCHOLZ

In 1973, Michael Walzer published an influential article on "dirty hands." Political actors, Walzer argues, sometimes "face a moral dilemma, a situation where [they] must choose between two courses of action both of which it would be wrong for [them] to undertake."[1] Walzer is concerned because the act is wrong in-itself, and because doing the act is harmful to the rule of law and the community. In the end, we can only mitigate the potential harms and we do so by entrusting the decision with the person who "has scruples about it," the person who knows that the action is wrong but recognizes it must be done anyway.[2] Following Albert Camus, Walzer states: "political action is so uncertain that politicians necessarily take moral as well as political risks, committing crimes that they only think ought to be committed. They override the rules without ever being certain that they have found the best way to the results they hope to achieve, and

---

1. Michael Walzer, "Political Action: The Problem of Dirty Hands," *Philosophy and Public Affairs* 2, no. 2 (1973): 160. https://www.jstor.org/stable/2265139.
2. Ibid,, 166.

we don't want them to do that too quickly or too often."[3] With Walzer, we hope that the politician is a person with integrity; the person who values the rules so highly that breaking them causes guilt, punishment, distress; the person who acts not to advance self-interest but for the good of others.

The problem apparent in the "dirty hands" scenario is not confined to the realm of formal politics, nor does it merely affect politicians. Indeed, political actors of all sorts sometime face uncertain choices that negatively affect the moral relations of those involved. A similar problem appears in solidarity, a problem that might be called pernicious solidarity, when the relation itself becomes dangerous for some of the participants. Like Walzer, we should be concerned not only about the potential direct harm of solidary actions, but also the potential indirect harm of those actions on the relation itself or on others who participate with us in solidarity.[4] The solidary relation might have an adverse impact on the social standing of some members more than others, it might disempower some members more than others, or it might exclude some people or issues that ought to be included. Walzer concluded that the best we could hope for is that the dirty hands politician might be a person with integrity, a person who understood that the choice must be made for the common good. For political solidarity, the question is: What does integrity demand of solidary actors? And is there a way to avoid pernicious solidarity or, if the relation appears dangerous to some, to understand the weight of that danger and seek avenues to mitigate it? The virtues of trust and equity are at the heart of these questions.

---

3. Ibid., 179–180.
4. Solidarity also needs to heed the relation to those affected by an injustice but who opt not to participate in solidarity as well. See Scholz, *Political Solidarity* (State College: Penn State Press, 2008), ch. 3.

SALLY J. SCHOLZ

Before discussing the problem further, I offer three examples of solidarities that became dangerous for some of the participants. In 2011, while revolutionary movements were sweeping through North Africa, the Occupy Wall Street movement took hold in the United States and eventually spread to major cities around the world. The movement, claiming to speak for the 99%, drew attention to the tremendous economic and political disparity between the wealthy and the poor, highlighting the fact that 1% of the population held approximately 40% of the wealth in the nation. In calling attention to material inequality, the activists sought to redirect attention to the majority and challenge the corrupting influences of wealth in politics.

Movements are not necessarily instances of solidarity, but Occupiers pledged solidarity in taking up the cause of fighting homelessness, a solidarity that drew attention to the injustices suffered by people who lack adequate housing. Occupiers created encampments in cities throughout the United States; the encampments aimed to shine a spotlight on and prioritize the needs of those who were vulnerable because of the lack of stable housing. By living together in camps, these cities-within-cities demonstrated solidarity by providing community among and between people without housing and housing-secure people. The encampments included hot meals, clothing, and tent-shelter, while also fostering local governance and education opportunities. At least some of these encampments were located in parks or public spaces that unhoused people regularly utilized themselves. The solidarity created by the Occupy movement brought attention to gross economic inequality and injustice in the United States and enacted the core principle of material equality at the heart of the movement's goals.

The movement was not without its critics, however. During its peak of activity in 2011–2012, different Occupy camps were also overtaken by relatively privileged university students who were committed to fighting for material equality, but who often displaced or effectively silenced some of the concerns from the poor and marginalized or their longtime advocates.[5] The enactment of solidarity was not inclusive enough and led to some significant aspects of social injustice being overlooked. Indeed, many unhoused people and longtime advocates for housing justice argued that Occupy's encampments made some people more vulnerable, not less. The encampments were ill equipped to provide for the mental health needs of some of the people without adequate housing, even disrupting services that were being provided by established shelter and advocacy agencies. The encampments were also frequently criticized for failures with regard to issues of race and gender.[6] When city officials forcibly cleared the encampments, people without housing, who had previously lived in the parks and public spaces undisturbed by local officials, were also swept out of the areas. Further, once the Occupiers were cleared, the underfunded shelter and service systems were left with the responsibility of re-establishing regular mental health and physical security for their clients. Although the National Coalition for the Homeless offered praise of the Occupiers for bringing attention to homelessness, they also noted the need for the Occupiers not to forget the lowest 1%, to continue to fight homelessness, and to advocate for the rights of the people without housing to continue to live in parks.[7]

The #MeToo movement offers another example of solidarity that becomes dangerous for some participants. In 2017, building on a sexual violence awareness campaign initiated by Tarana Burke, an actress used Twitter #MeToo to encourage survivors to share their experiences of sexual violence. The hashtag exploded and many survivors

---

5. I discuss the problems of privileged people in solidarity in *Political Solidarity*, chapter 5, "The Paradox of the Participation of the Privileged."
6. Ruth Milkman, "Millennial Movements: Occupy Wall Street and the Dreamers," *Dissent* 61, no. 3 (2014): 55–59.
7. See the National Coalition for the Homeless website: http://nationalhomeless.org/occupy-homelessness/ Accessed November 18, 2019.

shared their experience, claimed their voice, and dubbed #MeToo a supportive network—a solidarity—for survivors. The #MeToo campaign brought worldwide attention to a very serious problem that affects people across the globe. It also created a coalitional politics that united the unique experiences and activist pursuits of individuals into a collective.[8] The solidarity, however, also obscured the long history of efforts to raise awareness about violence against women and openly discuss issues of sexual harassment in the workplace. Indeed, the social media campaign obscured, for a time, the longstanding existing efforts by advocates in law, politics, economics, and social work to bring justice for survivors and to punish perpetrators.

The third example comes from the Black Lives Matter movement in the United States, which started in 2013 as a response to the murder of Trayvon Martin, an unarmed Black teen. During the summer of 2020, following the death of George Floyd at the hands of Minneapolis police officers, thousands of people joined Black Lives Matter in solidarity. Throughout the country and around the world, they gathered to protest peacefully, to push institutions and governments to enact change, and to make good on the promise of equality in the United States. In some cities, the protests continued for months and even years.

Among the nonviolent protesters in one city were a group of parents who called themselves the "Wall of Moms," linking arms in an effort to create a barrier between federal agents and protesters.[9] The Wall of Moms consisted of mostly white, suburban women, who declared their intentions as protesting racial injustice by using their bodies as a barrier, making themselves vulnerable during the

---

8. Alyson Cole and Sumru Atuk, "What's in a Hashtag? Feminist Terms for Tweeting in Alliance," *Philosophia* 9, no. 1 (2019): 26–52.
9. Some of the protests in Portland had violent elements, but the violence was attributed to anarchists seeking to co-opt the BLM protests.

protests. Another nonviolent activist, Reginald Richardson, Jr., pastor of Your Bible Speaks Seventh Day Adventist Church, noted that acting as a barrier in this manner ought to be encouraged among "our white brothers and sisters" who stand against racial injustice because "Black men and women will go to jail at a higher rate than our white brothers and sisters."[10] But even as the Wall of Moms functioned to protect Black protesters, it also became a focal piece—like the violence of anarchists—that detracted from the very cause they sought to support and ignored the contributions of Black moms both to this current protest and to years of being on the front lines of anti-racism protests.[11]

As one news source reported, the president of the Portland NAACP, Rev. E. D. Mondainé, told protesters, "The focus has been moved from where it is supposed to be and made to be a spectacle, a debacle."[12] Protests against racism became protests against federal involvement in local issues. Although their intentions were to protect peaceful protesters, the Wall of Moms, together with the anarchists and the federal agents meant to quell them, became the spectacle. Similar scenarios played out in other major cities around the country.

---

10. https://www.nbcnews.com/news/us-news/black-lives-white-spectacle-portland-protests-have-lost-focus-civil-n1234886.
11. In addition, the group was charged with allegations of anti-Blackness for excluding Black leaders and filing for nonprofit status without consultation. For more on the controversy, see Danielle Kurtzleben, "The Complicated History of Moms as the Face of Protest Movements," *NPR Morning Edition*, July 28, 2020. https://www.npr.org/2020/07/28/896088053/complicated-history-moms-as-the-face-of-protest-movements; and Alex Hardgrave, "Portland's Wall of Moms Crumbles amid Online Allegations by Former Partner, Don't Shoot PDX," *Oregonian*, July 29, 2020, https://www.oregonlive.com/news/2020/07/portlands-wall-of-moms-crumbles-amid-online-allegations-by-former-partner-dont-shoot-pdx.html.
12. https://www.nbcnews.com/news/us-news/black-lives-white-spectacle-portland-protests-have-lost-focus-civil-n1234886. See also E. D. Mondainé, "Portland's Protests Were Supposed to Be about Black Lives. Now, They're White Spectacle," *Washington Post Opinion*, July 23, 2020, https://www.washingtonpost.com/opinions/2020/07/23/portlands-protests-were-supposed-be-about-black-lives-now-theyre-white-spectacle/.

In short, the solidarity against systemic racism, racial injustice, and systematic violence by the police against Black bodies was usurped by actions and involvement of individuals, some of whom sought to protest racism, but whose involvement in the solidarity became harmful to the collective effort and the relationship of solidarity itself. As Mondainé explains, "There is more at stake here than who appears most often on nightly TV broadcasts. Everyone seeking to advance justice in Portland faces great danger."[13] Of course, because of systemic racism, Black people face greater danger in the protests even despite using primarily peaceful methods. Importantly, a solidarity movement is much larger than merely a series of protests. The purpose of Black Lives Matter is, as Kimberly Ann Harris puts it, "to repudiate Black demise and affirm Black humanity."[14] Recognizing that some solidary relations can be dangerous to the purpose of the movement or fellow actors compels us also to seek avenues to avoid such harms.

In all three cases, the specific actions taken were either morally neutral or morally good. These were cases of individuals and groups acting to address fundamental human needs and rights, to raise awareness of an injustice, and to protect a fellow human being. But in all three cases, something went awry. The actions themselves were not the cause of direct harm, but the actions were indirectly harmful to other participants in solidarity, to some people outside the solidary relation who experience the injustice or oppression, or to the purpose or goal of solidarity. The question of pernicious solidarities, then, asks whether the potential for indirect harms might be foreseen such that efforts may be taken to mitigate or avoid the harms entirely.

---

13. Mondainé, "Portland's Protests," 2020.
14. Kimberly Ann Harris, "What Does It Mean to Move for Black Lives?" *Philosophy Today* 63, no. 2 (2019): 276.

THE PROBLEM OF PERNICIOUS SOLIDARITIES

All three of the examples feature intentional actions by well-meaning people. The actions themselves are morally neutral or even morally good actions aimed at protecting the rights and bodies of others. But in each case, and in so many other instances of political solidarity, the solidarity is challenged because some participants end up carrying a heavier burden or are made more vulnerable because of the actions of others in solidarity. The risks of the solidarity are inequitably distributed, destroying trust and creating harm. Although one might fault specific actions or tactics within solidarity as harmful, or identify epistemic failures—including what Aili Mari Tripp, commenting on failures of transnational solidarities, identifies as "hubris, disregard of local context, a 'rescue' mentality, and distancing from the 'other' "[15]—the examples also feature valid efforts to act in solidarity.[16] Nevertheless, they also exhibit unintended effects that cause a tear or break in the solidary relation itself, a rupture that might not be noticed until it is too late for some participants. The harm that results is not a direct harm, but rather an indirect harm of solidarity.

This is the problem of pernicious solidarities: relations of solidarity that themselves carry potentially dangerous aspects for some participants. Like dirty hands, pernicious solidarities challenge how we think about the relation of solidarity. As Tommie Shelby discusses (Chapter 12 in this volume), there may be good arguments for excluding some people from solidarity. Like Shelby, though, I think

---

15. Aili Mari Tripp, "Challenges in Transnational Feminist Mobilization," in *Global Feminism*, ed. Myra Marx Ferree and Aili Mari Tripp (New York: New York University Press, 2006), 297.
16. Note, too, that all three cases involved either firsthand experience or genuine efforts to respond to the testimony of those who suffer injustice. Surely epistemic failures and hubris were present, but the practices of solidarity reveal something more is at stake here.

that would be a mistake. Although ideally it might be hoped that solidarities always avoid harm, the reality of politics and intersecting oppressions makes that unlikely. Thinking about the virtues associated with solidarity might provide some measures to minimize or mitigate the danger, even though we also must accept the very real moral burden when our efforts in solidarity cause it. Pernicious solidarity, like the dirty hands of a politician with integrity, is not necessarily a failure of solidarity simpliciter, but rather a solidarity that proves dangerous to some members or some outsiders and yet might otherwise be described as just. Knowing at least some of how it arises suggests methods to address it.

Of course, it is possible to look at the examples offered above as harms caused by (1) specific actions, (2) inaction, or (3) perceptions of action or inaction. Perhaps we could fault the Occupy participants, the #MeToo revealers, and the BLM protesters for failing to defer to others in the group, for not more completely joining their fate with those with whom they are united in solidarity, for co-opting the cause, or for remaining safe while others sacrifice. I appreciate such arguments; we need to be attentive to them. However, in this chapter, I set them aside and focus instead on what I take to be a normative principle of accepting the social risk associated with solidarity. Arguments about the efficacy of action or the failure of inaction, epistemic or otherwise, are frequently overridden by other concerns or alternate justifications. My aim in looking at what we can think of as the expectations of solidarity is to focus on a framework at the heart of solidarity that, rather than being overridden or explained away with an examination of faults or alternative justifications for intentions and actions, may be used to redirect the solidary relation when it goes wrong and guide it when it is working. This approach is similar to Shelby's argument (Chapter 12 in this volume) that we must look at the central values of solidarity; whereas he focuses on loyalty and trust in pursuit of justice, I focus on equity within the solidary relation.

Solidarity denotes a committed moral relation to others; political solidarity is "a committed unity of peoples on a range of interpersonal to social-political levels" connecting their actions for a cause.[17] Such a solidarity would be described as just if its intentions were social justice based, if its methods were considered neutral or even good (e.g., writing letters or boycotting products, peacefully protesting), and if it employed a logic of inclusion.

Solidarity requires a relatively comprehensive look at the interconnection between actions: how individual actions contribute to injustice, how actions in solidarity contribute to a cause for justice, and how actions affect relationships. Solidary actors are asked to think not only about the singular direct connections between actions and injustice, but about all the possible effects on the goal, the relation with those similarly committed, and the relation to those outside the solidarity. In solidarity, we willingly accept the burden of this complex task because we believe that other solidary actors are similarly engaged. This last sentence is, I think, the key to thinking about relations of solidarity that cause harm despite actions that are not themselves unjust.

It might be helpful here to set aside certain forms of dangerous in-group solidarities. In the *Second Discourse*, Jean-Jacques Rousseau discusses a group that plots together against the rest of society or against those outside their group. Rousseau uses the notion of a cabal to delineate groups that seek to consolidate power over and against another group or perhaps against random others who threaten either the existence of the cabal or the cabal's way of understanding the

---

17. Scholz, *Political Solidarity*, 58.

world.[18] The cabal is based on the restrictive or exclusive solidarity found in groups that place a high premium on policing membership, motivated by an ideology that seeks to diminish the excluded other. Tribalism, sexism, and racism, among other isms, create insular solidarities of this sort that, by their very nature and intent, exclude and cause harm. That which binds an association together can also pervert the power of the collective into enmity toward all those who do not belong. These conscious appeals to solidarity delineate clearly articulable borders of group inclusion often involving identity claims. Internal to the group, appeals to solidarity are used to maintain or strengthen the group bond or shore up commitment among individual members when their loyalty seems to be flagging. Solidarity, then, is used to demarcate an in-group, usually over and against an out-group.

The relation exists in order to cause harm or even the elimination of some other group or collection of peoples identified by their divergence from the in-group. Consider, for instance, the solidarity characteristic of xenophobic nationalisms. When the Hutu targeted the Tutsi in 1994, among other things, they claimed to be acting on Hutu solidarity. The demarcation of an out-group perceived to threaten the existence of the in-group creates a justification for violence or harm. In-group solidarity is dangerous—in addition to any group-prescribed harm to outsiders—in that the particular participants often consider their attitudes and actions to be motivated by intentions they consider to be good, for instance, the preservation of a cultural group or race.

In that case, the determination of the harm is a matter of justice and may be a matter of comparative justice. Civil society organizations

---

18. Jean-Jacques Rousseau, "Discourse on the Origin and Foundation of Inequality among Men," in *The Discourses and Other Early Political Writings*, ed. Victor Gourevitch (Cambridge: Cambridge University Press, 1997), 181.

that undermine liberal democracy, for instance, might exhibit a strong solidarity internal to their group, but the external or outwardly facing aim of the group is premised on excluding others from civil society generally. In a seminal article on the topic, Chambers and Kopstein discuss what they call "bad civil society," those civil society organizations that "advocate hate and bigotry."[19] Emphasizing the importance of studying "bad civil society," they note that the positive argument is often made that active participation in civil society is necessary for a robust flourishing of democracy. However, as they also note, "The lessons of trust and solidarity, of developing an 'I' into a 'we,' do not strengthen democracy when the trust, solidarity, and the 'we' are such that they do not go beyond the group in question."[20]

Cabals, or the type of in-group solidarity found in such things as xenophobic nationalisms, cultivate what Chambers and Kopstein call "particularist civility" in that they foster "all the goods that are associated with participation (trust, public spiritedness, self-sacrifice), but only between members of a particular group" and usually at the expense of an out-group.[21] Dangerously promoting an ideology of hatred toward others, cabals manifest a form of pernicious solidarity that is best dealt with using the tools of justice. In contrast, political solidarity of the sort discussed in the rest of this chapter is inclusive.

Making a commitment to political solidarity, individuals joining together to form a collective might reasonably assume that for each participant: (1) they are empowered to contribute in their unique way; (2) they will not be *unduly* subject to harm or vulnerability in other aspects of life because of their solidary relation in spite of recognizing that sharing social risk may involve loss; and (3) they or their

---

19. Simone Chambers and Jeffrey Kopstein, "Bad Civil Society," *Political Theory* 29, no. 6 (2001): 840.
20. Ibid., 841.
21. Ibid.

concerns will be included in the sphere of consideration when decisions are taken. Solidary actors want to feel that their efforts make a difference to the collective effort. They want to know that there is a realized trust among all similarly engaged solidary actors.

Realized trust is built and sustained through a shared practice of sharing the risk that political action entails. I suggest that solidarity expects equitable sharing of *social risk*, the benefits and costs of uniting with others for collective action. Although related, social risk differs from social capital, which may be understood as the "connections among individuals—social networks and the norms of reciprocity and trustworthiness that arise from them";[22] Putnam associates social capital with civic virtue. Social risk is the potential for loss given the networks within which one finds oneself enmeshed or which one chooses. Some loss is expected in any social togetherness (e.g., loss of time as one dedicates that time to a friend's needs, loss of free movement as one carries a child, loss of money as one purchases a meal or contributes to the cost of an outing) and not all loss is bad. Indeed, we willingly shoulder many forms of loss because we consider the social togetherness itself as valuable. These exchanges of loss are present in solidarity but they are not always as predictable or chosen as these examples indicate. The willingness to share *social risk* is the normative piece in solidarity; it indicates the tie that connects individuals as well as the acknowledgment that there will be risk because of our collective tie. Further, the willingness accepts that unique participants in solidarity will be affected by the collective relation differently; our commitment to share—to coordinate actions and understand individual actions as operating in concert with others—means that even while some participants might experience

---

22. Robert Putnam, *Bowling Alone* (New York: Simon & Schuster, 2000), 19; see also Chambers and Kopstein, "Bad Civil Society," 840.

increased risks at various times, risks are distributed so that no one is unduly burdened or made vulnerable because of the solidarity.[23]

The expectations of solidarity, then, may be explained as allowing one's efforts and well-being in a particular context to be interdependent with others ostensibly such that all others will similarly be interdependent with them in a collective whole—to equitably share social risk within the context of solidarity. Consider the context of collective decision-making for activism within solidarity. Participants cannot assume that they know the course of action to take or the most effective means to accomplish an end. Some effort must be made to assess the impact of decisions on other current and future solidary participants. Individuals thinking about whether to employ violence in a campaign for a cause, for instance, ought to include all those potentially affected by the decision in the sphere of consideration.[24] When a person joins with others in political solidarity, that person reasonably presumes that all others similarly committed to the solidary cause will include that person in the sphere of consideration when decisions are taken. The willingness to share social risk requires an assessment of risks among group members, even if the assessment is conducted individually.

Although decision-making is one facet, there are others that are similarly impacted by the willingness to share social risk. In joining together, the individual members use their power to struggle for a cause. The key to sharing risk is that it acknowledges and incorporates the variations of vulnerabilities that might affect a single person as well as the variations of vulnerabilities affecting all participants in

---

23. Sally Scholz, "Solidarity as a Human Right," *Archiv des Völkerrechts* 52, no. 1 (2014), 56; and "Solidarity, Social Risk, and Community Engagement," *American Journal of Bioethics* 20, no. 5 (2020): 76.
24. Elsewhere (and in contrast to Kolers, Chapter 4 in this volume), I have argued that violence is incompatible with the inclusive logic of solidarity; Scholz, "Political Solidarity and Violent Resistance," *Journal of Social Philosophy* 38, no. 1 (2007): 38–52.

the solidary relation. The repercussions of the solidary relations may fall on differently situated people differently. Willingness to share social risk is willingness to accept that action in solidarity may expose one to vulnerabilities or may exacerbate existing vulnerabilities but that others are similarly committing, and we will collectively readjust if any one of us is unduly harmed by our solidary relation. The sharing is done under the belief that social existence will be better if we take the risks together rather than if only a few shoulder the risks. It also implies that the sharing will be done in such a way that the solidary relation is continually re-evaluated, and social risks are redistributed. A "willingness to share" is distinct from "actually sharing" social risk. Not everyone in solidarity will actually share the same risks. Some participants will be more vulnerable because of their personal needs or their status in the larger society, some will be vulnerable because of the physical risks they undertake, others will be more vulnerable because of victimization or oppression, and still others will be vulnerable due to their personal circumstances. These accounts of vulnerability might also intersect in ways that compound the adverse effects. In political solidarity, however, each member comes from his or her particularity and willingly assumes the social risks involved in solidarity. A willingness to share social risks seeks the social conditions that minimize the social risk and potential vulnerability for everyone.

Although many accounts of solidarity appeal to deference as a means of fostering the humility and reflection needed, deference does not alleviate the burden on subordinated groups and may actually heighten it. Shelby articulates a number of problems with deference, including the lack of consensus about specific aims or means of practicing solidarity in spite of a "stable consensus on... fundamental values and goals." Even there, however, dissent has to be allowed in solidary relations, "no one should expect blacks to subscribe to the same political philosophy," and "debate and altered circumstances" revise and amend fundamental values and goals (in Chapter 12 of this volume). Kolers, on the other hand, defends deference in solidarity to include acting against one's conscience.[25] In that sense, deference burdens the very people it is meant to aid, while also removing important viewpoints from the processes of revision and emendation of solidarity's values, as well as crucial sources of power for the struggle. Rather than deference, solidarity ought instead to spotlight and amplify the voices and needs of the oppressed or those who suffer injustice.

As the examples from Black Lives Matter, #MeToo, and Occupy show, solidarity might become dangerous because of flaws in the assumption of social risk which cause an adverse impact on the social standing of some members more than others, disempower some members more than others, or exclude some people who ought to be included. I offer three such flaws: (1) the willingness to share social risk is inequitably distributed; (2) social risk is unjustifiably limited; or (3) willingness to share social risk is strategically withdrawn. If equity in solidarity is the willingness to share social risk, then each of these flaws points to a problem of equity. Of course, other things can go wrong or cause harm in solidarity as well. My aim is simply to offer some considerations, relevant to contemporary solidarity movements, that help to foresee possible harms and address them. These ideas contribute to the critical project of solidarity and the need continually to scrutinize the relation.

INEQUITABLE DISTRIBUTION OF WILLINGNESS TO SHARE SOCIAL RISK

> *This is a moment for serious action—to once again take up the mantle of the civil rights era by summoning the same conviction and*

---

25. Avery Kolers, *A Moral Theory of Solidarity* (Oxford: Oxford University Press, 2016), 71, 119.

determination our forebears did. We welcome our white brothers and sisters in this struggle. In fact, we need them. But I must ask them to remain humbly attuned to the opportunity of this moment—and to reflect on whether any actions they take will truly help establish justice, or whether they are simply for show.

E. D. Mondainé, "Portland's Protests" (2020)

Commenting on the Portland Black Lives Matter protests, E. D. Mondainé emphasizes the need for equity in the sharing of social risk. In many ways, the Wall of Moms sought to do just that: to take on risks by making themselves a barrier to deflect violence. They understood that Black people face a greater risk day-to-day in society and would certainly face heightened risk if arrested during the protests.[26] Mondainé pushes past the "show" of the protests to challenge participants in solidarity to accept the risks of confronting systemic racism: "In boardrooms, in schools, in city councils, in the halls of justice, in the smoky backrooms of a duplicitous government—that is where we will finally dismantle the gears of the brutal, racist machine that has been terrorizing black Americans and hollowing out the moral character of this nation since its inception."[27] Calling for humility and reflection in solidarity, Mondainé's comments illustrate that attention to the distribution of social risk is all too often missing.

A similar phenomenon is evident in society generally. Juliet Hooker diagnoses one of the causes of many white people's reaction to Black protest movements, including Black Lives Matter, as the "inability to cope with (often symbolic) losses and the racial

---

26. For a comprehensive study of the risks of arrest and incarceration confronting Black people, see Mark Westmoreland, "On the Beat: Profiling in the Racial Polity," doctoral dissertation, Villanova University, 2020.
27. Online editorial, https://www.washingtonpost.com/opinions/2020/07/23/p.

resentment that accompanies it."[28] This lack of willingness to share symbolic loss is a hindrance to racial justice in the United States. Quoting Danielle Allen, Hooker explains:

> Because public policy decisions will rarely benefit all citizens equally, those citizens "who benefit less than others from particular political decisions, but nonetheless accede to those decisions, preserve the stability of political institutions. Their sacrifice makes collective democratic action possible. . . . The hard truth of democracy is that some citizens are always giving things up for others." For such sacrifices to be legitimate, however, they must be evenly distributed among citizens.[29]

Although Hooker and Allen both are referring to democratic society writ large, the lesson they articulate is appropriate for political solidarity. The inability to accept loss affects the politics within struggles for justice as well. If the burdens are distributed unevenly, constantly falling on some participants rather than willingly shared, then trust erodes and the solidary relation becomes harmful or dangerous. Turning again to Black Lives Matter, Hooker argues that asking "subordinated groups . . . to bear primary responsibility for the work of racial justice" does not cohere with the commitment to equitably distribute the burdens of solidarity.[30]

In his review of the important book by Naomi Zack, *White Privilege and Black Rights*, Lawrence Blum argues that social movements are important because they serve as an intermediary between

---

28. Juliet Hooker, "Black Protest/White Grievance," *The South Atlantic Quarterly* 116, no. 3 (2017): 483.
29. Juliet Hooker, "Black Lives Matter and the Paradoxes of U.S. Black Politics," *Political Theory* 44, no. 4 (2016): 453.
30. Ibid., 456.

individual action and the larger social structure.[31] Acting together in solidarity holds greater hope because we take risks together rather than leaving it to only a few to shoulder the risks. Blum also argues that "[i]f a right has been violated, that should matter not only to the person whose right is violated but to all members of the polity within which that right is officially recognized."[32] While the stirring slogan of the movement functions as a reminder that Black lives are precarious, it also ought to remind us within the movement there are expectations of equity in the risks we share.

If there is inequitable distribution of the willingness to share social risk, then vulnerabilities based on social status or identity increase, and relations of solidarity become strained as those subject to these vulnerabilities carry more risk or even find themselves disempowered compared to those who do not.

Equitable distribution of social risk requires that those with power understand the situation and the experiences of those with whom they join in solidarity and use their power for the struggle. That may mean that they must shoulder more risk in the struggle because those whose situation is spotlighted carry greater risk because of their social identity. This conception of solidarity's expectations is evident in the statement from White Coats for Black Lives on Black Lives Matter. They describe partnering with community members, working together to dismantle systemic oppression, and advocating "for equitable social structures. The privilege that physicians possess within society and within the professional hierarchy of medicine provides them with power that can be used to spearhead policy changes to advance racial justice locally and nationally. Using this 'physician

---

31. Lawrence Blum, "White Privilege, Injustice, and the 'Black Lives Matter' Movement," *Radical Philosophy Review* 19, no. 3 (2016): 686; see also Scholz, *Political Solidarity*.
32. Blum, "White Privilege, Injustice," 687.

privilege' to advocate for social change is necessary if we are to eradicate the systemic illness that is racism."[33]

LIMITATION IN THE WILLINGNESS TO ENGAGE IN SOCIAL RISK

Another practice that destroys trust in the solidary relation is limiting the willingness to engage in social risk, especially when the limitations result in merely symbolic gestures from some participants while others are encouraged or even forced into positions that expose them to greater risk or exacerbate their vulnerabilities. Analyzing the relation between the Burke's Me Too survivor network and the hashtag #MeToo, Miranda Pilipchuk suggests that the hashtag's explicit call for survivors to disclose their sexual violence, while intentionally raising awareness of the problem, unintentionally creates a "hierarchy of victims." Pilipchuk argues that #MeToo's "project of public education through survivor disclosure may unduly burden survivors who do disclose, and creates a moral dilemma for survivors who do not wish to disclose."[34] Telling stories of the abuse can be empowering for some survivors. But disclosure of sexual violence is not always possible for survivors, perhaps because they remain in potentially volatile situations or they are not personally ready for that event. A solidarity movement is not merely about raising awareness; the demands of solidarity extend beyond that to address needs and change structures. In this way, those who choose to participate in #MeToo might be commended for sharing their stories and empowering a community of

---

33. White Coats for Black Lives, "#BlackLivesMatter: Physicians Must Stand for Racial Justice," *AMA Journal of Ethics* 17, no. 10 (2015): 978–982, doi: 10.1001/journalofethics.2015.17.10.sect1-1510.
34. Miranda Pilipchuk, "Good Survivor, Bad Survivor," *APA Newsletter on Feminism and Philosophy* 19, no. 1 (2019): 6.

survivors online, but unless they step out of their individual mode to also address social structures and needs in more concrete (less virtual) ways, their solidarity could actually be dangerous to current victims and harm the solidary relations with other survivors seeking to bring about change. This conscientious attentiveness to those affected by solidarity movements, as well as commitment to the cause that extends beyond the performative, distinguishes solidarity from other activist responses to injustice.

Practicing inclusivity in our delineation of the issues could help to mitigate the potential harms. When issues are framed in a way that limits the risks asked of participants (or gives them permission to limit their willingness to take on social risk), those limits keep participants from adequately responding to the situation that inspires their solidarity. This misframing can yield what Nancy Fraser calls "a special kind of meta-injustice, in which one is denied the chance to press first order justice claims in a given political community."[35] If the social risks pertinent to the nature or function of the group itself are not willingly engaged, then the solidary relation might become dangerous. Expanding the content of solidarity through practices of inclusivity aids in identifying and addressing potential harms, keeping the solidarity from becoming pernicious.

STRATEGIC WITHDRAWAL OF WILLINGNESS TO SHARE SOCIAL RISK

Finally, willingness to share social risk that is strategically withdrawn indicates instability in the solidary relationship that allows indirect harm to accrue to some. Trust in equitable sharing of social risks is a

---

35. Nancy Fraser, "Reframing Justice in a Globalizing World," in *Nationalism and Global Solidarities*, ed. James Goodman and Paul James (New York: Routledge, 2007), 173.

crucial part of maintaining solidarity. Solidary actors will sometimes have to withdraw from the solidary relation. But strategic withdrawal of the willingness to share social risk differs from the withdrawal from solidarity for personal or contingent reasons. Strategic withdrawal indicates a power that disregards both the "sharing" and the "willing" aspects. It occurs when an individual decides that acting outside of the solidary relation will yield more benefits to oneself than acting in the solidary relation. The cause per se is not necessarily abandoned but the choice of individual status over solidary relation places the individual's personal power at odds with the collective. Strategically withdrawing the willingness to share social risk is comparable to never actually being willing in the first place. Solidarities can be dangerous for some participants when they are engaged in what they take to be a solidary relation and yet the willingness to share a social risk is absent in a large portion of the relevant participants.

One could argue that the very motivation for the encampments of the Occupy movement was to share social risk among and between unhoused people and permanently sheltered people in a solidary relation to bring about social change. By renouncing their apartments and houses, some of the Occupy participants sought to live with and as the unhoused people to highlight the economic disparity between the wealthiest and the poorest in the United States. Yet when city officials broke up the camps, the Occupiers who had previously been without shelter continued to be, while the Occupiers who hailed from shelters returned to those. At least some of the permanently sheltered longtime advocates continued to work to raise awareness of the plight of unhoused people or create social change that addresses the conditions of homelessness as a way of living out their solidary commitment. However, the vast majority of the permanently sheltered Occupiers have moved on to other matters or other issues.

The relations of trust and vulnerability within the solidary relation mean that at various times other people will be in positions of authority or power over us, and we over them. The transient relations of power or authority and vulnerability ought not to become so pervasive as to keep a solidary actor from acting freely, or so unpredictable as to expose some members to undue risk. When the Occupy campers gave up the warmth of their homes temporarily, they failed to see how they impacted precarious situations of unhoused activists. Longtime activists from among the unhoused people as well as the sheltered people were frustrated in their efforts to address economic injustice by Occupy's lack of attention to disability, and racial and gender justice. In the political solidarity to fight homelessness and transform an unjust social system, the longtime advocates and many of the people lacking housing from marginalized communities were disempowered by the Occupy encampment. The Occupiers focused on the performance of the encampments (limiting their risk) while also withdrawing their solidarity when the performance was over. In the words of Angela Davis, solidarity must "embrace projects that address the sociohistorical conditions that enable" acts of domination to take place.[36] Strategic withdrawal from the solidary relation fails to address the conditions and might further enable acts of domination from within as well as from outside the solidary relation.

CONCLUSION

In all three cases of solidarity, the solidary relation emerged around a cause to stop violence, injustice, or inequality. Members acted in concert and their specific actions were well-meaning and morally good or neutral. We can surely identify epistemic weaknesses or failures, faulting them for their hubris and their insufficient information-gathering.

---

36. Angela Davis, "Transnational Solidarities," in *Freedom Is a Constant Struggle*, ed. Frank Barat (Chicago: Haymarket, 2016), 138.

However, there is more to the solidary relation than acting on reliable epistemic evidence or deferring to the immediate victims of violence, injustice, or tyranny. Solidarity entails an expectation that members share social risk with other actors in their solidary relation such that no one is made worse off by their relation of collective action. This expectation requires that we practice equity and trust within the solidary relation itself as we strive for justice and equality through political solidarity.

In the examples presented, the harm is not directly tied to the act. It is not just the troubling effects on the plight of people who lack housing that accrued during and after Occupy, on Black protesters in Portland's Black Lives Matters protests, and on victims of sexual violence in #MeToo. Among the harms may be found a harm to the relation of solidarity itself. If some members are disempowered or their vulnerabilities made worse due to the political solidarity, then we have to look at the relation itself. The willingness to share social risks is just that.

One of my guiding assumptions is that social justice work is difficult. There is no best way to do it and no single right way. Solidarity efforts are sometimes harmful or dangerous to solidary actors or those outside the solidary bond. Even well-intentioned solidarities that embrace a logic of inclusiveness grounded in justice risk creating unjustifiable burdens or perpetrating unconscious or unintentional harms. Yet allowing the fear of causing unintended harm to paralyze us from acting is also not a viable option in a world of injustice. Solidary actors live in the struggle. To live in the struggle means to accept the risks together with fellow solidary actors, to look out for each other—especially those who are most vulnerable—and to think beyond the current moment or performative action. The relation is important, but it is an ongoing arduous responsibility that requires equity, inclusivity, attentiveness, trust, and commitment. The hope, however, is that those so engaged will have done everything in their power to obviate or mitigate the potential dangers. Like Walzer's politician with dirty hands, we know that at times solidarity may become dangerous. But we hope that solidary actors act with integrity as they exist in moral life within solidary networks. Instead of focusing on what solidarity is, we ask how solidarities may cause harm, and in doing so, we open the way for more dynamic accounts of movements, individuals, and groups that are more critically aware of their limitations.

WORKS CITED

Blum, Lawrence. "White Privilege, Injustice, and the 'Black Lives Matter' Movement." *Radical Philosophy Review* 19, no. 3 (2016): 681–688. https://doi.org/10.5840/radphilrev201619372.

Chambers, Simone, and Jeffrey Kopstein. "Bad Civil Society." *Political Theory* 29, no. 6 (2001): 837–865. https://www.jstor.org/stable/3072607.

Cole, Alyson, and Sumru Atuk. 2019. "What's in a Hashtag? Feminist Terms for Tweeting in Alliance." *Philosophia* 9, no. 1 (2019): 26–52. doi:10.1353/phi.2019.0012.

Davis, Angela. "Transnational Solidarities." In *Freedom Is a Constant Struggle: Ferguson, Palestine, and the Foundations of a Movement*, ed. Frank Barat. Chicago: Haymarket, 2016, 129–146.

Fraser, Nancy. "Reframing Justice in a Globalizing World." In *Nationalism and Global Solidarities*, ed. James Goodman and Paul James. New York: Routledge, 2007, 168–186.

Hardgrave, Alex. "Portland's Wall of Moms Crumbles amid Online Allegations by Former Partner, Don't Shoot PDX." *Oregonian*, July 29, 2020. https://www.oregonlive.com/news/2020/07/portlands-wall-of-moms-crumbles-amid-online-allegations-by-former-partner-dont-shoot-pdx.html.

Harris, Kimberly Ann. "What Does It Mean to Move for Black Lives?" *Philosophy Today* 63, no. 2 (2019): 275–291. doi:10.5840/philtoday2019731265.

Hooker, Juliet. "Black Lives Matter and the Paradoxes of U.S. Black Politics: From Democratic Sacrifice to Democratic Repair." *Political Theory* 44, no. 4 (2016): 448–469. doi:10.1177/0090591716640314.

Hooker, Juliet. "Black Protest/White Grievance: On the Problem of White Political Imaginations Not Shaped by Loss." *The South Atlantic Quarterly* 116, no. 3 (2017): 483–504. doi:10.1215/00382876-3961450.

Kolers, Avery. *A Moral Theory of Solidarity*. Oxford: Oxford University Press, 2016.

Kurtzleben, Danielle. 2020. "The Complicated History of Moms as the Face of Protest Movements." *NPR Morning Edition*, July 28, 2020. https://www.npr.org/2020/07/28/896088053/complicated-history-moms-as-the-face-of-protest-movements.

Milkman, Ruth. "Millennial Movements: Occupy Wall Street and the Dreamers." *Dissent* 61, no. 3 (2014): 55–59. doi:10.1353/dss.2014.0053.

Mondainé, E. D. "Portland's Protests Were Supposed to Be about Black Lives. Now, They're White Spectacle." *Washington Post Opinion*, July 23, 2020. https://www.washingtonpost.com/opinions/2020/07/23/portlands-protests-were-supposed-be-about-black-lives-now-theyre-white-spectacle/.

Pilipchuk, Miranda. "Good Survivor, Bad Survivor: #MeToo and the Moralization of Survivorship." *APA Newsletter on Feminism and Philosophy* 19, no. 1 (2019): 5–12.

Putnam, Robert. *Bowling Alone*. New York: Simon & Schuster, 2000.

Rousseau, Jean-Jacques. "Discourse on the Origin and Foundation of Inequality among Men." In *The Discourses and Other Early Political Writings*, ed. Victor Gourevitch. Cambridge: Cambridge University Press, 1997, 111–188.

Scholz, Sally J. "Political Solidarity and Violent Resistance." *Journal of Social Philosophy* 38, no. 1 (2007): 38–52. https://doi.org/10.1111/j.1467-9833.2007.00365.x

Scholz, Sally J. *Political Solidarity*. State College: Penn State Press, 2008.

Scholz, Sally J. "Solidarity as a Human Right." *Archiv des Völkerrechts* 52, no. 1 (2014): 49–67. doi:10.1628/000389214X14056754359509.

Scholz, Sally J. "Solidarity, Social Risk, and Community Engagement." *American Journal of Bioethics* 20, no. 5 (2020): 75–77. https://doi.org/10.1080/15265161.2020.1745935.

Tripp, Aili Mari. "Challenges in Transnational Feminist Mobilization." In *Global Feminism: Transnational Women's Activism, Organizing, and Human Rights*, ed. Myra Marx Ferree and Aili Mari Tripp. New York: New York University Press, 2006, 296–312.

Walzer, Michael. "Political Action: The Problem of Dirty Hands." *Philosophy and Public Affairs* 2, no. 2 (1973): 160–180. https://www.jstor.org/stable/2265139.

White Coats for Black Lives. "#BlackLivesMatter: Physicians Must Stand for Racial Justice." *AMA Journal of Ethics* 17, no. 10 (2015): 978–982. doi:10.1001/journalofethics.2015.17.10.sect1-1510.

Chapter 8

Rethinking Solidarity through the Lens of Critical Social Ontology

CAROL C. GOULD

INTRODUCTION

In this chapter, I want to build on my earlier accounts of solidarity by tackling some of the hard questions that remain for any such account.[1] The resurgence of (putatively) solidaristic but harmful nationalist groups, or worse—white supremacist or neo-Nazi groups—poses the question of whether such groups really display solidarity at all, if solidarity is to be understood as a sort of norm, involving a virtuous practice of mutual aid. Or perhaps, the notion remains useful only in some descriptivist or value-neutral sense. How can a conception of solidarity that wants to remain sensitive to justice specifically rule out these perverse manifestations of group commitment? More generally, how should we frame the normativity of solidarity and how does

1. For my initial account, see Carol C. Gould, "Transnational Solidarities," *Journal of Social Philosophy*, Special Issue on Solidarity, 38, no. 1 (2007): 146–162, doi:10.1111/j.1467-9833.2007.00371.x; Carol C. Gould, *Interactive Democracy, The Social Roots of Global Justice* (Cambridge: Cambridge University Press, 2014), 99–131.

it apply to such exclusionary groups? If solidarity in fact involves a virtuous practice of standing with others and offering them mutual aid, can members of exclusionary and hateful groups nonetheless be said to exemplify such a virtue in their internal relations with each other, despite the profound harm they may cause for outsiders? I will suggest that a critical social ontology, which incorporates an analysis of power, can shed some light on these difficult questions. And finally, what are the implications of the norm of solidarity for understanding our various responsibilities not only to insiders but also to outsiders, including those who may be situated at some distance from the solidarity group itself?

I have discussed the question of solidarity and what we owe outsiders in another recent essay,[2] but hard questions continue to confront an adequate account of solidarity. I want to begin my analysis of some of these questions here by first recapping the distinction I have drawn between two major sorts of solidarity and investigating the two different sorts of social ontology they entail. The two are what I have called the unitary and the networking models of solidarity, the first taken to be exemplified especially by national political communities and also smaller associations, and the second manifest especially in social movements oriented to eliminating oppression. I will then move to a brief discussion of the normative features of solidarity as an activity of standing with others, and the sense in which it can be considered a virtue of individuals or groups. I will then make a turn to discuss the practices of solidarity groups (understood as social and historical emergent practices), and consider their connection to power, which I suggest is necessary in order to understand what is wrong with gangs, neo-Nazi groups, and other problematic cases.

---

2. "Solidarity between the National and the Transnational: What Do We Owe to 'Outsiders'?" in *Transnational Solidarity: Concept, Challenges and Opportunities*, ed. Helle Krunke, Hanne Petersen, and Ian Manners (Cambridge: Cambridge University Press, 2020), 22–41.

(Such an emphasis on power and social practice has often been missing in philosophical accounts to date, despite the fact that solidarity is distinctive among norms in social and political philosophy by being explicitly particularist and constructivist.) The chapter will conclude with some brief remarks on the implications of the analysis of solidarity in its networking form for the issue of collective responsibility. I will call my proposed alternative model one of "collectivizing responsibility," in place of corporate group agency accounts.

TWO FORMS OF SOLIDARITY AND THEIR SOCIAL ONTOLOGIES

I have previously distinguished unitary solidarity from networking solidarity, as ideal types of solidarity relationships. The first characterizes the relations among the members of a single community or group and is sometimes explicated by reference to the Three Musketeers slogan of "All for one, and one for all."[3] In fact, Raimo Tuomela explicitly relies on this slogan to analyze group solidarity, which he says involves "dispositions toward prosocial (e.g. helping) behavior" between members qua members, some degree of which is required in "all groups that are capable of action."[4] For him, "groups that function on the basis of 'we-thinking' (and not merely on individualistic 'I-thinking' or 'I-mode' thinking) are solidary groups."[5] He sees these groups as involving a collective commitment to the group and its ethos (along with some other conditions). This is suggestive

---

3. It should be noted that this slogan has older roots than Alexandre Dumas's novel of 1844, apparently going back to at least the seventeenth century, and serving as the traditional motto of Switzerland.
4. Raimo Tuomela, *Social Ontology: Collective Intentionality and Group Agents* (Oxford: Oxford University Press, 2013), 242–263.
5. Ibid., 244.

also of Margaret Gilbert's appeal to joint commitment as a sort of "glue" that binds people to each other, though the relevant accounts of these commitments differ between those two thinkers, and certainly Gilbert does not discuss solidarity in connection with her own view.

The formulation "All for one, and one for all" suggests a direct relationship among the members of the group to each other and implies a form of reciprocity (though not an instrumental one of tit-for-tat), or a form of mutuality that exists among them.[6] It resonates with Durkheim's notion of mechanical solidarity, which he discerned among the members of traditional forms of community in which each member stands to the group as a whole in the same relation, that is, as a member, and where there tend to be shared group norms. The notion that people's identity may stem (in part) from this group membership even has contemporary resonances in notions of national identity as marking people's sense of belonging to their own political community.

The "all for one . . ." formulation also suggests a commitment to mutual aid, which, like reciprocity, is a key feature of solidarity in both this sense and its alternative, networking, sense, as we shall see. Although there may be an implication of a direct relationship that exists between each member and the others (as is evident especially in small group contexts), this unitary form of solidarity may often be mediated by the shared goals of the group, around which they orient themselves. And Tuomela does include a role for such shared goals, specifically in terms of what he calls the ethos of a group around

---

6. My original analysis of the various forms of reciprocity is in Carol C. Gould, "Beyond Causality in the Social Sciences: Reciprocity as a Model of Non-Exploitative Social Relations," in *Epistemology, Methodology and the Social Sciences: Boston Studies in the Philosophy of Science*, vol. 71, ed. Robert S. Cohen and Marx W. Wartofsky (Boston and Dordrecht: D. Reidel, 1983), 53–88.

which the group is unified, involving "the constitutive goals, values, and purposes to which group life is dedicated."[7]

In my own account, this more unitary form of solidarity can sometimes be found in what I have called "common activities," which is a loose notion that encompasses a group or set of institutional arrangements organized around meeting a set of shared goals. In this context, solidarity can emerge in contexts of joint action (or can involve dispositions to joint action) in ways that are oriented to the realization of these ends and that are responsive to, and interdependent with, the actions of others. Often in institutional contexts, these actions are embodied in social practices and sets of rules that structure people's interactions and organize the mutual aid that transpires among them. It goes beyond simple coordinated action to include a disposition to such mutual aid. There is some degree of reciprocity involved in the members' relations to the shared goals, which includes instrumental (tit-for-tat) forms of reciprocity, but goes beyond them to incorporate some degree of mutual recognition of each as a member, and some elements of the fuller mutuality involved in explicit orientation to cooperation and support of others as a shared aim.

In fact, it is in some ways quite misleading to use the Three Musketeers phrase (or the motto of Switzerland) as an account of most forms of unitary solidarity, since the reciprocities involved in those may operate indirectly, even in traditional forms of solidaristic societies. As Mauss described in his early account of "The Gift," the solidarity, trust, and, indeed, the cohesion of the group can be generated not only through directly reciprocal actions, but by the ways that giving and receiving operate through a social group as a whole, that is, when some give to others who give to others who give to others. . . . This may already suggest that these unitary groups involve some networking aspects themselves, but it is nonetheless the case

---

7. Tuomela, *Social Ontology*, 15.

that members regard themselves as belonging together within the singular group, which at least partly defines their identity.

In the case of national identity, the solidarity involved has often been thought to arise from preexisting features of history, language, traditions, and cultures, although this is not essential for unitary solidarities. As Tuomela points out, these solidarities can arise from processes of collective commitment themselves. Where the commitments involve something like the adoption and institutionalization of a constitution for the society as a whole, solidarity may emerge from that, perhaps taking the form of what Habermas called "constitutional patriotism."

The social ontology implied in unitary solidarity may take a holistic form, as in older forms in which the members are internally related via their relation to the social whole. But it does not necessarily connote such holism, although it will involve internal or constitutive relations among the members of the group. In Tuomela's version, they are related to each other as a collectivity, with shared group reasons for action, and as collectively committed to the group and its ethos.[8] But this only requires a we-mode and we-thinking on the part of the individuals, rather than some sort of preexisting or overarching whole from which they derive their social roles and (supposedly) their very identities.

Against the notion of mechanical solidarity, Durkheim juxtaposed what he called organic solidarity, such as is manifest in the modern division of labor. This refers to a set of real connections and interdependencies among people but where those take the form of more dispersed networks, which may even operate behind their backs, as it were. For Durkheim, the people are tied together but also are ideally able to express their individuality through the jobs that they occupy (which he thought would be suitable to, and make use

8. Ibid., 241.

of, their diverse talents). So, the unity involved here is a differentiated one.

My own notion of network solidarity is itself primarily drawn from an existing social phenomenon, namely, social movements, and especially those oriented to overcoming oppression or exploitation. The account initially grows out of a reflection on labor solidarity, but extends more widely to other movements, for example, those for climate justice or for migrant justice, Occupy Wall Street, the #MeToo movement, or Black Lives Matter, as well as in a different context, the Via Campesina. The relevant networks may even pertain to connections among disparate civil society organizations. While these solidarity networks are increasingly transnational, they are also found within nation-states. Conversely, unitary solidarities can be transnational, as in the case of supranational organizations, as well in smaller cross-border communities, whether online or off.

I distinguish these network solidarities from the unitary ones in several respects, but they share with the latter the notions of reciprocity and mutual aid, although in somewhat different interpretations. Like most unitary cases, solidarity networks are also oriented to shared goals. In the case of many of these solidarity movements, the goals include the establishment of more just social relations, whether by way of eliminating oppression or exploitation, or countering coercion, or meeting people's human rights, or instituting more democratic forms of governance, among other such aims. The network solidarities may take agonistic forms, characterized by mutual support among those with shared interests regarded as standing opposed to the interests of others, for example, of labor to capital (although this relation is not always conceived as fully oppositional in this way). Increasingly, social movements see themselves as working to counter structural or systemic injustices, in varied senses of this term.

I have elsewhere elaborated the connection of solidarity to justice.[9] Here, we can note that these movements are not only constrained by considerations of justice but tend to aim at its realization. They do so by mobilizing connections not only among individuals but among groups, each of which attempts to make some contribution to the overall goal from its own perspective and drawing on its own competences and background. The groups (and sometimes individuals) stand in solidarity with each other in lending support to the overall effort. Solidarity here differs from charity in being—implicitly at least—reciprocal and as based on mutual aid. That is, even though these networks may involve relatively advantaged people working to counter oppression or disadvantage, there is an expectation of reciprocal support should that come to be necessary. Normatively, the groups should exhibit deference to those they are trying to support, in the sense of taking the lead from them in regard to the forms of assistance that would be beneficial.[10] This is required not only because those being aided are generally best acquainted with their particular situation and needs, but also as a mark of respect and to avoid potentially imperialist or dominating impositions on these others. Deference in this sense is nonetheless compatible with reciprocity. It requires making efforts to understand the distinctive features of the actual social context of those one is working to assist, so as not to assimilate their situation to one's own. I have also suggested that participation in such solidarity networks is motivated partly by a sort of social empathy, but it also has roots in indignation

---

9. Carol C. Gould, "Solidarity and the Problem of Structural Injustice in Healthcare," *Bioethics*, Special Issue on Solidarity: New Frontiers, 32, no. 9 (November 2018): 541–552, doi.org/10.1111/bioe.12474.
10. Gould, "Transnational Solidarities," 157. Avery Kolers develops this aspect of solidarity at length in his book *A Moral Theory of Solidarity* (Oxford: Oxford University Press, 2016).

at oppression, as well as in the rational recognition of the demands of equality and the importance of realizing people's human rights.[11]

Such a solidarity network can be widely dispersed and its constitutive groups may not always be specifically aware of each other as members of the network. In this sense, often there is no explicit process of coming to agreement on the shared aims or goals. These networks, moreover, are generally open to new participants in the cause, provided the newcomers are willing to do their part to help establish justice (or, in some cases, remediate or alleviate suffering). In normative forms of network solidarity, there is an expectation of equality among those engaged in the struggle and even an expectation of democratic modes of participation.

In previous work, I have suggested that the particular solidarity network one participates in is open to choice, given the impossibility of joining more than a few and the vast scope of injustice. Clearly, solidarity remains a particularist social phenomenon, on this view. Nonetheless, participation can have a universalist intent, as it were, to the degree that it aims at the fulfillment of the requirements of justice, understood as involving the overcoming of domination, oppression, and exploitation, or meeting people's basic human rights. These clearly normative aspects of solidarity will be discussed in the next section.

For now, we can observe that the social ontology of networking solidarity differs from the unitary type sketched above. It differs most notably from the original and traditional forms of unitary solidarity that are defined by a preexisting and comprehensive society in which people relate to each other as members. (Note that this traditional view finds some resonance in more recent expositions in political

---

11. Carol C. Gould, "Motivating Solidarity with Distant Others: Empathic Politics and the Problem of Global Justice," in *Oxford Handbook of Global Justice*, ed. Thom Brooks (Oxford: Oxford University Press, 2020), ch. 6.

theory, including, to a degree, some of David Miller's writing on national identity, Raz and Margalit's on encompassing groups, etc.) With networks, in contrast, the solidarities are actively constructed. The networks are also fundamentally open to new members, provided they are committed to the goals (understood in terms of justice or remediation). In this sense, the networks are indefinitely extendable rather than being understood in terms of a given whole. Clearly, there is no presumption of a preexisting community, based on culture or tradition, as a source of identity. Moreover, in contrast to the solidarities among individuals within a given group, networking solidarities often transpire between groups, where the groups themselves are not always themselves solidary (in contrast to Tuomela's account, on this point, where ingroup solidarity is generally a condition for external solidarity[12]).

If we consider the more modern readings of unitary solidarity, which do not see individuals as gaining their identities by occupying a place and a role within a preexisting community, we can nonetheless discern some differences in social ontology from the network solidarity model. In the unitary case, the group is still taken to be singular and bounded, and within it, individuals experience solidarity with others as fellow members. As with traditional unitary solidarity, their relations to each other are internal, and mediated by group membership. Network solidarities are not only constructed but are essentially open to any group or individual who wants to work for the cause. The relations among participants are internal via their commitment to the goals and norms or to forwarding their shared interests, but are not necessarily directly relationships with each other. Moreover, the solidarity actions of networks may be outward facing, involving relations among the groups toward another group or groups outside the network (or at least not yet a part of it), in contrast to the

---

12. Tuomela, *Social Ontology*, 247.

solidarity activity in unitary cases which remain relations among the members of the group. Although the relations within a solidarity network normatively should involve mutual recognition of each as a co-participant in the solidaristic project, this recognition also tends to be constructed over time rather than presupposed or expected as a feature of membership.

While the unitary solidarities within a group or social whole may in some cases suggest the relevance of a notion of group agency, with shared agency and possibly shared decision-making by the members, networking solidarities are better characterized as involving a looser form of what might be called collective agency among the groups or individuals participating in the network. To the degree that each group within the network makes relatively self-determined contributions based on their own goals and abilities, with only loose coordination with other groups, notions of corporate group agency are inapplicable. Yet, to the degree that the social movements or networks of civil society organizations often make use of various methods of coordinating their efforts and contributions with each other, the collective agency involved is certainly far greater than is involved in crowds (e.g., those who gather to collectively demonstrate or engage in protests).

The distinction between unitary and network solidarity may additionally be thought to coincide with one often drawn between social and political solidarity,[13] but I think that the latter distinction does not adequately capture the social ontological differences. After all, both forms of solidarity are social and both are political. The notion of "project-related solidarity" (Rippe[14]) comes a bit closer to

---

13. See, for example, Sally Scholz, *Political Solidarity* (University Park: Penn State University Press, 2008), 17–50. Scholz adds to these two a third basic type, that of civic solidarity.
14. Klaus Peter Rippe, "Diminishing Solidarity," *Ethical Theory and Practice* 1, no. 3 (September 1998): 355–374.

characterizing the networking type but makes it sound entirely episodic and ephemeral. This does not adequately account for the ultimately large and enduring aims of most social movements, or indeed, their openness to solidarity with other such movements, with the goals of establishing justice and not just alleviating a particular instance of suffering or harm (whether naturally or socially caused).

I have elsewhere discussed the limitations of the notion of a network itself, which derives from computer networking, and bears the limits of its inorganic origins. The metaphor of a web is probably better in some respects, retaining the multiple lines of connection. But in its organic form, at least, it also does not necessarily connote the openness of solidarity networks, though it does describe their constructed (spun) nature.[15] Moreover, the goals and norms that motivate the mutual aid and joint action in the case of solidarity networks are missing from these various technological or natural metaphors. In solidarity networks, they infuse and guide the interaction of individuals and groups.

SOME NORMATIVE FEATURES OF SOLIDARITY

With these or similar social ontological approaches to solidarity in mind, some may be tempted to propose a purely descriptivist account of solidarity as an empirical phenomenon, whether of the unitary or networking type. However, I am not at all sure that such a putatively value-neutral account is possible (or indeed helpful, were it possible). On such a "descriptivist" view, pernicious cases of violent

---

15. An alternative organic metaphor, suggested by Patricia Cipollitti in discussion, is that of a rhizome, with its connotations of an open-ended, non-hierarchical, non-linear, and heterogenous structure.

gangs, or white supremacist groups, or virulent nationalist states, or alternately, neo-Nazi networks (like the older Aryan Nation or the more recent Identity Evropa or System Resistance Network) would all be cases of solidarity, albeit immoral or unjust ones. But I think such an approach misunderstands the nature of solidarity as itself a norm (and as incorporating various sub-norms). Moreover, it fails to recognize the values that are inevitably part of any social ontology. Such an approach also will not help us much with criticizing those specific nefarious cases of "solidaristic" action, inasmuch as it would be limited to bringing external norms to bear in an "all things considered" approach.

A similar "all things considered" approach has been advocated by Margaret Gilbert in her account of the normativity of joint commitment as the basis of collective action. In that view, there is a nonmoral normativity or set of obligations and rights that follow from these joint commitments. But these can be qualified by moral considerations that may be brought to bear to criticize pernicious collective actions.[16] There is certainly something appealing about the idea of a bare normativity of joint commitments, when this is understood in the simple terms of providing some reasons for action. In Gilbert's approach, which sees joint commitments as primary and irreducible, making such commitments to others to jointly undertake some action binds us or obliges us (non-morally) to perform those actions, so much so that we are also obligated to seek the permission of the others if we no longer intend to follow through on the commitment. There are several criticisms one may make of Gilbert's claims here, especially since she seems to problematically model joint commitment on promising, with its relatively strong obligations and demands. In addition, the claim that there is an obligation to seek

---

16. For Gilbert's recent discussion, see Margaret Gilbert, *Rights and Demands: A Foundational Inquiry* (Oxford: Oxford University Press, 2018).

permission may not in fact conform to people's intuitions about actual cases, as recent experiments have claimed to demonstrate.[17] Nonetheless, if normativity is reduced to a minimal "having *a* reason to act," then it seems plausible to attribute this to our commitments to undertake joint actions.

For Gilbert, these non-moral obligations can be subjected to further scrutiny from a moral standpoint, although no account is given of what such a moral perspective entails. Moreover, it is not clear where social and political norms, like freedom, justice, and democracy, fit on such an individualistic view of morality. Clearly, however, they would be regarded as external to the social dimension of joint commitment, which Gilbert separates out as non-moral. My own sense is that this division does not do justice either to social ontology, which to my mind is always value-laden, or to the social and political norms themselves, which are not purely moral, at least in the way moral principles have been interpreted in modern and contemporary philosophy (primarily in terms of consequentialist, deontological, or virtue ethical perspectives). Nor, of course, are these social and political norms merely legal norms, which is the only other category that Gilbert recognizes. (The options for her are limited to non-moral social normativity, morality, and legality.)

Without going into the deep questions that are involved in a critique of that and similar views, we can focus on the question of the sort of normativity, if any, that is involved in solidarity. There is also the question of how solidarity fares in the company of freedom, justice, and equality. Is solidarity intrinsically valuable? If so, what can be said about these pernicious cases? Are those non-solidaristic? Is

---

17. Matthew Rachar and Javier Gomez-Lavin, "Why We Need a New Normativism: An Empirical Investigation into Collective Action," unpublished manuscript; and Matthew Rachar, "How We Act Together," doctoral dissertation, the CUNY Graduate Center, April 2019 (ProQuest Dissertations, 2019, 13860025).

something wrong with the very sociality of the participants? Or can these cases only be criticized from the standpoint of an external norm (even if not only a narrowly moral one)? Note that similar problems could be raised with regard to social cooperation, which might seem to be a good thing, one notably missing from much of contemporary society, especially given our individualistic economic life. However, there are certainly many pernicious cases of social cooperation as well, so one must proceed carefully here.

A fuller account of the problems with negative solidarity groups has to await a consideration of the impact of power and coercion in the next section, but for now, we can focus on the question of what could be construed as normative solidarity, especially in regard to our central focus on networking solidarities.

We can observe that even Tuomela's supposedly neutral characterization of solidarity in its unitary form involves significant normative dimensions, at least in what he calls "an ideally functioning paradigmatic we-mode group." He says that it exemplifies (following Lindenberg): (1) cooperativeness versus free-riding; (2) fairness (in the division of tasks and the fruits of cooperation); (3) commitment to the group's ethos and to helping each other; (4) trustworthiness and loyalty; and (5) considerateness to fellow members.[18] Even more interesting for our purposes, a strong solidarity group is said to be based on equality (though more weakly solidarist groups are only based on equity). Moreover, insofar as the group is based on collective commitment and oriented to shared goals, the participation of the members is intentional and voluntary and, we could add, in that sense free. And although oppressed groups are described as non-autonomous, standard solidarity groups are characterized as self-determining, and indeed in paradigmatic cases as democratic.[19]

---

18. Tuomela, *Social Ontology*, 251–254.
19. Ibid., 17, 30, 251, 257.

Clearly, these robust normative features that are clearly evident in Tuomela's account (and in that of other theorists) go well beyond the bare reasons for action that result from joint commitment in Gilbert's view. These normative aspects will prove important, especially when we put them in relation to actually existing solidarity groups, as they emerge socially and historically. Even if these normative characteristics are presented via an account of "paradigmatic solidarity groups," they are nonetheless held to pertain to other solidarity groups, though most often to a lesser degree.

In my own account of network solidarities, normative features of the account include forms of non-instrumental reciprocity, including mutual recognition and a disposition to mutual aid; the presupposition of equality among the individual members and the groups as well, except insofar as some of the latter may be regarded as taking some sort of leadership role; deference to those who are receiving assistance; and most notably a commitment to justice, understood as the elimination of oppression and exploitation, and as involving the recognition and fulfillment of people's human rights. Participation in a specific solidarity movement is voluntary and people are free to leave it. The network would also ideally use participatory, consensual, and generally democratic means for making decisions, both within and across groups that make it up.

These networks also exemplify the standard solidarity features of "pro-social" or cooperative action, and participants show a willingness to bear some costs,[20] if only through the use of their time and effort. To the degree that their solidaristic action is oriented to goals,

---

20. For a discussion of solidarity that makes such a willingness to bear costs central to it, see Barbara Prainsack and Alena Buyx, *Solidarity in Biomedicine and Beyond* (Cambridge: Cambridge University Press, 2017), 52. For a critique of this centrality, see Gould, "Solidarity and the Problem of Structural Injustice in Healthcare."

the activity of the individuals and groups can be regarded as chosen and indeed as non-coerced.

I have elsewhere argued that we need to cultivate a disposition to solidarity. Although solidarity remains a particularist notion, oriented to particular groups or involving relations among such groups, we can propose that the disposition to stand in solidarity with others in the interest of justice, or even perhaps to stand in solidarity with any human being who may be in need of it, can be developed as a general feature of character.[21] Here, solidarity at a global level remains a limit concept, designating a horizon of imaginative possibilities, whether in the sense of an identification with every human being or in a collective sense as an identification with human life on earth.[22] Nonetheless, the readinesss to feel empathy with others and to stand with them in meeting needs through mutual aid could be developed as a disposition or a trait of character that is not merely particular but is in principle open to all generally.

The mention of character here suggests that in its normative sense, the practice of solidarity can be considered a virtue of an individual and the solidaristic activity of groups can be viewed as a type of virtuous practice. Like other virtues, solidarity is likely developed through practice itself, along with the right sorts of education. It involves cultivating the right sorts of attitudes of mutual care and concern, respect, and a recognition of interdependence. Beyond that, it requires developing a willingness to freely engage in concrete actions in support of others, and carrying through on that willingness in particular contexts, in the interest of eliminating hardship and oppression and working with others toward establishing justice.

---

21. Gould, "Transnational Solidarities," 155; and Gould, *Interactive Democracy*, 127–128.
22. Gould, *Interactive Democracy*, 127–128.

POWER, COERCION, AND THE CORRUPTION OF SOLIDARITY

With the social ontological analysis in mind, along with the general outlines of the normative framework, we can now turn to our central question and consider how white supremacist groups, violent gangs, virulent nationalist states, or neo-Nazi networks measure up to the requirements of solidarity. It would be easy to criticize these groups normatively, but interestingly we can wonder whether they meet even a putatively descriptive understanding of solidarity, as on Tuomela's account. Needless to say, one major problem—probably *the* major problem—with these groups concerns their exclusionary character, and very often their deeply problematic actual treatment of outsiders. Nonetheless, I think even if we remain with the "internal" features of these groups, that is, the relations interior to the group, we see some problems emerging as to whether they measure up to existing accounts of solidarity.

To assess this requires that we consider actual social factors and especially the differential power among the members that undermines the claim to equality (or even equity) held to characterize solidarity groups. This is most evident in nationalist states, especially of the fascist variety, which are marked by extreme differences in power among the participants. But it is evident also in many gangs and white supremacist groups that are generally organized with leaders, often with a hierarchical arrangement as well. And while it may be tempting to regard all the members as freely choosing not only to participate, but also to follow the leaders and thus in some sense to authorize their power, in fact these groups often operate against a background of coercion and power relations that make membership virtually mandatory. Even more evident is the fact that once an individual joins such a group, whether by choice or because of necessity, it can be very hard to leave it.[23]

This difficulty in leaving gangs, as well as ultranationalist or white supremacist groups, suggests that they could be viewed as "total institutions" from a sociological point of view.[24] While this term, originally introduced by Erving Goffman, has mainly been applied to institutions like prisons, military boot camps, or monasteries, which govern all of a person's life, there is also some ground for applying it beyond those to social institutions from which there is essentially no escape. In this way, even if the entry into gangs and white supremacist groups may be voluntary (to a degree), the continuing participation of the members is not. The recognition of these as total institutions in this sense, with the form of background coercion that this entails, casts doubt on the adequacy of the description of solidarity groups as involving the freedom and equality of members.

This problem with the analysis of the nature of solidarity arises, I think, from adopting a social ontology that remains uncritical, by disregarding the role of differential economic and political power or social status within existing societies. Indeed, these theoretical approaches may read into the analyses of the nature of social reality the features of an ideally normative social life, or at least, of unrepresentative forms of social life. Even where the model of solidarity is held to have its prime exemplification, namely, in "families and certain work and sports teams," according to Tuomela,[25] it is evident that

---

23. Daryl Harris, Russell Turner, Ian Garrett, and Sally Atkinson, "Understanding the Psychology of Gang Violence: Implications for Designing Effective Violence Interventions," *Ministry of Justice Research Series* 2/11 (2011). Retrieved from www.justiceacademy.org/iShare/Library-UK/research-gang-violence.pdf; Scott H. Decker, David C. Pyrooz, and Richard K. Moule, Jr., "Disengagement from Gangs as Role Transitions," *Journal of Research on Adolescence* 24 (2014): 268–283, doi:10.1111/jora.12074; Bryan F. Bubolz and Pete Simi, "Leaving the World of Hate: Life-Course Transitions and Self-Change," *American Behavioral Scientist* 59, no. 12 (2015): 1588–1608, doi:10.1177/0002764215588814.
24. I owe this observation to Michael Gould-Wartofsky, in discussion.
25. Tuomela, *Social Ontology*, 254–255.

power differences between men and women or between managers and workers (or even between managers and players) often play an important role and undercut the putative equality.

Indeed, the recognition of the power differentials within various groups that supposedly evidence mutual aid and solidaristic support among members also bears on the age-old claims to this presence of virtue among group members, even when the group carries out criminal or coercive acts toward outsiders. We are familiar with the analogous claims summed up in the idea of "honor among thieves" (from Plato onward[26]). Nonetheless, as we have just observed, many such putatively solidaristic groups are in fact hierarchical and the aid they provide is not always fully mutual, with some (e.g., the leaders) demanding or getting more than others (e.g., newcomers or underlings). Without a genuine recognition of the equality of members, the practice of solidarity can become somewhat or altogether one-sided, with the practitioners not exemplifying the relevant virtue of character in such cases.

These observations concerning the role of power in undercutting solidarity suggest the need for what one might call a *critical social ontology*. Such a critical theory would not only analyze basic processes that are manifest in ordinary interactions but would attend also to the background structures of injustice and the differences in power that frame and affect those everyday interactions in practice. Such an approach would also be self-critical about the ways that the interests, standing, and social context of the theorists themselves might affect their theorizing.

Clearly, as a particularist phenomenon that arises and marks several of our associations, solidarity would need to be placed in relevant social and historical contexts. This is not to say that norms are at all

---

26. Plato, *Republic*, I. 351.

irrelevant to its formulation, but these too need to be understood as partly emergent.

For our narrower purposes here, we need to acknowledge the ways that background power and existing economic and political structures that constrain people's freedom can deeply infect groups and their potential for solidaristic functioning. The model of a free and equal association of people who operate democratically, which Tuomela and others attribute as a basic structure of group action,[27] is clearly a normative version of solidarity, whether unitary or networking. To my mind, to recognize the normative dimension is not a negative thing and elements of this vision may well be displayed even in corrupt forms of solidarity, as well as in our ordinary interactions (e.g., with regard to mutual recognition of agency in ordinary life).[28] In fact, there is much to be said in favor of developing an adequate normative version of both the unitary and networking types of solidarity and much work remains to be done in that enterprise. But it is not at all clear that we can speak of violent gangs, ultra-nationalist groups, or virulently nationalist states, as examples of a neutral and "empirical" solidarity either, unless that term is stripped of many of the features that have been attributed to it. Moreover, the problem here is not simply that those phenomena embody solidarity, but one not properly qualified by justice or morality. Rather, the criticisms I raise suggest that those cases should not be considered solidarity groups at all, at least where these take the idealized forms that they do in accounts such as Tuomela's.

Of course, this is not to say that there may not be some actual cases of solidarity groups that fully measure up to Tuomela's description (at least for a time), or to the Three Musketeers motto (e.g., a group

---

27. Tuomela, *Social Ontology*, 17, 30, 251.
28. Erving Goffman, *Relations in Public: Microstudies of the Public Order* (New York: Basic Books, 1971), 5–18; Gould, *Interactive Democracy*, 43.

of close friends). And there may be solidarity networks aiming at justice that do exemplify a commitment to consensus or at least more minimal forms of democratic decision-making and whose members treat not only each other but those they are working to assist in line with the requirements of mutual recognition and mutual aid. Perhaps the groups making up the network also freely choose their joint and several actions toward the goals they shared, as would be required by the model. Here, we can see that a normative account can helpfully explicate both some of the values involved and how these values are related to each other.

But I suggest that lack of attention to the role played by power relations and to the injustice of background conditions poses a problem not only for the theory of solidarity but for the potential solidarity within these groups themselves. Power differences can infuse and undercut the actual social relations among the members of the group or those that can exist between groups, for example by enabling group members to display sexist or racist forms of interaction that undercut any genuine solidarity among the full set of members. This tendency can be found in actually existing unitary groups and in social movements, including those oriented to social justice. While this is certainly not a new observation (consider the critiques of the anti-war movement of the 1960s, and of Occupy Wall Street,[29] etc.), I think that considerations of this sort have not much been applied to cases of solidarity, which so far have been treated in recent literature most often exclusively in positive and idealized terms.

Recognizing the ways that power differences and background structural injustice can affect the sociality and potential solidarity among group members could potentially help in dealing with perhaps the most difficult aspect of the theory of solidarity, namely, the

---

29. See the discussion in Michael Gould-Wartofsky, *The Occupiers: The Making of the 99 Percent Movement* (Oxford: Oxford University Press, 2015).

relation to non-members or outsiders. It has seemed to many that solidarity, at least in its unitary form, or even simply in virtue of being a particularist phenomenon, necessarily has to be exclusionary, if not also necessarily involving the group's setting itself against an "other." While I cannot address this issue at length here (and have discussed it elsewhere[30]), we can speculate that the nefarious treatment of outsiders can be harmful to the people who do so in much the same way that has been claimed for oppressors in contexts of race or gender (whatever immediate psychological or material benefits they may derive.)[31] But for more benign exclusions, for example, where an oppressed group seeks to organize to take some concerted action on its own behalf, we could certainly see an argument for the legitimacy of partiality, again on grounds of their actual social standing in the contemporary historical context.

To discern when such partiality and limited exclusion are justified, I think we need to appeal to a notion of justice that serves as the overall guide for evaluating solidarities.[32] Indeed, I suggest that the conception of justice involved has to have a certain cosmopolitan element to it. This would apply differently to each of the senses of solidarity discussed above.

For networking solidarities that in fact aim at justice, their mode should be disposed to openness where possible. As indicated, they would be willing to link up with other groups or individuals who are

---

30. Gould, *Interactive Democracy*, 119–131; and Gould, "Solidarity between the National and the Transnational."
31. See, for example, Derald Wing Sue, *Microaggressions in Everyday Life: Race, Gender, and Sexual Orientation* (Hoboken, NJ: Wiley, 2010).
32. I have myself argued for an interpretation of justice as what I have called equal positive freedom, or prima facie equal rights of access to the conditions of self-transformative, or self-developing, activity, where these conditions can be specified in terms of human rights (on a certain interpretation, but including economic, social, and political ones). But I do not think that there needs to be an agreement on a specific conception such as this among those who act in solidarity.

committed to overcoming injustice. Such a network is by its nature an open and processive notion. This is not to say that exclusions might not sometimes be justified, but there would be a presumption in favor of openness.

In the case of unitary solidarities, which tend to be relatively closed, I have elsewhere argued that they need to be understood as framed by a similar commitment to the equal freedom of all and to seeing their human rights fulfilled. I have adapted Robert Goodin's notion of assigned responsibility for this context (without accepting his consequentialism overall), to explain the idea that partiality (as well as delimited institutional arrangements more generally) can be justified in economic and political contexts, provided others equally can meet their needs and fulfill their rights effectively in similar partial ways (e.g., within nation-states).[33] Where people cannot do so, as when states fail to provide for people's basic human rights, there is an important role for networking solidarities and social movements which act in the interest of justice. The underlying idea here, which I cannot develop in this chapter, is that as fundamentally interdependent beings we have responsibilities to meet each other's human rights but that the devolution to smaller scale institutional contexts makes sense as a practical requirement and can be justified in those terms. But where there are serious lacks in this process and existing groups or states fail to fulfill these rights or meet these needs, others need to step in.

---

33. Robert Goodin, "What Is So Special about Our Fellow Countrymen?," *Ethics* 98, no. 4 (1988): 663–686, https://www.jstor.org/stable/2380890. For my own discussion, see Carol C. Gould, *Interactive Democracy: The Social Roots of Global Justice* (Cambridge: Cambridge University Press, 2014), 191; Gould, "Solidarity between the National and the Transnational"; and Gould, "Motivating Solidarity with Distant Others." I note that Margaret Kohn also appeals to Goodin's notion in her Chapter 10 in this volume.

CAROL C. GOULD

NOTES ON COLLECTIVIZING RESPONSIBILITY IN SOLIDARITY NETWORKS

In conclusion, we can suggest a few implications of the account of the two forms of solidarity, and especially of networking solidarity, for understanding collective responsibility. Existing accounts of such responsibility in the recent philosophical literature have tended to focus on corporate group agents, with a view to holding them to account for their wrongful actions.[34] These corporate agents may display some forms of what we have called unitary solidarity, but, as Tuomela observes, they generally do not display the "paradigmatic" solidarities possible in smaller group agents like families or teams.[35] Nation-states, similarly understood as unitary group agents, have also been called upon to rectify historical injustices and to otherwise correct for the harms that they have brought about.

A reflection on responsibility within solidarity networks suggests that accounts of shared or collective responsibility need to be considerably broader than these. It is not merely that existing approaches tend to be limited to backward-looking issues of liability for harm, as Iris Marion Young has argued.[36] Beyond this, these accounts fail to see that responsibility can be (and I would argue, often needs to be) conceived in a processive and ongoing way. I call this a model of *collectivizing responsibility*.

We can see this alternative model in the activity of solidarity networks, as discussed above, often (though certainly not always) operating transnationally. In contrast to (relatively) unitary solidarity groups, which are conceived as already existing, the network

---

34. See, for example, Christian List and Philip Pettit, *Group Agency: The Possibility, Design, and Status of Corporate Agents* (Oxford: Oxford University Press, 2011), 153–169.
35. Tuomela, *Social Ontology*, 242–243.
36. Iris Marion Young, *Responsibility for Justice* (Oxford: Oxford University Press, 2011).

solidarities that are aimed at rectifying injustices (like practices of oppression or exploitation) involve processes of constituting the group itself in an ongoing way, in being open to all those who want to take up responsibility to assist others by joining the group in solidarity with them and with each other.

In these contexts, moreover, people's initial impulses to take responsibility for addressing existing harms and for rectifying social and institutional injustices can provide a motive force for forming the solidarity groups themselves and also can help guide the network's ongoing activity. In a sense, the process of taking responsibility can be seen as binding together the people involved, and thus as helping to construct the groups themselves, in a manner that stands opposed to existing models that instead hold existing groups to be collectively responsible. The processes of acting in solidarity with others can in turn enhance participants' sense of responsibility with which they began the process, as well as solidifying them as a group in a collective responsibility project. That project may also involve explicitly distributing responsibilities for its success among the groups that make up the network.

I suggest that this alternative model could be especially useful for understanding collective responsibility for addressing global harms like climate change and global economic injustices. But its further development would have to await another paper.

Chapter 9

The Cost of Belonging

Universalism versus the Political Ideal of Solidarity

VÉRONIQUE MUNOZ-DARDÉ

What *is* solidarity?[1] The idea of solidarity has both a descriptive and a normative dimension. 'Solidarity' is a term which marks out an affective dimension by which members of a community feel a sense of belonging or community among themselves, and which is taken to express or to ground a sense of duty toward other members of that same community, be it one's family, profession, social class, urban environment, nation-state, species, or whatever.

As David Wiggins reminds us, 'solidarity' in English borrows its meaning from French. For the meaning of the word in French consider the following definition:

---

1. This chapter is an extensively reworked version of a paper for the workshop on "Solidarity: Its Nature and Value," organized by Andrea Sangiovanni and Juri Viehoff in May 2019 at the European University Institute, Florence. For comments and suggestions, many thanks to Hannah Carnegy-Arbuthnott, Justin Broakes, Victoria Camps, David Charles, Naomi Eilan, Cécile Fabre, Niko Kolodny, Dan Khokhar, Cécile Laborde, Mike Martin, David Miller, Rowan Mellor, Angel Puyol, Joseph Raz, Andrea Sangiovanni, Tommie Shelby, Amia Srinivasan, Rowland Stout, Nikhil Venkatesh, David Wiggins, Lea Ypi and audiences at the EUI, the Nuffield Political Theory Workshop, Berkeley, UCL, and Barcelona.

Solidarity is no other but a relation which joins and combines interests, a sort of mutual insurance through which all are generally protected, and each person in particular safeguarded against bad luck. To have solidarity is to be responsible for each other.[2]

This seems to give a good sense of the role of solidarity within well-functioning social institutions. But in itself it doesn't really tell us what, if any, the *value* of solidarity is, or how this mutual concern should be grounded in what matters. That unclarity, one might feel, is reflected practically in our ordinary political discourse. In political debate, appeals to solidarity seem to reflect the sense that 'solidarity' is a warm, if fuzzy, word: its connotations are almost invariably positive and its demands not to be resisted, despite, or perhaps because of, its fuzziness.

In this chapter, I'll explore and try better to articulate the political ideal of solidarity. Solidarity plays a central role in a lot of our political discourse. Our sense of solidarity with others, our group identifications, seems to be essential to the political activities and associations which structure social and political life. Since it is difficult to see how we could live without such identities, we must recognize that these are to some extent at least a legitimate aspect of political life: solidarity is one among our political ideals. But I want here to press the question further: Is solidarity a value, as most take liberty to be, and many have supposed equality is? Elsewhere I have argued that while

---

2. "La solidarité n'est autre chose qu'un rapport qui rattache et confond les intérêts, une sorte d'assurance mutuelle où tous sont protégés en général et chacun garanti en particulier contre les mauvaises chances. Être solidaire, c'est être responsables les uns pour les autres." Gerald Antoine, *Liberté, égalité, fraternité* (Paris: UNESCO, 1980), 154–155, my translation; quoted in David Wiggins, "Solidarity and the Roots of the Ethical," *Tijdschrift voor Filosofie*, 71ste Jaarg., no. 2 (2009): 253. Generally speaking, in French, but not necessarily in other languages, solidarity is one of the keywords to refer to social rights. This is in part due to the nineteenth-century influence of the *solidaristes*, as I'll briefly explain in the following section.

questions of equality are politically urgent, they are not to be understood as grounded in some distinctive value of equality.[3] And in the present chapter, I want also to argue that we should question whether solidarity could be a value in its own right. This is not to say that solidarity is without value or without significance: on the contrary, it is an important and indispensable political ideal. Solidarity expresses and structures the kinds of association we need to live well within a social and political setting. But the proper explanation of the central role of solidarity in political life equally highlights the essentially partitive nature of this ideal. And it is this aspect of solidarity which rules out any fundamental role for it in an ethical theory grounded on equal and universal respect.

Emphasizing the essential partitive structure of the concept of solidarity may leave some liberal thinkers uneasy with the partiality in concern that that engenders. This might lead some to wish to reject entirely any ideal of solidarity. I think we should reject such an injunction. Any plausible account of our ethical thought must allow morality to include the partiality to be found in our familial, romantic, and friendly relations. Solidarity as a political idea imposes no more on us than that. So, I invite us to trace a path through the middle here: we must be alive and not unduly critical of the central role that ideals of solidarity play within political life; we must not mistake the instrumental role it plays for any fundamental ethical concern; but in rejecting its partitive essence as part of the ground of ethical life, we should not thereby repudiate partiality.

---

3. Véronique Munoz-Dardé, "Equality and Division: Values in Principle," *Proceedings of the Aristotelian Society*, supplementary volume 79 (2005): 255–284.

SOLIDARITY IN THE HISTORY OF POLITICAL THOUGHT

Let us start with the history of the term in social and political thought. One of the first explicit theoretical efforts at defining the idea of solidarity is found in Emile Durkheim. He describes modern societies as the result of a historical evolution toward more individual autonomy, and at the same time toward more interdependence and complementarity of social tasks. The result of this process, as he sees it, is that there *isn't* a loss of social cement in modern societies. Instead, solidarity based on similarities of tasks and values typical of traditional societies gives way to a form of solidarity based on the complementarity of tasks and cooperation in society at large.[4] Ideally, in this form of modern solidarity, a person focused on one task can feel that they are useful in doing their part, so to speak, in bringing about what we might today call the fruits of social cooperation, echoing John Rawls. Durkheim considers that societies need some kind of durable bond, or solidarity. He finds its possibility in the regulation of the distributive structures and a system of protection for all individuals and, in particular, the least well-off, in the political community as a whole. As individuals become more independent from traditional solidarities, more universal forms of social protection take their place.[5]

---

4. Durkheim's distinction is between what he calls *mechanical* and *organic* forms of solidarity. Similar ideas are found in Weber, Tönnies, and before them Adam Smith. See Émile Durkheim, *De la division du travail social* [1983] (Paris: PUF, 1930) and *L'éducation morale* (Paris: Felix Alcan, 1925). See also Marie Claude Blais, *La solidarité: Histoire d'une idée* (Paris: Gallimard, 2007), ch. 8 ; and Serge Paugam, *Repenser la solidarité: L'apport des sciences sociales* (Paris: PUF, 2007).
5. See Stephen Lukes, *Émile Durkheim, his Life and Work: A Historical and Critical Study* (London: Allen Lane, 1973), ch. 7, 137–178; and Lisa Herzog, "Durkheim on Social Justice: the Argument from 'Organic Solidarity,'" *American Political Science Review* 112 (2018): 1, 112. Herzog emphasizes Rawlsian themes that we shall return to below.

This view already contains some of the core elements which will occupy us below. It starts with small-scale examples of solidarity and on that basis hypothesizes a more generalized social bond to replace and remedy the deficiencies that arise out of more partial allegiances. It also highlights the need for, and importance of, sentimental ties among individuals in society for systems of solidarity to work.

In this, Durkheim was essentially focused on illuminating how the norms of social cohesion actually function. It was left to the *solidaristes*, the movement initiated following Alfred Fouillée by Léon Bourgeois at the end of nineteenth century, to translate Durkheim's ideas into a normative account, and into a political ideal.[6] Bourgeois stresses interdependence, and points out that, from the moment we are born, we depend on others and cannot satisfy any need without "drawing on the immense reserve of utilities accumulated by humanity."[7] For the *solidaristes*, there is a form of contract, or 'quasi-contract' between individuals in a given society and also between generations, and the state must put in effect this contract by guaranteeing social rights as well as forms of social insurance against risks. Alive to the fact that there is no actual consent, be it expressed or tacit, at the root of what they call a 'quasi-contract,' Bourgeois and his followers nonetheless appeal to the idea found in the Law of obligations for services rendered that are not the result of a contract or promise, but where utility or fairness demand that they be regarded as if they were. An example of such quasi-contracts is when the Law imposes a debt on a party who has benefited from the provision of services even if these services are not the result of an explicit contract: equity demands that these benefits be regarded as if they were the result of a contract.

---

6. Léon Bourgeois, *Solidarité* [1986] (Villeneuve d'Ascq: Presses du Septentrion, 1998), 45. See also Blais, *La solidarité*, ch. 1; and Serge Paugam, "Solidarité," in *Dictionnaire des inégalités et de la justice sociale*, ed. Patrick Savidan (Paris: PUF, 2018), 1536ff. On this period, see Jean-Fabien Spitz, *Le moment républicain en France* (Paris: Gallimard, NRF essais, 2005).

7. Bourgeois, *Solidarité*, 45: "l'immense réservoir des utilités accumulées par l'humanité."

There is nonetheless still a question whether there has been *voluntary acceptance* of the benefits: Bourgeois and his followers are not fully clear on this point. That is, they find it reasonable to assume that individuals accept the benefits of the division of labor, and so owe a social debt. So the question of whether they underplay the non-voluntary dimension of belonging to one's political community remains.[8] Be that as it may, their school of thought eventually played a key role in the genesis of organized systems of social insurance in the early twentieth century across Europe. And the legacy of the *solidaristes* is that the language of social solidarity still underpins the idea of social rights, at least in the French language.

With Durkheim and the *solidaristes* we see an illustration of some of the most attractive ways in which we can employ the term, and how otherwise disparate claims for social assistance among the needy come to be institutionalized as reciprocal forms of social insurance. That use has now spread to other languages and cultures, including in the English-speaking world.[9]

An element of solidarity as a need and vehicle within social life has, as was already noted by Durkheim, a sentimental dimension: in order to serve its purpose, feelings of belonging need to be shared throughout the group. Like fraternity, with which it is sometimes

---

8. Contemporary discussions of political obligations in the light of tacit, voluntary, acceptance of benefits which have nonetheless not been requested are already present in germ in the *solidaristes*. See Charles Andler, "Du quasi-contrat social et de M. Léon Bourgeois," *Revue de Métaphysique et de Morale* 5, no. 4 (July 1897): 520–530. See also, in Chapter 3 of this volume, Andrea Sangiovanni's analysis of Bourgeois's philosophical ideas. On the other hand, as Sangiovanni notes, there is also a resemblance between Bourgeois conception of a 'quasi-contract' and Rawls's *hypothetical* contract.

9. See Philippe Van Parijs, "Solidarity, Diversity, and Social Justice," in *The Strains of Commitment: The Political Sources of Solidarity in Diverse Societies*, ed. Keith Banting and Will Kymlicka (Oxford: Oxford University Press, 2017), 425, for a brief note on how the French term *solidarité* spread to other languages over time. Van Parijs notes that in "the graphs provided by <books.google.com/ngrams>, the 0.001 mark was reached by the French 'solidarité' around 1850, by the Italian 'solidarietà' around 1890, by the Spanish 'solidariedad' around 1905, by the German 'Solidarität' in 1950 and by the English 'solidarity' only in 1980."

contrasted, but with which it has served similar purposes in the history of political movements,[10] solidarity can ground this shared feeling of belonging in a whole host of divergent ways. One can build solidarities by focusing on common features and values: this is what Durkheim thought was characteristic of 'mechanical,' that is, traditional, solidarities. However, the *solidaristes* highlight a different narrative: even in the context of diversity of values and identities, a common response to a shared need is enough to create a solidaristic narrative. This is the *first* dimension of the concept where one finds some contention regarding the meaning of the term: some theorists expressing concerns, for example, that social solidarities and the welfare state are undermined by perceived increased diversity, and others highlighting the hope that 'inclusive' solidarities[11] can nonetheless be forged around just institutions.

A *second*, related, aspect of the nineteenth-century movement is that it equivocates over the voluntariness of members' belonging to a group. As we saw, Bourgeois underplays the difference between contracts where benefits have been tacitly accepted, even if not requested, and obligations that the citizens of a state have toward each other. However, Bourgeois also stresses many involuntary aspects of the human condition, such as interdependence, as part of his account. And the legacy in political history of the *solidaristes* is to be found in the various forms of welfare state created in the last century and a half, all of which typically protect members of a political community. That we belong to this or that political community is generally not voluntary: we find ourselves in the same boat as others, sharing some need for social protection, but without a common endeavor other

---

10. On this point, see Marcel David, *Le printemps de la fraternité: Genèse et vicissitudes 1830–1851* (Paris: Aubier, 1992). See also François Dubet, "Fraternité," in *Dictionnaire des Inégalités*, 592–598.
11. The term 'inclusive solidarity' is used by Will Kymlicka and Keith Banting in the introduction of *The Strains of Commitment*, 11ff.

than that of defining and sustaining forms of solidaristic help. So, is voluntariness at the heart of solidarity, or simply incidental?

A *third* aspect of contention has to do with the scale of the community of solidarity. The incipient welfare states of the nineteenth century were typically nation-based. However, the language of solidarity can apply to small-scale solidarities and there is also, at least in principle, a tendency to extend solidarity in the other direction, to the whole of humanity. Indeed article 22 of the Universal Declaration of Human Rights declares that "Everyone, as a member of society, has the right to social security and is entitled to realization, through national effort and international co-operation and in accordance with the organization and resources of each State, of the economic, social and cultural rights indispensable for his dignity and the free development of his personality."

Article 22 of the Declaration of Human rights highlights a *fourth* possible area of contention or ambiguity: Who is supposed to have solidarity with whom? Who is supposed to give help, and to whom? There are at least two competing models: (i) mutual help of members who are both contributors and beneficiaries; and (ii) help from those members who are able to provide it to those members who need it whatever their level of contribution. Following Van Parijs, we could term the first type of solidarity *Bismarckian*, a reference to the type of mutual insurance put in place in Bismarck's Prussia, and the second type *Beveridgean*, after the famous Beveridge report *Social Insurance and Allied Services* of 1942 which served as the basis for the generous welfare state set up by the Labour Government elected in the United Kingdom after the Second World War.[12]

---

12. See Philippe Van Parijs, "Au delà de la solidarité: Les fondements éthiques de l'État-Providence et de son dépassement," in *Repenser la solidarité*, 246, for the distinction between what he terms a *Bismarckian* notion of solidarity between and for workers, and a *Beveridgean* conception. (Van Parijs himself favors a third possibility, universal basic income, inspired in the ideas of Thomas Paine.) "Dans le modèle que j'appellerai bismarckien, les travailleurs renoncent obligatoirement à une partie de leur rémunération présente pour constituer un

A final, *fifth*, element of the contest over solidarity, to which we'll return below, is that it is characterized by a dynamic which emphasizes one's responsibilities toward insiders to the group. However, we saw that article 22 of the Declaration of Human Rights potentially extends social solidarity to all members of humanity: so, in some discourse exhibiting this trait, there are no more outsiders to be contrasted with. The social models of the nineteenth and early twentieth centuries ground social solidarity in special ties, feelings of common belonging, and communal responsibility with people we share a political community with. But if all that fuels the sense of solidarity is the necessary cooperation of many to attend to claims of need of some, then it may seem that solidarity demands to be extended to more general duties of mutual aid or impartial benevolence we owe others as members of humanity. Whether this more recent development of the ideal of solidarity is coherent is a question to which we turn below.

All of these divergent elements and opposed narratives persist in our political theory, and in the political rhetoric of solidarity. The word is used to justify the existence of extended social rights such as those exemplified in the National Health Service, and, perhaps continuous with this, it figures to underpin the idea of reciprocity between European states to sustain social rights. Expanding and perhaps diluting this dimension, the Treaty of Maastricht calls for a deepening of "the solidarity between [European] peoples while respecting their

fond qui interviendra dans le paiement des soins de santé dont ils auront besoin et qui leur fournira un revenu lorsqu'ils auront passé un certain âge ou lorsqu'un accident, la maladie ou le chômage involontaire les empêcheront de travailler. Dans le modèle que j'appellerai beveridgéen, tous les titulaires de revenus primaires (du travail ou du capital) renoncent obligatoirement à une partie de leurs revenus pour constituer un fond qui fournira à tout membre de la société un niveau minimum de ressources, y compris la prise en charge des soins de santé dont il a besoin, au cas où il ne serait pas capable d'atteindre ce minimum par ses propres moyens, en raison par exemple de son âge, d'un handicap, d'un accident, d'une maladie ou de l'impossibilité de trouver un emploi suffisamment rémunéré."

history, their culture and their traditions." At a wholly international level a 'solidarity' tax was introduced in 2006 to provide help for AIDS in Africa, and the UNHCR calls for 'concrete acts of solidarity' by governments in order to provide solutions for the refugees. The idea of solidarity is used by both sides of the dispute on Brexit, to define the contested boundaries of collective belonging and responsibility. Solidarity underpins opposing narratives and constituencies within feminism, where the question of *who* is in solidarity and *with whom* is acute and constant, as it is in about every solidaristic social movement, ... the list could go on. If we are to better understand how the positive valence works through creating allegiances among selective groups, we probably need to take a step back.

The first thread through this discussion is questioning whether we should take solidarity to introduce a *distinctive* value in the political realm. Although it is sometimes contrasted with it, fraternity is often treated as cognate with solidarity. And so, it is tempting to think that the holy triad of liberty, equality, and fraternity group together and highlight for us the distinctively political values that we should find at the heart of any well-functioning society. Elsewhere I have argued, in part taking my lead from Harry Frankfurt and Joseph Raz,[13] that we should question whether equality really is a value in its own right, whatever political ideal, or instrumental worth, it might embody. For rather different reasons, I shall argue here that we should also question whether 'solidarity' could be the name of a distinctive value, or set of values, within ethical theory.[14] But this is not to question in

---

13. Although Raz shares many of the criticisms of Frankfurt, he is more circumspect about allowing any label or slogan to summarize his critical stance. See "Equality," in *The Morality of Freedom* (Oxford: Oxford University Press, 1988), ch. 9, and "On the Value of Distributional Equality," Oxford Legal Research Paper Series (2008).
14. Again, this is not to deny the valuable instrumental effects of solidarity. For an exploration of the impact of solidarity e.g. on constraining inequality, protecting vulnerable members, and fostering social trust, see David Miller, "Solidarity and Its Sources" in *The Strains of Commitment*, 61ff.

either case that we should be concerned with equality or solidarity as political ideals. And in the middle section, I'll set out to show why we should think of solidarities as an essential element in political society. In turn, that leads me to the third and final concern of this chapter: within liberal theorizing there is an anxiety about the status of solidarity. So, I want to close by evaluating the question whether liberal thought should have a principled opposition to solidarity.

THE PARTITIVE DIMENSION OF SOLIDARITY

Our brief exploration of historical uses of the idea of solidarity situates it between mere contract for mutual benefit and an ideal of abstract benevolence directed at the whole of humanity. However, it may seem that it is in the logic of the move from small, *mechanical*, solidarities to a more evanescent sense of solidarity that arises in diverse and highly complex societies where we will find the political ideal of solidarity takes on the latter connotation of universal benevolence. This seems to be the move advocated by David Wiggins in one of the most interesting efforts to date to give a philosophical analysis of the idea of solidarity.[15]

Wiggins is among those who wish to contrast fraternity and solidarity. He introduces the distinction so: as soon as we speak of fraternity, we find that there is a *special* consideration that each of the brothers owes the others. Solidarity, by contrast, is a universal sense of human benevolence. And Wiggins wishes to give this universal solidarity an anti-consequentialist reading: for him true benevolence neither aggregates nor maximizes. In this, Wiggins takes inspiration

---

15. See David Wiggins, "Solidarity and the Roots of the Ethical," and *Ethics: Twelve Lectures on the Philosophy of Morality* (London: Penguin Books, 2008; Cambridge, MA: Harvard University Press, 2008), ch. 9.

from Philippa Foot, who defines solidarity between human beings as a morality "which refuses to sanction the automatic sacrifice of the one for the good of the many," and does "not want evil, serious evil, to come on another, even to spare *more* people the same loss." The kind of solidarity between human beings is thus defined, Foot adds, "as if there is some sense in which no one is to come out against one of his fellow men."[16]

Wiggins comments on these claims of Foot as follows:

> We should see Foot's solidarity requirement as spelling out one non-negotiable corollary of the transition that human beings make from mutual recognition under the aspect of personal beings to a social morality that requires personal beings to *live out* that recognition in a solidarity that is all of a piece with the recognition that requires each personal being to recognize the other one as participating in that morality and equally requires the other one to recognize him or her as a participant in it. […] *This* is the source of the supposition … that one who participates in an ethic expressive of that recognition will be disposed (in the way Foot describes) to refuse to contemplate the automatic sacrifice of one personal being for the good of the many or to sanction the exchanging of the serious suffering of the one personal being for the lesser sufferings of a larger number […]. In so far as aggregative considerations gain admittance to a social morality that rests on the solidarity of recognition, such considerations must enter only on terms that respect the ethic itself and sustain

---

16. Philippa Foot, "Morality, Action and Outcome," in *Morality and Objectivity*, ed. T. Honderich (London: Routledge, 1985), quoted in David Wiggins, *Ethics: Twelve Lectures on the Philosophy of Morality*. In this article, Foot develops ideas which are also the focus of "Utilitarianism and the Virtues," and "Killing and Letting Die." Utilitarianism, she contends, is a deficient moral theory and, in particular, the coherence of the idea of good states of affairs from a moral point of view ought to be called into question.

its basis. From the same solidarity, moreover, it is another short step to the idea of reciprocity between personal beings, and to Hume's idea that gratitude is a natural (not an artificial) virtue.[17]

For Foot and Wiggins, then, the idea of solidarity emphasizes first and foremost an anti-consequentialist thought: if you really feel solidarity with other individuals, you wouldn't wish them sacrificed to the aggregative maximizing tendencies characteristic of consequentialist reasoning. It also takes the form of the natural virtues of benevolence and gratitude.[18] The two are connected. Both Foot and Wiggins are opposed to the consequentialism of utilitarianism: the view that goodness, utility, or welfare, suitably aggregated, are what morality requires that we should bring about. This view goes together with the idea that the property through which we establish a comparison, and a ranking, of policy options is welfare conceived as a characteristic of states of affairs as such. Foot, and Wiggins following her, use the term 'solidarity' to commend the virtue of universal benevolence to us in a form that is stripped of any of the connotations of traditional utilitarianism, or any of the sophisticated consequentialist revisions of it in recent theorizing.

In this setting, we must contrast differing conceptions of welfare and benevolence. The conception of welfare involved in the utilitarian account is that of an impersonal value, a value attached directly to

---

17. Wiggins, *Ethics: Twelve Lectures on the Philosophy of Morality*, 245.
18. Wiggins finds the roots of this meaning of solidarity as universal benevolence again in French thought. See "Solidarity and the Roots of the Ethical," 252: "In the ethical sense it reaches England and America in the 1840s. It comes through the Fourierists. For a typical Fourierist utterance, far wide of formulations such as Foot's, see Hippolyte Renaud, *La solidarité: Vue synthétique de la doctrine de Charles Fourier*, . . . : 'Tous les hommes doivent se ranger à la loi: c'est qu'il n'en est pas donné à quelques-uns d'être heureux pendant que les autres souffrent; c'est que tous les membres de la grande famille sont liés en un seul faisceau par un grand principe: la SOLIDARITÉ [. . .] nous aurons à faire comprendre que les intérêts des hommes sont en tout point rigoureusement identiques.'"

the outcome brought about, in contrast to a conception of the welfare of particular individuals, and how some things can thereby be good for a given individual. Correspondingly, benevolence becomes an impartial concern for the level of welfare realized within such a state of affairs, rather than a concern with the plight of particular individuals. Yet it seems incoherent, Wiggins and Foot complain, for the natural virtue of benevolence, once generalized as a social virtue, to be conceived in such a way as "to be positively dangerous to moral subjects whose vital interests will be outweighed by the less vital interests of others more numerous than they." We must take benevolence to be an attitude essentially directed toward individuals, and welfare to be an aspect of individuals alone, and not individuals aggregated together in some overarching state of affairs. Foot and Wiggins harness talk of solidarity in the service of this anti-utilitarian and anti-consequentialist dialectic:

> To those who are impassioned [by utilitarian ideas], solidarity will say again: it is morally and reasonably impossible for you to recognize each human being as owed your abstention from intentional assault—and then, in your aggregative reasoning, to acquiesce in what you could see for yourself, if only you looked, is scarcely different from intentional assault. How can you not see that the categorical prohibitions that flow from solidarity have a prior claim over benefits that make their appeal only to an unconsidered generalization of benevolence?[19]

Before critiquing this way of talking of solidarity, let me first say that I unreservedly share the anti-consequentialist thought. Having to protect individuals against the relentless pursuit of the best state of affairs, when we understand this state of affairs precisely as that which

---

19. Wiggins, "Solidarity and the Roots of the Ethical," 256.

promotes things which are good for individuals, is indeed deeply problematic. But I think Wiggins's discussion illustrates an underlying problem with taking solidarity to be fundamental in our ethical armory and so making this explicit allows us to draw a general moral here, that stands apart from Wiggins's own specific commitments. We may side with Wiggins in his debate with utilitarians about the understanding of benevolence, and yet resist putting this in terms which evoke the ideal of solidarity.

My first concern is purely a dialectical one. Foot and Wiggins wish to highlight that there are more ways to understand the notions of welfare and benevolence than are to be found in utilitarian and consequentialist discourse. But how useful is it to underline this by introducing a distinctive use of the term 'solidarity'? Utilitarians and consequentialists of all stripes may legitimately retort that they do not fall short of the ideal of solidarity. Rather, they have a different conception of what solidarity demands, one which can be only be defeated by proper argument rather than mere invocation of a term. Foot and Wiggins, of course, have arguments to launch against the coherence of the views that they oppose. But such arguments can be framed without any appeal to the notion of solidarity in addition. So, the merits of their particular positions will not stand or fall on whether we append the epithet of solidarity distinctively to their conceptions of welfare and benevolence.

And this leads me to the second, and more substantial concern, whether the concept of solidarity can be shaped properly into the form that Foot and Wiggins need it to take. As the brief historical sketch above illustrated, the common role of appeals to solidarity in our political discourse emphasizes an 'us' whose interests we should focus on, and about whom we should be feeling suitably warm. In all actual situations of political activity and the demand of mobilization, that 'us' comes with a 'them': others that we can be contrasted with. That is to say, we should think of the common role of invoking solidarity in political language as *partitive*: dividing the world into some and others. When we come to the discussion of the positive function of solidarity, we'll see reasons to think that this aspect of the concept is not accidental. For the moment, I shall rely just on the thought that we have no reason to suppose it accidental. So, if our appeal to the notion in ethical thought requires us to leave aside this partitive function, we might rather fear that we have simply changed the topic.

And that, I suggest, is the central problem with Wiggins's discussion, and the Foot proposals lying behind it. In invoking the circle of all humanity (and, no doubt, beyond that, were Wiggins to encounter other species that he could not deny the same ethical standing to), Wiggins is seeking to leave out any contentious 'them' with which 'we' might feel a contrast. But do we really have *fellow*-feeling with others, where it makes no sense to suppose that there are others with whom we do not have this bond? When someone invokes common humanity or asks us to imagine those in plight as if they are our brothers, then rather than showing that the circle of concern encompasses all, they instead acknowledge the motivational force of our partial ties and seek to gain the motivational advantage of that in the context of addressing urgent needs.

This is not to question whether we should have proper concern for the rest of humanity. Clearly the plight of the global poor and the desperate conditions of many migrants highlight a shameful stain on current political reality within the West. The question is whether that concern is illuminated by talk of solidarity, beyond the recognition as such of the status of being of moral worth and being an object of benevolent concern. In the political arena, it is clear that solidarity means so much more than this. So, we are in danger of losing our distinctive sense of the notion, if we simply rearrange the concept so as to lose this partitive element.

Is the partitive element to be found in common invocations of solidarity really alien to the ethical domain, and is any such acknowledgment of the partitive element essential to any conception of solidarity? Clearly, Wiggins makes no use of it and wishes to insist that solidarity as such is with all of humanity. But, our notional objector may continue, that is part of the eccentricity of Wiggins's position. And that underlines why Wiggins does not provide the route to an understanding of the value of solidarity. It does not show, however, that we can make no sense of solidarity within the ethical realm. For example, one might imagine a suitably cartoonish version of the ethical, perhaps inspired by Schmittian ideas, which appeals to a contrast between friends and enemies, the strong and the weak, or some other such division: which sees the moral realm as some see the political, as a place of constant contest, in which there must be not only some winners but also some definite losers. If we were to think of the world in terms of such contest, then it might also make sense to think of the world in terms of groupings where we identified now with the weak or now with the strong: celebrated being a winner; sighed at being a loser.

Implicitly my resistance to Wiggins's appropriation of the concept of solidarity also presupposes the rejection of such a picture of the ethical, and hence of what our ethical theories should be aiming at. And this chapter is not the place to engage in the debate about how we should think of ourselves either as all members of the Kingdom of Ends, or contestants in the latest iteration of *I'm a Celebrity, Get Me Out of Here*. I am content for this discussion simply to conditionalize the moral here to the claim that if one acknowledges a suitably inclusive conception of the ethical domain, then in turn, one has reason to exclude solidarity from among the ethical concerns, however forceful a political ideal it remains.

And so, that makes more pressing the second question, whether being partitive really is essential to any conception of solidarity in the ethical realm. Now it is important to see here that the proponent of solidarity as fundamental faces a dilemma: if they insist that the us/them dynamic that we find in typical political discourse of solidarities is inessential, then they need to explain how solidarity amounts to a concept distinct from other ethical notions that we already clearly possess and understand somewhat better. For example, if we follow Wiggins in just extending the concerns of solidarity to all humanity, and potentially wider, to all members of the Kingdom of Ends, do we not then just have the idea of reciprocity and recognition that is at the heart of much of the discussion of relational theories of the ethical?

No wonder that some have the suspicion that solidarity can add something here only by inviting us to draw a distinction between those we stand in solidarity with and some un-named other. We clearly do not feel generally inclined to think of the moral in a manner which has at root the possibility of excluding some from consideration or moral status. To give just one example, Rawls prefers to put reciprocity rather than solidarity at the center of his conception of a just society. (The difference principle "expresses a conception of reciprocity"; the theory of right and justice "is founded on the notion of reciprocity which reconciles the points of view of the self and of others as equal moral persons."[20])

But, of course, at the level of sentiment there is an important, and motivationally significant element, that we find in solidarity and that is not predicted in just talking of recognition and reciprocity. Can't we imagine that positive element arising without us making any use of a partitive element which draws a contrast between an 'us' and a 'them'? Two possibilities immediately spring to mind. On the one hand, think of a group of people suddenly beset by an imminent,

---

20. Rawls, *A Theory of Justice*, rev. ed. (Cambridge, MA: Harvard University Press, 1999), 88 and 424. For a fuller discussion of the idea of reciprocity, see *Political Liberalism* (New York: Columbia University Press, 1993), Lecture 1, §3, particularly 16–17.

but impersonal threat: perhaps the inhabitants of a small Caribbean island together discover that their lives are to be upended by an erupting volcano, or a destructive tornado. The calamity which besets them gives the islanders a cause to come together and prevail, to be shored up by a sense of fellow-feelings with others in their plight. In this case there is a focus for concern with the other, against which they rally, but the other is no person, or no agent.[21] Here we have the positive feelings and motivation of solidarity without the negative elements of exclusion. On the other, consider a kind of case raised to me by Niko Kolodny. Solidarity can be vicarious: we can express our standing in solidarity with the members of an oppressed or marginalized group. Consider, for example, solidarity with victims of racism by people who are not the butt of racist attitudes themselves. Non-black participants to demonstrations carrying placards stating "Black Lives Matter" express their solidarity with the sufferings of a group they do not belong to. Clearly the non-black participants do not see themselves as part of a group in contrast to others. Here again, we have the sense of standing together, the positive aspects of solidarity, but no reason to suppose that the negative elements, excluding non-members as other, need play any role.

Such examples no doubt help explain why it is so tempting to reach for the notion of solidarity in explaining some of our universalist impulses. But neither really can show that we can leave behind the partitive structure of solidarity and still hold on to a distinctive notion in our ethical thought. The case can be laid out more clearly with the second kind of example, but the worries raised apply equally to the first.

What the example of vicarious solidarity highlights is something interesting about vicarious emotions and feelings in general. The kind of genuinely vicarious pride of parents for their children lacks

---

21. I owe this example to Andrea Sangiovanni.

the kind of egotistical preoccupation that pride in your own achievements possesses. With the competitive character that school can take on, one may be concerned with one's children's success and failings in a too engaged manner: one thinks of them as reflecting on the merits of team 'us.' But genuinely vicarious pride is selfless in a distinctive way: you feel proud on behalf of your child and from their perspective, whether they can see what is good about their achievements or not. Now, the fact that such vicarious pride is possible, and in such a pure form is not egotistical and self-directed, really doesn't show that pride in general is not a form of self-appraisal. What it shows is that we can displace the proper subject of such an emotion and feel on behalf of another. And that is the lesson that we should draw about vicarious solidarity. Someone who feels solidarity with some oppressed group does not thereby feel themselves to be part of an 'us' which is directed against a 'them,' the group of oppressors. In feeling the solidarity, they displace the subject of the feeling onto some member, perhaps arbitrarily conceived, of the oppressed group, and in that perspective, the contrast between 'us' and 'them' plays its role. We do not escape the partitive structure of solidarity, it is rather made clear: there is an 'us' among this group, the victims of oppression, inasmuch as there is a 'them,' those who are the causes of oppression.

The difficulty of avoiding the enriching role of the imaginary equally plays a role in the first example. Suppose we do not start with a sudden event or disaster, as with an eruption or tropical storm, but simply with the general plight of people. One can think of human life as just misery heaped upon misery, and one can imagine some orator seeking to inspire the folk to do better with their lot. Perhaps in their Beckettian misery, the people together have some fellow-feeling which motivates them in a drive to improve life. Would this be solidarity? It makes sense to think so, if we can think of these people as a distinctive group who find their lives a dispiriting challenge. But once we define a definite group, then we have the structure of these versus the rest of humanity. If we avoid that interpretation by supposing that each conceives of humanity's lot as a whole as miserable, and in need of improvement, then we begin to lose the sense of there being any role for solidarity here, rather than just the concern that people should live life well, a concern with benevolence.

So, that suggests that it is essential that we think of the original case in terms of some distinctive thing or event against which those in solidarity are acting: it matters that we can identify the volcano or the tornado which is responsible for our downfall, and against which we can stand. And once we put it in these terms, then it is natural to think in terms of solidarity being appropriate here precisely because one has personified the cause of distress and thereby treated it as an other. One might reflect here on the recent, and growing, popularity of zombie stories in popular culture: in the cinema, in television series, and in video games. While this trope has had some life for centuries, the focus on the zombie apocalypse and one's need to survive it seems a broad popular obsession of only the last decade or so. One might suspect that it is no coincidence that in the same period, it has become extremely unfashionable to construct narratives around traditional national enemies, be that the Bosch, the Yellow Peril, or the dread Soviets. Zombies look a lot like people, and one can violently interact with them as one might one's enemies. But in being only the living dead, zombies are no longer people, and so one lacks any concern for them and their rights which might check one's behavior toward genuine enemies. In this way, one might think of zombies as quasi-persons within fictional narratives, protagonists which allow for the pleasure of violent agency against them without any questionable moral consequences. In the same spirit, we may think of the volcano or the tornado as a quasi-agent, an enemy against which we can unify in solidarity, but with respect to which there is no moral consequence in deeming it the other. If this is the right way to think of the appropriateness of talk of solidarity here, then we still have not managed to describe a genuine case in which solidarity is the distinctive response to our plight and yet in which the partitive structure has been left behind.

We can, of course, deny that partition. Vicarious solidarity builds on our universal moral concerns for justice, reciprocity, and so forth. The concerns that lead us to vicarious solidarity need in no way be partitive. But that doesn't succeed in showing solidarity to have a non-partitive character. At best, if we substituted for the feelings of solidarity the universalist concerns which lead to them, we would simply be returned to the other horn of the dilemma and the reduction of solidarity to other universal moral concerns. None of this leads to the rejection of vicarious solidarity as an important political motor, but one which is instrumental to the realization of other concerns.

I've argued that we can't hold on to what is distinctive in the concept of solidarity without acknowledging that it has a partitive aspect: that it draws some together by excluding others. It won't do to reserve the label 'fraternity' for that notion and apply the label 'solidarity' instead to some notion of universal concern. We already have perfectly good notions which are strictly universal, our interest in the recognition and reciprocity of the Kingdom of Ends; the weak, but entirely pervasive feelings of benevolence which check our insensitivities toward other human beings. The history of the term teaches us that 'solidarity' is a term that applied in the context of social and political strife, and in that original usage, necessarily some partition was drawn. If we stick with a conception of the ethical as universal and impartial, nothing like the structure of solidarity can be at its foundation. So solidarity cannot be, as liberty is, one of our fundamental values.

If it is not a value, what else can it be? I've already suggested that we should think of it as a political ideal. What does the distinction between ethical value and political ideal amount to? Well, the reasons for thinking of solidarity as instrumentally central to political action are the concerns of the next section. But first, let me say a couple of words on what makes something a *value*. Of course, if all it takes for a value to be such is for there to be a positive evaluative narrative associated to it, then both equality and solidarity are political values. Moreover, there may not be any good argument to the conclusion that in our metaphysics of value there is no place for equality or solidarity. But the claim is not that. Rather, my guiding thought is that in order to treat something as a value it has to do some basic *explanatory* work in our ethical thought. When it comes to equality, we can follow Frankfurt and Raz at least in this: the value of equality does surprisingly little to explain and illuminate our commitment to, say, egalitarian policies of distribution.[22] The value of equality is not the crucial input in our deliberation: rather the needs and welfare of people are what motivates distributing equally, and that is true more generally of an egalitarian political ideal. The import of denying equality the status of a value is to recognize that we care about equal distributions because there are other values which are traduced where distributions are systematically unequal.

The case of solidarity is different. The worry here is not that we can substitute through for solidarity with some other value which really carries the load. The concern is, rather, if we took solidarity as such, rather than say universal concern, as fundamental, then we

---

22. See also the conclusion of T. M. Scanlon's lecture on "The Diversity of Objections to Inequality" in *The Difficulty of Tolerance: Essays in Political Philosophy* (Cambridge: Cambridge University Press, 2003), 218: "[R]elief of suffering, avoidance of stigmatizing differences in status, prevention of domination of some by others, and the preservation of conditions of procedural fairness are basic and important moral values. Within the framework of the principle of equal consideration they provide strong reasons for the elimination of various inequalities. Taken together these values account for at least a large part of the importance that equality has in our political thinking. They may account for all of this importance, or there may be an important role to be played by a further moral idea of substantive equality. But it remains unclear exactly what that idea would be."

would be compelled to divide the world in ways that *conflict* with our other ethical concerns.

Once we leave aside an entirely abstract realm of ethical thought and situate ourselves in the context of genuine social strife and concern, one where an 'us and them' has already been gifted to you—as in the cases of racism and the possibility of a resulting black solidarity so eloquently described by Tommie Shelby (Chapter 12 in this volume)—then there can indeed be a positive political way in which you think of solidarity with some and not others.

To say that solidarity is not a value, therefore, is not to say that it does not matter. It is certainly not to deny that it is a political ideal and idea which is alive and essential to healthy political discourse. But if it is wrong to think of it in terms of value, what other sense can we make of it being an ideal? That is the question I now want to sketch an answer to.

IN WHAT SENSE CAN SOLIDARITY BE A POLITICAL IDEAL IF IT IS NOT A VALUE?

It will help to say a bit more about the distinctive nature of the emotional commitment which underlies the sense of collective responsibility characteristic of solidarity. Let us begin with a thought that Joel Feinberg has made explicit about sentiments of solidarity. He writes:

> A group has solidarity to the degree that its members have mutual interests, bonds of affection, and a 'common lot.' The mutual interest may be a specific overlap of shared interest, or it may be a community of interest of the sort that exists when each member's integrated set of interests contains the integrated interest set of each of the others. Such 'community' is often associated with bonds of sentiment directed toward common objects

or with reciprocal affection between the parties. Finally, the parties share a common lot insofar as their goods and harms are necessarily collective and indivisible. Where there is solidarity there is no hurting one member without hurting them all; and because of the way their interests are related, the successes and satisfactions of one radiate their benefits to the others.

[. . .] There is perhaps no better index to solidarity than the occurrence of vicarious pride and shame. These attitudes occur most frequently in group members on behalf either of the larger group, or of some other member(s) of the larger group, of which they are a part. Individuals sometimes feel proud or ashamed of their families, ancestors, countries, or races; and all or most members of groups may feel pride or shame over the achievements or failures of single members.

[. . .] We are inclined to congratulate or 'condemn fraternally' only when we feel some degree of solidarity with the other parties. The *solidarity is a necessary condition of the vicarious emotion, which is in turn an index to the solidarity*.[23]

Feinberg's focus on collective responsibility is narrower than our concerns, and anyway is directed at issues which would take us elsewhere. There may well be conceptions of collective responsibility which do not function as Feinberg's picture suggests. But what I want to take from these passages is the idea that solidarity features both in the way in which it is *expressed* in certain specific feelings or sentiments such as vicarious pride and shame, when a group bonds together, but is also something which comes to be *strengthened* through that expression.

Broadly, the thought I want to explore is that which should see solidarity as a political ideal because it frames for us a set of affective

---

23. Joel Feinberg, "Collective Responsibility," *The Journal of Philosophy* 65, no. 21 (1968): 674–688, at 677–678, emphasis added.

responses which can both give expression to a well-functioning social grouping and can operate to motivate people to act positively in group-related ways which thereby help fulfill the ends of political society. We cannot really imagine political life going well without suitable groupings within it which are bound together through appropriate feelings of belonging.

I suggest that we need to think of solidarity as operating in at least two complementary ways within political society. On the one hand, individuals find themselves through various of their identities to be part of certain socially recognized groups. Identifying with such groups gives rise to feelings of solidarity, and such a sense of solidarity can play a role within political action. On the other hand, at least within a well-functioning society, one can feel oneself in a position where one is both opposed to some other group in terms of some political contest on some decision, or in pursuit of some resource, but nonetheless one recognizes the legitimacy of the opponents' position. In this case, one can think of solidarity as a sense of belonging to all those who are part of the society in question. And in this case, the expression of solidarity is a way of modifying the antagonistic and competitive feelings that political dispute can give rise to.

We can see such a thought at work in Durkheim, and more recently in John Rawls's *Theory of Justice*. Rawls doesn't use the idea of solidarity in outlining his theory of justice. However, he theorizes mechanisms of reciprocity associated with sentiments of fraternity. He explains, that is, how sentiments of fraternity are *possible*, and how they are *necessary* for stable solidarity arrangements to be generated and stably sustained. So, Rawls's framework is a useful way to explore how these sentiments of solidarity can function.[24]

---

24. For a discussion of the role of sentiments of fraternity in *A Theory of Justice* see my "Fellow Feelings: Fraternity, Equality and the Origin and Stability of Justice," *Daimon, Revista Internacional de Filosofía* 7 (2018): 107–123.

As is well known, Rawls suggests that sentiments of fraternity can be cultivated through principles which can be justified to all, and in particular to the least well-off. Rawls sees the existence of a fraternal ethos as one of the necessary elements of stability of just principles. The interesting point, however, is that an ethos of fraternity (or solidarity) is what *results* from appropriately justifiable principles of justice. (Contrast the view we find in G. A. Cohen's assertion that a fraternal sentiment, or motivation, is missing from Rawls's picture of principles of justice.)

Rawls starts from the threats to political solidarity: at the one end, the egoism of the 'haves'; at the other, the sense of exclusion of the 'have-nots.' This sense of exclusion explains why, for Rawls, some welfare state arrangements fall short of justice: not enough is done so that "the least advantaged feel that they are a part of political society." As a result, if we belong to one of the excluded categories, "we grow distant from political society and retreat into our social world. We feel left out; and withdrawn and cynical, we cannot affirm the principles of justice [...]. Though we are not hostile or rebellious, those principles are not ours and fail to engage our moral sensibility."[25] How, then, do we strengthen the sense of solidarity? This is one of the most directly political questions of Rawls's theory, one which resonates with special intensity in troubled times such as ours.

Some philosophers see their role as laying down the rules of the ideal city. By contrast, Rawls begins from certain features of human societies and hypotheses about our moral psychology to envisage what the characteristics of a just society might be. For Rawls, as for Hume, justice is an artificial virtue which is made both possible and necessary by certain features of human societies. Like Hume, Rawls

---

25. John Rawls, *Justice as Fairness: A Restatement* (Cambridge, MA: Harvard University Press, 2001), 127–128.

considers that human beings are such that they have a sense of solidarity and benevolence toward each other; that sentiment is however weak: hence the need for the artifice that rules of justice provide. This is Rawls's first empirical hypothesis: the fact of a weak sense of benevolence of human beings toward each other makes justice both possible and necessary. In the context of each political community, this initial sentiment manifests itself in an inclination to meet the needs of the badly-off; in the same manner, sisters and brothers in a family often tend to help the badly-off among them. Call this first rationale 'the lifeboat': the idea that morality requires that we meet the needs of the *badly-off*, at least within the political community.

This initial fraternal inclination is however not operative without a favorable institutional framework. Again, Rawls no less than Hume stresses the artificial nature of political society and that its virtues lie in this artifice. A political society, if well run, ought to have institutions such that the badly-off receive the resources necessary for flourishing. Given limited resources, a proper attention to the need of the least well-off will render certain inequalities problematic. If some enjoy superfluous goods while the needs of others are unmet, society is not well run. This tendency toward lesser inequality is supplemented by a further thought: if people in a given society cooperate to produce goods and services, they should receive a just share of the product of their social cooperation. Call this second rationale 'the boat we built': fairness requires that the least well-off do as well as possible. Enter the principle of fraternity: social and economic inequalities are to be to the greatest benefit of the least-advantaged members of society. (We saw Durkheim already anticipating such a thought.)

To these initial points, Rawls adds two further empirical hypotheses. The first is that it is part of our moral psychology, of our basic makeup, that we attach value to our institutions being justifiable to others in the political community. The principle of fraternity, or that is to say, the Difference Principle, meets that demand for justification. Rather than an exhortation to the better-off that they do more to deliver more welfare or to maximize equality, it is a principle that can be shared by the better-off and the least well-off: all can see it as a rule which expresses an interest they have that society be run to meet the needs of each, the needs of all.

The final empirical hypothesis is that the weak sentiment of benevolence present in human beings is fortifiable by rules which are publicly justified and regarded as just. Hence the idea of an ethos of fraternity, or of solidarity. The good which *results* from the Difference Principle is a shared fraternal ethos: an endorsement of shared norms of cooperation; and this in turn makes rules of justice more stable, through approval of compliance with the rules. A just society, thinks Rawls, is one in which members shape their society together. The *have-nots* see themselves in a position to claim resources on the basis of this collective enterprise: society does not only do the best by them, but it is also a society which they partake in shaping. In turn, the *haves* see it as reasonable for the have-nots to make that claim, because they identify with the community as a collective enterprise, and see their interest in a well-run society satisfied. Organizing a society alongside the Difference Principle thus results in all seeing themselves as properly belonging.

We might suggest at least three dimensions in which feelings of solidarity provide for a well-functioning polis, without meaning to rule out further functions or other elaborations and refinements. First, as our brief discussion of Rawls brings out, there are both positive and negative grounds for generating a sense of group membership. Rawls's stress on the idea of the fruits of cooperation offers a ground which can only be understood positively: the individual moves from the recognition of something of value to a sense of belonging with others in having collectively had some claim to have a causal role in bringing this about. On the other hand, Rawls's other ground, the sense of sharing a common fate through somehow being passively thrown together, emphasizes a sense of common fate which can also arise just from involuntary belonging: living on this, allegedly small, island, or having the same hair color, the same sex or ethnicity, and so forth. And this sense of common fate can be given both a positive and a negative gloss. One may feel pride in one's tribe and express outwardly the valence of this identification. Or one might rather come to know one's belonging through discovering how others think of one, and how they group you together with others to be treated in some negative way.

Once there is such identification, then there is the possibility of distinctive motivation to act to help others who are part of the same group, and to pursue ends together. One of the most important, but difficult to articulate properly, aspects of such group-identification is the way in which solidarity can *reduce the amount of political deliberation*. In many representative democracies, particularly those with alternating parties, there is a need to create coalitions of interests in order to have effective political agency.[26] Were one simply to vote on preference, issue by issue, then no aggregation of interest need come about. On the other hand, the demands on one's time to decide the shape of a governmental manifesto would potentially be ever increasing. The Rousseauian idea of justification to others of our joint political institutions is fundamental; however, in the hands of some it gets transformed into an idyll where the shape of teaspoons and the exact number of grains of sugar to be added to a cup of tea can rationally be debated and collectively decided upon: most of us shrink from such unmoderated political engagement. The chance to be committed to some political end simply because that is what *we* believe in should

---

26. For a discussion of some aspects of the role of solidarity in political agency, see Andrea Sangiovanni, "Solidarity as Joint Action," *Journal of Applied Philosophy* 32 (2015): 340–359.

not be underestimated. Solidarities allow for efficient coalition of interests and ends within a political society.

That is to say, in many forms of well-ordered political society, we would look for *nested solidarities* among political agents. For political deliberation to be effective and to be responsive to the various social groupings to be found within a society, we must expect there to be solidarities among the group identities that exist there. At the same time, for the political contest to be suitably constrained, and for us to avoid any tyranny of the majority, or of the loudest, there needs to be a mutual recognition of the claims of others. So, the society itself needs a solidarity which cuts across these sub-groups and can help lead the various different members to recognize their commonality.

It is at this level of political sociology and collective affective science that we should locate solidarity as an essential element in the happy body politic. While some libertarians dream of direct democracy, with individual consumers advising their personal connected AI of their vote in the privacy of their isolated dwellings, we might rather recognize that successful social interaction requires that we recognize ourselves as both part of some group or groups that has/have political significance, as well as one among all the others who are party to this political engagement and dispute.

Suppose, then, that we think of solidarity in this way—not as some fundamental value to which our political strivings must answer, but as an ideal of political life, in the sense of one of the effective sentimental mechanisms by which we can provoke coordinated decision and action within political society. Should we then rest content with the centrality of solidarity in political life? It is time now to address the concern running through liberal theory that a genuinely egalitarian liberal should reject all talk of fraternity or solidarity, and simply embrace thoughts of universality.

CONCLUSION: LIBERALISM AND THE POLITICAL IDEAL OF SOLIDARITY

Solidarity has not been the central focus of liberal discussion. But more than that, many such writers seem to evince a reluctance to embrace any demands that arise from solidarities. If the sketch of the last section is correct, then we should anticipate in well-functioning polities, solidarity plays a key role. Are concerns with solidarity ones which draw on questions of *principle*, or are they principally worries about the *practicality* of organizing our politics around fellow-feeling?

There are, I suggest, two obvious grounds of concern resting on matters of principle. The first we touched on in our discussion of Wiggins and the impulse to create a properly universal form of solidarity. At that stage, I noted that our political discourse in terms of solidarity exploits a partitive element: an intended audience is moved by thoughts about an *us* to be contrasted with some *them*. The principled concern here would be against enshrining that contrast within our picture of the ethical realm. Social interactions constantly reflect differences of group and the very real presence of hierarchies and differential power relations. But the patterns of duties and obligations on us all, one might think, leave aside such differences as non-ideal. We are all together members of the Kingdom of Ends, and our actions must be justifiable to each and to any. Such a picture of the pattern of moral demands would be upset if we took as part of the fundamental concern our segmentation into groups. On such a picture, some might properly be stigmatized as the other: the same concern would not be due them as one's in-group. Any universal principles would be derived in part through the concerns of how one could make the in-group flourish.

As I have already indicated, if this is the ground of a principled rejection of solidarity as a political ideal to guide our conception of political order, then I think we should indeed reject solidarity. We should not suppose that solidarity forms one of the basic structuring principles of ethical life. To the extent that notions of solidarity are essentially partitive, we should rather conclude that solidarity cannot be expressive of a distinctive ethical viewpoint. What I have urged, though, is that such a conclusion should not lead us to reject solidarity as part of our political vocabulary and ideals: it is through appeals to solidarity and fraternity that we build effective coalitions, the possibility of collective political agency. Solidarity may properly be grounded in the political world even if it is not further reflected in the foundations of moral thought, in terms of some further distinctive value, or some way of structuring the pattern of care.

This is not the only source of principled concern, or so some would press. If our solidarities are motivationally effective, then they will move us to action which is directed in favor of some, helping or furthering the interests of an 'us,' and leaves us indifferent to the concerns of others, not moving us to pay the same attention to the claims of those who are merely 'them.' The critic may then object that this leads to a pattern of concern and of behavior which is necessarily *partial* and that that in itself, from a moral perspective, is objectionable.

But we should equally resist this objection. The fact that one is partial in concern and action does not itself seem to be a forceful complaint.[27] Those who took the universalizability of practical commands as the mark of the distinctively moral may have been inclined to suppose that all genuinely moral or ethical demands are themselves impartial, requiring even and equal treatment of all people. But it is clear that such a picture of the ethical misrepresents the relations in which we stand to many of those around us. One responds to the

---

27. See Joseph Raz, "Identity and Social Bonds," Joseph Raz (edited by Ulrike Heuer). 2022. The Roots of Normativity. Oxford: Oxford University Press. (chapter 11).

needs of one's partner not because they happen to occupy the role of being one's partner and one is sensitive to a universal principle that humans should attend to the cares of those in romantic connection to them. Rather, in loving that person in the way one does, their needs and cares become an object of focus, and that shapes one's practical concerns and what one does about them. Human life is necessarily partial, one's attention is drawn to some things and not to others. A proper description of the demands of morality must take such facts into account.

It is in the natures of both friendship and solidarity that I cannot bear such relations to absolutely everyone in the world. But the difference between friendship and solidarity is located in *the reasons to exclude*. That I have a special relation to my loved ones doesn't need justification, but if asked why I care particularly about my grandson and not in the same way about all the other kids in his class, my reason is that I love him. It is this which gives him a special standing in my concern. I do not thereby have reasons to exclude others. Solidarity, by contrast, relies on a logic of the following sort: we are us and they are them. It works particularly well, or so I tend to think, when we are in a group where the reason to be in solidarity is involuntary: that you are oppressed, excluded, but also trapped in the same situation, bound to others you haven't chosen but with whom you face a similar fate. (This is what Tommie Shelby would call 'thin' solidarity.[28]) That we face a similar fate gives us cause to be in solidarity. But there is the temptation, well-illustrated in social movements such as feminism, to say too much about why what binds us is positive features and why what excludes the others is negative features (the enemy and friend narrative). In loving my grandson, it is this positive relation alone which is the ground of my attitude; in the relation to others I am in

---

28. See Tommie Shelby, "A Tale of Two Tenths: Race, Class, and Solidarity," Chapter 12 in this volume.

solidarity with, it is the boundary between the in- and the out-group which is the focus.

But more importantly there is a (universal) value in friendships. Is there such a value in groups of solidarity? I have answered in the negative (other than instrumental to the political). The value in friendships is focused on the loved ones. If we say the same for solidarity, then we treat it as a larger group of friends. But if we think there is more, or something else, then that is a matter of groups of Fs versus not-Fs. And that being the grounds of concern goes against universalism.

So, the complaint that solidarities issue in a pattern of partial concern and action cannot in itself be a principled basis of rejection. However, the critic may continue, it is not merely that solidarities give rise to partiality in this way. Solidarity, as we have stressed above, is essentially partitive: it involves treating some as 'us,' belonging to an in-group, and others as 'them,' excluded. This categorization need not be part of the partiality of concern with loved ones. That one loves one's partner or one's sibling may be the ground of the pattern of concern that one has, but this is not to say that one treats it as a further reason for the concerns that one has. So one doesn't divide the world into those one loves, and those one doesn't. The refined objection to solidarity, then, may insist that it is this *additional* structural feature of solidarity which is of concern: that it invites one to think of the practical world in terms of such categories, and hence to offer justification for one's lack of concern, or one's outright hostility, to some.

I do not want to deny that there is a genuine practical concern here, and it is to that which I wish to turn in just a couple of sentences. What is at issue at this point, though, is whether there is an objection of *principle*: Does thinking of others through the lens of solidarity necessarily conflict with a properly ethical outlook on the world? And here, still, I want to suggest that the case has not been made. It may well be essential to the invocation of solidarity that one focuses on some as belonging to one's in-group and in need of distinctive concern and lets one treat others as outside of this charmed circle, not in a position to make demands, or anyway not in a position to make demands of the same urgency. But the objection needs something more than this: it requires that this sorting of the world that solidarity provides also further provides a rationale for one's differential attitudes: that one can say that one ought to look after these people because they are one's own, and that one ought to reject the claims of others because they are mere outsiders. This further level of justification in terms of the structure of groups, this idea that one ought to look after one's own because they are one's own, doesn't automatically flow just from the partitive structure of solidarity itself. Solidarity can be socially and politically useful to us through directing our attention in partial ways without that in addition generating *further reasons* to justify this partiality.

And so, one can respond to the critic by insisting that we don't have this additional layer of reasons. We are not required when moved by feelings of solidarity to think of some people as merely other and thereby less important. Rather, our solidarity simply makes us think with greater focus of some people, and to find ourselves more engaged by their concerns. It needs no deeper rationale than that, no need to find this pattern vindicated through the greater objective importance of my group over others.

But that is not to deny that there clearly is a matter here of great practical importance. For the mere fact that our concerns can be structured partitively, to be concerned with an in-group and to draw a contrast with an out-group, can allow for just such corrupting thoughts. On the one hand, the drawing of this division allows us now to focus attention on the in-group, or now to direct our attention outward. Likewise, we can associate with either direction a positive or a negative valence. We can seek to increase the bonds of solidarity by getting members of our group to feel better about each other through such membership. Or we can look to increase the bonds by casting aspersions on those who are not us.

Many of the positive consequences of solidarity flow from the positively valenced in-group focus: one thinks particularly of these people, one is moved by their claims, one identifies with their ends as one's own. The out-group in such thought is marked simply by one's lack of attention to them. But in much political discourse, people are effectively bonded together and moved to collective action more easily by the opposite strategy: highlighting an other toward whom various negative feelings can be generated.

This seems clearly part of the focus of recent critiques of populism. Talk of 'we the people' pretends to an inclusivity of all within political society, while clearly encouraging its audience to exclude those who are in political disagreement with the movement. So, we have a contrast of us and them, where the them is taken somehow to be illegitimate.

It is definitely the case that the presence of solidarities in our social lives and our political discourse allows for such negative uses, which leads to the stigmatization of some, and the potential escalation of negative consequences. So, it might well be true that in a world without solidarities, these risks would be diminished. But, I think, we should hold off supposing that this is the appropriate lesson to draw. Thinking in terms of solidarity allows for such negative projects, but it really doesn't mandate it. Moreover, there is much in political life which clearly flourishes in the context of recognizing one's distinctive alliances. Therefore, I suggest, we should rather see this as one of the practical risks of thinking in terms of solidarity. Our broader ethical concerns should lead us to police the ways in which we think about the body politic in terms of solidarity.

Liberal thought has often been driven by positive impulses of universalism and the recognition of our shared duties and claims. In this context, it can feel unsettling to recognize that we nonetheless have sentiments which bind us together with only some and not others. One response to this, we have seen in Wiggins and Foot, is to seek to remove the partitive elements of solidarity: we are to find fellow feeling with all humankind, or with all persons. I've suggested that this bleaches out of solidarities precisely that which is politically essential to them. Faced with this recognition, it is tempting to find the liberal unease with the claims of our various identities as nothing more than a distaste with the political.[29] The only ways that we have learned to be political agents and successfully to act collectively is by finding solidarity with some against others. To wish to leave that aside and focus just on what is universal and common to all seems nothing more than an impulse to leave the political aside entirely.

---

29. For a discussion of liberal anxieties with identity solidarity, see T. M. Scanlon, "Ideas of Identity and Their Normative Status," manuscript. See also Tommie Shelby, *We Who Are Dark: The Philosophical Foundations of Black Solidarity* (Cambridge, MA: Harvard University Press, 2005).

Chapter 10

Solidarity

The Link between Facts and Norms

MARGARET KOHN

In the early days of Covid, signs started appearing in my neighborhood: *we are all in this together*. Some commentators pointed out that this wasn't accurate. Frontline workers and vulnerable, often racialized, people experienced the crisis quite differently from professionals zooming in from vacation properties. The critics were right, but the factual claim of interdependence was often intended as the foundation for a normative argument about obligation to others. It is this politically potent but philosophically confusing blending of fact and norm that I try to unpack in this chapter.

From the very beginning, the concept of solidarity connected descriptive accounts of interdependence with political theories of obligation. This may look like faulty logic, but it was an effective strategy for motivating fellow citizens. In late nineteenth-century France, a group called the solidarists justified investments in public health, housing, and sanitation using both self- and other-regarding arguments. Citizens should care about the well-being of others, but they would also benefit themselves because disease would not spread as quickly in a healthy population. Solidarism was an alternative to the individualism of classic liberalism and the collectivism of socialism. The solidarists argued that industrial society had created highly productive forms of interdependence that could enable human flourishing, but they also thought that this potential would only be realized if the social virtue of solidarity prevailed over egotism and greed. The solidarist philosopher Alfred Fouilée thought that Kantianism was a dead-end. It couldn't provide a justification of positive duties and it couldn't motivate citizens to discharge negative duties. The solidarists used a combination of descriptive sociology and normative theory to establish solidarity as a distinctively democratic virtue, one that justified the nascent welfare state.

Solidarist ideas also play a role in social liberalism, social democracy, and even American pragmatism, but solidarism, in a narrower sense, refers to a group of philosophers, political economists, and politicians allied with the Radical Republican group in the National Assembly in France.[1] They embraced a form of civic solidarity founded neither on ethno-nationalist identity nor on constitutional patriotism but rather on a theory of social property. Solidarism advanced a theory of quasi-contractual obligation based on social debt. The solidarists argued that the productivity of industrial and commercial societies was due to the advanced division of labor and the technology and infrastructure inherited from the past.[2] They were troubled by the fact that this vast and growing social wealth was accompanied by high levels of destitution and suffering and concluded that the benefits of social cooperation had been allocated unfairly. Based on the principle of restorative justice,[3] the solidarists

---

1. Hayward, "The Official Social Philosophy of the French Third Republic"; Spitz, *Le moment républicain en France*.
2. Kohn, "The Critique of Possessive Individualism," 2016.
3. Fouillée, "La Fraternité et la justice reparative"; Fouillée, "Le progrès social en France."

argued that those with too much owed a debt to those with too little.[4] At the same time, solidarity was understood as a virtue, the willingness to discharge a collective obligation to repair unjust social institutions. The solidarists also proposed ways to inculcate this virtue in citizens, notably through public education and the shared enjoyment of public infrastructure.

The primary contribution of this chapter is a defense of civic solidarity that draws on the arguments of the solidarists, but also engages the work of contemporary thinkers in order to clarify the relationship between the descriptive and normative dimensions of solidarity. The first section introduces key arguments from the political theory literature, with a particular focus on Habermas's shifting account of the relationship between justice and solidarity. The second section reconstructs the main objections to civic solidarity, and the final section argues that the solidarist approach, in conjunction with the 'assigned responsibility' model of political obligation, can satisfy the main objections.

SOLIDARITY—BETWEEN FACTS AND NORMS

Solidarity suggests a willingness to carry out acts in order to support others.[5]

The term 'solidarity' is French in origin, and it was used to indicate commonality and mutual obligation. Contemporary philosophers have understood the normative significance of solidarity in different and sometimes contradictory ways. The main approaches fall into three categories: the interpretive-constructive, the affective, and the praxis-based. The interpretive approach was endorsed

---

4. Blais, *La solidarité*; Audier, *La pensée solidariste*.
5. Rippe, "Diminishing Solidarity."

by Richard Rorty, who argued that solidarity is "made rather than found, produced in history rather than recognized as an a-historical fact."[6] According to Rorty, solidarity expands our sense of we-ness as far as possible.[7] Individuals extrapolate from the experience of caring for family to caring for neighbors, and the underlying principle, which may be reciprocity or the prevention of suffering, is stretched to apply to more distant others.

John Rawls endorses what I call the affective approach. In the voluminous literature on John Rawls, little attention has been paid to his account of solidarity, yet the concept plays an important role in his justification of the difference principle.[8] Rawls explains, "The difference principle, however, does seem to correspond to a natural meaning of solidarity: namely, to the idea of not wanting to have greater advantages unless this is to the benefit of others who are less well off."[9] Rawls also connects fraternity to the problem of moral motivation. This is significant, given that critics have identified an inadequate account of moral motivation as an important weakness of Rawls's abstract approach. In *A Theory of Justice*, Rawls associates fraternity with "sentiment and feeling" and the desire to live together with others on terms that are mutually beneficial. Ultimately, however, Rawls's discussion is confusing because he fails to clarify the relationship between solidarity (the affective dimension) and justice.

While Rawls introduces solidarity only briefly, Habermas examines the concept in depth. In his writings on solidarity, there are three different approaches: the earliest one emphasizes praxis and 'ethical life'; the middle period highlights discourse; and the final iteration is similar to Rorty's interpretive account. In the context of an early

---

6. Rorty, *Contingency, Irony, and Solidarity*, 195; Rorty, "Solidarity or Objectivity."
7. Rorty, "Solidarity or Objectivity."
8. Estlund, "Debate: Liberalism, Equality, and Fraternity"; Rawls, *A Theory of Justice*.
9. Rawls, *A Theory of Justice*, 292.

essay on Kohlberg, Habermas introduces the idea that solidarity is embedded in social relations and calls it "the reverse-side of justice."[10] Abstract morality is the face of justice, and the reverse side includes the concrete institutions and practices of everyday ethical life. In later work, Habermas still calls justice and solidarity "two sides of the same coin,"[11] but he also specifies that discourse binds these two sides together. Justice is produced through reason-giving, but the practice of deliberation is also a 'social bond' that fosters a sense of belonging to a community of communication. In a recent lecture on the European Union, however, Habermas rejects his earlier approach and argues that solidarity is forward-looking and inventive, and should not be construed as a product of existing social relations. In order to decide whether this new account is a rejection or a modification of the earlier theory, we must examine them more closely.

In an early essay entitled "Justice or Solidarity: On the Discussion of Stage 6," Habermas notes that solidarity concerns not only the welfare of individuals who share a way of life, but also "the integrity of the way of life itself."[12] He suggests that solidarity, rooted in "the certainty of intimate relatedness in a shared life context,"[13] is intrinsically valuable. How should we understand the connection between abstract moral principles, particular obligations to others, and concrete ways of life? The connection could be understood in at least three different ways: functional, duty generating, or motivational. The connections fostered through intersubjective relations could be a kind of functional social capital that makes it possible to fulfill moral obligations. For example, an individual may have a duty to care for vulnerable elderly people, but if he is a member of a church, it

---

10. Habermas, "Justice and Solidarity," 244.
11. Habermas, *Autonomy and Solidarity*, 251.
12. Habermas, "Justice and Solidarity," 244.
13. Ibid., 246.

is easier to discharge this obligation since he knows specific elderly people and understands their needs. Alternately, intersubjective relations could generate a duty. I could have an obligation not to wrong strangers and an obligation to provide assistance to members of my group. Finally, social connections could strengthen the motivation to perform a duty. The term 'motivation' describes how committed one is to an undertaking.[14] I could have a duty to help the needy, but I only discharge this duty in relation to my neighbor because I care about his suffering, which provides the motivation to act.

In a lecture published under the title "Plea for a Constitutionalization of International Law,"[15] Habermas rejects part of the praxis/discursive account.[16] He denies that solidarity must be embedded in concrete ways of life, an approach that he now describes as "depoliticizing." In a footnote he writes, "I no longer uphold the assertion that 'Justice conceived deontologically requires solidarity as its reverse side.'"[17] His new position is that justice requires the *creation* of solidarity-enhancing institutions and practices. This reversal comes in the context of a lecture about solidarity in the European Union. Habermas favors European solidarity but also recognizes that it doesn't emerge naturally from concrete ways of life in member states. Habermas points to the "offensive character" of solidarity, by which he means that political solidarity is constructive and forward looking.

What then is solidarity? According to Habermas, solidarity must be distinguished from both legal and moral duties. He links solidarity to ethical life (*Sittlichkeit*) and 'supererogatory' duties that extend what we owe to other people in general.[18] For example, caring for a

---

14. Taylor, "Solidarity: Obligations and Expressions."
15. Habermas, "Plea for a Constitutionalization of International Law."
16. Pierce, "Justice without Solidarity?"
17. Habermas, "Plea for a Constitutionalization of International Law," 12.
18. Ibid., 10.

distant sick relative is neither a moral nor a legal duty, but it is an other-regarding action that one might be motivated to carry out on the basis of social ties. He also notes that solidarity is akin to *Sittlichkeit,* but it corresponds to political communities rather than pre-political associations like the family.[19] We could summarize his position as follows:

> Solidarity should be understood neither as a natural foundation for moral and political obligation nor as a synonym for an abstract principle of justice.
> Solidarity is linked to ethical life (concrete practices of social integration and sources of moral motivation) but not exclusively to traditional forms of ethical life.
> Solidarity has a creative dimension and is not determined by natural affinities.

Habermas does not explain precisely how these fit together, but I think it is possible to make sense of them by returning to Rorty's interpretive approach to solidarity. Solidarity is neither a fact about the social world nor an abstract principle; instead, it is an interpretation of our social relations that attaches us to more extensive obligations to others. Solidarity adds new obligations and stretches and expands our ethical practices through reflective judgment based on narrative or analogy. Understood in this way, solidarity is not the reverse side of justice, as Habermas originally suggested, but rather a social virtue and the glue that attaches people to a widening circle of imagined communities to whom we have obligations.

This reconstruction of the concept of solidarity provides support for Habermas's suggestion that solidarity is the struggle "to discharge

---

19. Ibid., 11.

the promise invested in the legitimacy claim of any political order."[20] A political order is legitimate if it is an order in which the benefits and burdens of social cooperation are shared fairly. It must also have institutions that provide individuals with equal opportunities to defend different views about what constitutes fairness and how to achieve it. This much is not too controversial but the terms 'struggle' and 'promise' require further attention. These terms suggest that the legitimacy of the political order is not fully realized and perhaps that it cannot be. A promise is something that will be achieved in the future, and the term 'struggle' implies that it will be difficult to realize it.

Habermas explains the "forwarding looking character" of solidarity by pointing toward the tension between existing norms/institutions and the force of "systematic interdependencies" which are not always recognized or acknowledged. Habermas's point is that European economic integration has exceeded normative and political integration. Interdependence generates dependency and domination that must be controlled through democratic institutions, but the construction of political institutions is difficult because the required affective solidarity is absent. The solution is to establish practices that forge practical connections and feelings of solidarity and also to interpret facts about interdependence through an expansive interpretation of our existing values.

Solidarism provides an illustration of how this interpretive approach can be applied to civic solidarity. Writing in the late nineteenth century, the solidarists emphasized two key facts: the vast social wealth produced through a complex division of labor and the persistently high levels of destitution that accompanied it.[21] They also offered an interpretation of these facts that drew on, and transformed, existing norms. The destitution experienced by members of

---

20. Ibid., 11.
21. Bourgeois, *Solidarité*.

the working class seemed to contradict the promise that legitimized the social order: that social cooperation should benefit all participants, or at least ensure a minimal level of well-being.[22] In the emerging commercial, industrial societies of the late nineteenth century, existing forms of ethical life such as charity and gleaning were unable to prevent destitution. A new, civic commitment was needed.

The solidarists argued that economic interdependence bound the members of society together and produced overall social benefit. Furthermore, they claimed these benefits rested on trust and stability, which would be impossible to maintain in an economic system with high levels of domination, inequality, and poverty. Yet the facticity of interdependence was not a natural foundation for moral and political obligation. If it were, then the political project of solidarism would not have been necessary. Solidarism was a creative set of arguments intended to convince elites that their enjoyment of jointly produced benefits justified a corresponding obligation to share some of the benefits. The solidarists claimed that a more equal allocation of social property would be good for the group and a higher contribution from the wealthy was reasonable.

The solidarist concept of 'quasi-contractual debt' was an interpretation that linked facts and norms. In *Solidarité*, Léon Bourgeois argued that value produced by society was actually due to contributions inherited from past generations in the form of technology and social infrastructure.[23] According to the solidarists, individuals deserve the fruits of their labor but not a disproportionate share of this inheritance. The vast inequalities of wealth are evidence that some people have taken a disproportionate share of this patrimony. The argument in favor of expanding the scope of obligation to strangers relies on a certain kind of analogy between the family and the

---

22. Bouglé, *Le Solidarisme*.
23. Bourgeois, *Solidarité*.

society. Bourgeois doesn't argue that society *is* the same as a family, nor does he say that individuals *should* treat familial and social obligations in the same way. Instead, he suggests that in light of a key similarity between the family and state (the fact that we receive unearned benefits from both), citizens should apply the norms of gratitude in a more expansive way. They should recognize reciprocal obligations to needy members of society. To summarize, solidarity is an interpretation of ethical life that expands the scope of obligation. Furthermore, by linking self-interest to collective identity, it heightens the motivation for civic action. Solidarism was a particular form of solidarity focused on civic solidarity and the recognition of social rights, an approach that is still worth defending today.

CRITIQUES OF SOLIDARITY

Solidarity was the key concept in the late nineteenth century, but it plays a much less visible role today. Perhaps this eclipse is due less to the coherence of the concept and more to the harmful consequences of solidarity when put into practice. Solidarity has been the focus of some explicit critiques, and relevant objections to solidarity come up in related literatures on communitarianism, constitutional patriotism,[24] and liberal nationalism.[25] Jacob Levy's article "Against Fraternity: Democracy without Solidarity" provides a particularly clear articulation of the objections to the concept of solidarity.[26] In this section, I will summarize three main critiques of civic solidarity: the liberal-pluralist; the anti-communitarian; and the ingratitude

---

24. Yack, "The Myth of the Civic Nation"; Markell, "Making Affect Safe for Democracy?"
25. Mason, *Community, Solidarity and Belonging.*
26. Levy, "Against Fraternity."

critiques. In the final section, I will address the most relevant and challenging features of the critiques in more detail.

The pluralist critique holds that solidarity is impossible because shared identity is disappearing in modern political communities.[27] Modern polities are complex societies with high levels of diversity. Citizens and residents do not have the opportunity to meet face to face. Bureaucratic institutions undermine the importance of networks of mutual aid. Moreover, racial, religious, ethno-cultural, and ideological heterogeneity make it difficult for citizens to even imagine themselves as belonging together. As Levy put it, "The inhabitants of a political community are more like strangers who find themselves locked in a very large room together than they are like an extended family or a voluntary association united in pursuit of a common purpose."[28] According to the pluralist critique, civic solidarity rests on an inaccurate picture of modern societies, which, in reality, are deeply divided by demographic differences (race, ethno-cultural identity, immigration status) and normative disagreements (religion, political values).

There are two main ways of responding to the pluralist critique. The first response concedes the empirical accuracy of the pluralist account but insists that it is irrelevant because the most persuasive justifications of solidarity rest on 'joint action' rather than shared identity. If you are locked in a room together, you still have to find a way to live together and solidarity will help. According to Andrea Sangiovanni, the reciprocal obligations of solidarity are produced through our joint action as authors of political and social institutions.[29] Solidarity need not be grounded in a collective identity such

---

27. Mason, *Community, Solidarity and Belonging*; Alexander, *The Antinomies of Classical Thought*, 303.
28. Levy, "Against Fraternity," 107.
29. Sangiovanni, "Solidarity as Joint Action."

as ethnicity or nationalism. The French solidarists also advanced a version of the joint action approach, one that emphasized the shared enjoyment of common wealth inherited from past generations and the joint production of social wealth in the present.

The second response to the pluralist critique also accepts the descriptive account but derives a different normative conclusion. It emphasizes that the pluralism of modern society makes a politics of solidarity necessary. This response builds on Durkheim's sociology. Durkheim thought that solidarity was mechanical or autonomic in traditional societies.[30] In pre-modern times, individuals produced things largely for their own consumption, but other people did the same, which meant that an individual's way of life was very similar to that of other members of her society. A sense of common values and identity reflected a shared way of life. In modern societies, however, the reverse is true. The division of labor is complex and each individual depends entirely on others for his or her basic needs. At the same time, each task is distinct and this differentiation of tasks leads to differentiated identities. The result is a high level of interdependence but a low level of mutual identification. For Durkheim, there were both positive and negative sides of this development. The positive side was the increasing opportunity for individual freedom and autonomy. The downside, however, was what he called anomie, a kind of alienation caused by the loss of orienting values. In modern, pluralistic societies an explicit project of solidarity becomes necessary.[31]

Pluralists have the following concern: if the absence of solidarity is described as a lack of shared identity, then the remedy for this lack will be the promotion of ethno-nationalism or thick civic identity. The worry is that the binding force of shared identity undermines the ability to recognize obligations to diverse others. Durkheim himself

---

30. Durkheim, *The Division of Labor in Society*.
31. Ibid.

was a Dreyfusard and an opponent of the ethno-nationalism sweeping France in the late 1800s. He thought that the idea of law or right, rather than ethno-nationalist identity, could itself be a way of binding citizens to the state.[32] Nevertheless, the history of the Dreyfus affair reminds us that shared identity is often created in relation to a constitutive outside. Civic nationalism, of course, is an attempt to avoid this type of division by fostering identity around the constitution and the law, but critics argue that this is more difficult than proponents assume.[33] If justice is attached to membership in a polity, then it becomes all too easy to treat outsiders as people not worthy of protection of the law.[34]

According to Levy, the best way to avoid the exclusionary effects produced by solidarity is to reject the concept altogether. He claims that nothing is lost and much is gained through this minimalist approach. People can still enjoy the benefits of the rule of law because a limited state can be justified on the basis of rational self-interest alone. He argues that even a robust redistributive state can be defended in much the same way, as a feature of a peaceful system of social cooperation.[35] Redistribution *can be* justified as a feature of a peaceful system of economic and social cooperation—that is part of the solidarist project—but very different systems with much greater levels of economic inequality and poverty can be justified too. The relationship between political ideology (social democracy, conservatism, and liberal-individualism) and redistribution has been the focus of a vast scholarly literature. In his influential *Three Worlds of Welfare Capitalism*, Esping-Andersen demonstrated that the solidaristic welfare states took a distinctive form (the provision of tax-funded

---

32. Durkheim, *Emile Durkheim on Morality and Society*; Durkheim, *Durkheim on Politics and the State*.
33. Miller, *On Nationality*.
34. Levy, "Against Fraternity," 111.
35. Ibid., 115.

universal benefits) and subsequent research has shown that such programs are the most effective at limiting economic inequality.[36]

Klaus Rippe also argues that solidarity is unnecessary because the state itself is a sufficient source of social integration. Liberal democracies are able to secure justice without relying on the anachronistic and conceptually imprecise virtue of 'solidarity.' He argues that adequate levels of social integration can be secured through commercial relations and participation in voluntary associations and political institutions. How we assess this claim depends on the meaning of adequate social integration. From a purely functionalist perspective, the claim may be correct. Law, citizenship, and commerce may be strong enough to prevent the dissolution of society, but the term 'adequate' can also be interpreted in a normative sense. Adequate social integration, in this deeper sense, means something like a widespread belief that the existing order is a fair system of social cooperation, or at least that the social order incorporates adequate mechanisms for rectifying injustices. The rise of populist movements and economic inequality suggests that there is a crisis of both social integration and social justice.[37]

Rippe's descriptive claim about the character of social integration in modern societies is not that different from the solidarist approach; the disagreement stems from their respective assessments of its adequacy, both in terms of stability and legitimacy. Following Durkheim, the solidarists argued that the high level of functional integration did not automatically generate a corresponding recognition of interdependence. Modern society enables freedom and individuality, but such individuality, if unmoored from its social foundation, can turn into selfishness, indifference, and ultimately social dissolution. This

---

36. Esping-Andersen, *The Three Worlds of Welfare Capitalism*; Rueda and Pontusson, "Wage Inequality and Varieties of Capitalism"; Pontusson, "Once Again a Model."
37. Piketty, *Capital in the Twenty-First Century*.

seemed particularly obvious in the *Belle Époque* when extremely high levels of economic inequality were accompanied by utter destitution among the poor and rising levels of violent class conflict. Durkheim argued that abstract humanism was, at most, a very weak source of normative guidance and social integration. Solidarists such as Célestin Bouglé proposed strengthening social ties through the legal protection of social rights.[38] This initially seems like an odd position, at least when it is viewed in light of a long line of leftist criticism that treats rights as atomizing, but Bouglé thought that legal rights need not lead to atomization. If the doctrine of social right is the glue that binds society together, then it must be defended as a collective ideal.

The liberal-pluralist critique emphasizes that solidarity is unnecessary or impossible. The anti-communitarian critique, on the other hand, holds that it is normatively unappealing. Klaus Rippe rejects the view that traditional modes of solidarity based on the family and the village are normatively desirable. Rippe's critique of solidarity, however, is based on the fallacy of composition, which is the mistake of conflating a part (a particular form of solidarity— communitarianism) with the whole (solidarity in general). Rippe argues that traditional forms of social integration such as the village and family did not necessarily produce just forms of cooperation, nor are they well suited to addressing large-scale social challenges today. This is correct, but it is akin to rejecting the principle of democracy because earlier versions excluded women or relied on slave labor.

The anti-communitarian argument, however, is an exaggerated form of a more plausible argument that any type of solidarity rests on a constitutive outside. Binding group members closer together inevitably reinforces exclusion and marginalization of outsiders. In a prescient essay on constitutional patriotism, Patchen Markell explained the paradox of civic solidarity like this: "Even the reproduction of

---

38. Bouglé, *Solidarisme et libéralisme.*

civic affect proceeds by tying its citizens to historical institutions and concrete cultures that are never quite equivalent to the universal principles they purport to embody."[39]

Markell is right, but this is an ontological objection, and even though it cannot be overcome, its negative effects can be mitigated. By that I mean we should endorse a form of civic solidarity that motivates the greatest commitment to vulnerable members while producing the least indifference to non-members. Solidarity takes many forms, from the solidarity among workers in a revolutionary movement to the solidarity among citizens in a social democratic welfare state. The question is less whether we need solidarity than what kind we need. The solidarist approach does not try to recreate the 'mechanical solidarity' of the village community nor does it rest on the kind of ethno-nationalist identity that is most likely to justify the exclusion of outsiders. The best one is an account that draws out the normative and practical significance of the modern division of labor.

Recent empirical research has pointed to an inverse correlation between ethnic diversity and support for redistribution, and some have even suggested that the tension between redistribution and multiculturalism constitutes 'a progressive's dilemma.'[40] While this research suggests a general trend, there is also a great variation across different countries and contexts. In his study of multiculturalism in Canada, Banting finds remarkably little tension between ethnic diversity and support for redistribution. Banting suggests that state-led efforts to foster an inclusive identity have played an important role in bringing about this outcome.[41] Embracing multiculturalism as a form of civic identity can diminish tension between multiculturalism and redistribution, and a particular kind of narrative about solidarity

---

39. Markell, "Making Affect Safe for Democracy?"
40. Kymlicka, "Solidarity in Diverse Societies."
41. Banting, "Is There a Progressive's Dilemma in Canada?"

can play a role in this process. Some kind of solidarity is necessary to motivate citizens to support the sharing of risks and benefits, but the basis of civic solidarity need not be the traditional community or the ethno-cultural nation. If we understand solidarity the way Rorty and the later Habermas do, as something creative, then we can tell a story about the facticity of interdependence that activates latent propensities to care about others.

In "Diminishing Solidarity," Rippe introduces a third line of critique, focused on the normative foundation of solidarity: 'gratefulness argument.' Why do members of a community or polity have obligations to one another that exceed the obligation to follow the law? The gratefulness argument is a reciprocity-based argument that obligation is a way of repaying society for benefits received by the individual. Rippe summarizes the gratefulness argument as follows:

1. The human being is dependent on social existence within a community.
2. The individual owes her values to the community.
3. This dependence upon the community generates rights and obligations for the individual. She has a right to a proportion of the goods generated by the community. She also has obligations toward the community, as well as toward other members of that community.
4. This network of joint rights and obligations is known as solidarity.[42]

This is a fair approximation of the normative argument made by the solidarists, and, if Rippe provided an adequate critique, then it would be strong grounds for rejecting solidarism. His critique, however, is not persuasive.

42. Rippe, "Diminishing Solidarity," 71.

Rippe rejects the first two premises, arguing that they rest on a false analogy. He calls this logical fallacy "the non-sequitur from the Family to the Nation." He accepts the widely shared moral intuition that we owe a debt of obligation to our parents or caregivers. Since each person received care and sustenance without providing anything in return, the principle of reciprocity implies that each person has a debt to discharge. Where he differs from the solidarists, however, is his view of the identity of the creditor. He thinks the debt is owed to the direct caregivers, usually parents, but not to society.

Rippe gives three reasons for rejecting the analogy between a debt to one's family and a debt to society. First, he challenges point two, explaining that the nation is not the primary source of individuals' values. He denies that the nation plays a fundamental role in individual development equivalent to that of the family. The case for 'civic solidarity,' however, does not rest on the claim that the community or state is the primary source of *values*. In liberal states, the role of the government in the reproduction of values is supposed to be limited to the cultivation of a disposition to tolerance and willingness to peacefully resolve conflict. The more plausible argument is that the individual owes the community or state for her education and for the material conditions that enabled her to develop and exercise her capacities.[43] The family's ability to convey its values rests on the foundation of a socially guaranteed minimum of material and intellectual capital.

Next, Rippe objects to claim 3, insisting that most exchanges of goods are based on mutual advantage and do not produce residual obligations. According to Rippe, networks of commercial relations create and circulate the things that people need to live, and the market mechanism ensures that adequate compensation is given to those

---

43. Alperovitz, *Unjust Deserts*.

who provide these goods and services. Once the market price is paid, there are no residual obligations.

Rippe also considers the significance of goods that do not circulate as commodities, such as language. He argues that while citizens may benefit from things like language and culture—things Charles Taylor called irreducibly social goods—these benefits do not generate a corresponding obligation. According to Rippe, "Our dependency on it [language] and our gratefulness towards it are far more similar to the dependency on and the gratefulness for the existence of the sun than of a family."[44] Since we do not have obligations to the sun, we do not have obligations to society.

This argument is not convincing because it rests on a false analogy. Language, history, and culture are not like the sun. The sun is a natural object that pre-dates human existence. Language, history, and culture are human creations, which contribute to the value of human products. This social dividend is obvious if we compare the difference between what an individual can produce alone on a desert island and her proportionate share of the things produced through the division of labor. The aggregate productivity of the division of labor and the corresponding larger individual share are due to social cooperation, which is made possible by language and culture.

Levy also challenges the gratefulness argument, but his critique focuses on the misalignment between the source of the duty (society) and the beneficiary (fellow citizens, the state). According to Levy, the problem with the gratefulness/shared inheritance approach is that it does not provide a foundation for *civic* solidarity.[45] Even if human beings do benefit from accumulated irreducible social goods such as technological knowledge, infrastructure, and social capital, any resulting debt is not owed to fellow citizens. By this he means

---

44. Rippe, "Diminishing Solidarity," 371.
45. Levy, "Against Fraternity," 108.

that the members of any particular polity are not united by a demarcated society to which individuals owe gratitude for these inherited advantages.[46]

This section has shown the weaknesses of most of the objections to solidarity and identified two objections to civic solidarity that deserve fuller consideration. The first is the claim that the benefits enjoyed by members of society do not justify reciprocal obligations to society. The second is the claim that even if there are social obligations, they are not tied to a specific polity. Similar arguments were made by nineteenth-century liberals in France, and the final section of this chapter revisits the philosophy of solidarism for some convincing responses.

THE DEFENSE OF SOLIDARISM

In his book *La Proprieté Sociale*, the solidarist philosopher Alfred Fouillée explained why the individual has a debt to society.[47] The premise of his argument is the claim that property is composed of an individual and a social share. The individual share corresponds to the individual's contribution to the value of the product. The social share is composed of the value of the raw material and the social infrastructure. Following Locke, Fouillée thought that all property was originally common to all mankind. When individuals produced things by mixing labor with raw materials, the resulting entitlement was only partial. The individual could claim the value of the improvement through labor but not the value of the raw materials. In early stages of society when there was lots of common property, there was no scarcity and therefore the value of raw materials, including land, seemed

---

46. Ibid., 108.
47. Fouillée, *La propriété sociale et la démocratie*.

small compared to the labor invested. In latter stages, however, when demand outpaced supply, causing the price of materials to rise, it became clear that those who had taken what they did not legitimately own (e.g., increasingly scarce land and raw materials) owed a debt to those who had no similar access to the common stock.[48]

The second source of social debt is social infrastructure. According to the solidarist theorist Charles Gide, the value of a piece of urban land provides a clear illustration of the way that social infrastructure contributes to value.[49] If two brothers each buy a parcel of land for the same price, but one parcel happens to be located in an area that subsequently develops into a metropolis, the value of the urban parcel will become one hundred or even one thousand times higher than the rural one, even though neither brother invested any labor. All of the increase in value is due to the proximity to value created by others, including roads, factories, schools, and shops. The increase in value is produced socially, but under the system of private property, it is appropriated by the titular owner. According to solidarists, this rent or unearned increment is a way of privatizing social value and therefore it creates a debt to society.[50]

Tom Malleson and Igor Shoikhedbrod describe this socially produced value as the understructure of economic production, which includes physical, political-legal, cultural, knowledge, and care infrastructure.[51] This understructure magnifies the productive capacity of individuals. While it is difficult to quantify the proportionate share credited to these social inputs, economists[52] estimate that as much as 80 percent of the economic growth over the last century is due to technological processes rather than the inputs of labor or capital.

---

48. Fouillée, *La propriété sociale et la démocratie*.
49. Gide and Rist, *A History of Economic Doctrines*.
50. Bouglé, *Solidarisme et libéralisme*.
51. Malleson and Shoikhedbrod, "On the Very Idea of Private Property."
52. Abramovitz, "The Search for the Sources of Growth."

Like the solidarists, Malleson and Shoikhedbrod argue that property is not produced by atomistic individuals but rather by individuals who are embedded in a social structure that provides both direct and indirect contributions to their productive activities, which are often uncompensated.[53] Direct contributions include the technology and know-how needed to produce things. Indirect contributions include everything that is necessary to reproduce life itself.

The understructure should not be viewed as something natural like the sun, which we can use freely without generating any corresponding obligation.[54] The understructure should be seen as more akin to a rental than a gift.[55] When we make use of the understructure, we are benefitting from the labor of others, and the principle of reciprocity requires a corresponding obligation. In other words, when we benefit from the understructure we incur a debt.

A critic might accept this argument in the abstract, but still insist that this obligation is owed to humanity in general, but not to citizens of a particular state. According to Levy, if the benefit is not created by a particular polity, then the debt is not owed to the state, and it is not an adequate way to ground civic solidarity. This objection is partially, but not entirely, correct. Some components of the understructure, things like roads and schools and national health care and courts, are public goods that are organized and paid for by the state. Much like individuals owe obligations of reciprocity to family for the care they received, citizens owe obligations to the state for its role in providing health services, education, and other forms of care, but the term 'understructure' describes something much more expansive. It includes elements of culture and knowledge that are better understood as a commons[56] rather than

---

53. Malleson and Shoikhedbrod, "On the Very Idea of Private Property."
54. Ibid.
55. Sternberg, "The Knowledge Inheritance Theory of Distributive Justice."
56. Hardt and Negri, *Commonwealth*.

state-provided public goods. Furthermore, the physical infrastructure of a particular country may have been funded by land, labor, and materials expropriated in distant colonies and in that case any debt would be owed to distant others rather than members of one's own polity.[57] Civic solidarity doesn't seem like the best way to discharge these debts.

My response is that the social property argument is best understood in conjunction with the assigned responsibility model of obligation.[58] General obligations are most likely to be discharged when they are assigned to particular agents. There are good reasons to focus on the needs of those close to us. Less geographic distance decreases the transaction costs of providing aid. Often, we respond more effectively and appropriately to the needs of people we know. Finally, shared political institutions enable people to deliberate together about the extent of their responsibilities and the best ways to meet them. The debt is owed to society but, in the absence of a global institutional structure capable of discharging redistributive obligations, it makes sense to start by using the instrument of existing state institutions. A pragmatic focus on existing institutions, however, does not preclude 'social property'–based arguments about debts to non-citizens. Contemporary theorists of global justice build on this approach when they emphasize the associative duties generated by the legacy of colonialism and the fact that much of the wealth created in Europe during the industrial revolution was originally funded by the proceeds of slave plantations.[59]

---

57. Ypi, Goodin, and Barry, "Associative Duties, Global Justice, and the Colonies."
58. Goodin, "What Is So Special about Our Fellow Countrymen?"
59. Williams and Palmer, *Capitalism and Slavery*; Pogge, *World Poverty and Human Rights*; Ypi, Goodin, and Barry, "Associative Duties, Global Justice, and the Colonies"; Wenar, *Blood Oil*.

CONCLUSION

Solidarity among citizens is the necessary precondition for the practical realization of social rights in a democracy. Unlike negative rights, which are a way of ensuring the state does not become an agent of domination, social rights require positive action by citizens to share resources. We prioritize the needs of others because we care about their flourishing and the world we share. The motivational force of solidarity comes from the way it connects obligation with affective attachment and self-interest. The sense of obligation stems from the fact that every person alive was born dependent and vulnerable and survived due to care provided by others. We reach adulthood with a vast debt of care, including an obligation to care for the material and social worlds, but it is not self-evident what this requires in practice, which is why interpretation, imagination, and deliberation are necessary.

The concept of solidarity is somewhat Janus-faced. It binds us to others, thereby motivating us to overcome egoism and engage in actions that benefit others. At the same time, there is a constant danger that the very ties that bind us to people near us will make distant others seem more distant and alien. An interpretive approach to solidarity does not fully resolve this conundrum, but it does provide a way of addressing it. It urges us to constantly consider whether the concrete practices that connect us to specific others might rest on principles that apply more broadly. It is also important to remember that solidarity by itself is unlikely to bring about a most just society. The powerful do not give up their power and privilege out of a sense of *noblesse oblige*. The fight against anti-black racism reminds us that struggle almost always comes before solidarity and confrontation precedes recognition. We see this pattern in the labor movements in the nineteenth century that demanded the things that the solidarists helped secure, and it is true for the movements for racial justice today.

WORKS CITED

Abramovitz, Moses. "The Search for the Sources of Growth: Areas of Ignorance, Old and New." *The Journal of Economic History* 53, no. 2 (1993): 217–243.

Alexander, Jeffrey C. *The Antinomies of Classical Thought: Marx and Durkheim (Theoretical Logic in Sociology)*. London: Routledge, 2014.

Alperovitz, Gar. *Unjust Deserts: How the Rich Are Taking Our Common Inheritance*. New York City: New Press, 2008.

Audier, Serge. *La pensée solidariste: Aux sources du modèle social républicain*. Paris: Presses universitaires de France, 2010.

Banting, Keith G. "Is There a Progressive's Dilemma in Canada? Immigration, Multiculturalism and the Welfare State: Presidential Address to the Canadian Political Science Association, Montreal, June 2, 2010." *Canadian Journal of Political Science/Revue Canadienne de Science Politique* 43, no. 4 (2010): 797–820.

Blais, Marie-Claude. *La solidarité: Histoire d'une idée*. Paris: Gallimard, 2007.

Bouglé, Célestin. *Solidarisme et libéralisme: Réflexions sur le mouvement politique et l'éducation morale*. Paris: É. Cornély, 1904.

Bouglé, Célestin. *Le Solidarisme*. Charleston, SC: Nabu Press, 2010 [1907].

Bourgeois, Léon. *Solidarité*. Paris: Hachette Livre BnF, 2013.

Brunkhorst, Hauke. *Solidarity: From Civic Friendship to a Global Legal Community*. Translated by Jeffrey Flynn. Cambridge, MA: MIT Press, 2005.

Coulthard, Glen, and Leanne Betasamosake Simpson. "Grounded Normativity/Place-Based Solidarity." *American Quarterly* 68, no. 2 (2016): 249–255.

Dean, Jodi. "The Party and Communist Solidarity." *Rethinking Marxism* 27, no. 3 (2015): 332–342.

Durkheim, Émile. *The Division of Labor in Society*. Glencoe, IL: Free Press, 1960.

Durkheim, Émile. *Emile Durkheim on Morality and Society*. Edited by Robert N. Bellah. Chicago: University of Chicago Press, 1973.

Durkheim, Émile. *Durkheim on Politics and the State*. Edited by Anthony Giddens. Stanford, CA: Stanford University Press, 1986.

Esping-Andersen, Gøsta. *The Three Worlds of Welfare Capitalism*. Princeton, NJ: Princeton University Press, 1990.

Estlund, David. "Debate: Liberalism, Equality, and Fraternity in Cohen's Critique of Rawls." *Journal of Political Philosophy* 6, no. 1 (1998): 99–112.

Fouillée, Alfred. "La Fraternité et la Justice réparative selon la science sociale contemporaine." *Revue Des Deux Mondes (1829–1971)* 37, no. 2 (1880): 281–311.

Fouillée, Alfred. "Le Progrès social en France." *Revue Des Deux Mondes (1829–1971)* 153, no. 4 (1899): 815–843.

Fouillée, Alfred. *La propriété sociale et la démocratie*. Paris: Hachette, 1884.

Gide, Charles, and Charles Rist. *A History of Economic Doctrines from the Time of the Physiocrats to the Present Day*. Lexington, MA: Heath, 1915.

Goodin, Robert E. "What Is So Special about Our Fellow Countrymen?" *Ethics* 98, no. 4 (1988): 663–686.

Gooding-Williams, Robert. *Look, a Negro!: Philosophical Essays on Race, Culture, and Politics.* London: Routledge, 2013.

Gould, Carol C. "Transnational Solidarities." *Journal of Social Philosophy* 38, no. 1 (2007): 148–164.

Habermas, Jürgen. "Justice and Solidarity: On the Discussion Concerning Stage 6." In *The Moral Domain: Essays in the Ongoing Discussion between Philosophy and the Social Sciences*, ed. Thomas Wren. Cambridge, MA: MIT Press, 1990, 224–251.

Habermas, Jürgen. *Autonomy and Solidarity: Interviews with Jürgen Habermas.* New York and London: Verso, 1992).

Habermas, Jürgen. "Three Normative Models of Democracy." *Constellations* 1, no. 1 (1994): 1–10.

Habermas, Jürgen. "Plea for a Constitutionalization of International Law." *Philosophy & Social Criticism* 40, no. 1 (2014): 5–12.

Hardt, Michael, and Antonio Negri. *Commonwealth.* Cambridge, MA: Belknap Press, 2011.

Hayward, Jack Ernest S. "The Official Social Philosophy of the French Third Republic: Léon Bourgeois and Solidarism." *International Review of Social History* 6, no. 1 (1961): 19–48.

Kohn, Margaret. "The Critique of Possessive Individualism: Solidarism and the City." *Political Theory* 44, no. 5 (2016): 603–628.

Kymlicka, Will. "Solidarity in Diverse Societies: Beyond Neoliberal Multiculturalism and Welfare Chauvinism". *Comparative Migration Studies* 3, no. 17 (2015): 1–19.

Levy, Jacob T. "Against Fraternity." In *The Strains of Commitment: The Political Sources of Solidarity in Diverse Societies*, ed. Will Kymlicka and Keith G. Banting. Oxford: Oxford University Press, 2017, 107–124.

Malleson, Tom, and Igor Shoikhedbrod. "On the Very Idea of Private Property: Towards a Socialist-Feminist Retrieval." Working paper, 2020.

Markell, Patchen. "Making Affect Safe for Democracy? On 'Constitutional Patriotism.'" *Political Theory* 28, no. 1 (2000): 38–63.

Mason, Andrew. *Community, Solidarity and Belonging: Levels of Community and Their Normative Significance.* Cambridge: Cambridge University Press, 2000.

Metz, Karl H. "Solidarity and History. Institutions and Social Concepts of Solidarity in 19th Century Western Europe." In *Solidarity*, ed. Kurt Bayertz. New York: Springer, 1999, 191–207.

Miller, David. *On Nationality.* Oxford: Clarendon Press, 1995.

Pierce, Andrew J. "Justice without Solidarity? Collective Identity and the Fate of the "Ethical" in Habermas' Recent Political Theory." *European Journal of Philosophy* 26, no. 1 (2018): 546–568.

Piketty, Thomas. *Capital in the Twenty-First Century.* Cambridge, MA: Belknap Press, 2014.

Piven, Frances Fox, and Richard Cloward. *Poor People's Movements: Why They Succeed, How They Fail.* New York: Vintage, 1978.
Pogge, Thomas W. *World Poverty and Human Rights*, 2nd ed. Cambridge: Polity, 2008.
Pontusson, Jonas. "Once Again a Model." In *What's Left of the Left: Democrats and Social Democrats in Challenging Times*, ed. James Cronin, George Ross, and James Shoch. Durham, NC: Duke University Press, 2011, 89–115.
Rawls, John. *A Theory of Justice: Revised Edition.* Cambridge, MA: Harvard University Press, 2009.
Rippe, Klaus Peter. "Diminishing Solidarity." *Ethical Theory and Moral Practice* 1, no. 3 (1998): 355–373.
Rorty, Richard. *Contingency, Irony, and Solidarity.* Cambridge: Cambridge University Press, 1989.
Rorty, Richard. "Solidarity or Objectivity." In *Knowledge and Inquiry: Readings in Epistemology*, ed. K. Brad Wray. Peterborough, ON: Broadview Press, 2002, 422–437.
Rueda, David, and Jonas Pontusson. "Wage Inequality and Varieties of Capitalism." *World Politics* 52, no. 3 (2000): 350–383.
Sangiovanni, Andrea. "Solidarity as Joint Action." *Journal of Applied Philosophy* 32, no. 4 (2015): 340–359.
Scholz, Sally J. *Political Solidarity.* University Park, PA: Penn State University Press, 2012.
Shelby, Tommie. *We Who Are Dark: The Philosophical Foundations of Black Solidarity.* Cambridge, MA: Harvard University Press, 2005.
Spitz, Jean-Fabien. *Le moment républicain en France.* Paris: Gallimard, 2005.
Sternberg, Elaine. "The Knowledge Inheritance Theory of Distributive Justice." *Economic Affairs* 30, no. 1 (2010): 33–37.
Taylor, Ashley E. "Solidarity: Obligations and Expressions." *Journal of Political Philosophy* 23, no. 2 (2015): 128–145.
Wenar, Leif. *Blood Oil: Tyrants, Violence, and the Rules That Run the World.* Oxford: Oxford University Press, 2015.
Williams, Eric, and Colin A. Palmer. *Capitalism and Slavery.* Chapel Hill: University of North Carolina Press, 1994.
Yack, Bernard. "The Myth of the Civic Nation." *Critical Review* 10, no. 2 (1996): 193–211.
Ypi, Lea, Robert E. Goodin, and Christian Barry. "Associative Duties, Global Justice, and the Colonies." *Philosophy & Public Affairs* 37, no. 2 (2009): 103–135.

Chapter 11

Transnational Solidarity

A Durkheimian View

ALEXANDER SOMEK

1. INTRODUCTION

As is well known,[1] the concept of solidarity has one most prominent descriptive usage; more commonly, however, is it invoked prescriptively or in a less imposing normative mood.

The descriptive use of the term emerges in nineteenth-century French sociological theory[2] and addresses the phenomenon that modern societies are integrated—held together—in spite of giving more room than ever before to individual choices. What explains this new form of social integration, according to Durkheim, is the social fact that the division of labor gives rise to altruism and an inchoate feeling of responsibility toward other members of society.

---

1. See, for example, Kurt Bayertz and Susanne Boshammer, "Solidarität," in *Handbuch der Politischen Philosophie und Sozialphilosophie*, ed. S Gosepath, W. Hinsch and B. Rössler, vol. 2 (Berlin: De Gruyter, 2008), 1197–1201.
2. See Steinar Stjernø, *Solidarity in Europe: The History of an Idea* (Cambridge: Cambridge University Press, 2009), 26.

Even though this engagement with solidarity is chiefly interested in *explaining* why societies are not torn apart by the anarchical forces of individual ambition, it nonetheless establishes a tight connection between solidarity as a virtue[3] and an institutional context from which it arises and that helps to sustain it. It links the existence of certain attitudes with the integration of society.

Prescriptive uses, by contrast, generally invoke solidarity in order to muster support for other people and to engage a readiness to incur sacrifices on their behalf.[4] In this respect, acting in solidarity is different from pursuing intentionally one's individual self-interest.[5]

It should not come as a surprise, however, that the most intriguing uses of "solidarity" combine a descriptive and a prescriptive or less strongly articulated normative element. This is the case for attempts to identify and to use, purposely, structures of interaction that are supposed to bring about solidarity *qua* cohesion that is supported by individual virtue as a desired result. They are based upon the intuition that the moral demands of solidarity can be best satisfied based on modes of cooperation that somehow trigger sympathy or compassion among the participating members.

The deliberate creation of such structures is, in a sense, more than an exercise in large-scale nudging. Supposedly, these structures establish the conditions necessary for generating moral attitudes behind the backs of individuals. The idea is that, while each individual engages with others for his or her own benefit, eventually, if all goes well, everyone begins to care about all others.

---

3. As a virtue, solidarity is a mindset that translates into dispositions, for example, the disposition to support the oppressed. See Andrea Sangiovanni and Juri Viehoff, Introduction to this volume.

4. For a recent and highly sophisticated philosophical reconstruction of the appropriate conditions, see Andrea Sangiovanni, "Solidarity as Joint Action," 32 *Journal of Applied Philosophy* (2015): 340–359.

5. For a well-received philosophical account of solidarity as a duty to support "the underdog," see Avery Kolers, *A Moral Theory of Solidarity* (Oxford: Oxford University Press, 2016).

In this vein, since the days of the Schuman Declaration,[6] European integration has been predicated upon the confidence that increasing economic interpenetration and interdependence will in the long run give rise to solidarity among the peoples of Europe. Such a transnational solidarity is supposed to involve not only abstention from violence in the conduct of international affairs, but also a growing readiness, on the part of Europeans, to make sacrifices for the benefit of nationals of other Member States and on behalf of the larger European house.[7]

Within and outside the European Union, however, the quest for transnational solidarity is notoriously set to end in disappointment and trailed with appeals to keep our hopes up. The following contribution would like to show why this is not accidentally the case. Transnational solidarity is, where it exists, composed of three elements: *doux commerce*, cosmopolitan concern for individual suffering, and faith in a future union. These three elements are genealogically connected. Taken together, they indicate the absence of "organic" solidarity in a transnational context.

As the language used already indicates, this conclusion is reached by drawing on Durkheim's classical framework.[8] Durkheim assumed

---

6. See https://www.robert-schuman.eu/en/doc/questions-d-europe/qe-204-en.pdf.
7. For a rather skeptical perspective on whether this form of "positive solidarity" has already arisen, see Graham Butler and Holly Snaith, "Negative Solidarity: The European Union and the Financial Crisis," in *Transnational Solidarity: Concept, Challenges and Opportunities*, ed. H. Krunke, H. Petersen, and I. Manners (Cambridge: Cambridge University Press, 2020), 128–165 at 131, 162–163. For a more optimistic outlook, see Floris de Witte, *Justice in the EU: The Emergence of Transnational Solidarity* (Oxford: Oxford University Press, 2015).
8. Methodologically, the contribution offers hermeneutics with a *de dicto* attitude. It is based on the confidence that interpreting the thoughts of another author is a way of discovering the truth. See Robert B. Brandom, *Tales of the Mighty Dead: Historical Essays in the Metaphysics of Intentionality* (Cambridge, MA: Harvard University Press, 2002), 99–102. Any interpretation engages in a conversation with the author. This activity is not external to human reason, rather, it is essential to its exercise. See Hans-Georg Gadamer, *Wahrheit und Methode: Grundzüge einer philosophischen Hermeneutik*, 4th ed. (Tübingen: Mohr 1975), 350–360; Cristina Lafont, *The Linguistic Turn in Hermeneutic Philosophy*, trans. J Medina (Cambridge, MA: MIT Press, 1999), 95–107.

plausibly that prior mutual sympathies (e.g., among members of a nation) and joint reactive attitudes toward deviant behavior (i.e., what he called "mechanical" solidarity) are necessary in order for market integration and the division of labor to generate another, supervening form of social connection. In his view, decentralized social cooperation that builds on existing sympathies and reactive attitudes gives birth to "organic" solidarity. Its terms and conditions, as it were, are articulated in widely shared ideas concerning the just distributions of goods and a fair allocation of opportunities.[9] The relevant ethics of reasonable and equitable competition is indicative of a closer connectedness than the prudent etiquette of *doux commerce*, which, in spite of its gentle manners, has no mercy with losers.

At the same time, Durkheim seems to have also believed that an effective and mature division of labor is already pregnant with another form of solidarity that is remarkably cosmopolitan in its orientation. Its manifestations are fleeting and transient, as its relevant emotional cord is struck by accidental encounters with individual misfortune. Owing to its focus on the individual, its sensibility is not tied to the institutional context of a particular community or an ethos of fair and equitable dealings. This explains why its operation is in principle severed from existing structures of cooperation and collective action. Like the elementary forces of cohesion that precede organic solidarity—forces that are manifest in collective reactive attitudes[10]—its mode of operation is mechanical. It comes to the fore in emotions that are triggered by the spectacle of human misery.[11] Substantively, it is difficult to reconcile it with the bounded

---

9. See Lisa Herzog, "Durkheim on Social Justice: The Argument from 'Organic Solidarity,'" *American Political Science Review* 112 (2018): 112–124.
10. See P. F. Strawson, "Freedom and Resentment," in *Perspectives on Moral Responsibility*, ed. J. M. Fischer and M. Ravizza (Ithaca, NY: Cornell University Press, 1993), 45–66.
11. See Lilie Chouliaraki, *The Ironic Spectator: Solidarity in the Age of Post-Humanitarianism* (Cambridge: Polity, 2013) at 2, 45.

horizon of the genuine organic solidarity from which it nonetheless emerges.[12]

2. *DOUX COMMERCE*

These are the famous words from the Schuman Declaration:[13]

> L'Europe ne se fera pas d'un coup, ni dans une construction d'ensemble: elle se fera par des réalisations concrètes, créant d'abord une solidarité de fait.
>
> Europe will not be made all at once, or according to a single plan. It will be built through concrete achievements which first create a de facto solidarity.

What is to be achieved, obviously, is "une solidarité de fait."[14] It is rather obvious what solidarity does not designate here, namely, any readiness to share one's fate.[15] The "solidarité de fait" is merely expected to avoid another cataclysmic catastrophe. The next sentence provides the context that clarifies.

> Le rassemblement des nations européennes exige que l'opposition séculaire de la France et de l'Allemagne soit éliminée: l'action entreprise doit toucher au premier chef la France et l'Allemagne.

---

12. See, for example, *Richard Vernon, Cosmopolitan Regard: Political Membership and Global Justice* (Cambridge: Cambridge University Press, 2010).
13. See note 6.
14. On the historical genealogy of this idea in French thought, see Herman-Josef Große Kracht, *Solidarität und Solidarismus: Postliberale Suchbewegungen zur normativen Selbstverständigung moderner Gesellschaften* (Bielefeld: Transkript, 2017), 199, 242.
15. See Sangiovanni, "Solidarity as Joint Action," note 4 at 347.

> The coming together of the nations of Europe requires the elimination of the age-old opposition of France and Germany. The action undertaken must primarily affect France and Germany.

The submission made in the Schuman Declaration is, therefore, modest. The *de facto* solidarity would make countries abstain from actively harming others. This, at any rate, would be the first step. There may be further steps. Since the Declaration is framed in anticipation of greater economic interpenetration in the fields of coal and steel it is fair to say that the solidarity envisaged in the Schuman Declaration is somewhat reminiscent of the old *doux commerce* idea.[16] The dispositions necessary in order to engage permanently in mutually beneficial dealings with others is expected to drive out more martial human impulses and to enhance industriousness, suppleness, and probity.[17] But we should not expect more than that.

Generally, in a commercial society, humans are supposedly inclined to be serviceable to others at least as long as being so reaps adequate rewards. Hopefully, commerce and industry will give rise to a strong distaste for the turmoil and turbulence associated with war and bloodshed.[18] In this vein, the first achievement of Schuman's solidarity would have to be a negative one: abstaining from the use of force. People stick together in order to sort their differences out. They respect one another.

---

16. See Montesquieu, *The Spirit of the Laws*, trans. A. M. Cohler, B. C. Miller, and H. S. Stone (Cambridge: Cambridge University Press, 1989), XX.1. at 338.
17. See Albert O. Hirschman, *The Passions and the Interests: Political Arguments for Capitalism before Its Triumph* (Princeton, NJ: Princeton University Press, 1977), 59–63.
18. For a brief description of the *doux commerce* thesis, which had its heyday in the eighteenth century, see Albert O. Hirschman, "Rival Interpretations of Market Society: Civilizing, Destructive, or Feeble?," *Journal of Economic Literature* 20 (1982): 1463–1484 at 1465.

3. NEGATIVE AND POSITIVE SOLIDARITY

Schuman's rather modest submission is consistent with Émile Durkheim's view of what he calls "negative" organic solidarity (which he later does not even count as solidarity proper).[19]

Generally, organic solidarity has its source in an increasing division of labor.[20] In its negative form, it is just about mutual non-interference. It facilitates social interaction as though this concerned the smooth and collision-free movement of planets. Society is "in order" as long as each gets out of the way of the other.

What makes Durkheim so intriguing, however, is his remarkable submission that negative solidarity cannot stand on its own feet. Rather, it presupposes *positive* solidarity. Here are Durkheim's words:[21]

> In reality, for men to acknowledge and mutually guarantee the rights of one another, they must first have a mutual liking, and have some reason that makes them cling to one another and to the single society of which they form a part. Justice is filled with charity, or to employ once more our expression, negative solidarity is only the emanation of another solidarity that is positive in nature: it is the repercussion of social feelings in the sphere of "real" rights which [the feelings, A. S.] come from a different source.

---

19. See D 166, 168, 171–172, 468; E 91, 92, 94, 310–311. I am quoting from the German and the English translation using either "D" for the German or "E" for the English version. The relevant translations are *Über soziale Arbeitsteilung: Studie über die Organisation höherer Gesellschaften*, trans. L. Schmidts, 2nd ed. (Frankfurt am Main: Suhrkamp, 1992) and *The Division of Labor in Society*, trans. W. D. Hall (New York: Free Press, 2014).
20. See D 109, 200, 478; E 50, 116, 317.
21. E at 95.

While much remains strange and obscure in this statement—for example, one cannot but wonder why people would ever have reason to respect the rights of strangers—it also demonstrates why Durkheim's theory continues to attract our interest. This statement holds out the promise that there is already *more* of a connection among people and *greater* mutual benevolence even though we perceive only mutual non-interference. Durkheim reassures us of this promise by claiming that organic solidarity is initially "unconscious."[22]

Indeed, Durkheim insinuates that solidarity[23] is the source of feelings, while law and morality are proper ways of articulating their normative significance:[24]

> […] [M]oral rules […] enunciate the basic conditions of social solidarity. Law and morality represent the totality of bonds that bind us to one another and to society, shaping the mass of individuals into a cohesive aggregate.

It does not contradict this finding that Durkheim explains solidarity's effect entirely in moral terms, namely, as regulating the action of man "by something other than the promptings of his own egoism."[25] Moral and legal precepts are the *effect* that the growing division of labor has on individual consciousness while the division itself —in particular

---

22. See D at 469. See E at 311: "Conscience is a poor judge of what occurs in the depths of one's being, because it does not penetrate that far."
23. Very often in Durkheim's text, "solidarity" does not designate a virtue (see above note 3) but the force of the social that precedes individuation and hence gives the lie to "atomism." On the latter, see, prior to Charles Taylor, G. W. F. Hegel, *Elements of the Philosophy of Right*, trans. H. B. Nisbet (Cambridge: Cambridge University Press, 1991), §§197, 303, pp. 197, 343–344. "Atomism" reconstructs society based on the primacy of individuals and individual choices.
24. E at 310. For a similar approach, see David Wiggins, "Solidarity and the Root of the Ethical," *Tijdschrift voor Filosofie* 71 (2009): 239–269.
25. E at 311.

when it gives rise to conventional dealings with one another[26]—is the cause of organic solidarity.

It remains largely unclear, at first glance, how and why the division of labor is capable of exercising this normatively guiding effect. Durkheim goes to some lengths in explaining that even though the division of labor is undoubtedly economically beneficial, solidarity as a virtue and its attendant sentiments are not a matter of rational insight into the long-term benefits of social cooperation. Hence, what gives rise to solidarity is not the smart realization that morality is in one's own best self-interest.[27]

4. MECHANICAL SOLIDARITY

What translates the *de facto* interdependence among people into a sense of obligation toward others, however, seems to remain just as mysterious as the origin of connectedness in the case of mechanical solidarity. Durkheim sometimes claims that mechanical solidarity rests on similarity.[28] Actually, he explains that it emerges when the image of the other and the image of oneself coalesce into one. Indeed, he left it to his sociology of religion to explore the mechanism of fusion.[29]

It is not, however, entirely clear who or what the agent of the underlying synthesizing activity is. The impression of similarity does not in and of itself lead to a merger. The only candidate for such an agent that we encounter in Durkheim's text is the "collective

---

26. See D 435; E 286.
27. See, notably, David Hume, *A Treatise of Human Nature*, ed. E. Mossner (London: Penguin Books, 1985), III.2 at 540–544.
28. On similarity qua source of mechanical solidarity, see D 109; E 50–51.
29. See Émile Durkheim, *The Elementary Forms of Religious Life*, trans. C. Cosman (Oxford: Oxford University Press, 2001).

consciousness," which is the totality of shared beliefs concerning what one must not do.[30] It seems as though this consciousness, which is regenerated in religious effervescence and ecstasy, carries out the fusion for us, for Durkheim frequently presents it as acting upon us *qua* force that has the power to obliterate individuality completely.[31] In a like manner, when we are affected by emotional outrage over a criminal act or the fear of foreign intruders we are beside ourselves and totally taken over by sentiments that we have inasmuch as we are encumbered by the collective consciousness of one particular society.[32] Hence, it would be consistent with this role of collective consciousness to regard the identification with those whom I believe to be like "us"—my fellow Austrians, for example—as triggered by this very force. But none of this emerges clearly from Durkheim's analysis.

5. ORGANIC SOLIDARITY

When it comes to explaining organic solidarity, however, Durkheim provides us with better clues. His remark that, "however the result is accomplished,"[33] the division of labor produces among people the feeling of being constrained by the legitimate demands of others suggests that he is after an invisible hand effect.[34] Repeatedly, we are told that solidarity emerges from a spontaneous division of labor and that spontaneity is essential to it.[35] He suggests, for example, that the rules governing fair competition follow in and of themselves from the

---

30. See D 181; E 82.
31. See D 181–182, 156, 466, 364; E 82, 101, 263, 309.
32. See D 151, 224, 413; E 77–78, 132, 269–270.
33. E 46.
34. An invisible hand effect is of human making, but not of human design. See Edna Ullmann-Margalit, *Normal Rationality: Decisions and Social Order*, ed. A. Margalit and C. Sunstein (Oxford: Oxford University Press, 2017), at 130.
35. D 256, 434, 444–445; E 158, 286, 294.

division of labor.³⁶ Generally, Durkheim says that it is sufficient for individuals to devote themselves to special functions and they will "discover inevitably" that they are in solidarity with other people.³⁷

But what must appear, undoubtedly, as a hastily diagnosed and not terribly well corroborated invisible hand effect indicates also something that cuts anthropologically deeper. This is revealed rather early in Durkheim's *Division of Labor*³⁸ where he discusses what a simple exchange "implies and what results from it."³⁹ In his view, the fact that we depend on exchanges reveals an essential incompleteness about us.⁴⁰ We can be whole only if "[. . .] [t]he image of the one who complements us becomes inseparable within us from our own."⁴¹ Moreover, Durkheim actually suggests that an exchange—at any rate, if it occurs regularly and repeatedly—is, semiotically speaking, a *symbol* of a deeper condition of individual incompleteness. Once people have, if only intuitively, grasped the significance of exchanges, they come to see themselves as parts of a larger whole, and this means that, within their conception of who they are, being part of the whole becomes an essential component of their identity. People put themselves, inevitably, at the center of the world; but they do so intelligently only if they also de-center their position within it.

At a later point in the theory, not just single exchanges, but the division of labor as a whole is cast in this symbolic role. Durkheim suggests that by virtue of the division of labor, human beings come to realize their dependence on society.⁴²

---

36. D 434; E 286.
37. See E 158.
38. See above note 19.
39. E 50.
40. Cast in the idiom of Axel Honneth's social philosophy, one could say that it also indicates that our freedom is not an individual possession but socially shared. See his *Freedom's Right: The Social Foundations of Democratic Life*, trans. J. Ganahl (Cambridge: Polity, 2014).
41. E 50.
42. See D 470; E 311–312. At the same time, the whole can come to itself only on the basis of parts that conceive of themselves in this manner. See D 429; E 292.

It must appear, therefore, that Durkheim regards social solidarity as an ontological matter. Against this background, "organic" is indeed the adequate attribute for this type of cohesion. Their ontological quality of being a part of a whole is revealed to individuals through the normative language of morality and law, for compliance with the relevant precepts allows them to be who they *really* are. Pathologies and anomies excluded, people will be at ease with themselves and content with the way they live if they embrace their dependence on others and take some active interest in their well-being. Stated in Hegelian parlance, this means that organic solidarity is possible only if by virtue of morality and law people are *for* themselves what they are *in* themselves.

6. THE MECHANICAL ROOT OF ORGANIC SOLIDARITY

Durkheim leaves no doubt that organic solidarity has to grow out of a preexisting connectedness:[43]

> Work is not shared out between independent individuals who are already differentiated from one another, who meet and associate together in order to pool their different abilities. It would be a miracle if these differences, arising from chance and circumstance, could be so accurately harmonized as to form a coherent whole.

Market dealings are rendered as interactions among strangers and tend, thereby, to obliterate what makes them possible. The genealogy

---

43. E 216.

of organic solidarity suggests, however, that certain ideas of justice governing a liberal society are either transformations of a more archaic and arcane form of connectedness or at least depend for their emergence on these roots:[44]

> What draws men together are mechanical forces and instinctive forces such as the affinity of blood, attachment to the same soil, the cult of their ancestors, a commonality of habits etc. It is only when the group has been formed on these bases that cooperation becomes organized. [...] It is true that once cooperation has made its appearance, it tightens social bonds and imparts to society a more complete individuality. But this integration supposes another sort that it replaces. For social units to be able to differentiate from one another, they must first be attracted or grouped together through the similarities that they display.

Apparently, just like competitive market dealings are sustainable only if they are constrained by organic solidarity, the latter depends for its emergence on the blind instincts of its mechanical counterpart.[45]

This genealogical connection holds true, according to Durkheim, for the creation of larger units that might transcend the bounds of the nation.[46] They do not simply emerge on the basis of exchanges. Rather, they first have to be "blended together in the sense of a single and identical common consciousness so that the process of differentiation can begin or begin again."[47] In this context, Durkheim

---

44. E 217.
45. Not by accident, Durkheim observes the requisite struggle between individualization and "normalization." See D 344–345; E 223–224.
46. See D 341, 475–476; 219, 315–316.
47. E 217.

contrasts a future European society with the establishment of mere "mutuality" among nations, that is, conditions under which states cooperate merely for the sake of mutual advantage.[48] In a long footnote[49] Durkheim explains that transnational commerce that is based on mere mutuality may leave existing social segmentation in place. The economic division of labor can thus develop without any appreciable change in the social structure.[50] Such *doux commerce* merely makes strangers disposed to sort out their differences peacefully. At the same time, their mutual benevolence is likely to be highly circumscribed.

Organic solidarity, by contrast, is rooted in a deeper and more opaque form of connection. It is an extension of an existing sympathy among members of society to contractual relations of exchange and to the competition for opportunities and goods. Since, indeed, the interacting persons become less alike, it appears as though organic solidarity is taking over from its mechanical predecessor. Nevertheless, remnants of mechanical solidarity remain in place and come to the fore when the question has to be answered as to who belongs in the circle of beneficiaries. All of a sudden, "similarity" and "likeness" claim their relevance again if only at a remove, for example, when they are inferred from a certain length of participation in society.[51]

---

48. See D 342; E 219–220.
49. See D 342–343 footnote 31; E 221.
50. Quite remarkable is his observation about how acquiring the requisite professional training leaves the foundations of the psychological life of the individual quite unaffected. This gives us Durkheim's explanation for why people who have been socialized in illiberal cultures can successfully participate in a global market economy or any market economy, for that matter.
51. See, for example, on "a certain degree of integration into society" as a condition of eligibility for student loans, Case C-209/03, The Queen (on the application of Dany Bidar) v. London Borough of Ealing, Secretary of State for Education and Skills [2005] ECR 2005 I-02119, para. 57.

7. COSMOPOLITAN SOLIDARITY: THE INDIVIDUAL

Not surprisingly, mechanical and organic solidarity remain difficult to disentangle. Yet, upon closer inspection it turns out that Durkheim must have been after a quite remarkable phenomenon, which he himself may not have understood all too well.

The diversity of human activities in a context of interdependence explains why individuals can conceive of themselves as *parts* that require complementation by other such parts. And yet, the potentially infinite interaction of parts can only give rise to the impression among these parts that they are parts *of a whole* if their perception of mutual partiality is complemented with the sense of unity. Such unity, however, cannot be generated by the parts themselves or grow out of potentially infinite structures of horizontal interaction. It can only be nurtured by the similarity that underlies mechanical solidarity. This explains why an interconnection of parts that is not unified by the prior ties of reactive attitudes can yield merely *doux commerce*, which is essentially indifferent to the well-being of these parts. The connection among the parts remains, thus understood, external.

At the same time, the force that accounts for the fact that the external relation among strangers is rendered as an internal relation among, say, compatriots or those living in the same region is itself external to the form of horizontal interaction within the division of labor. It is the mechanical solidarity among those who by virtue of their reactive attitudes mutually consider each other alike. Put in other words, the external relation among parts is transformed into something internal (i.e., a genuine concern for others) by something that is itself external to the internal relation. It should not come as a surprise, therefore, that the residual energies of mechanical solidarity become easily diverted from social justice qua articulation of organic solidarity among parts to the well-being of these parts themselves.

In order for that to happen, individualization merely has to reach up to the level at which each perceives individuality as what makes all individuals alike.

In this vein, Durkheim observes that the intensity of "collective sentiments" within the division of labor decreases generally with the exception of sentiments concerning the individual.[52] He claims that the respect for individuals even rises to the level of religious veneration.[53] Durkheim gives us only hints as to why he believes this to be the case. The inevitability and opportunity for individuals of having to find their niche of specialized activity encourage them to explore new things on their own initiative. Socially, individuals become thus rendered as "autonomous source of action."[54] They are able to enact credibly such independence if there is, indeed, some special talent or ability that appears to be distinctively their own. Since survival and well-being under conditions of intense division of labor depend essentially on being a self-directing and self-enacting individual,[55] the collective consciousness of society adopts this type of being as its core ideal. The collective consciousness reduces itself, according to Durkheim, to the "cult of the person" and of personal dignity;[56] it no longer serves the function of tying the individual to one particular

---

52. See D 205, 222; E 119, 130. Durkheim is also quite explicit about the social nature of obligations. The obligation that an individual has toward itself is in fact an obligation toward society. See D 470, E 311–312.
53. See D 227, 478; E 133, 316. See also Emile Durkheim, *Physik des Rechts und der Sitten: Vorlesungen zur Soziologie der Moral*, trans. M. Bischoff (Frankfurt am Main: Suhrkamp, 1991), at 102, 163. For a fresh elaboration of this Durkheimian theme, see Hans Joas, *Die Sakralität der Person: Eine neue Genealogie der Menschenrechte* (Frankfurt am Main: Suhrkamp, 2011).
54. E 314; D 474.
55. It gives rise to the respective "governmentality" that we now associate with neoliberalism. See Nikolas Rose, *Powers of Freedom: Reframing Political Thought* (Cambridge: Cambridge University Press, 1999).
56. See D 470; E 311–312.

society.⁵⁷ What Durkheim anticipates here are evidently varieties of cosmopolitan concern.

Hans Joas has gone so far as to claim that this new and universal mechanical solidarity rests on the belief in the "sacredness" of the person.⁵⁸ This explains why the spiritual and bodily integrity of human beings appears to be of utmost concern. Violating this personal integrity is just as taboo as the intrusion of a sacred space or the desecration of a holy object.⁵⁹

Durkheim, however, unearths a remarkable dialectic. The rules of distributive justice adhered to in a society depend for their realization on relatively closed social units. They lend expression to organic solidarity and hinge substantially on conditions of reciprocity. If you serve me, I serve you. If you benefit us, we are there for you. We respect your individual effort if you adapt to what we want. Amending Durkheim, one is inclined to add: If you fail owing to the vagaries of market forces, I will be there for you because my well-being depends on your having taken the risks involved in market-participation. Not by accident, organic solidarity is spelled out in terms of merit, equality of opportunity, leveling the playing field of fair play.⁶⁰ But in order to be *relevant* to others, one has to be experienced as belonging to the world of which one is (merely) a part. At the same time, the overwhelming relevance of interdependence creates pressure to specialize. Specialization fosters individuality. At the end, the individual becomes the one moral idea to which the collective consciousness of *all* market-integrated societies attributes supreme value. Remarkably, the individual comes to occupy the

---

57. See D 228; E 228.
58. See Joas, *Die Sakralität der Person*, note 53 at 85.
59. The assimilation of human dignity to sacredness may be duly doubted. Violations of human dignity are not trailed with the sense that the perpetrator has aroused the wrath of the gods or is in any other way doomed.
60. See D 462; E 306.

center of a collective consciousness that *transcends*, oddly enough, the *bounded* and *desert-oriented* confines of organic solidarity.[61] The cult of the individual breaks the shackles of reciprocity. This explains why, cast in Durkheimian terms, *justice*, which readily recognizes inequalities as long as these are based upon some form of desert or mutual advantage, is eventually superseded by *charity* that accords equal value to all human beings regardless of their merits or accomplishments.[62] The ultimate focus of this new form of mechanical solidarity is located at levels below and beyond any integration in organic terms. It engages the respect for individuals without regard to their membership in a group or concrete achievements.

8. TRANSNATIONAL SOLIDARITY IS FRAGILE

Mechanical solidarity is the soil out of which organic solidarity can grow. But once organic solidarity has developed within bounded societies, mechanical solidarity becomes boundless from within. Its focus comes to rest on the individual. The moral sentiments unleashed by the Syrian refugee crisis are testament to a cosmopolitan concern that reflects universal mechanical solidarity. Indeed, its articulation may even be made easier by the fact that solidarity extends to relatively distant strangers. In their case, the love of humanity[63] is not circumscribed by controversy about the merits or demerits of beneficiaries. It is easier, indeed, to be kind to a distant stranger with whom one does not share a history than with compatriots whose demands strike one as presumptuous in light of their failings. It is in this context that

---

61. The relation between solidarity and justice is difficult to disentangle in Durkheim's work. See Herzog, "Durkheim on Social Justice," note 9.
62. See Durkheim, *Physik*, note 53 at 303.
63. See ibid.

the "communication of solidarity becomes simultaneously the communication of cosmopolitan dispositions," that is, the readiness to benefit strangers without any expectation of reciprocation.[64]

The cosmopolitan transcendence of particular social worlds, however, comes at a cost. It lacks support from adequate structures of social action. This is the case, not only because their realization would require a more centralized mode of global governance; we are also not sure as to how we might weigh adequately other values against the universal respect for the human person. Ordinarily, existing institutions have already done the balancing for us. But these institutions seem to be increasingly inadequate in the face of the global omnipresence of individual suffering.

We can now identify more clearly two of the elements of which transnational solidarity is composed, namely, *doux commerce*, on the one hand, and cosmopolitan concern, on the other. Where transnational solidarity basically amounts to *doux commerce* it can merely amount to civility and not to solidarity, properly understood. This is reflected in the ethos underpinning various Euro crisis settlements.[65] States are ready to support others more or less self-interestedly so long as the beneficiaries are pledging to repay their debts.

Universal mechanical solidarity is at stake, by contrast, in the context of the refugee crisis. But one should not be surprised to see that some states appear to be impervious to it, for this form of solidarity is beset with its own problems. It operates, indeed, mechanically. It is chiefly triggered by images or stories that give rise to a compassionate response.[66] We all remember the image of the Syrian boy whose

---

64. See Chouliaraki, *The Ironic Spectator*, note 11 at 2, 45.
65. See Butler and Snaith, "Negative Solidarity," note 7.
66. See Chouliaraki, *The Ironic Spectator*, note 64. It may be objected that by classifying such a response as "solidarity" the concept becomes inflated and thereby recklessly assimilated to charity. Yet, the genealogy of such cosmopolitan concern in Durkheim's work suggests that the response bespeaks mechanical solidarity, for it manifests what people take themselves to be: either compatriots or "deracinated" individuals.

dead body was washed to the European shore. We cringe. The major emotional vehicle of such solidarity is pity. While the mechanical quality of our emotional response explains its strength, it also makes it vulnerable to individual or collective attempts to turn the trigger off either by looking away or by demonizing those who suffer as evil or dangerous people. Moreover, as Nietzsche perceptively observed,[67] there is something inherently aggressive about pity. It hits us over the head from without and gives rise to feelings of guilt. Not by accident, we feel emotionally attacked by people whom we suspect to reckon with our compassion. We resent them. The wholesale moral vilification of the indigents and outsiders is the reply of resentment.

9. IMAGINE NO COUNTRIES

In light of the ascendancy of the second form of mechanical solidarity, its organic counterpart begins to look hidebound and partial. Nevertheless, cosmopolitan concern is often fortuitous and only weakly supported by existing political structures. As a result, this new form of solidarity amounts to a negative sum that explains the consciousness ("mindset") of the contemporary liberal bourgeoisie. It pairs haphazard cosmopolitan concern with a waning belief in the priority of concern for compatriots, for such a belief becomes difficult to reconcile with the urgency to benefit strangers that are far less well off.

Undoubtedly, in this form, transnational solidarity is perplexingly underdetermined. In an attempt to fix this, an attitude has emerged that can be called, for want of a better concept, *fluid organic solidarity*. Sketches of it can be found in the works of Claus Offe and

---

67. See Friedrich Nietzsche, *Die fröhliche Wissenschaft*, 2nd ed. (Leipzig: E. W. Fritsch, 1887), at 42.

Jürgen Habermas. It emerges from attempts to reconcile context-transcending moral intuitions with *imagining* future "organic" connections.

One can put up with feeling obligated to share goods or resources with others if this feeling is complemented with the expectation that sharing is in one way or another also *somehow* in one's own interest.[68] The ways in which people imagine their interest to be served may range from future reciprocation by those whom they benefit or some diffuse belief in beneficial indirect effects. The *faith* that one or the other might come to pass is essential. If solidarity were perceived entirely as a one-way street and not as tied to what one believes to be durable forms of interconnection, it would most likely cease to exist. This psychological factor explains why the moral high ground of universal mechanical solidarity is abstract.[69] If only certain members of society were to pay for benefits while a potentially unlimited number of others with whom the payers feel unconnected benefited, redistributive programs would simply not be sustained. Owing to a lack of closure or reciprocation, the paying members would no longer rationalize transfers by telling themselves that they will somehow—in the future or indirectly—partake of the benefits. A world in which compatriots and foreigners alike had equal claims to welfare would be composed of Nozickian minimal states. In such a world, the government may not even make efforts to educate their population, to have them learn languages and to acquire the discipline indispensable for earning a living. The Western European dreamlands to which refugees feel for very good reasons attracted would cease to exist in

---

68. See Claus Offe, "Pflichten versus Kosten: Typen und Kontexte solidarischen Handelns," in *Transnationale Solidarität: Chancen und Grenzen*, ed. J. Beckert et al. (Frankfurt am Main: Campus, 2004), 35–50, at 40–43.
69. "Abstract" in the Hegelian sense of "one-sided." See G. W. F. Hegel, "Who Thinks Abstractly?," in *Hegel: Text and Commentary*, trans. W. Kaufmann (Garden City, NY: Anchor Books, 1966), 113–118.

their current form. Solidarization along the universal mechanical dimension would be trailed by de-solidarization along the organic dimension. Social programs would be replaced with what one writer pithily called the "hypocrisy of helping the poor."[70] There would be charity on the part of those who benefited from the demise of social programs, but it would actually go to places where reports of doing good produced the best public relations.

Offe's observations actually offer a clue as to how fluid organic solidarity can grow out of a faith in anticipated connectedness. Habermas[71] reminds us, correctly, that the solidarity of the working class was an attempt to redeem relations of mutual support that had become obsolete in the course of industrialization. Workers were forming alliances for their mutual support across the divides of competitive labor markets. The internal logic of binding oneself and others, however, amounts to the same. Acting in an ethically appropriate way or extending solidarity to others means doing more than one owes to strangers, while doing so is, perhaps, also in one's own long-term interest in the event that the ties of solidarity become tighter and fasten into shared understandings of justice.[72]

And yet, it is precisely the problem of proletarian solidarity that teaches us why a more ambitious form of transnational solidarity is possibly destined to remain a noble dream.

---

70. See Paul Theroux, "The Hypocrisy of 'Helping' the Poor," *New York Times*, October 2, 2015.
71. See Jürgen Habermas, "Democracy, Solidarity and the European Crisis," https://www.academia.edu/4259473/Democracy_Solidarity_And_The_European_Crisis_By_Jürgen_Habermas (last visited October 8, 2020). See also his *Philosophische Texte*, vol. 3: *Diskursethik* (Berlin: Suhrkamp, 2019) at 353.
72. For a reconstruction of the relevant reasons for action, see Sangiovanni, "Solidarity as Joint Action," note 4.

10. EXALTED PROLETARIAN SOLIDARITY

The major problem of proletarian solidarity has always been that on the level of the actual consciousness of groups the proletariat appears to be less homogeneous than it really is from an economic point of view. Hence, the brotherly and sisterly sentiments that do not exist even though they ought to exist have to be somehow supplemented in order to make proletarian solidarity real. As is well known, for Leninism it was a foregone conclusion that class-consciousness had to be mediated by an intellectual and political vanguard that integrates the daily business of class struggle with the pursuit of "the final aim." The party was supposed to be the external deposit, as it were, of that class consciousness of the proletariat which did not actually exist. By being guided by the party, the proletariat was to come to exist objectively *for itself* even if its members did not subjectively recognize who they were *in themselves*.

Lukács conceded that in exercising its function to synthesize various groups into one class, the members of the party must have been perceived as acting like the elect leaders of a sect. From its members it had to demand the full embrace of "ancient liberty,"[73] that is, the readiness to submit their "whole personality" to the movement.[74] It also had to expect from the working class a quasi-religious readiness to incur sacrifices for future generations.

Evidently, an attitude of this type is not congenial with our twenty-first-century self-loving liberal subjectivity. Proletarian solidarity lends itself *systematically* to *authoritarian* uses. This is manifest already in the act in which the party identifies itself as the external

---

73. See Benjamin Constant, "On the Liberty of the Ancients Compared with That of the Moderns," in *Political Writings*, ed. B. Fontana (Cambridge: Cambridge University Press, 1988), 307–328.
74. See Georg Lukács, *Geschichte und Klassenbewusstsein: Studien über marxistische Dialektik*, 10th ed. (Neuwied: Luchterhand, 1988), 486, 488, 508.

deposit of the class consciousness of the masses. The revolutionary vanguard comes into existence on the basis of its self-identification and self-authentication.[75] Once it is constituted, it decides for itself for whom it speaks since its central task is to synthesize groups into the proletariat and to mold their class consciousness. The latter is, as Lukács memorably explained, not a psychological fact but a historical possibility to be actualized by the party. It stands for viewing society in a manner that is adequate to the social position of a social class.[76] It is, thus understood, entirely correct to view society from the perspective of the bourgeoisie in the terms of liberal political economy. This outlook matches the social position of the bourgeoisie. It is nonetheless *false* consciousness in the sense that it does not permit to solve the problems that have historically arisen.[77] By contrast, while the actual consciousness of the proletariat may well be wrong when it is diverted by more short-term concerns, the possibility of viewing society from its point of view gives in principle access to the objectively adequate view of historical developments.[78] The empirical consciousness of proletarians may often be confused. It is the task of the revolutionary vanguard to straighten it out. Such an epistemic authoritarianism remains largely indifferent to what the folks on the ground may think.

In its vanguard party format, proletarian solidarity is not a sibling of liberty. It is no longer right for us. Just like we are no longer material for ancient liberty,[79] we are not material for the elite party either.

---

75. See Lukács, *Geschichte und Klassenbewusstsein*, note 74 at 499–500.
76. See ibid. at 444.
77. See ibid. at 448.
78. See ibid. at 450.
79. See Nietzsche, *Die fröhliche Wissenschaft*, note 66 at 286.

11. CONCLUSIONS

With that we arrive at the following conclusions:

First, organic solidarity comes in various colorations: it can seem to be what it in fact is not, in which case it is merely *doux commerce*, but also genuine or fluid. Only in its first and third form is it relevant to the transnational setting.

Second, the transnational setting is marked by an ascendancy of cosmopolitan concern with individual suffering, which, as Durkheim suggests, supervenes on organic solidarity.

Third, transnational solidarity is manifest in various attempts to integrate cosmopolitan moral intuitions with the workings of fluid organic solidarity. The latter stands for imagining mutually beneficial connectedness where one has not perceived it before. For example, it is revealed in attempts to envision and to construct future reciprocity with strangers, in particular by taking tentative first steps. It is a way of overcoming at an entirely symbolic level the loss of solidarity that is inherent in combining *doux commerce* with cosmopolitan concern.

Fourth, cosmopolitan moral sensibilities may push for anticipating connectedness and reciprocity in spite of inertia by local populations and groups. This is reminiscent of the predicament of proletarian solidarity, at any rate, in its most exalted form. Since the solidarity inherent in class consciousness is underdeveloped in the relation of various groups, it has to be actively synthesized by the communist party. However, supplementing fluid organic solidarity with morally (or historically) elitist leadership results in authoritarianism. It is inconsistent with our penchant for modern liberty. This leaves us with the interplay of cosmopolitan sensibilities and fluid organic solidarity as the only defensible form of enacting solidarity in a transnational setting.

Fifth, interconnection, taken by itself, is insufficient to create organic solidarity. What matters is identification with being part of a whole. Identification with "Europe" would be key to the emergence of a genuinely organic solidarity. It may have been the mistake of the founders of the Union to assume that such identification would simply spring from economic interconnectedness as such.

Of course, it may be suggested that solidarity ought to be extended to all with whom we happen to be interconnected. But even assuming that we ought to extend solidarity beyond national bounds, the sheer fact of interconnection does not provide us with a sufficient moral reason to do so. In the larger scheme of things, we are all interconnected with ISIS, Hamas, American libertarians, and, in particular, with the National Security Agency (NSA). But this does not mean that we owe them any support.

Chapter 12

A Tale of Two Tenths

Race, Class, and Solidarity

TOMMIE SHELBY

This chapter tackles one of the biggest challenges to contemporary black political solidarity: *class differences among black Americans*.[1] In light of such differences, many Marxists are sharply critical of black solidarity and antiracist identity politics.[2] They are convinced, for example, that this form of politics, if it has any value at all, largely serves the interests of the black professional class. The black working

---

1. For helpful feedback on this chapter, I am grateful to the participants in the Workshop on Solidarity held at the European University in Florence in 2019 and to this volume's editors, Andrea Sangiovanni and Juri Viehoff. Versions of this chapter were presented at Dartmouth College, University of Michigan, University of North Carolina at Chapel Hill, University of Pennsylvania, and the American Philosophical Association Eastern Division Meeting, and I'm grateful for the questions and comments I received on those occasions.
2. See, for example, Adolph Reed, Jr., "Black Politics after 2016," *Nonsite* 23 (2018); Adolph Reed, Jr., "Antiracism: A Neoliberal Alternative to a Left," *Dialectical Anthropology* 42 (2018), 105–115; Adolph Reed, Jr., and Merlin Chowkwanyun, "Race, Class, Crisis: The Discourse of Racial Disparity and Its Analytical Discontents," *Socialist Register* (2012), 149–175; Walter Benn Michaels, *The Trouble with Diversity: How We Learned to Love Identity and Ignore Inequality* (New York: Macmillan, 2016); Jacqueline Jones, *A Dreadful Deceit: The Myth of Race from the Colonial Era to Obama's America* (New York: Basic Books, 2013); Cedric Johnson, "The Panthers Can't Save Us Now," *Catalyst* 1 (Spring 2017), 57–85.

class would, these leftists insist, do much better to find allies among the broader multiracial working class and in the labor movement.[3] Such Marxists also maintain that race-based politics wrongly subordinates class to "race" rather than viewing racism and class exploitation as inextricably related and fundamentally structured by capital-labor relations. I believe these criticisms are serious and merit a considered response. In fact, I share some of the skepticism that thinkers on the left have toward identity politics and antiracist activism. But I think they often take their criticisms too far and consequently undervalue black solidarity, which is, in my view, still absolutely vital. In an attempt to show this, I draw on some insights from W. E. B. Du Bois, Martin Luther King, Jr., and Cornel West.

One limitation of this leftist critique—and the central theme of this chapter—is that it relies on a paradigm of solidarity that has its source in the Marxist theory of working-class politics. This conception generally gives too much weight to the role of shared material interests in binding a group together politically, thus ignoring other reliable sources of group cohesion. And it gives too little weight to the ethical considerations and moral virtues that sometimes dispose people to put aside narrow self-interest to act for the common good.

Let me distinguish three subgroups in the U.S. black population. The first group is similar to what Du Bois referred to as "the talented tenth."[4] This is the black professional class. College education, high-status occupations, and high incomes define them. These are the black doctors, lawyers, engineers, bureaucrats, executives, and small business owners. I refer to them as *black elites*. The second group is similar to what Du Bois referred to, in *The Philadelphia Negro*, as "the

---

3. There is a similar left black nationalist critique of the black professional class that charges this stratum with self-hate, a pathological thirst for white acceptance, and insufficient love for black peoples, particularly for the black working class and the black poor.
4. See W. E. B. Du Bois, "The Talented Tenth," in *The Future of the Race*, ed. Henry Louis Gates, Jr., and Cornel West (New York: Vintage, 1997), 133–158.

submerged tenth."[5] The group is made up of those in chronic poverty. These are blacks who have very limited education and work experience, and many of whom are jobless, dependent on public assistance, have access to only dead-end jobs that pay below a living wage, or earn income through activities in the informal economy.

The majority of black Americans do not fall into either of Du Bois's "tenths." They are instead solidly working class and employed in the formal economy, and their situation is precarious though less dire than the marginalized black poor. But the black elite and the black poor are both relatively large, provide a stark contrast, and are often thought to be sharply at odds, making the relationship between them a good test case for the viability of black solidarity in the post-Obama era. If black elite-poor solidarity is possible, solidarity between the black professional class and the black working class should also be viable, as the division between these two segments of the black population is, overall, less antagonistic.

In speaking of the black elite and the black poor, I am referring, not to class background or origins, but to current class position. Some defenders of black solidarity deny that a serious class divide exists by calling attention to the fact that many black elites come from working-class and even poor families and that they continue to have deep ties to their poor kin. Many black elites provide regular financial support to their disadvantaged family members and go to great lengths to help them when they are in urgent need (bailing them out of jail, caring for their children, paying their rent so they won't be evicted, providing financial loans, etc.). This has led some to conclude that most black elites must strongly identify with the black poor. But this would be a hasty inference. Solidarity with one's poor kin does not necessarily extend to the broader black poor. And though people

---

5. W. E. B. Du Bois, *The Philadelphia Negro: A Social Study* (Philadelphia: University of Pennsylvania Press, 1996), 311.

often help disadvantaged kinfolk out of a sense of familial obligation, many resent having to do so. Moreover, some black elites believe that because they were able to pull themselves out of poverty without such assistance, other blacks, including their kin, could and should do the same.

Whatever the merits of Marxist class analysis, it is evident that class position does not strictly determine a person's political commitments. Even Marx allows that "communist consciousness," while emanating primarily from the proletariat, "may, of course, arise among the other classes too through the contemplation of the situation of this [proletarian] class."[6] There are black elites who are progressive, even radical, in their politics, and some have sacrificed much to advance the cause of racial justice and to help other blacks in need. Indeed, some of the harshest left-wing critics of black political solidarity are themselves members of the professional class, often holding tenured positions at elite private universities. Do they regard themselves as exceptional, that rare breed of radical that can empathize and act with the working class? If so, what accounts for their exceptionalism? If they do not regard themselves as exceptional, what justifies their belief that other black elites couldn't be brought around to a similar position?

We should also note that many among the black poor are political reactionaries and prey on and exploit other vulnerable blacks. As West rightly reminds us, "there are numerous instances of 'field negroes' with 'house negro' mentalities and 'house negroes' with 'field negro' mentalities."[7] So although we shouldn't ignore sources of class-based tension and conflicts of interest, nor should we romanticize the political consciousness of the poor and working class.

---

6. See Karl Marx and Fredrick Engels, *The German Ideology*, in *The Marx-Engels Reader*, 2nd edition, ed. Robert Tucker (New York: Norton, 1978), 193.
7. Cornel West, *Race Matters*, 25th anniversary edition (Boston: Beacon, 2017), 98.

Still, utopianism (in the bad sense) is a danger. Yes, we can't be certain of a person's politics if all we know is their class position. But there might be a strong *correlation* between class position and political commitment such that skepticism toward interclass black solidarity is warranted. We might put the question like this: Are the differences in material interests, social status, and political power between black elites and the black poor such that political solidarity between these two groups is unwise or impractical?

In *We Who Are Dark: The Philosophical Foundations of Black Solidarity* (2005), I suggested the answer to that question is "no." In particular, I argued that black solidarity is still viable despite class division in the U.S. black population and notwithstanding the geographic separation of black elites from disadvantaged black communities (sometimes called "ghettos"). I must confess, though, that I am not confident about this. But nor am I fully persuaded by Marxist critiques of black solidarity. So, here I return to the subject.

I will consider seven challenges to the viability of black solidarity. Some are old, dating back to the early twentieth century. Some are more recent, with roots in the Civil Rights/Black Power era. And some are new, coming in the wake of Barack Obama's presidency.

CHALLENGE 1: BLACK ELITES DON'T BENEFIT FROM MAINTAINING SOLIDARITY WITH OTHER BLACKS

Some argue that it is not in the interests of black elites to commit to black solidarity or to push a racial justice agenda. Black professionals, despite the odds, have managed to succeed in the highly stratified and competitive U.S. social order and are largely insulated from the most burdensome or lethal forms of racial injustice. They live comfortable lives, often in integrated communities, and enjoy considerable social status. They get along reasonably well with other white elites and have been largely incorporated into the mainstream of American society. And they are keenly aware that "playing the race card" (or even proudly asserting "Black Lives Matter") tends to alienate, and even anger, many of their white peers and that most whites regard black solidarity as unjustified and possibly even racist.

To be sure, black elites are sometimes subjected to racial insults and slights (sometimes called "micro-aggressions"), and racial bias might cost some a recognition, reward, promotion, or job opportunity. But, in the wider scheme of things, these are minor inconveniences and temporary setbacks in an otherwise good and prosperous life. And, all things considered, black elites may be better off downplaying racial issues than joining fellow blacks in militant modes of resistance.

To address this challenge, we first need a working conception of solidarity. What characteristics must a group of people exhibit to be correctly said to have "solidarity"? I believe solidarity has five core components:

1. *Mutual identification:* group members openly empathize and publicly identify with one another other.
2. *Special concern:* members come to the aid of others in the group (especially to the aid of the worst off among them), even if this might call for some personal sacrifice.
3. *Common values or goals:* a set values or objectives are widely shared in the group and known to be widely shared.
4. *Loyalty:* group members stick by one another and abstain from actions that would undermine the group's basic aims.
5. *Trust:* group members are confident that others within the group are doing, or will do, their part to defend the group's values and to advance its fundamental goals.

These five elements comprise a type of *commitment*, one that an individual may undertake or refuse. This commitment is a pledge or vow—a way of sincerely binding oneself to others in a cause. Having made such a pledge, one's fellows in solidarity ("comrades," we might call them) may rightfully hold one accountable. Solidarity has the same normative structure whether the cause is racial justice, gender justice, or economic justice.

Among the moral duties we are all bound by is the *duty of justice*. This is the duty to support just social arrangements and to help bring about social justice where it fails to exist. If an individual seeks to correct a structural injustice, they will, typically, need to do so in concert with others. Because such efforts almost always face strong opposition, it is generally useful, and sometimes essential, for those most directly burdened by the injustice to form bonds of solidarity among themselves. The fundamental purposes for which these bonds are formed are to advance the cause of justice, to defend group members against unjust treatment, and to provide in-group mutual support.

Third-party bystanders can of course sometimes make good comrades, and there may even be members of the dominant group who will defect and come over to the side of the oppressed. Yet, the most trustworthy and loyal allies will often be drawn from the oppressed group itself, given their obvious personal stake in the liberatory effort and their mutual understanding born of the shared experience of subordination. I contend that the duty of justice is the *normative* ground of black political solidarity. It is the fundamental principle from which the claims of solidarity are derived. It is the primary reason why blacks can be justified in making the mutual commitment of solidarity to one another.

Some may value or seek solidarity with others because of its intrinsic merits (e.g., because of the sense of community it provides).[8] However, it is perfectly legitimate to embrace or seek it, at

---

8. For more on this point, see Lawrence Blum, "Three Kinds of Race-Related Solidarity," *Journal of Social Philosophy* 38 (2007): 53–72.

least initially, because of its *extrinsic* value (for instance, because it may help in resistance to injustice). In light of solidarity's value as a tool for correcting or mitigating injustice, it is rational for one to commit oneself to solidarity with others (provided that others similarly situated are willing to reciprocate) and thereby to be bound by its norms.

I do not believe (as some black nationalists do) that blacks have a fundamental duty to form and sustain political unity. Black solidarity in the pursuit of racial justice is, however, a *morally permissible* and *sometimes effective* way to carry out the duty of justice. When one undertakes this commitment of solidarity, one thereby commits oneself to in-group obligations of loyalty, special concern, and mutual trust. Although black solidarity may not be the only way to fulfill the duty of justice, it is an approach that has proved valuable in earlier struggles against slavery and Jim Crow.

In *Race Matters* (1993), West doesn't often use the language of "solidarity." He writes instead about a "politics of conversion" and a "love ethic." A politics of conversion is similar to a pledge or vow in that it calls for the converted to sincerely accept that there is hope for fundamental change and meaning in collective struggle to achieve justice. This political conversion is maintained through a love ethic, which goes beyond a commitment to a shared conception of justice. This ethic, he explains, is about cultivating and sustaining agency in the oppressed by keeping alive the memory of past achievement and successful resistance and by affirming the humanity of the downtrodden.[9] Those who fully embody this love ethic have self-respect, courage, and integrity.

Whether one uses the language of solidarity or love ethic, the thing to notice is the role of *moral commitment* and *individual virtue* in creating and sustaining meaningful collective resistance to

---

9. West, *Race Matters*, 19, 37.

oppression. If a member of the black elite acts politically *solely* out of self-interest, then either they don't understand what solidarity involves or they reject its requirements. It may be that, from a strictly cost-benefit standpoint, the personal costs or risks to many black elites of openly fighting anti-black racism, racial inequality, and black poverty outweigh the personal benefits of participating in the collective effort. However, if black elites are so unprincipled and selfish that they are willing to compromise with racial injustice to protect their relative privilege, then a solidarity that includes them would be ineffective or worse.

On the account of solidarity I defend, self-interest is, at best, only a *supporting* reason to commit to solidarity. Such interests cannot do their work alone—that is, apart from ethical considerations or moral motivation. Although black people share many important interests, their interests are not entirely aligned. Even where there are interests in common, free-riding on the sacrifices of others would inevitably occur in the absence of loyalty to the group and its cause.

I don't doubt that openly condemning racial injustice increases white racial resentment and hostility toward blacks. However, on grounds of justice, integrity, and self-respect, black elites should not accommodate themselves to these sentiments. Insofar as black elites are moved by considerations of justice and their identification with other blacks, consideration of self-interest can supply a secondary reason to contribute to the group's historical struggle against racial domination.

There is, ultimately, no philosophical solution to this challenge. The most that philosophers can do is to explain why there are *good practical reasons*, moral and prudential, for blacks to cultivate and maintain solidarity despite existing class cleavages. The viability of black solidarity, across class lines, turns on whether there are a sufficient number of black elites willing to carry the collective project forward even if this would involve some personal sacrifices or risks.

TOMMIE SHELBY

CHALLENGE 2: BLACK SOLIDARITY IS A FORM OF "IDENTITY POLITICS" THAT REIFIES "RACE" AND ROMANTICIZES SO-CALLED BLACKNESS AND THEREBY OBSCURES CLASS DIFFERENTIATION AND DIVERGENT INTERESTS AMONG BLACKS

Many who call for "black unity" uncritically rely on the dubious race concept when doing so. They fail to appreciate that there are no races but only a distorting racial ideology that legitimizes material inequality and economic exploitation by infusing social meaning into superficial physical traits. Race-thinking makes "blackness" (like "whiteness") seem magical, like a necessary feature of a meaningful and valuable life. Those in the thrall of "blackness" downplay differences among blacks, exaggerate differences between blacks and whites, and aggressively guard the boundaries of black identity. These dynamics generate an unhealthy in-group conformity and silence dissent from a presumed (though largely illusory) group consensus. And, given the centrality of "race," racism becomes the singular focus of political energy, marginalizing the significance of other forms of injustice, particularly those arising from political economy.

To respond to this set of concerns, we first need clarity about the "black" in "black solidarity" and the relation of blackness to "race" and identity. The five elements of solidarity previously outlined—mutual identification, special concern, common values/goals, group loyalty, and mutual trust—constitute solidarity's general *form*. All robust kinds of group solidarity, including working-class unity, have these characteristics. We can distinguish different types of solidarity by two things: (1) the criteria used for determining membership in the group; and (2) the specific values or goals to which these members jointly commit themselves. These two features constitute the *content* of solidarity.

So who is "black" for purposes of black solidarity? It is helpful to distinguish thin from thick blackness. *Thin blackness* is a category within a historically specific and socially imposed classification scheme. One needn't believe in races as biological kinds to accept that there is such a social system of classification and that this classificatory scheme has practical consequences for those who fall under it. The category "black" serves to mark off a set of individuals within the United States on the basis of their having sub-Saharan African ancestry and sharing certain visible, inherited physical characteristics (chiefly dark skin and tightly coiled hair). Thin blackness is an indelible mark, a salient social fact, and generally carries social stigma. A person cannot choose whether to be black or to stay black in the thin sense.

Thick blackness, on the other hand, is a social identity—say, an ethnic or a cultural identity—that can be adopted, altered, or lost. It is often embraced as a *positive* dimension of a person's self-concept. Black identities are generally components of a conception of the fundamental aims of human life. Given a thick conception of blackness, it can make sense to encourage someone to "stay black" or to hold firmly to their black heritage. It can also be coherent (though not necessarily fully justified) to say that, though someone is unambiguously black in the thin sense (i.e., clearly satisfies conventional ascriptive criteria for the racial classification), they aren't "really" black (that is to say, don't exhibit or subscribe to our favored conception of thick blackness).[10]

The thin/thick distinction is meant to distinguish the unchosen aspects of blackness from those dimensions that are subject to

---

10. Some disputes over who is "really" black are best understood as disagreements about what the relevant ascriptive criteria are or about whether a particular person satisfies the criteria.

individual will. The distinction is not meant to deny that unchosen factors—whether biological or cultural—shape who we are. Not only is racial classification a matter of birth, many of us have been or will be socialized into a practice of cultural blackness. We can't change these facts about ourselves. What we can do, though, is decide what significance we will attach to these facts, and in particular we can choose whether to positively identify with and thus affirm our blackness as a component of our self-concept and ongoing conscious practice, even if we sometimes unwittingly or involuntarily exhibit its hallmarks.

I have argued that blacks, in the thin sense, should *not* demand a shared thick black identity as a condition of solidarity. Nor should blacks treat the conservation or valorization of thick blackness as a defining element of black solidarity. This does *not* mean that blacks must abandon all recognizable genres of thick blackness if they are to share bonds of solidarity. Nor does it mean that those who choose to celebrate their thick blackness cannot draw on their identity as a source of strength or inspiration in the fight for justice. And I am emphatically *not* saying that thin blackness and the stigma it carries is all there is to being black.

I would, however, urge greater *tolerance* toward different views about the meaning and value of thick blackness. And, perhaps more controversially, I believe that such tolerance should be extended even to those who, though thinly black, reject all modes of blackness as defining their positive sense of self. The criteria for thin blackness is all that is needed to determine group membership; and thick blackness should not be a requirement for full standing in the group.

Moreover, the category of thin blackness is all that is needed to enforce antidiscrimination law, because the targets of anti-black racism are those who are thinly black, where this thin blackness is a putative sign of inferiority, a mark of a supposedly deeper difference. In this way, we emphasize the link between the *criteria* for who is black with the *point* of black political solidarity, which is to resist and possibly end racial injustice. The attribution of thin blackness makes all blacks vulnerable to racism and thus makes the common experience of racial mistreatment possible. It is this common *experience*, not thin blackness, that generates spontaneous black bonds.

The precise content of black solidarity is defined, not only by its criteria for group membership, but also by its *specific aims and values*. This content has appropriately shifted with historical circumstances. In past eras, blacks have focused their energies on ending slavery, Jim Crow, and ghettoization and on fighting racism and discrimination generally. In the current era, blacks are still faced with many challenges, some old, some new. There is continuing discrimination in housing, lending, employment, and law enforcement. There is a wide range of troubling racial disparities (e.g., in wealth, educational opportunity and educational achievement, access to health care and health outcomes, and employment and incarceration rates), which are, in part, a legacy of the racial subordination and exploitation of past eras. There is the persistence of ghetto poverty and its associated ills—teenage pregnancy, joblessness, high drop-out rates, unstable families, crime, and mass incarceration.

There are also deep in-group cleavages, not only along the lines of class, but also along the lines of gender, sexuality, generation, and national origin. And there is a general social climate within the United States in which most people, even many who are ostensibly committed to racial equality and antiracism, are simply tired of hearing about black people's grievances and problems—which we might call "race fatigue"—and are now inclined to believe that blacks continue to lag behind whites largely because of self-defeating attitudes and a refusal to take advantage of existing opportunities. Any attempt to specify the appropriate content for contemporary black solidarity must take into account these and other social factors that define the post–civil rights era in the United States.

In view of the circumstances that blacks currently face, I suggest that the content of black solidarity be defined in terms of a joint commitment to antiracist values and to the goals of reducing racial disparities and ending ghetto poverty. In a phrase, black solidarity in the post–Jim Crow era should be fundamentally about advancing a racial justice and antipoverty agenda.

I conceive of "black interests," within the context of group solidarity, as interests for which it is reasonable to expect all blacks to commit to advancing and that blacks share because they are black. Because the duty of justice is binding on all, it is reasonable to expect blacks (and those who aren't black) to do their part to correct ongoing racial injustices and to remedy harms due to past race-based wrongs. Because they are black (in the thin sense), all blacks have a tangible and durable self-interest in ending racial injustice, especially those forms rooted in anti-black prejudice and bias. Thus, it is rational (in the instrumental sense) for blacks to support a joint effort to further this cause, provided they have reason to believe this cooperative venture has some prospects for success.

It is undoubtedly true that not every racist idea or type of racial injustice affects all blacks. And among the forms of racism that do affect all blacks, they obviously do not affect all blacks in the same way or equally. Moreover, there are racist stereotypes that target specific black subgroups rather than all blacks (e.g., the stereotype of the poor black female welfare cheat or the stereotype of the young black male criminal). However, the widespread assumption that blacks are intellectually inferior, lazy, and prone to violence certainly affects all blacks *negatively* even if it does so in different ways. And the stereotype of the young black male criminal can negatively affect blacks that are not young or male.[11]

---

11. See Khalil Gibran Muhammad, *The Condemnation of Blackness: Race, Crime, and the Making of Modern Urban America* (Cambridge, MA: Harvard University Press, 2010).

The specific political content of black solidarity is now, and has always been, *contested* among blacks. Such disagreement, which is often deep, is not simply about which *strategies* would be best (something to be expected within any solidarity group) but also about *basic values and ultimate aims*. Not all blacks have the same conception of social justice, not even of racial justice, and blacks disagree about the degree to which racial injustice remains a problem and about the underlying causes of black disadvantage. These facts should neither surprise nor alarm us. After all, blacks are a *people*, not a political party. There is no official political platform, nor could there be. And no one should expect blacks to subscribe to the same political philosophy. Still, I think that blacks do have interests that converge around the agenda I've outlined and that there is a stable consensus on these fundamental values and goals, which largely cuts across ideological differences.[12] Black solidarity can, and should, be maintained despite these inevitable disagreements about ideals, objectives, and strategy.

There is nothing in this account that precludes or discourages debate about the specific values and goals that should underpin black solidarity. Even the black consensus—what in my book I call the "implicit black constitution"—is not immune to revision or amendment. In fact, it has changed over time in response to debate and altered circumstances. I do however believe that we should be slow

---

12. Though few in number, there are black conservatives who believe that racial justice has already been achieved and that continuing black disadvantage is the result of some combination of blacks' self-defeating attitudes and behavior and of an overly generous welfare state predicated on white liberal guilt. Since black solidarity is rooted in opposition to what is taken to be an unjust social order, black conservatives will naturally refuse to join the effort, and black progressives (from liberals to radicals) will have little reason to regard black conservatives as reliable allies. The two sides may, however, sometimes agree to support specific social service programs or in-group self-help initiatives. For comparative research on black conservative political attitudes, see Andrea Y. Simpson, *The Tie That Binds: Identity and Political Attitudes in the Post-Civil Rights Generation* (New York: New York University Press, 1998); and Michael C. Dawson, *Black Visions: The Roots of Contemporary African-American Political Ideologies* (Chicago: University of Chicago Press, 2001), 281–313.

to make changes and that the burden of proof should be on those who propose such changes. Why? Two reasons.

First, these consensus values and goals (and not "race" or "identity") are the glue that holds the group together, and this group cohesion (when accompanied by sufficient numbers) is the primary source of the group's political power and efficacy. I am not saying that blacks, as a collective, would be powerless without black solidarity—multiracial coalitions and *modus vivendi* black politics are still available. But I think it is fair to say that a black politics that eschews black solidarity would be needlessly discarding what historically has been the group's greatest weapon of self-defense and group advancement.

Second, as blacks debate what values and goals they should be committed to in the post–Jim Crow era, they should not regard themselves as starting from scratch. There has been a long, black debate over many generations about how to respond to white domination and its consequences. Through this historical debate blacks have forged their current political consensus. At the risk of sounding like a Burkean conservative, I believe there is *wisdom* in these traditional black ideas. There is, no doubt, error too, some of which I sought to expose and correct in my book. But ultimately, my goal is to draw out and defend the essential truths of black political common sense.

Without common values and goals, we cannot make sense of group loyalty and mutual trust, which are partly constitutive of solidarity. Loyalty and trustworthiness are to be judged by fidelity to group values and goals. The traitor or "sell-out" is the person who fails to be faithful to the group's values and goals. And I think most blacks have a rough sense of what these values and goals entail even if they disagree about their precise content. My aim in identifying and defending these shared values and goals is rooted in the objective of demonstrating the cogency and viability of black solidarity in the face of skepticism, not in a desire to provide indubitable foundations for black political practice or to prevent debate about the content of black solidarity.

Blacks could of course jointly commit themselves to promoting a social justice agenda far beyond racial justice and antipoverty—and by all means should. But for a variety of reasons that I explain in *We Who Are Dark*, such a *joint* commitment to a broad progressive agenda is unlikely to form among blacks. We simply cannot expect that kind of political cohesiveness within such a diverse and internally stratified population. I still think a progressive form of black solidarity is possible and desirable, but I don't want to downplay or ignore its limits.

CHALLENGE 3: BLACK ELITES GENERALLY HAVE CONTEMPT FOR THE BLACK POOR OR, AT BEST, ACT ON THE BASIS OF PATERNALISTIC NOBLESSE OBLIGE

Many black elites don't identify with the black poor. Indeed, many abhor (what they take to be) the black poor's habits, attitudes, and lifestyle. They believe that poor blacks tend to have self-defeating values, behave irresponsibly, and fail to take advantage of available opportunities. The result, they feel, is that the race looks bad, stereotypes are reinforced, and therefore black identities are further stigmatized and black lives are devalued. Moreover, black elites often resent the fact that "ghetto" modes of blackness are viewed in the wider society as representative of black life. So they seek to distance themselves from poor black people or support measures that aim to make the black poor conform to "mainstream" values. From the point of view of the black poor, this stance is naturally unacceptable and insulting, thus making fruitful solidarity infeasible.

Even if these moral criticisms of the black poor have merit, the *social structure* that poor blacks have inherited and confront is manifestly unfair. Moreover, the black poor, like many other blacks, are burdened by the legacy of past racial injustices. Thus, even if the black poor could do more to help themselves, as a matter of simple justice they are nonetheless entitled to good schools, better job opportunities, decent housing, and a fair criminal justice system. Disapproval of the choices that poor blacks make in response to their unfair circumstances does not justify abstaining from actions that would improve the circumstances—the unjust social structure—they face.

It is well known that class differences correlate strongly with differences in lifestyle and tastes. Blacks are not immune to this. But I see no reason to suppose that blacks must have a similar lifestyle or approve of one another's lifestyles to share a commitment to fight racial injustice. Blacks can respect (or at least tolerate) diverse ways of living as a black person while working together to remove unfair burdens that group members face.

Moreover, blacks don't have to love each other to have solidarity. Now here West might disagree. Much will depend on whether feelings of affection and affinity are necessary components of his proposed love ethic. West does tell us that a love ethic is *not* a matter of "sentimental feelings" or tribal allegiance.[13] Here I read him as following King, whose love ethic is not a matter of passion but of mutual respect and empathy. But West also emphasizes, and praises, the fact that Malcolm X's love for black people was not "abstract" but passionate and concrete—which partially explains why he remains a revered figure among black Americans.

The commitment of solidarity should, I think, be distinguished from the *feeling* of solidarity and also from *liking* those with whom one has solidarity. The commitment can of course be accompanied or prompted by feelings of affection or affinity toward fellow members of the group. And it is entirely appropriate to have such feelings toward

---

13. West, *Race Matters*, 18.

one's comrades. But these feelings are *not* the foundation of solidarity. Such positive sentiments are neither necessary nor sufficient: one can be steadfast in one's commitment and yet lack the feelings; and one can possess the feelings without undertaking or honoring the commitment.

In addition, the feeling of solidarity is often a spontaneous emotional response and not an act of will. But the commitment that often springs from such sentiments need not be unreflective and is never involuntary. Those with the feeling of solidarity—just like those who fall in love—must still decide whether, when, and how to act on this sentiment. Feelings of affection and affinity can no doubt create greater cohesion within a group. And such sentiments can be a powerful motivating force when the going gets tough. But solidarity is, ultimately, an ethical commitment.

Some might concede that feelings of solidarity are not sufficient for sustained collective resistance but insist that such feelings are *necessary*. Our will is too weak to remain steadfast in their absence, they might say. Yet here the comparison with working-class unity is instructive. Marx insisted that *solidarity* is the fundamental principle of the labor movement, and he thought such solidarity can and must bind together workers of different countries.[14] This kind of solidarity could certainly rest on common values and objectives, the common experience of oppression, and perhaps shared enemies. It could not, however, rest on feelings of affection and affinity, given how large and diverse the international working class is. It would not therefore be fair for Marxists to fault black solidarity for failing to possess virtues that working-class solidarity is incapable of exhibiting.

---

14. In a speech delivered in Amsterdam on September 8, 1872, at a congress of the International Working Men's Association, Marx says, "Citizens, let us think of the basic principle of the International: Solidarity. Only when we have established this life-giving principle on a sound basis among the numerous workers of all countries will we attain the great final goal which we have set ourselves." See Karl Marx, "The Possibility of Non-Violent Revolution," in *Marx-Engels Reader*, 524.

TOMMIE SHELBY

CHALLENGE 4: BLACK ELITES CARE ABOUT RACISM BUT DON'T HAVE A STAKE IN ENDING BLACK POVERTY

It might be thought that although black elites have a vested interest in defending civil rights, preserving affirmative action, and enforcing antidiscrimination laws, they do not have a stake in ending black poverty and its associated ills. After all, black elites are no longer forced to live in segregated poor neighborhoods and are not relegated to the low-skilled labor market. They do not depend on public assistance to meet their basic needs. Their highly valued and scarce skills, which enable them to get high-paying jobs, protect them from the precarious lives of the black poor. Though black elites may empathize with the plight of the black poor, there is little reason to believe that they are invested in actively fighting poverty.

Conversely, the black poor are primarily concerned with "bread and butter issues." They need to acquire jobs that pay a living wage and to find affordable housing in safe neighborhoods. They need decent schools for their children and basic public services. They need access to inexpensive and efficient public transportation. They feel they are facing a police state that is highly punitive and violent toward the black poor. And the most dangerous stereotypes target the black urban poor, not blacks in general. Black elites and the black poor are not therefore having the same "black experience." In light of these differences in interests and priorities, it is not realistic to expect solidarity that cuts across this vast class divide.

The existence of black slums, the achievement gap in education, high black jobless rates, and racialized mass incarceration are all, in the minds of many, conspicuous confirmation of familiar negative black stereotypes—that blacks are unintelligent, lazy, irresponsible, imprudent, and violent. Those in the grip of these stereotypes are often disposed to interpret these disturbing racial disparities, not as a sign that there are further racial injustices to address, but as empirical support for their low opinion of blacks and as justification for their resistance to policies that might create greater racial equality. Therefore, sharply reducing these disparities and eradicating ghetto poverty *is* in the interests of black elites.

If black identities are stigmatized because of their association with intellectual inferiority, indolence, irresponsibility, folly, and crime—as they clearly are—then black elites have a stake in breaking that association. As Du Bois often lamented, the black population in America is generally judged by the behavior and condition of its most debased members, and the condition of the worst-off is treated as a sign of the inferiority of blacks as a whole. Moreover, the black elite (or at least some of their kin) are sometimes *mistaken* for members of the black poor and mistreated as a result. This can have deadly consequences for advantaged blacks when the abuse comes at the hands of the police. Such facts give black elites a practical reason to be personally invested in the eradication of ghetto poverty.

However, quite apart from their personal stake in eliminating black urban poverty, black elites should, on grounds of solidarity, do their part to alleviate the burdens of the black poor. Recall that solidarity entails special concern—a commitment to aid one's comrades in need even if in doing so one receives no reciprocal benefit. It would be utopian and impractical to expect broad-based solidarity in the absence of shared interests. To be sure, there will always be some heroic and self-sacrificing individuals who will commit to solidarity with others in the cause of justice despite having little if anything to gain personally. But most of us are not moral heroes. We often need incentives to live up fully to our political commitments. In the absence of a personal stake in the outcome of a political struggle, we can find ourselves without the will to contribute much to the fight. But, as I have emphasized, it would also be a mistake to attempt to ground solidarity solely in shared interests.

TOMMIE SHELBY

CHALLENGE 5: BLACK ELITES HAVE AN INCENTIVE TO PAY LIP SERVICE TO BLACK UNITY BUT THEN SUPPORT POLITICAL MEASURES THAT ADVANCE THEIR NARROW CLASS INTERESTS

Many black elites do take pride in being black and don't like being regarded as "uncle toms" or sell-outs. They resent having their blackness questioned, and they know that poor blacks often view them with suspicion if not disdain. Insofar as they value their black identity and affiliation with other blacks, they have an incentive to *appear* to support the most disadvantaged in the group whether or not they actually have this commitment.

They may say all the right things in public, using the familiar rhetoric and tropes of black political culture, and express their blackness through recognized cultural markers and consumption patterns while actually supporting policies that favor the affluent. West makes a similar point about the public performance of black anger and appeals to black sentimentality and nostalgia.[15] Recognition of the divergent interests between black elites and the black poor might lead the latter to reasonably wonder whether they can actually trust black elites. The interests of the two groups might be thought to diverge so sharply that the black poor are rightly concerned that black elites, despite their professed commitment to group solidarity, will not care enough about the needs and priorities of the worst off in the group.

This question turns on whether we have reason to believe that black elites, in virtue of their relative privilege, have an insincere or a weak commitment to black solidarity such that when asked to sacrifice

---

15. West, *Race Matters*, 38.

or risk some of their advantages, they will betray their downtrodden brothers and sisters. This problem is real. The right response to it, though, is not to write off all black elites as untrustworthy. Rather, given these legitimate concerns, the black poor should demand some positive signs of good faith, trusting only those black elites with a demonstrated commitment to racial equality, rather than giving every black elite that avows solidarity the benefit of the doubt. Less weight should be given to ethno-cultural signs of blackness when it comes to determining who is a good comrade. More weight should be placed on concrete evidence that would-be allies are committed to advancing the cause of racial justice and reducing black poverty.

King considered this problem. He argued that nonviolent direct action erases class distinctions by making all sectors of the community vulnerable to being convicted on public order violations and perhaps sharing a jail cell. His general point could be extended to calling on black elites to share the same neighborhoods and schools with the black poor.

CHALLENGE 6: BLACK ELITES VIEW THE WORLD THROUGH A NEOLIBERAL LENS

Many now understand freedom and fairness as no more than economic mobility using market mechanisms uninhibited by discrimination. In light of this, some Marxists argue that black elites regard the social conditions that would advance *their* interests as identical with the conditions that would advance the interests of the black population as a whole. Too often, black elites view their own individual successes as victories for the group and as positive signs of racial progress. In other words, black elites have a systematic class bias in their political perspective. Regardless of their level of goodwill and commitment to the black cause, this bias distorts their judgment about what would be best for the black poor.

I would not deny that there is such bias. However, provided blacks do not tie their solidarity to a Du Boisan talented tenth doctrine, this bias need not undermine solidarity. Instead of elite-driven politics, there should be no presumption that elites are the "natural leaders" of the collective effort or that elites should set the group's agenda. As West emphasizes throughout *Race Matters*, black politics, like all politics, should be rooted firmly in critical dialogue and democratic accountability, where all participants, regardless of class, have equal standing. Those persons who are chosen to lead various initiatives should be responsive to the criticisms of those they expect to follow them; and those who choose to follow others' lead should submit these leaders' political proposals to close scrutiny, checking not only for conflicts of interest and bias, but making sure that these proposals treat the interests of all segments of the group as equally important.

The threat of elite bias could be significantly mitigated through the mechanisms of a black counter-public, where issues that affect the group are openly debated and the voices of the marginalized are not silenced or ignored. Yet, the democratic ethos among blacks is not currently as robust as it could or needs to be. And the suppression of open black debate—sometimes by black elites themselves—that occurred during the Obama years may have done lasting damage.

CHALLENGE 7: GIVEN THE DIVIDED ALLEGIANCES OF THE BLACK ELITE, THE BLACK POOR (WHO ARE REALLY MEMBERS OF THE WORKING CLASS) SHOULD SIMPLY MAKE COMMON CAUSE WITH WORKERS OF OTHER RACIAL GROUPS

To secure the interests of the black poor, a radical transformation of society needs to occur. Although black elites oppose racial discrimination, they have an obvious stake in preserving the *economic* status quo—that is, the concentration of wealth in the hands of the few (and the power that comes with it), low taxes on high-income earners, and great income inequality, where the benefits of economic growth go largely to investors and the professional-managerial classes. Moreover, as West points out, black elites' preoccupation with white peer recognition could lead them to be overly invested in standards of evaluation or "merit" that buttress our highly unequal social order. Indeed, if black elites were to get what many seem to want most—namely, their "racially proportionate" share of status, income, and wealth—this would still leave a whole lot of broke black people. Even if the black poor were to face no racial prejudice and their fortunes were no worse than poor whites, they would still be *poor* and thus at the mercy of the rich and powerful.

This assessment, it seems to me, is basically correct. The black poor should seek multiracial working-class solidarity and participate in the labor movement. But they should also maintain solidarity with other blacks to fight racial injustices and anti-black racism. There are no perfect allies awaiting the black poor. There are deep cleavages within the working class as well, as many among the white working class seem to identify more strongly with rich whites than with disadvantaged people of other races. And therefore it seems to me, as it did to Du Bois in the 1940s, that the black proletariat should not abandon its traditional ties to progressive elements among the black elite.

In "The Paradox of African American Rebellion," West takes a position on the black elite that still strikes me as entirely apt.[16] He argues that the black freedom struggle cannot be re-energized without a critical mass of the new middle class. Black elites possess vital skills, resources, and power, and most blacks look to them for leadership. But black progressives and the black working class must hold the black elite accountable and push them beyond their neoliberal reformism. And yet, West suggests, reliance on the black elite is only a *temporary* measure, a pragmatic compromise until more reliable progressive forces can be mobilized and organized.

CONCLUSION

There is no question that black solidarity is currently fragile. Blacks are not as cohesive as they were during past eras, when very few could expect to acquire significant wealth, status, or power and almost every black person's life prospects were far below that of the average white person. It can be difficult to trust those that clearly benefit from the status quo and have something to lose by participating in the collective struggle. Black unity cannot therefore be the emancipatory tool it once was. Nostalgic calls for the degree of solidarity characteristic of the civil rights era are unhelpful. And we cannot expect

---

16. Cornel West, "The Paradox of the African American Rebellion," in *Is It Nation Time?: Contemporary Essays on Black Power and Black Nationalism*, ed. Eddie S. Glaude (Chicago: University of Chicago Press, 2002), 22–38.

black solidarity to be the solution to every social injustice that affects blacks. It is not the best vehicle for all the hopes and aspirations of progressives. Yet when it comes to demanding racial justice, greater racial equality, and an end to ghetto poverty, I believe that black solidarity still serves a vital progressive function.

INDEX

For the benefit of digital users, indexed terms that span two pages (e.g., 52–53) may, on occasion, appear on only one of those pages.

A Theory of Justice, 50–53, 271, 287
altruism, and solidarity, 65–68, 108
Annas, Julia, 114–18, 120–22, 129n.41, 133n.53
Arendt, Hannah, 89–90
Aristotle, 21–22, 113–14, 122–23, 134–35
assigned responsibility, 243, 306

Black Lives Matter, 1–2, 189–90, 198–200, 209–13, 226, 341–42
Black nationalism, 338n.3, 344
Black solidarity, 337–38, 341
   Black solidarity, and black identity, 347–49
   Black solidarity, content of, 351–52
   See also working class: Black
Black unity, 344, 346, 358–59, 362–63
Bommarito, Nicolas, 150–52
Bourgeouis, Leon, 29–30, 58–59, 60–61, 94–95, 250–53, 292–93
Brüderlichkeit, 5, 54

Camus, Albert, 63–64n.10, 194–95
Catholic social thought, 18–19, 27, 171–80
   Catholic social thought, and solidarity, 176–77, 181–89, 191–93

   See also Good Samaritan, parable of; principle of subsidiarity
Christianity, 60–61, 86
civil rights movement, 15, 18–19, 209–10, 341, 349, 356, 362–63
class, *See* working class
class struggle, 50, 333
coercion, solidarity and, 237–43
Cohen, G.A., 51n.32, 76n.21, 272
Commitment, solidarity as, 20, 28, 87, 95–97, 100–1, 148, 160–62, 225, 342–45, 353, 354–55
   See also joint commitment
common goals, and solidarity, 23–24, 102–3, 153–54, 208–9, 223–24, 228, 342, 352–53
common good, 40–41, 177–80, 181, 183–84, 185–88, 338
communitarianism, 32–33, 192–93, 293–94, 298–99
community, 44–46, 60–62, 246, 299–301
   imagined community, 24–25, 77–78
   and solidarity, 108–9, 152–55, 253
Comte, Auguste, 7, 57–58, 59–60
consequentialism, solidarity and, 233, 256–57, 258–60

INDEX

constitutional patriotism, 93–94, 96–97, 225, 293–94
  See also Habermas, Jürgen; Markell, Patchen; solidarity: civic
context-dependence, solidarity as, 44–54
corruption, of solidarity, 237–43
Covid-19, 171–76, 177–, 78–, 284

Dean, Jodi, 95n.13
debt. See social debt
deference, as part of solidarity, 208–9, 227–28
deliberation, 79, 80, 275–76, 307
difference principle, as expression of solidarity, 50–51, 76n.21, 263, 273–74
  See also Rawls, John
dignity, 123–24, 174–77, 179, 183–85, 187–88, 326–27
diversity, as a challenge to solidarity, 77–79, 251–52
division of labor, 160, 225–26, 295, 311–12, 314–15, 317–19, 320–21, 325–27
  See also Durkheim, Emile
doux commerce, 30, 313–14, 315–16, 323–24, 325, 329, 335
Dreyfus Affair, 295–96
Du Bois, W.E.B., 337–39, 357, 360, 361–62
Durkheim, Emile, 30, 48, 59–60, 249–52, 295–96, 297–98, 311–12, 313–15
  and collective consciousness, 319–20, 326–27
  and negative and positive organic solidarity, 317–19
  See also division of labor; solidarity: cosmopolitan; solidarity: mechanic; solidarity: organic
Dworkin, Ronald, 5–6, 127–28

elites, and solidarity, 30–31, 292, 353–55, 356–57, 358–60, 361–62
empathy, and solidarity, 25–26, 108, 227–28
equality, 115, 228, 234, 235, 237–38, 247–48
  power differences within groups as a threat to, 239–43
  status and, 112–13, 119, 122–24, 128, 263

value of, 267–68
  See also virtue ethics, equality and essentialism, 101
ethical life (Sittlichkeit), 287–88, 289–91
eudaimonism, 113–14, 123–25, 129
  solidarity as a challenge to, 133–34
  See also Aristotle
European Union, solidarity in, 80, 287–88, 289, 291, 313, 335–36
exclusion, 97–99, 105, 241–42, 272, 277–78, 279–80, 296–97, 298–99
  See also partitive, solidarity as

Feinberg, Joel, 269–70
fellow-feeling, vs. solidarity, 108, 354–55
feminism, See solidarity: feminist theories of
Foot, Philippa, 256–61, 282–83
Fouillée, Alfred, 29–30, 284–85, 303–4
fraternity, 251–52, 255–57, 271–74, 287
  and solidarity, 5, 267
Friedan, Betty, 99–100
friendship, and solidarity 134–36, 279–80
functionalism, and solidarity, 155–68

Gilbert, Margaret, 222–23, 232–33
  See also commitment, solidarity as; joint commitment
Good Samaritan, parable of, 190–93
  See also Catholic social thought
group action, 240
group agency, 157–58, 230, 244

Habermas, Jürgen, 225, 286, 287–91, 330–32
Harris, Leonard, 112–13, 123–25
Hooker, Juliet, 210–11
hooks, bell, 98–100
humanity, 261–62
  shared, 9–11, 53, 187
Hume, David, 55, 272, 273
Hurka, Thomas, 21

identification, solidarity and, 63–64, 89, 97–98, 274–76
  mutual, 342
  See also national identity
identity politics, and solidarity, 346–53

INDEX

inequality, and solidarity
injustice, 28, 50, 52–53, 200, 203, 244–45, 343–44
   patriarchal, 100–1
   racial, 344–45, 350
   See also solidarity: and unjust groups
institutions, *See* solidarity: and social institutions
insurance, 70–76, 250–51
interdependence, 64, 181, 183–84, 185–86, 207–8, 243, 249, 284, 291, 292, 325, 327–28
   See also Bourgeouis, Leon
intersectionality, and solidarity, 98–99, 100n.24, 105, 106–7

joint action, 9, 85–86, 89, 224, 294–95
joint commitment, 232–33, 234–35, 346–47, 350, 353
   See also Gilbert, Margaret
justice, relation between solidarity and, 50–53, 109, 227–28
   duty of justice, 343
   social solidarity and social justice, 69–76, 93–94

Kantianism, 55, 284–85
Kantian optimization, 67–68
Kateb, George, 90–93
King, Martin Luther Jr., 190–91, 337–38, 354, 359

Leibniz, Gottfried Wilhelm, 46–47
Leroux, Pierre, 57–58
Levy, Jacob, 293–94, 296–97, 302–3, 305–6
Liberalism, 88–89, 91–92, 284–86
   solidarity as incompatible with, 91–92
loyalty, 74, 89–90, 234, 342, 346–47, 352–53
Lukács, Georg, 333–34

Mafiosi, 15
Markell, Patchen, 298–99
Marx, Karl, 50, 340
Marxism, 16, 30–31, 355, 359–60
   criticism of Black solidarity, 337–38
   and proletarian solidarity, 333–34, 335
   See also working class

McCain, John, 139–41
MeToo, 1–2, 189–90, 197–98, 202–3, 209, 213–14, 217, 226
mutual aid, and solidarity, 220–21, 223–24, 227–28, 235, 253, 254, 294
mutual obligation, 286–87
mutual recognition, 44–45, 240–41, 257–58, 276
mutual sympathies, and solidarity, 103–4, 313–14

national identity, 62, 223, 225, 228–29, 295–96
   See also constitutional patriotism; identification, solidarity and
Neoliberalism, 48–49, 126, 359–60, 362
network solidarity, 235–36, 242–43, 244–45

Occupy Wall Street, 196–97, 215
Offe, Claus, 330–32
ontology, critical social, 239–43
oppression, and solidarity, 3, 95–96, 99–100, 136–37, 200–2, 212–13, 227–28, 264–65, 344–45
   See also solidarity: and social movements; solidarity: and unjust groups

partiality, 248, 278–79
partitive, solidarity as, 247–48, 260–62, 266–67, 277, 280–82
   See also exclusion
political obligation, 286, 290, 292
Pope Francis, 173–80, 187–88, 189–90, 191–93
Pope John Paul II, 185–87
Pope Leo XIII, 172–74
poverty, Black and solidarity, 30–31, 350
principle of subsidiarity, 188–89
privilege, white, 211–12

Race, 196–97, 241–42, 337–63
Rawls, John, 37–38, 50–51, 76n.21, 249, 263, 271–75, 287
   See also A Theory of Justice
Raz, 228–29, 255–56, 267–68
reciprocity, solidarity and, 23–24, 40, 223, 224, 227–28
   reciprocal debt to family, 301
   solidarity as counterfactual, 66–67

INDEX

redistribution, 71–72, 79, 296–97, 299–300
responsibility, collectivizing, 244–45
responsibility, solidarity as mutual, 24–25
Rippe, Klaus, 297–98, 300–2
Roemer, John, 67–68
Rorty, Richard, 6, 286–87, 290–91
Rousseau, Jean-Jacques, 203–4, 275–76

sacrifice, 26–27, 144–49
  self-sacrifice, and solidarity, 20, 140–41
sacrifice, non-solidaristic, 147
Schuman Declaration, 58n.7, 313, 315–17
Seneca. *See* Stoics
Shklar, Judith, 88–90, 92–93
sisterhood, and solidarity, 98–107
social debt. *See* solidarism
socialism, 86, 179–80, 182–83, 284–85
social risk, and willingness to share it, 27–28, 201, 206–9
  and inequitable distribution of willingness to share, 209–13
  and limitation in the willingness to engage, 213–14
  and strategic withdrawal of willingness to share, 214–16
  and vulnerabilities, 207–9
solidarism, 29–30, 250–51, 284–85, 291–93, 294–95, 297–98, 304
  and social debt, 27, 29–30, 250–51, 285–86, 292–93, 304
  See also Bourgeois, Leon; Fouillée, Alfred
solidaristes. *See* solidarism
solidarity
  accounts of, 8–9
  as action, 38–39
  challenges to, 84–86
  civic, 93–96, 291–92, 301, 302–3, 305–6 (*see also* constitutional patriotism)
  concept vs. conception, 5–7, 36–38
    conceptions of solidarity and normative contexts, 44–54
    moralised conceptions of solidarity, 15
  conceptual uniqueness of, 12–13
  cosmopolitan, 242–43, 314–15, 325–29, 330 (*see also* Emile Durkheim)
  critics of, 293–303
    anti-communitarian critique, 298–300

  ingratitude critique, 300–3 (*see also* exclusion)
  liberal-pluralist critique, 294–98
  disposition towards, 236 (*see also* virtue, solidarity as a)
  duties of, 53
  feminist theories of, 18–19 (*see also* sisterhood, and solidarity)
  grounds of, 1–2, 16
  limits of, 33–34
  mechanical, 223, 251–52, 256, 319–20
    and its relation to organic solidarity, 322–24
  motivation-based accounts of, 149–55
  and mutual responsibility, 56–61
  negative vs. positive, 234, 317–19
  networking account of, 221–25 (*see also* solidarity: unitary)
  non-sacrificial, 147 (*see also* sacrifice non-solidaristic)
  organic, 7–8, 30, 59–60, 225–26, 313–14, 320–22
  solidarity, organic, and its relation to mechanical solidarity, 322–24
  pernicious, 195, 201–9 (*see also* solidarity: and unjust groups)
  as a political ideal, 247–48, 255–56, 267–68, 270–71, 276, 277–78
  scope of, 10–11, 17
  and self-interest, 65–68, 307, 312, 319, 331–32, 344–45, 350 (*see also* altruism, and solidarity)
  silent, 15–16
  and social institutions, 70–71
  and social movements, 226, 241 (*see also* Black Lives Matter; MeToo; Occupy Wall Street; oppression, and solidarity)
  transnational, 51–52, 201, 226, 313, 329, 330–32, 335
    fragility of, 328–30 (*see also* solidarity: cosmopolitan)
  types of, 7–8
  unitary, 7–8, 221–31, 243, 244–45 (*see also* solidarity: networking account of)
  and unity, 157–58, 162–63, 164, 203

and unjust groups, 204–5, 220–21, 231–32, 237–43
as a value-laden practice, 85–87
value of, 247–48
vicarious, 264–65, 267, 270
state-level solidarity, 92–94
See also solidarity: civic
Stoics, 115–19
sympathy, 100, 312, 324

Thoreau, Henry David, 92
trust, and solidarity, 14–15, 95–96, 195, 206–7, 214–16, 342
destruction of trust, 213–14
Tuomela, Raimo, 222–23, 225, 234–35, 238–39, 240, 244

universal basic income (UBI), 75–76, 253–54n.12
Universal Declaration of Human Rights, 174, 253–54
universalism, 264, 280, 282–83
utilitarianism, 125
See also consequentialism, solidarity and

value, instrumental of solidarity, 11, 17–18, 28–29, 87
value, non-instrumental of solidarity, 11, 17–18, 87, 233–34, 235
virtue, civic and solidarity, 20–21, 29–30, 206–7

virtue ethics, equality and, 112–13, 115, 121–22, 128–29
See also Aristotle; eudaimonism
Virtue, solidarity as a, 18–22, 25–26, 124–25, 186–87, 311–12
individual virtue, 344–45
as a morally neutral virtue, 41–42, 231–32
as a social virtue, 290
See also solidarity: disposition towards virtue, solidarity as a meta, 19–20
virtues, and their unity, 128–33

Walzer, Michael, 194–95
welfare state, 70–72, 93n.9, 251–53, 272, 284–85, 299, 351n.12
West, Cornel, 337–38, 340, 344, 354, 358, 360, 361–62
Wiggins, David, 112–13, 125–28, 246–47, 256–62, 282–83
withdrawal, strategic, 214–16
woman, as a category, 103–5
See also solidarity: feminist theories of
working class, 38, 71–73, 291–92, 332–55
Black working class, 337–38, 339–40, 361–62
See also Marxism: and proletarian solidarity

Young, Iris Marion, 101–3, 105–7, 244

Zhao, Michael, 152–55

The manufacturer's authorised representative in the EU for product safety is
Oxford University Press España S.A. of el Parque Empresarial San Fernando
de Henares, Avenida de Castilla, 2 – 28830 Madrid (www.oup.es/en).

Printed in the USA/Agawam, MA
December 13, 2024

878851.003